Praise for *Secrets of the Best Chefs*

"Adam Roberts is an original: smart, funny, talented, endlessly inquisitive, an A student, and, happily for us, an A+ teacher. Everyone from beginner cooks to sure hands will learn something new on each page."
—**Dorie Greenspan, author of *Around My French Table***

"Adam Roberts is the affable and infectiously curious friend we all wish we had with us in the kitchen—the one who prods us with questions, entertains us with amusing tales, and makes us feel better when our cake flops. After he spent a year hanging out with some of the best chefs in America, we get to enjoy the fruits of Roberts's labor, and feel that we, too, are cooking at home with Alice Waters, Brandon Pettit, and José Andrés."
—**Amanda Hesser, food writer and founder of Food52**

"One of the best and most approachable books on chefs' cooking I've seen—showcasing recipes anyone can master, without fussy techniques or fancy equipment."
—**David Lebovitz, pastry chef and author of *The Sweet Life in Paris***

"*Secrets of the Best Chefs* is almost guaranteed to make you a better cook."
—**Colman Andrews, editorial director of TheDailyMeal.com and author of *The Country Cooking of Italy***

"I really like this book; it's packed with the kind of insights and tips that stay with you for a lifetime of cooking, and written from a sophisticated yet friendly and relatable point of view."
—**Ted Allen, author of *In My Kitchen***

SECRETS OF THE BEST CHEFS

SECRETS OF
THE BEST
CHEFS

RECIPES, TECHNIQUES, AND TRICKS FROM AMERICA'S GREATEST COOKS

Adam Roberts

ARTISAN

Published by Artisan
A division of Workman Publishing Company, Inc.
225 Varick Street
New York, NY 10014-4381
www.artisanbooks.com

Published simultaneously in Canada by
Thomas Allen & Son, Limited

Library of Congress Cataloging-in-Publication Data
Roberts, Adam D.
  Secrets of the best chefs : recipes, techniques, and tricks from
America's greatest cooks / Adam Roberts.
     p. cm.
  Includes index.
  ISBN 978-1-57965-439-9
  1. Cooking. I. Title.
  TX643.R63 2012
  641.5—dc23   2011051780

Art direction/design by Kevin Brainard

Printed in China
First printing, August 2012

10 9 8 7 6 5 4 3 2 1

To all of the chefs and home cooks who let me
into their kitchens and into their lives

Contents

xii **Preface**

1 **Introduction**

2 **What You Need to Proceed**

5 **A Note About the Recipes**

6 **Ten Essential Rules
for Cooking Like a Chef**

8 **Jonathan Waxman**

Gnocchi with Eggplant and
Tomatoes

Arugula Salad with Heirloom
Tomatoes

Fish Stew with Cod, Swordfish,
and Mussels

14 **Angelish Wilson**

Vegetarian Collard Greens

Chowchow

Fried Chicken

Fresh Pecan Pie

22 **Brandon Pettit**

Homemade Pizza Dough

Pizza Sauce

Margherita Pizza

The Brooklyn Pizza

Sausage and Pickled Pepper
Pizza

32 **Alice Waters**

Farmer's Market Salad with
Garlic Vinaigrette

Charred and Cheesy Garden
Salad Tacos

Olive Oil–Fried Eggs with
a Crown of Herbs

38 **Bobby Hellen**

Yogurt-Marinated Leg of Lamb

Lamb Stock

Leftover Lamb BLT

44 **Lidia Bastianich**

Ziti with Broccoli Rabe and
Sausage

Frico with Potato

Mussels and Clams Triestina

50 **Grace Young**

Beef with Tomato Stir-Fry

Fried Rice with Dried Scallops
and Shiitake Mushrooms

Stir-Fried Bok Choy with Ginger

56 **Peter Dale**

Shrimp and Polenta with Chorizo

Chickpeas and Okra with Harissa
and Yogurt

Pineapple with Lime Sugar,
Cane Syrup, and Pomegranate
Seeds

62 **Einat Admony**

Fried Olives with Labneh and
Harissa Oil

Shakshouka

Baba Ghanouj Bruschetta with
Citrus Herb Salad

68 Nancy Silverton

Prosciutto San Daniele with
  Warren Pear and Pomegranate
  Seeds

Mozzarella with Meyer Lemon,
  Celery Salad, and Alici di
  Menaica

Mozzarella in Panna with Pesto
  and Slow-Roasted Tomatoes

74 Harold Dieterle

Hearts of Palm Salad with Mango
  and Macadamia Nuts

Chicken with Rosemary, Fennel
  Pollen, and Balsamic-Braised
  Radicchio

Creamed Corn

**82 Vinny Dotolo
    & Jon Shook**

P'tit Basque with Chorizo and
  Grilled Garlic Bread

Funky Lettuce Salad with
  Beets, Feta, and Creamy Meyer
  Lemon Dressing

Sweet-and-Sour Balsamic-Glazed
  Spareribs

88 Gina DePalma

Lentil Soup with Sausage,
  Chard, and Garlic

Bagna Cauda with Vegetables

Lemon Semifreddo with
  Blackberries and Honey

94 Melissa Clark

Crostini with Sugar Snap Peas,
  Radishes, and Anchovies

Trofie with Basil and Cilantro
  Pesto

Seared Duck Breast with Garam
  Masala and Grapes

100 Tim Artz

West Indies–Style Hot Sauce

Spinach Calzone with Two
  Cheeses

Chicken Croquettes

106 Rebecca Charles

Scallop Chowder

Smoked Fish Salad

Cracker-Crusted Cod with
  Corn, Sugar Snap Peas, and
  Tomatoes

112 Gary Danko

Buckwheat Blinis with Smoked
  Salmon and Caviar

Asparagus Soup with Spinach
  and Tarragon

Blueberry Crostada

**120 Alex Raij
    & Eder Montero**

Fried Eggplant with Honey

Spring Vegetable Confit

Chickpea and Salt Cod Stew

128 Alain Allegretti

Cavatelli with Pesto, Peas, and
  Ricotta Salata

Pan-Seared Branzino with
  Fennel Salad

Chocolate Cherry Clafoutis

134 Samin Nosrat

Buttermilk-Marinated Roast
  Chicken

Pasta Dough

Butternut Squash Tortellini

144 Anthony Martin

Beet Salad with Pecans, Herbs,
  and Apple

Lamb Shanks Roasted with
  Root Vegetables

Orange-Poached Peaches with
  a Graham Cracker Crust

150 Ana Jovancicevic

Braised Rabbit with Carrots
  and Mushrooms

Gibanica with Feta, Goat Cheese,
  and Kajmak Cheese

Plum Dumplings with a Brown
  Sugar Crust

158 Sara Moulton

Chicken Liver Mousse

Stuffed Chicken Breasts

French Apple Tart

166 Marco Canora

Light-as-Air Potato Gnocchi

Braciola (Rolled Beef with Garlic and Parsley Braised in Tomato Sauce)

Raw Dandelion Salad with Hard-Boiled Eggs and Pickled White Anchovies

174 Roy Choi

Choi's Favorite Banana Milk Shake

Sweet Chili Sauce

Stir-Fried Chicken Henhouse Bowl

180 Michel Richard

Mushroom Stock

Potato Risotto

Mushroom-Crusted Chicken Breasts with Mushroom Jus

186 Susan Feniger

Kaya Toast

Black Pepper Clams

Lamb Meatballs (Kafta) with Baked Feta and Pomegranate Molasses

194 Christopher Israel

Radish Salad with Toasted Pumpkin Seeds and Pumpkin Seed Oil

Chanterelle and Cremini Mushroom Gratin

Swiss Chard and Ricotta Dumplings

200 Tony Mantuano

Tagliatelle with Cherry Tomatoes

Stuffed Focaccia

Pantesca Salad

208 Renee Erickson

Sautéed Medjool Dates

Poached Halibut with Pistachio–Meyer Lemon Pesto

Mussels with Cider, Cream, and Mustard

214 Omar Powell

Oxtail Cassoulet

Jamaican Squash Soup with Chicken and "Spinners"

Jamaican Rum Cake

224 Jessamyn Waldman Rodriguez

Country Bread (Pain de Campagne)

Bread Salad with Tuna, Capers, and Olives

Chilaquiles

232 Kevin Davis

Trout David

Salt-and-Pepper Shrimp

Crispy White Asparagus with Orange and Marcona Almonds

238 Asha Gomez

Chai Tea

Beef Ularthiyathu

Thoren with Carrots and Green Beans

Yogurt Rice

246 Chuy Valencia

Tomatillo Chicken Tamales

Ceviche

Flank Steak with Guajillo Chili Sauce

254 Tom Douglas

Spinach Salad with Pear, Curried Cashews, and Bacon

Crab Cakes with Lemon and Dill

Porcini-Crusted Rack of Lamb with Celeriac-Potato Gratin

262 Anne Quatrano

Herb-Cured Duck Breast with Baby Turnips and Meyer Lemon

Pasta Fagioli

Baba au Rhum with Grapes and Crème Fraîche

270 Hugue Dufour

Bone Marrow and Escargot

Smoked Herring Caesar Salad

Tortilla Española with Chorizo

276 Michael White

Tortellini with Pork in Creamy Meat Ragù

Garganelli with Speck and Cream

Cavatappi with Mussels

284 Amanda Cohen

Carrot Dumplings

Celery Salad with Mushrooms and Grapes in a Celery Leaf Pesto

Red Tomato Spaetzle in Yellow Tomato Coconut Sauce

292 Linton Hopkins

Pickled Black Radishes and
   Vidalia Onions

Sautéed Georgia Trout with
   Watercress Puree and
   Mandarin Salad

Braised Winter Greens
   with Tasso and Pickled
   Banana Peppers

300 Charles Phan

Steamed Chicken with Preserved
   Black Beans and Ginger

Caramel Shrimp with Lemongrass,
   Thai Chili, and Ginger

Stir-Fried Bok Choy and Shiitakes
   with Garlic and Rice Wine

306 Anita Lo

Tuna Carpaccio with Kohlrabi Slaw

Eggplant Two Ways

Almond Jelly with Candied Fennel
   and Grapefruit

314 Daniel Patterson

Raw Vegetable Salad with Aged
   Goat's-Milk Cheese

Orange, Yellow, and Purple
   Carrots Braised in Brown
   Butter

Grilled Brassica with Dandelion-
   Green Vinaigrette

322 Curtis Duffy

Crab and Cucumber

Chilled Corn Soup

Short Ribs Braised in Coconut Milk

330 José Andrés

Citrus Gin Cocktail

Juiced Gazpacho

Salt-Crusted Pork Loin with
   Ibérico Ham and Asparagus

336 Naomi Pomeroy

French Onion Soup

Porcini-Rubbed Roast Beef
   with Demi-Glace and
   Caramelized Turnips

Lentilpalooza

Beast Stock and Demi-Glace

344 Hugh Acheson

Chicken Thighs Braised
   in Cider Vinegar with Fennel
   and Radish

Seared Scallops with Mustard
   Greens, Parsnip Puree, and
   Beurre Blanc

Cured Pork Belly with Kimchi
   Rice Grits

**354 Nils Noren
& Dave Arnold**

Eggs on Eggs

Rib-eye Steak Cooked Sous-Vide

French Fries

362 Elizabeth Falkner

Puntarelle with Candied Bacon,
   Soft-Cooked Eggs, and Ricotta
   Salata

Yogurt with Blood Oranges,
   Raspberries, Cherries, and
   Chocolate

Red Velvet Cupcakes with Cream
   Cheese Frosting

370 Afterword

371 Resources

374 Acknowledgments

376 Index

Preface

When I was twelve years old, my parents moved us from Oceanside, New York, to Boca Raton, Florida, into a coral-colored house that had four ovens. I like to joke that my mom, a graduate of the Fashion Institute of Technology, used two of those ovens to store her handbags and the other two to store her shoes. Suffice it to say, my family didn't cook.

When people ask me, then, how I came to be a food writer, I have a simple answer: "I went to law school."

It was in law school, after long, dull days discussing *promissory estoppel* and *res ipsa loquitur,* that I found myself standing in my kitchen, craving some sort of visceral release. That release came when I chopped my first onion, threw it into a pot with ground beef, cumin, chili powder, and a can of tomatoes, and made chili from a Betty Crocker cookbook. My roommate at the time told me that it looked like dog food, but that didn't matter: I was hooked on cooking.

Ten years later, I'm still hooked. And the lifeline I threw myself in my third year of law school—a food blog that I started called *The Amateur Gourmet*—is now my full-time profession, a way to document my adventures as an enthusiastic eater and a passionate home cook.

Since starting my blog (and despite my upbringing), I've discovered that I have some talent in the kitchen. Friends clamor for a seat at my table, where I serve them piles of super-garlicky Caesar salad, steaming bowls of pasta, and hacked-apart pieces of aggressively seasoned roast chicken. Homemade chocolate-chip cookies are de rigueur in my house, and every so often, I try my hand at an apple pie. (I'm better at cookies.)

As much as I enjoy making these comfort foods, more often than not I'm stumped in the kitchen when it comes to taking everything to the next level—making the pasta from scratch, for example, or knowing (and understanding) the proper way to truss a chicken. Luckily for me, over the course of writing my blog, I've had the chance to meet a wide variety of chefs, many of whom are incredibly generous when it comes to answering my cooking questions.

Which is how I got the idea for this book.

What if I spent a year of my life traveling the country, cooking shoulder-to-shoulder with the best chefs and home cooks all over, gleaning as much knowledge, experience, and inspiration as I could in the process? Why, such an adventure might be instructive, edifying, and empowering not only for me, but also for you, the reader. A project like that could make all of us better cooks.

You are now holding the result: this book. Here in these pages, I've attempted to distill the breathtaking amount of culinary wisdom that these giants in the kitchen have to share. Once you start reading these essays and cooking these recipes, you'll throw out your old bag of tricks and start thinking about color and texture, where your ingredients come from, how best to combine them, and how, once they're combined, to present everything in the most beautiful way possible. But we're getting ahead of ourselves.

The point is: the child of a noncooking, shoes-in-the-oven family went on an epic cooking odyssey and now gets to share this wealth of culinary knowledge with you. Come along with me, then, as we learn to cook like the chefs in this book do. Some of the recipes may be intimidating, but just remember where I started. If an amateur like me can make this extraordinary food, you can make it too!

Introduction

In every cook's life, there comes a moment. It's not a moment you can anticipate, but it's certainly one you can prepare for. It's the moment when you stop following recipes to the letter and start cooking based on what you know.

Maybe it's because of all those cooking shows where angry chefs rail against kitchen rookies for oversalting the cod or underseasoning the étouffée, but we've become a nation of nervous Nellies in the kitchen. Most people deal with their kitchen nerves by slavishly following recipes to the point where if a recipe calls for a half teaspoon of paprika and they only have a quarter teaspoon, they'll turn off the oven and order a pizza.

That's no way to cook.

This book is an attempt to change all that. Consider this book an insecurity killer, a confidence booster of epic proportions. For a year, I cooked with the best chefs and home cooks in America. In the process of visiting eleven cities and fifty kitchens, I learned a thing or two about producing quality food at home. It has nothing to do with recipes and everything to do with trusting yourself in the kitchen.

Great cooks are confident people. In a restaurant setting, chefs are leaders: they command roomfuls of fellow chefs and, through their leadership, feed hordes of hungry masses night after night. Great home cooks also project great confidence, as they often face an even tougher crowd: picky spouses and cranky children.

And though I'm becoming more confident in the kitchen, my status as a self-taught, amateur home cook with no formal training makes me an ideal candidate to soak up all the knowledge and wisdom that these chefs and cooks have to offer. Because, like you, I'm just a normal home cook—not a noteworthy chef redefining the face of gastronomy—I notice things most cooks and chefs do and take for granted. And I've distilled it all for you in these pages.

I've cooked with chefs from a wide variety of cultural backgrounds (French, Jamaican, and Chinese, to name a few), with varying degrees of experience (from young chefs to chefs in their sixties), and who cook for unusual reasons (like Brandon Pettit [page 22], who gave up a career in music to make pizza).

Some of the chefs use old-fashioned cooking gear (food mills, copper bowls); others use more futuristic devices (immersion circulators, Cryovac sealers). Some chefs have ingredients delivered to their restaurants; others grow the produce that they use themselves. Some chefs work hard to make everything new (carrots cooked in hay stock, corn soup with a coconut dome made with liquid nitrogen); others work hard to properly execute and improve upon classic dishes (potato gnocchi, pasta fagioli, chicken liver mousse).

In all these cases, one thing is very clear: all of these cooks and chefs who are so notable for their food are also notable for their personalities. I was surprised to discover that it's a strong sense of self more than anything else that allows you to make extraordinary food at home. To put it simply: if you make the food that you like to eat, you'll make food that others like to eat. You just have to trust that the food that you like to eat is food worth eating.

To become a great cook, you have to tap into the part of you that knows, on a deep level, what you want something to taste like and then get it to taste that way. That's what all of the chefs in this book do, and that's what I try to do now too. Don't look outward for the answers; look within.

Think of this book as a prompt, a catalyst for self-reliance in the kitchen. With countless stories, lessons, pictures, and more than 150 recipes, I want to help you trust yourself behind the stove. The next time you're making a recipe that calls for a half teaspoon of paprika, and you only have a quarter teaspoon? You'll shrug it off and use something else.

You won't have to measure. And when you stir it in, you'll take a taste just to make sure. And if it tastes good to you (and why shouldn't it? You're a good cook!), it will taste good to everyone.

That's the secret, the ultimate wisdom I gleaned from cooking my way across America. It's a funny thing to say at the start of a cookbook, but it's true:

Don't rely on the recipes. Learn to trust yourself.

What You Need to Proceed

Despite the wish list on your friend's wedding registry, you don't need fancy equipment to cook good food at home. When I asked Hugh Acheson (page 344) what his favorite kitchen tool was, he shrugged off the question: "It's not about tools. You should be able to cook something good with just a fork and a cast-iron pot."

While there's something to be said for keeping things extra simple, it's also important to have enough tools on hand to make cooking at home as easy as possible. Here, then, is my list of the essential equipment that every cook should have in his or her kitchen.

A good knife

You've heard it before, but it bears repeating: your best tool in the kitchen is a good, sharp knife. Now, a good knife doesn't necessarily mean an expensive knife. You can get a very decent, functional knife for less than fifty dollars. In fact, at the beginning, it's probably advisable to do so. Get a medium-size chef's knife that fits comfortably in your hand (Harold Dieterle, page 74, recommends a German knife for beginners and a Japanese knife for more experienced cooks) and keep it sharp. To do that, either buy a sharpening stone (see Susan Feniger, page 186) or get it professionally sharpened every so often. (When I started, I used the AccuSharp; now I use a Japanese whetstone.) Also, steel your knife

before using it (see Sara Moulton, page 158). Wash your knife immediately after you're finished with it and keep it dry and safe in a knife rack.

A good cutting board

You may not think much about the cutting board that you use to cut your vegetables, but chefs do. And most of them know something that you might not: a bad cutting board can damage your knife. Some chefs—Rebecca Charles (page 106), for example—have custom-made cutting boards built into their counters. For most people, I recommend a large rubber cutting board that not only is kind to your knife but also can withstand lots of scrubbing in the sink without warping.

A wooden spoon

Every great chef and home cook has a favorite wooden spoon. Mine has a square shape and can neatly work its way around the edges of a pan.

Pots and pans

Don't go crazy spending money on pots and pans. Here's a basic list of what to have (though there's no need to buy them all at once).

Two 12-inch stainless-steel skillets. One with a lip so you can toss the contents easily, and one with a higher rim and a lid for

braising. All-Clad is the way to go, if you can afford it.

One 12-inch nonstick skillet. Ideal for making omelets, crepes, or anything that has a tendency to stick.

A cast-iron skillet. A favorite among chefs because of the way it retains heat, this is also an excellent tool for replicating the effects of outdoor grilling indoors. Lodge brand is a good option.

One large metal pot. Nothing fancy; just something you can use to make sauces, soups, beans, rice, and anything else that can't be made in a skillet.

A stockpot. Though this takes up a lot of space, it's essential, especially when you start making stocks.

A Dutch oven. My favorite cooking vessel, this is fantastic for braising, cooking pasta, frying, you name it. The Le Creuset brand is incredibly resilient.

A wok. A wok takes up extra space, but when you try the wok recipes in this book, you'll understand why for much of the world, this isn't just an essential kitchen tool, it's *the* essential kitchen tool. (See Grace Young, page 50, for wok-buying details.)

Mixing bowls

Assorted mixing bowls are omnipresent in restaurant kitchens and should be part of your home kitchen too. Use them for tossing salads (see Jonathan Waxman's technique, page 12), storing ingredients, whisking dressings, sifting dry ingredients into, and allowing dough to rise.

A regular spatula, a rubber spatula, a whisk, and a spider

These are handy tools to have. A regular spatula can be used to flip things, and the rubber spatula can be used to fold ingredients together, to reach the hard-to-get-to crevices in a pot or a bowl, and to smooth the top of a cake batter before it goes into the oven. The whisk is ideal for incorporating batters, whipping cream, and folding. A spider is a terrific tool for lifting pasta out of a pot and placing it directly in the sauce.

Baking pans and cookie sheets

If you like to bake, it's good to have three cake pans, all the same size, so you can make layer cakes, and a loaf pan for making various kinds of breads (banana, zucchini) and loaf-style cakes. It also pays to have a springform pan with a removable bottom. Pie plates are useful not only for making pie but also for holding the dredge when you make fried fish or fried chicken. (A glass pie plate is good for actual pie or to use in place of a gratin dish.) Rimmed cookie sheets (aka half-sheet pans) are underrated kitchen tools: yes, they're great for making cookies, but—even better—they're also great for roasting vegetables. Try taking broccoli florets (dry them thoroughly), tossing them with olive oil, salt, and pepper, and placing them on a cookie sheet in a 425°F oven for 15 to 20 minutes. You'll never eat broccoli any other way again.

A blender or a hand blender

As great as you might be with your knife, there's no way, working by hand, to create a puree or soup as smooth as one processed with either a blender or a hand blender. A Vitamix blender is prized by chefs because a Vitamix is as powerful as it gets. But it's by no means necessary; a standard blender or hand blender will work with almost all of the recipes in this book.

A food processor

Because of its design, a food processor works differently than a blender. Its wide shape and wide blade ensure that everything gets worked in at once (with a blender, the ingredients have to fall to the bottom to come into contact with the blade). Thus, with a food processor you can easily chop up vegetables and bring together pie dough and pasta dough. With the blade attachment, you can shred ingredients (like carrots for a carrot cake or cabbage for coleslaw), and because it comes apart so neatly, a food processor is easy to clean.

A KitchenAid mixer

It's possible to make cookies, cakes, and cupcakes without a KitchenAid stand mixer, but having one makes life so much easier. Especially when it comes to bread-making, a KitchenAid with a dough hook attachment is a lifesaver and one piece of kitchen equipment that is hard to live without once you've had one.

As far as how to stock your pantry, it's a good idea to always have the following on hand:

Extra virgin olive oil

Keep one cheaper bottle for cooking (Colavita is a good choice) and one more expensive bottle for salads and for drizzling on finished foods (I like Frantoia for that purpose).

Butter

Using unsalted butter is preferred because it lets you control the seasoning in your cooking, adding as much or as little salt as tastes best.

All-purpose flour

I recommend King Arthur brand.

Kosher salt

I prefer Morton coarse kosher salt, though most chefs use a finer kosher salt (coarse is my own strange predilection). Taste a few and decide which you like best.

Black peppercorns
Keep a bunch on hand for grinding fresh with a good pepper grinder.

Red pepper flakes
For adding a little heat to pasta dishes, pizza, and soups.

White and brown sugar (both dark and light)
For baking or adding a touch of sweetness to savory dishes.

Eggs
Preferably organic, free-range, purchased at a local farmer's market.

Garlic
Whole heads are always better than anything that is sold pre-chopped.

Spices
Your spice cabinet should contain whole nutmeg, cinnamon, ground cloves, chili powder, smoked paprika, regular paprika, cumin, coriander, turmeric, cayenne pepper, and fennel seeds. It's important to replace these every 6 to 12 months, because, like all foods, they lose their potency over time.

All kinds of vinegar
It's good to have a lot of vinegar to choose from; keep cider, red wine, balsamic, white wine, champagne, and sherry vinegar on hand.

Soy sauce
Add to dishes for a hit of umami and salinity, especially when you're stir-frying.

Vegetable oil and canola oil
Good for making salad dressings and homemade mayonnaise, for recipes that require deep-frying, or when you want a neutral flavor.

A good spicy mustard
Try Roland or another French brand.

A Note About the Recipes

All of the recipes in this book are based on the notes that I took while cooking alongside each chef and home cook over the course of this journey. When adapting and testing each recipe in my modest-size (read: tiny) home kitchen, I took into account such factors as affordability, practicality, and whether or not a specific step that a chef taught to me was realistic to re-create at home. The end result is recipes that retain all the excitement and brilliance of the original chef recipes but with a slightly more down-to-earth approach.

All of the recipes are annotated (see words underlined in yellow) to include my own discoveries and helpful chef tidbits to ensure success.

Organization-wise, the easier recipes come at the beginning and the slightly more difficult recipes come at the end. So yes, Jonathan Waxman's Arugula Salad with Heirloom Tomatoes (page 12) is much easier to execute than Naomi Pomeroy's French Onion Soup made with homemade veal stock (page 338). But just because something is easier to execute doesn't mean you should be sloppy or careless in making it. In some ways, the simpler stuff is *more* difficult because each distinct element resonates louder. So bring your A game to all of the recipes in this book and you will be richly rewarded.

Ten Essential Rules for Cooking Like a Chef

These are the most compelling and universal lessons that I learned from cooking with some of the best chefs in the world. Taken together, these tips should paint a clear portrait of what it means to know what you're doing in the kitchen.

01 Taste as you go.

If there's one lesson to take away from this entire book, this is it. Cooking is not about blindly adding this and that and hoping that what you're making comes out okay. Engage with the food you're making and taste it every step of the way. When it's not to your liking, adjust it. Chefs don't measure how much olive oil, butter, salt, pepper, or vinegar they add to a dish; they use these to adjust food as it cooks. To enrich food, they add fat. To heighten the flavor, they add salt. For a spicy kick, they add pepper. And for a sour edge, they add acid. It's not just a neat trick to know about; it's your job to use these tools to make your cooking great. Once you understand that, your food will taste better forevermore.

02 Put ingredients on display.

Too many times, we shop with a recipe in mind and come home with bags of ingredients to make that recipe, and whatever is left over gets shoved into the fridge. Great chefs and home cooks go to the market and buy what's beautiful and in season. Then—and here's the kicker—they *display* what they buy in baskets or bowls so that this food not only serves to make their homes beautiful (baskets full of radishes and turnips, bowls spilling over with Meyer lemons), it serves as inspiration for cooking. Applying this to your own life, keep a basket on your kitchen counter and fill it with whatever you find at the market (purple potatoes, Bosc pears, parsnips, and apples in winter; heirloom tomatoes, chilies, squash, and corn in the summer), and use it to inspire what you cook.

03 If it looks good before you cook it, it will taste good after you cook it.

So many times while I was writing this book, chefs would assemble something that they were about to roast in the oven or steam in a steamer and I'd say, "That already looks good." It's not an accident. Food should look good at every stage, and if it doesn't look appetizing before you cook it, you may want to rethink what you're making.

04 Use your internal timer.

Chefs were often amused as we cooked together because I'd nervously remind them that they had something in the oven. I'd fret when a timer wasn't set. But all good chefs have a well-developed sense of everything that is happening in the kitchen at all times. It's encoded in their DNA. With practice, you can learn to have this internal timer too.

05 Control the heat.

Very rarely do recipes talk about that knob on your stove that controls the heat, but great cooks know that knob very well. Seldom do they set the heat to "high" or "medium" or "low" and leave it alone. As they cook, they monitor what's happening and adjust the heat accordingly. Recipes can't dictate a specific heat setting for every moment of cooking, which is why you have to be alert, pay attention, and adjust the knob based on what you observe going on in the pan.

06 Use your ears.

Food will speak to you if you listen. Samin Nosrat (page 134), for example, stopped our conversation while she was roasting her buttermilk-marinated chicken (see page 136) to say, "Oh, the chicken's talking to us." What she heard was a loud sizzle, which suggested the oven was too hot, so she lowered the temperature. When I made Angelish Wilson's Chowchow (page 17), I heard lots of gurgling and stopped it just before it boiled over. Your ears are an important tool for cooking.

07 **Don't use pepper the way you use salt.**

Most of us who cook at home think of salt and pepper as a constantly complementary duo: wherever we put salt, we can also put pepper. But that is not often the case in the professional kitchen. Most chefs rarely use pepper, and when they do, they use it in dishes that they think will benefit from a hit of the seasoning. Even then, they seldom use it at the beginning of the cooking process. Add pepper at the end of cooking just to impart some complexity and some heat.

08 **Use the Internet.**

There's this notion that chefs are infallible, that when it comes to food, they know everything. That's very much not the case. Most of the chefs I met while writing this book were humble, always eager to learn more. And when they really don't know something, they look it up on the Internet (just like most of us do at home). Naomi Pomeroy (page 336) told me that whenever she wants to learn a new technique, she turns to the Internet and does her research there. Her food, which is already terrific, is that much better because of all the new things she's willing to learn.

09 **Clean with fluidity.**

Doing the dishes is the most dreaded of kitchen tasks, but one of the most essential lessons I took away from my time cooking with great chefs is that doing the dishes is not a separate act from cooking. It's all part of the same fluid sequence of motions: mix ingredients in a bowl, dump the contents into a pan, put the bowl in the sink and run water in it while you put the pan in the oven. Then, while the pan is baking, wash the bowl and wipe down the counters (clean counters make cooking so much more pleasant). Once you make cleaning part of your cooking process, you'll find it difficult to do it any other way.

10 **Remember, everyone makes mistakes.**

On the subject of chefs being fallible, there were many times when a chef would mess up. Elizabeth Falkner, for example, was so engrossed in talking to me (I'm very engrossing!) while candying her bacon for a puntarelle and candied bacon salad (see page 364) that at one point I interrupted our conversation to ask: "Is that pan supposed to be on fire?" We had a good laugh about it, and the remarkable thing is how quickly she recovered. The fiery pan went in the sink, a new pan went on the stove, and just a few minutes later we had a beautiful pan of candied bacon ready to go. The lesson is: no one cares if you mess up in the kitchen; it's how you recover that matters most.

Jonathan Waxman

Chef-owner, Barbuto
New York, New York

Up in the air the salad goes—arugula, multicolored cherry tomatoes, olive oil, and lemon juice—and down it splashes, most of it landing in the big metal bowl, as I intended, and some of it sloshing over the side. Chef Jonathan Waxman, with a bemused look on his face, says, "Good. Now try again."

We are in the kitchen of Barbuto, Waxman's West Village restaurant, and as the summer sun streams through big glass windows, the master imparts his culinary knowledge to me, his eager student. Waxman, who's often credited with introducing California cuisine to New York City in the 1970s and who mentored a young Bobby Flay, is a born teacher. Instead of showing off his legendary cooking chops during our time together, he has me do everything. I came here to learn from the master and, apparently, the best way to learn how to cook like a master is to actually cook.

So Waxman has me begin with a large red heirloom tomato.

"You're going to cut the core out with this knife," he says, handing me a large chef's knife with a long blade. "Hold it like a pencil and you'll get laser accuracy."

I carefully maneuver the knife around the core, Waxman looking over my shoulder and correcting my grip before I hurt myself. Then he has me repeat the process with several more tomatoes, after which I dice them.

I ask questions and Waxman tells me I worry too much. The edict seems to be

"Don't take this too seriously," even though the food we're making, when it's finished, is pretty serious.

We proceed to a stove, where Waxman shows me how to tip a whole bottle of olive oil upside down, stemming the flow of oil with my thumb. The oil heats in a pan, and then I add eggplant, which I also have diced myself.

"Don't shake the pan yet," he warns. "You lose heat and disturb caramelization."

When the eggplant's browned all over, I add tomatoes to the pan and then add gnocchi to a separate hot pan. "How long does the gnocchi cook?" I ask.

"Why do you need to know that?"

"Umm . . . I guess so we can time the sauce to finish when the gnocchi finishes?"

Waxman shakes his head. "People shouldn't look at clocks when they cook. You don't time it; you just *feel* it." Indeed, when the gnocchi is brown and feels like it's done, it goes into the pan with the tomatoes and eggplant, along with some scallions and a Fresno chili. Voilà: the alchemy of lunch.

And so it goes as I prepare several dishes (including that salad in the big bowl) that we ultimately serve to Waxman's staff. Waxman doesn't say much—he just watches me—and by the time we're done, I feel empowered and remarkably capable.

By trusting me to do everything, Waxman makes me a better cook.

"Cooking's the opposite of science: it's alchemy."

Gnocchi with Eggplant and Tomatoes

Serves 4

Summer ingredients rarely want to be cooked, but this is the dish to make when you want to coax deep flavor out of the eggplant and tomatoes that you bring home from the market. You can't be afraid of fat here; the butter and olive oil are essential for cooking the eggplant. "It soaks them up," explains Waxman, "and they help it cook properly." The gnocchi itself can be store-bought and frozen; it'll brown straight from the freezer in a pan of hot fat and finish cooking in the sauce.

- Even though there's a recipe for homemade gnocchi in this book (page 168), that gnocchi is too delicate to hold up to this intense cooking technique.

- If you can't find a Fresno chili, try using a red jalapeño or, if you're a heat fiend, a habanero.

Extra virgin olive oil (about ½ cup)

1 medium eggplant, cut into medium cubes

Kosher salt and freshly ground black pepper

Unsalted butter, at room temperature (5 to 6 tablespoons)

2 large red heirloom tomatoes, cored and cut into a large dice

1 pound store-bought gnocchi

1 Fresno chili, minced

1 scallion, chopped

Coat a stainless-steel sauté pan with olive oil (about ¼ cup). Raise the heat, and just before it starts smoking, add the eggplant and don't move it around. Season with salt and pepper. After a few minutes, when the eggplant has had time to color, shake the pan. If the eggplant is sticking (and it very well might), add a knob of butter (let's say 1 tablespoon) and shake the pan again. Let the eggplant keep cooking until it detaches, and then toss the eggplant around by shaking and flipping it in the pan. Lower the heat slightly.

After a few more minutes, when the eggplant is golden brown on all sides, take a large piece out and cut into it. Taste it: if it's cooked all the way, or almost all the way, you're ready for the next step. This is a good time to adjust the seasoning too.

Add all the tomatoes and their juices. Season with more salt and pepper, add a glug of olive oil, and toss.

While that's simmering, start the gnocchi. In another sauté pan, heat 3 tablespoons olive oil and 2 tablespoons butter until very, very hot (almost to the smoking point). Add the gnocchi and shake the pan to make one even layer. Season with salt and pepper and allow the gnocchi to cook until it caramelizes, about a minute. When it's golden brown on one side, toss the gnocchi over using a spoon and cook on the other side. (Careful: as it heats, the gnocchi will become delicate.)

To finish, add the gnocchi to the pan with the sauce, along with the Fresno chili, scallions, another tablespoon or two of butter, and a splash of water. Toss on medium heat (careful not to break up the gnocchi) and then pour onto a large platter. Serve hot.

Arugula Salad with Heirloom Tomatoes

Serves 4

"People are too scared when they make salad," Waxman told me. "You have to relax, think about ingredients." This salad has just a few ingredients, and that's the way Waxman likes it. "People overload salad," he continued. "They put in mustard, shallots, all that crap. But the best salads have the fewest ingredients." Because there are so few ingredients in this particular salad, source the best you can find (tomatoes are best in late summer). Tossing them all in the air isn't just a way to show off; it prevents you from damaging the lettuce and tomatoes with salad tongs.

- Waxman slices around the core of the lemon as you would the core of an apple; this results in lemon segments that are easier to juice and that have fewer seeds.

A dozen heirloom cherry tomatoes (preferably multicolored), sliced in half along the equator (with the stem as the top of the globe)

1 large red heirloom tomato, diced

2 to 3 big handfuls of arugula (washed and spun dry)

Extra virgin olive oil

Lemon juice (a few squeezes from 1 lemon)

Kosher salt and freshly ground black pepper

Put the tomatoes and the arugula in a very large bowl. Use your thumb to stop the top of a bottle of olive oil and turn it completely upside down. Drizzle a generous amount of oil over everything until it's lightly coated. Squeeze the lemon into the bowl and sprinkle salt and pepper over everything.

Now toss: flip the tomatoes and greens on themselves by making a swooping motion with the bowl (much like flipping an omelet). Taste for salt, pepper, and acid and adjust. Serve quickly, before the acid from the lemon wilts the arugula.

Fish Stew with Cod, Swordfish, and Mussels

Serves 4

The first time I ever made a seafood stew, it was a disaster. I overloaded a pot with fish and potatoes and left it on high heat for so long that half an hour later, the fish was so overcooked it resembled Sally Field's performance in *Not Without My Daughter*. The secret to Waxman's remarkable fish stew (which he talked me through, improvisationally, after a fisherman delivered an enormous portion of swordfish) is that you only need to cook it *just enough*.

Extra virgin olive oil

2 cloves garlic, smashed

1 large shallot, minced

1 baby fennel bulb, stems cut into small pieces and the bulb diced (if you can't find baby fennel, use half a regular fennel)

Kosher salt and freshly ground black pepper

1 medium fillet of swordfish, skin cut off, cut into cubes

1 medium fillet of cod, skin left on, cut into cubes

6 to 8 mussels, scrubbed and debearded

6 to 8 heirloom cherry tomatoes, sliced in half

½ glass (about 2½ ounces) white wine

Juice of ½ lemon

1 to 2 tablespoons unsalted butter

Heat the olive oil in a medium pot on medium heat and add the garlic and shallot. Cook briefly, until aromatic, and then add the fennel. Season with salt and pepper and continue to cook, tossing occasionally, until tender.

Add all the fish, season again, toss, then add the mussels, tomatoes, wine, lemon juice, and butter. Cover the pan and shake. Cook for a minute or two, until the mussels open and the fish is just cooked inside.

Pour onto a large platter and serve hot.

● Waxman is very particular about how to smash garlic properly. Place a clove on the corner of the cutting board, hover the flat end of a chef's knife over it, and then punch the blade with the bottom of your fist. The garlic should be smashed so thoroughly, it looks practically minced.

● Nothing's worse than finding grit in your mussels. To ensure that this doesn't happen, soak the mussels in a bowl of cold water with a spoonful of flour in it an hour before cooking. The flour helps draw out the grit; rinse the mussels off before using.

● When I asked Waxman what kind of white wine, he scoffed, "It doesn't matter!" Though, I suspect, if prodded, he'd agree that a dry white is preferable to something fruity.

Angelish Wilson

Chef-owner, Wilson's Soul Food
Athens, Georgia

Wilson's Kitchen Know-How

IF YOU WANT to impart chicken flavor to a recipe but don't want to use stock, save the juices from the roasting pan after you've finished roasting a chicken. Add some water, turn up the heat, and stir to work in the bits from the bottom, but don't reduce too much. Save the liquid and use it to flavor casseroles and other recipes that call for stock.

WHEN USING a frozen piecrust (and there's no shame in that), there are a couple of ways to dress it up so it looks like the real thing. Step 1: Brush the top crust with softened butter; that'll help turn it brown in the oven. Step 2: For a sweet pie, sand the top with sugar, to disguise any unattractive spots and give it an extra sparkle.

TO MAKE an intense lemonade, here's a trick: use real lemons, water, and sugar and then add a tablespoon of lemonade powder. The small amount won't be detectable but will amp up your lemonade flavor that much more. Also, add a teaspoon of lemonade powder to cherry pie to impart a citrusy kick.

In 1981, when she was twenty-nine years old, chef Angelish Wilson offered to help her dad—a man who spent his life working two jobs, building railroads and cutting hair—fulfill his dream of opening a restaurant. "Daddy loved to cook and have gatherings," she tells me at a table in that very same restaurant, thirty years later. "We already cooked big at home. We just had to add a little more."

Cooking big, it turns out, isn't just Wilson's business philosophy, it's her life philosophy. After she and her brother Homer took over the business in 1992, Wilson let go of her dream of becoming a nurse and embraced her role as a leader and a feeder of her community here in Athens, Georgia. (She's prominently featured on the Web site of the Southern Foodways Alliance, an organization that celebrates the diverse food cultures of the South and that honored Wilson in 2006.)

"A lot of students come here from UGA," says Wilson as she begins prepping her famous fried chicken. "They all call me Mamma."

One look at the steam table, and you can see why so many flock here to fill their bellies. Compartments overflow with collard greens, macaroni and cheese, squash casserole, fresh corn, and green beans, all of which Wilson makes from scratch. "We knew when we opened that we wanted to serve a home-cooked meal," says Wilson. "This is where everyone could come to have a good time."

During pecan season, customers are known to bring Wilson fresh pecans from their own trees, which she turns into her classic pecan pie (see page 21). When she makes chowchow (see page 17), that punchy peppery Southern relish, customers come with jars to fill from her master batch.

Clearly, for Wilson, cooking big is a way to constantly surround herself with people. And nothing works better on that front than turning on the deep fryer and adding chicken.

Wilson's fried chicken is pretty remarkable in its simplicity. Pieces of chicken are seasoned with salt and pepper and allowed to sit for a few hours. Then Wilson takes each piece of chicken, dunks it in water, and rolls it around in all-purpose flour. The water has two functions: it rinses off excess seasoning and it helps the flour stick. She places the chicken in 370-degree oil and cooks it for twenty minutes.

"Don't drop the chicken in," she warns. "Place it in."

When the chicken comes out, it's covered in a crispy, crackly golden crust. She serves me up a plate with more chicken than I can eat, a huge heap of her vegetarian collard greens (see page 16), a spoonful of the spicy chowchow, and, like a trophy on top, a hot piece of corn bread. Wilson handing me this plate feels like a big hug.

And a big hug is what I get when it's time to leave.

Wilson, who hasn't had the easiest life—her fiancé passed away and her son was recently declared legally blind—proves that food itself only goes so far. It's the spirit with which you make it and serve it that matters most.

"You're gonna ask me, 'How long does it cook?' and I'm gonna say, 'Til it looks pretty.'"

Vegetarian
Collard Greens

Serves 2 to 4

Collard greens are almost always flavored with some kind of pork product (usually a ham hock or tasso), but Wilson has so many vegetarian customers, she came up with a version of collard greens that has no meat at all. ("And you don't miss the meat, do you?" she asked me when she served me a big heap. The answer was no.) Turns out Wilson's secret ingredient is a commercial product that's readily available almost everywhere: Lawry's Seasoned Salt. Add the greens a handful at a time and keep in mind that they really cook down, so buy more than you think you'll need.

2 to 3 big bunches of collard greens

2 tablespoons Lawry's Seasoned Salt (or more, to taste)

A pinch of kosher salt

A big pinch of freshly ground black pepper

A pinch of crushed red pepper flakes

A pinch of sugar

1 onion, finely chopped

Wash the collard greens really well under cold water. Remove and discard the tough stems and slice the leaves; then wash the leaves again under cold water in a strainer (it's essential to get all the dirt off).

Fill a large pot with water (about 8 cups) and bring it to a boil. Add all the seasonings—both salts, the pepper, the red pepper flakes, and the sugar—and taste the water to make sure it's flavorful. Add the onion and the collards, a handful at a time.

Lower the temperature slightly and cook the greens for at least 15 minutes until they're tender. You can only know by tasting them. As you taste, adjust for salt, pepper, red pepper, and sugar. When the greens are cooked to your liking, serve 'em up with a spoonful of spicy chowchow.

Chowchow

Makes a very big batch (good for sharing with friends!)

This isn't so much a recipe as it is a formula, a way to turn peppers and cabbage into a spicy relish. The level of spiciness is entirely up to you. When I tried Wilson's chowchow for the first time, my eyes nearly popped out of my head it was so hot. My own version, which you might call "Wimpy Northerner's Chowchow," contains a mix of spicy peppers and bell peppers to make it tamer. Some might want to include green tomatoes in the mix (which is traditional); if you do, just chop a few and add them to the pot with a splash more vinegar and sugar. Try mixing chowchow with mayo and putting it on sandwiches. It makes a killer spread.

● I prefer using a few red jalapeños, a few green jalapeños, and an orange bell pepper (for color).

1 cabbage, chopped into big chunks (discard the tough bits of core)

1 pound assorted peppers (jalapeño, Fresno, banana, bell, whatever you like), roughly chopped (seeds and membranes removed)

4 onions, roughly chopped

2 tablespoons kosher salt

1 teaspoon freshly ground black pepper

½ cup sugar

1 teaspoon whole allspice

1 cup cider vinegar

Crushed red pepper flakes (optional)

Start by cooking the cabbage in a pot of boiling water. Cook it for just a few minutes; you want it to still be firm, and cooking it just helps it blend later on. Use a spider to remove it to a bowl of ice water. Dump the hot water out of the pot, but don't clean it: you can use that same pot to cook the chowchow.

In a food processor, in batches, blend the peppers, the cabbage, and the onions just until you have a nice chunky texture (you don't want it too pulverized). It should look like confetti.

Add all the blended vegetables to the pot with the salt, black pepper, sugar, allspice, and vinegar. Bring to a boil, lower to a simmer, and cook for 1 hour, stirring every so often. (You don't want it to get too dry; so if necessary, add more vinegar.) Make sure to taste as you go: Does it need more sugar? More salt? More heat? If it needs more heat (unlikely!), you can add a pinch of red pepper flakes too.

After an hour, when the chowchow has thickened somewhat and there's less liquid than when you started, take it off the heat and let it sit at room temperature for 3 hours. This helps the flavors develop.

If you plan to use the chowchow right away, put it in a clean jar and store it in the refrigerator. If you want to put it up for later, follow the canning directions on page 134. Serve with collard greens.

Fried Chicken

Serves 4 to 6

I'm a big fryer of chicken, and I've done it all kinds of ways. I've soaked chicken in buttermilk, I've flavored the base with garlic powder and cayenne pepper, I've pan-fried it, I've oven-fried it; you name it, I've done it. This method, which is in many ways the simplest, is now my go-to method. Season the chicken with just salt and pepper, giving it some time to seep in, and then dip it in water, roll it in flour, and fry it in very hot oil. The water is the most unexpected and unusual step, but it's one of those mysterious recipe things you just trust once you do it. As always, when deep-frying, watch the oil: you don't want it to bubble over, so use a Dutch oven or a stockpot and only fill it halfway. Add the chicken one piece at a time, monitoring the bubbles. If the oil is bubbling up high, be patient and fry the chicken in batches.

1 to 2 (4-pound) chickens cut into drumsticks, breasts, thighs, and wings

Kosher salt and freshly ground black pepper

1 to 2 cups all-purpose flour

1 quart vegetable oil

Three hours before you want to fry, clean the chicken: get rid of any feather remnants (you'd be surprised; they're there) and organs (like heart or liver). Pat the chicken very dry with paper towels and then season all over with salt and pepper. Cover and refrigerate until 1 hour before frying, then remove from the refrigerator and bring to room temperature.

Set up two bowls: one full of room-temperature water, the other full of the flour. Also, start heating the oil. In a large stockpot or Dutch oven, pour in the vegetable oil. (It shouldn't come up any more than halfway; ideally, it'd be a third of the way up. You don't want that hot oil to bubble over!) Using a deep-frying thermometer, heat the oil until it reaches 370°F.

Now, piece by piece, dip the chicken in the water and then in the flour (the water helps the flour stick). Make sure the chicken is thoroughly coated in flour; you don't want water to come in contact with the oil. Carefully lower the floured chicken into the oil and cook for 15 to 20 minutes, turning every so often, until, when you cut into a piece, the meat is all white and not at all pink. (The breast will cook faster than the legs or thighs.) Use the thermometer to maintain the oil temperature between 365 and 370°F.

Use tongs or a spider to lift the chicken to a plate lined with paper towels and then serve very hot. If you're planning to fry chicken again soon, you can allow the oil to cool and strain it into a container, where it will keep for several weeks.

- Knowing how to cut up a chicken is a skill worth having; it's cheaper than buying chicken in parts and also is better because the chicken will be fresher. Use a sharp knife and start by cutting off the wing at the joint where the wing meets the body. Then use the knife to separate the thigh and leg together, bending the chicken around to find the joint. Once again, bend the chicken to find the joint that attaches the leg to the thigh and cut that apart. Use a pair of kitchen scissors to cut out the backbone; then you're left with the breast, which you should cut in half both vertically and horizontally. When you're finished you should have 10 pieces of chicken for frying (2 legs, 2 thighs, 2 wings, and 4 pieces of breast). Save the backbone for stock.

- The oil could catch fire if it bubbles over and could spread all over your kitchen, so be very careful when deep-frying.

- Try serving it with honey; it's not necessarily traditional, but it's good.

Fresh
Pecan Pie

Makes one 9-inch pie

Here is a gooey, oozy, candy bar–like pecan pie that benefits greatly from two ingredients that go well with pecans: orange zest and lemon zest. Those of you who frown upon using a frozen piecrust can use Sara Moulton's (page 164) or Gary Danko's (page 118) recipe for making your own. But the filling here is really the star of the show. In fact, my friend Ameer, who normally hates pecan pie, said this pie converted him. He went back for a second piece.

1 prepared piecrust, store-bought or homemade

1 cup Karo light corn syrup

1½ cups sugar

A pinch of kosher salt

3 large eggs

¼ cup melted unsalted butter (4 tablespoons)

1 teaspoon pure vanilla extract

1 tablespoon grated orange zest (optional)

1 tablespoon grated lemon zest (optional)

1½ cups whole pecan halves

Whipped cream or vanilla ice cream, for serving

Preheat the oven to 350°F. Place the prepared piecrust on an aluminum foil–lined cookie sheet and set aside.

In a large bowl, stir together the corn syrup, sugar, salt, eggs, butter, vanilla, and, if you're using them, the orange and lemon zests. Once that's homogeneous, add the pecans and make sure they're all coated.

Pour the pecan mixture into the prepared pie shell (don't overfill it; you want the filling to come just up to the top). Bake for 45 minutes, or until the filling is set. You'll know it's done when you shake the cookie sheet and the filling doesn't wobble in the center.

Remove to a cooling rack and allow to come to room temperature. Serve with whipped cream (flavored with bourbon, if you have it) or a scoop of vanilla ice cream. Covered loosely with plastic wrap, the pie will keep at room temperature for 2 to 3 days.

Brandon Pettit

Chef-owner, Delancey
Seattle, Washington

Perfection is a lofty goal for any artist, whether a painter, a dancer, a musician, or a chef.

What defines perfection? Technical precision? Yes, partly; but in art, as in cooking, there has to be something else too. Thomas Keller, in his writings, calls it "finesse." Carrie Bradshaw, in her writings, calls it the "za za zu." Whatever it's called, Brandon Pettit, chef and owner of Delancey in Seattle, Washington, strives for it every day.

"A musician can spend eight hours a day on one paragraph of music," says Pettit, who knows something about music, having pursued his Ph.D. on the subject. "The attention to detail required in music is greater than what you find in most restaurants."

As if to prove his point, Pettit applies a musician's dedication and focus to each of the pizzas he makes in the wood-burning oven at Delancey. When I eat there, the night before we cook together, he joins me at my table to chat; but any time an order comes in for another pizza, he leaps to his feet. He cooks every pizza at Delancey himself.

"Time slows down when I make a pizza," says Pettit. "It takes three minutes to make a pizza, but for me, it feels like ten."

How did this obsession begin? When Pettit first moved to Seattle to join his wife, food writer Molly Wizenberg, he was unhappy with the pizza that he found.

"Any random corner pizza place in New Jersey was better than the 'good stuff' I found here," he tells me. "Pizza here was underdone; there was no char, no salt in the dough; the sauce was a cooked sauce. It wasn't bright at all."

At home, Pettit started experimenting with making his own pizza. He read an essay in Jeffrey Steingarten's book about tricking one's oven to heat hotter than normal (a scalding-hot oven is important for excellent pizza) by wrapping the thermostat with cold, wet T-shirts. Twenty minutes later, the T-shirts were on fire and Wizenberg forbade him from trying it again.

But Pettit persisted, recalling something he had learned in music school about Aaron Copland's music teacher Nadia Boulanger. "She said, 'If you want to write a piano sonata, listen to every sonata out there. Then pull your favorite things from all of those, pick the best, and use that in your own work.'" Pettit applied this to pizza by traveling the country and sampling the nation's best pizzas.

"I liked the texture of the pizza at John's on Bleecker Street in New York," he says. "I liked the cheese from Di Fara on Avenue J in Brooklyn. The sauce from Cafe Lago in Seattle."

The pizza at Delancey is the apotheosis of Pettit's pizza passion. Each pie comes out crisp and crackling from the wood-burning oven (no wet T-shirts visible), the sauce bright red, the whole thing slicked with olive oil. To my mind, it rivals some of New York's best pizza, but Pettit himself isn't completely satisfied.

"It's not as good as I want it to be yet," he confesses before I go. "I'm still getting better every day."

"Picking the bassoon part out of an orchestral score is the same as picking out what spices are in a really good curry."

Homemade
Pizza Dough

Makes enough for 5 pizzas

The Delancey pizza dough recipe is proprietary, but Pettit gave his approval of this recipe I adapted from Tim Artz (page 100). In fact, Pettit has no problem with the home cook using a store-bought pizza dough. He's less concerned with the recipe itself than he is that you treat your pizza dough properly. That means letting it rise for the requisite amount of time so the flavors can develop. That also means stretching it as thin as you can so you don't get a big bready blob when you bake it. To know if the dough is going to be flavorful, do what Pettit does: taste it raw. Its level of saltiness and sourness will dictate how to flavor what you top it with.

½ teaspoon dried yeast

2½ cups water, slightly warmer than room temperature

2 to 2½ cups all-purpose or double-zero pizza flour, plus 2½ to 3 cups for later (plus more, as necessary)

1 tablespoon coarse salt

1 tablespoon olive oil

The night before you plan to make the pizza, mix the yeast and the water together in the bowl of a stand mixer with the whisk attachment on medium speed until the mixture is fluffy, about 1 minute. On medium speed, mix in 2 to 2½ cups of flour until the mixture is slightly thicker than pancake batter (this is called your "sponge"). Cover with plastic wrap and let it sit at room temperature overnight.

The next morning, add the salt and olive oil to the sponge and, with the mixer on medium-low speed (and using the dough hook attachment), begin adding more flour, ½ cup at a time. Let the flour fully integrate before adding another ½ cup. When the dough stops sticking to the sides of the bowl, you've added enough flour (it's better to add less flour now than too much). Continue kneading the dough in the mixer for 10 to 15 minutes, until it has a smooth, elastic surface. Cover the bowl with plastic wrap and let sit at room temperature for at least 4 hours (or until the dough rises to the top of the bowl).

Divide the dough evenly into 5 pieces (each piece should be 10 to 12 ounces), rolling each one into a round. Place them on a large oiled cookie sheet (you may want to use two because the dough expands) and cover again with plastic wrap; allow to rise, again, at room temperature for another 3 to 4 hours, until bubbles appear on the surface.

Make sure that the oven is preheated to its highest setting (usually 500°F) and that you have all the toppings ready to go: you want to do everything all at once so the pizza can slide easily into the oven.

• Any dough you don't use can be wrapped tightly in plastic wrap, frozen, and defrosted overnight in the refrigerator for use the next day.

On a floured surface and with floured hands, flatten a round until it's a circular shape. Stretch it out and then, using the back of your hands, lift the dough up and continue to stretch it out. Allow it to rest on your knuckles and let gravity do the work for you, rotating it around and around as it continues to stretch. If you're brave, you can toss the dough in the air to stretch it; but it's not necessary. What is necessary is to get the dough as thin as you can get it before topping it. The thinner it is, the faster it'll cook and the crisper it'll be. If you're using a pizza stone, make the dough into a round shape. If you're using a cookie sheet, stretch it into a large oval to cover the length of the sheet.

When your dough is stretched very thin, lay it on a wooden pizza peel coated with a little flour (you can also use cornmeal here) or on the cookie sheet. You're ready to proceed to any of the following pizza recipes. (You can use this same dough for the calzone on page 103.)

Pizza Sauce

Makes enough for 2 to 3 pizzas

The flavors in this pizza sauce are big because they mellow as they cook. When you taste the sauce it should be slightly too salty and slightly too acidic. At home, it's also important that the sauce add big flavor to the pizza because you're compensating for your oven's lack of heat (a commercial pizza oven goes up to 800 or 900°F; you're lucky to get your home oven up to 500°F).

1 (28-ounce) can whole, peeled Alta Cucina or San Marzano tomatoes

Red wine vinegar (optional)

Kosher salt

Sugar

Dry oregano (the kind that they sell on the stalk)

1 clove garlic, pressed through a garlic press

Strain the tomatoes and place them in a large bowl.

This is where you have to use your palate to guide you: If the tomatoes are very acidic, don't add any vinegar. If they're not very acidic, add a splash. Continue flavoring the tomatoes with a big pinch of salt, a pinch of sugar, a light sprinkling of oregano, and the garlic.

Using a hand blender, blend the mixture until it's the consistency of a chunky tomato soup. (A regular blender will get it too watery and a food processor would leak.)

Taste the mixture and adjust to make it slightly too salty and bright. Use immediately or store, refrigerated, for up to 3 days.

- If you don't have a garlic press, use a knife to mince the garlic the way Gina DePalma does for her bagna cauda (see page 91). Use salt to help you make a paste.

- You can use the tomato liquid to make an excellent sauce for pasta. Just add it to a pot with a pat of butter, a clove of garlic, and a pinch of salt and simmer until thick.

Margherita Pizza

Serves 2 to 4

There are two secrets to an excellent Margherita pizza (named after Italy's Queen Margherita and visually representative of the colors in the Italian flag): (1) good tomato sauce (see Pettit's pizza sauce, page 27) and (2) the best olive oil you can afford, drizzled on the pizza hot out of the oven. In summer, Pettit adds garden-grown basil at the end of cooking; in winter, he uses greenhouse basil and adds it right before the pizza goes into the oven.

Homemade Pizza Dough (page 24)	4 or 5 fresh basil leaves
1 cup Pizza Sauce (page 27)	Good olive oil (to add before cooking)
1 ball fresh mozzarella	Excellent olive oil (to finish pizza)

Get the oven as hot as you can get it (most likely, 500°F). If you have a pizza stone, place it in the cold oven and allow it to preheat for at least 30 minutes.

Pour some sauce onto the center of the prepared pizza dough and spread it out with a ladle, taking it close to the edge. You want just a thin layer of sauce or your pizza will be soggy.

Using your fingers, break apart the fresh mozzarella over the pizza surface and scatter around whole fresh basil leaves. Drizzle with the good olive oil.

If using a pizza stone, open the oven and carefully shimmy the pizza from the pizza peel onto the stone's surface. If using a cookie sheet, place the pizza in the oven.

Bake the pizza for approximately 10 minutes, until the cheese is brown and bubbly and the crust is golden brown.

Remove from the oven and slice into wedges or squares (a pizza cutter is handy for this). Drizzle with excellent olive oil, and eat it hot!

It helps here to have an oven with a window because you don't want to let heat out as you check the pizza. Time it so that if you do have to open the oven, you do it toward the end of cooking rather than at the beginning.

The Brooklyn Pizza

Serves 2 to 4

This is a balanced, nuanced version of the classic New York–style pizza that inspired Pettit to open Delancey in the first place. You may be surprised by the brands of cheese Pettit suggests—Polly-O? Grande?—but he assures me that the best pizza makers in the country use these brands too because they have so much flavor. When you serve it and your family asks what kind of pizza you made, tell them, with your best New York accent, "It's a Brooklyn pizza, you got a problem with that?"

**Homemade Pizza Dough
(page 24)**

1 cup Pizza Sauce (page 27)

½ cup aged mozzarella (look for Polly-O or Grande brand), cut into ½-inch cubes and pulsed in the food processor

**1 ball fresh mozzarella
(Grande or Lioni brand)**

Good olive oil

½ cup freshly grated Parmesan cheese

Get the oven as hot as you can get it (most likely, 500°F). If you have a pizza stone, place it in the cold oven and allow it to preheat for at least 30 minutes.

Pour some sauce onto the center of the prepared pizza dough and spread it out with a ladle, taking it close to the edge. You want just a thin layer of sauce or your pizza will be soggy.

Rub the aged mozzarella between your hands and sprinkle over the pizza in a thin layer. Pinch off chunks of the fresh mozzarella and scatter around. Drizzle with olive oil and place the pizza in the oven, either from the paddle onto a pizza stone or via a cookie sheet.

Bake for 10 minutes, or until the cheese is brown and bubbly and the crust is golden brown. Remove from the oven and sprinkle with the Parmesan. Cut into wedges or squares and serve.

Sausage and Pickled Pepper Pizza

Serves 2 to 4

If the first two pizza recipes (page 28 and opposite) are a welcome taste of the familiar, this is a pizza that takes you by surprise. It's really a beautiful study in contrasts: the meaty, fatty sausage against the zingy, spicy pickled peppers. You could probably buy commercially packaged pickled peppers (something like pickled jalapeños), but making your own pickled peppers is *so* easy and *so* worth it. Even though you may be tempted to, don't overload the pizza. Less is more, even when it comes to pizza.

A splash of olive oil, plus more for drizzling

3 or 4 links of pork sausage, out of the casing

Homemade Pizza Dough (page 24)

1 cup Pizza Sauce (page 27)

½ cup aged mozzarella (look for Polly-O or Grande brand), cut into ½-inch cubes and pulsed in the food processor

1 ball fresh mozzarella (Grande or Lioni brand)

A scattering of pickled peppers

Heat the olive oil in a sauté pan and shape the sausage meat into a patty. Cook the sausage on both sides until slightly browned on the outside and still pink in the middle. Remove the sausage to a plate and allow to cool.

Get the oven as hot as you can get it (most likely, 500°F). If you have a pizza stone, place it in the cold oven and allow it to preheat for at least 30 minutes.

Pour some sauce onto the center of the prepared pizza dough and spread it out with a ladle, taking it close to the edge. You want just a thin layer of sauce or your pizza will be soggy.

Crumble the sausage on top of the pizza sauce and then sprinkle with the aged mozzarella, pinches of the fresh mozzarella, and a scattering of the pickled peppers (depending on how hot and vinegary you like it). Drizzle with olive oil and place in the hot oven (either on the pizza stone or on a cookie sheet) for 10 minutes, or until the cheese is brown and bubbling and the crust is golden.

Remove from the oven, drizzle with olive oil, and cut into wedges or squares. Serve hot.

● Memorize the recipe for pickled peppers; not only are they great on pizza, they're great in eggs (deviled, scrambled, over easy), on chicken, in chili, you name it. It's as simple as this: buy a pound of red chilies (Fresno, red jalapeños; they don't have to be red, but the red adds nice color), seed them, and slice them into ¼-inch rounds. Place them in a bowl with 2 shallots, thinly sliced. Bring 2 cups white wine vinegar to a boil with ½ cup sugar, 3 tablespoons water, 2 sliced garlic cloves, and a big pinch of salt. Pour the boiling vinegar over the chilies, cover, and let stand for 5 minutes. Uncover, cool to room temperature, and pour into a jar. They'll keep like that for several weeks in your refrigerator.

● You make a patty to get the cooking process started for the sausage without cooking it all the way through (otherwise, it would dry out).

Alice
Waters

**Owner, Chez Panisse; and founder,
Chez Panisse Foundation
Berkeley, California**

Waters's Kitchen
Know-How

THE BEST VEGETABLES come, in season, from farmer's markets, but what do you do if there's not a farmer's market in your town? There are several solutions: Seek out a local farmstand. Find out where you can go nearby to pick fruits and vegetables. If all else fails, find neighbors who grow things and see if you can buy from them or trade with them.

A TOASTER OVEN isn't just for toasting bread. It's an energy-efficient small box of heat, and you can use it to roast beets or to melt cheese on cheese tacos.

IT'S TOO SIMPLE to require a recipe, but still worth mentioning because it's so good: when I noticed a green orb in Waters's vegetable basket, she revealed it to be a watermelon radish. She peeled away the outside and cut it into wedges ("It looks just like a little watermelon," she pointed out) and then squeezed lime juice over it and sprinkled it with salt. "It's a very hard recipe," joked Waters as she served it up. But in its simplicity, it's outrageously good: a perfect marriage of three ingredients.

When most people think of a great chef, they think of a master technician, an intense white-jacketed maestro, storming around a kitchen, lighting things on fire, and screaming, in French, because the *fumé* is boiling too rapidly.

That's certainly one path that leads to great food. The other is one that was forged by Alice Waters at her legendary restaurant Chez Panisse in the 1970s—a path that she still forges today. It has nothing to do with scars and burns and kitchen tirades and everything to do with sourcing the best ingredients and bringing them together in a simple way. It's a path informed, almost entirely, by good taste.

"Taste is a huge part of what I do," says Waters, from the kitchen table of her home in Berkeley. "That's what the restaurant has always been about. If you get really tasty things, it's so easy to cook."

And while most chefs spend their careers honing their technical skills (path #1), very few chefs or home cooks work on developing their palates. This is an easy feat to accomplish, however, in Waters's home kitchen, where everything that surrounds her is an exercise in good taste.

For example, let's talk about her vinegar. "I've tried and tried," she tells me, "to find a great wine vinegar, but I still haven't." Her solution? She makes her own in a wooden barrel that sits on the floor near a window. "You start with a vinegar mother and then add wine to it. At the end of a dinner party, if you have wine left over, you just pour it into the vinegar barrel."

The resulting vinegar, which I taste on a simple salad that Waters makes with purple carrots, celery, and radish, is positively haunting, it's so good. I say "haunting" because hours later, when I journey back to San Francisco, I can't get the taste of that vinegar out of my head. It has all the complexity of a great wine—which, when you think about it, makes sense because it's made with great wine.

That's just the tip of the iceberg. All of her vegetables—shallots, avocados, turnips, jalapeños, radishes—come from the farmer's market, and they're piled up in authentic straw baskets from Africa. The eggs are fresh, organic, and pasture-raised ("Find a farmer you trust," Waters advises); her olive oil comes from Stephen Singer, her ex-husband, who imports it from Tuscany. She pours some into a wineglass and we both taste it. "It burns the back of your throat," she points out. "And it's full and rich and coats your mouth."

Even when Waters makes something as simple as cheese tacos (the second dish she teaches me), she uses the best ingredients. The tortillas are stone-ground handmade organic tortillas from Primavera; the cheese is a local Monterey Jack. "I'm looking for the things that really make a difference," says Waters. "Certain things that taste remarkably different."

After frying eggs in olive oil, crowning them with a ring of fresh herbs from her garden, and serving them for lunch on whole wheat toast rubbed with garlic, she takes a glass teapot and fills it with mint leaves.

"I never had a green thumb and I still don't, but I befriend people who have green thumbs."

"This is my favorite recipe," she tells me, adding boiling water to the leaves from a kettle.

This is fresh mint tea, as simple as it gets, and she pours it into small glasses for us to sip. "Interesting," she says as she tastes. "This mint is *lemon balmy*. It's different from the mint you get in spring, which is more assertive."

I must confess that my mint tea tasted, at first, just like mint tea; but after thinking about it, I suppose it did taste lemon balmy. Noticing a detail like that doesn't just happen, but being aware of a detail like that is what comes at the end of path #2, a path that I find myself traveling upon leaving the home of Alice Waters.

Farmer's Market Salad with Garlic Vinaigrette

Serves 2 to 4

When Alice Waters makes a salad, you pay attention. "One of the failings of salad," she says as she combines garlic pounded with a pestle in a mortar with her homemade vinegar, "is sometimes it's too oily." She adds a small amount of olive oil to her dressing, way less than you might guess, and then spoons it over a salad made with shaved farmer's-market vegetables and mesclun from her backyard. She constantly tastes and adjusts the dressing with salt, more vinegar, more oil. "Stick your fingers in it," she tells me so I can taste it too. Needless to say, the dressing matters slightly less than the vegetables; use the very best you can get (this is the salad to make after a trip to the farmer's market).

See Hugh Acheson's tip for starting a vinegar at home on page 344.

1 clove garlic

Kosher salt

Red wine vinegar (preferably homemade)

Balsamic vinegar

Freshly ground black pepper

Olive oil

Any combination of purple, orange, and yellow carrots

Any combination of radishes

1 or 2 white turnips

1 celery stalk (plus the leaves)

A few handfuls of mesclun

Make the dressing in a mortar. Add the garlic clove and a pinch of salt and pound it with a pestle mercilessly until you get a garlic paste. Spoon in some red wine vinegar, a splash of balsamic (for sweetness), and another pinch of salt and one of pepper and stir to combine. Taste with your finger and adjust the seasoning to your liking. Stir in a small splash of olive oil and set aside.

In a large bowl, use a mandoline slicer to shave in the carrots (try not to peel the carrots too much so they retain their color). Use the mandoline to slice in the radishes and turnips. Cut the celery thin on a cutting board (it's too fibrous to work on the mandoline). Dress everything with a spoonful or two of the dressing and then add the mesclun. Toss the salad with your hands until everything is nicely coated and distributed, adding more dressing as necessary. Serve right away, before the mesclun wilts.

Charred and
Cheesy Garden
Salad Tacos

Makes 4 tacos

I have to admit, Waters took me by surprise when she opened a package of corn tortillas, gripped one with a pair of tongs, and held it over an open flame. Alice Waters making tacos? But these tacos, once again, have all the hallmarks of Waters's food: the recipe is simple, the ingredients are top-notch, and everything is assembled with delicacy and finesse. The best part is that you can char the tortillas ahead; put them on a cookie sheet, and when your guests arrive, top them with cheese and stick them in the oven. This recipe is also great for kids.

4 organic, stone-ground (preferably handmade) corn tortillas

1 cup shredded Monterey Jack cheese, shredded on a box grater's widest setting (use the best local cheese you can find)

Leftover Farmer's Market Salad with Garlic Vinaigrette (opposite)

1 avocado, pitted, peeled, and sliced

Kosher salt and freshly ground black pepper

Preheat the oven to 425°F (unless you're using a toaster oven, in which case skip this step).

Using a pair of tongs, hold each tortilla over a gas flame until it gets charred around the edges and puffs up a little. Place on an aluminum foil–lined cookie sheet or toaster oven tray.

Top each tortilla with some of the shredded cheese (not so much that it'll ooze over the side) and place in the oven or the toaster. Bake or toast just until the cheese melts.

While that's happening, chop up some of the dressed mesclun from the Farmer's Market Salad.

To finish, take the tacos out of the oven and top each with a little of the salad and some avocado. Sprinkle with salt and pepper, fold them in half, serve them up, and eat them quickly; they taste best hot.

Olive Oil–Fried Eggs with a Crown of Herbs

Serves 2 to 3

I love to cook breakfast on the weekends, but almost always the food that I make is brown (pancakes, waffles, French toast, granola) or gray (oatmeal). That probably explains why this dish—a simple dish of fried eggs topped with lots and lots of herbs—was such a startling discovery when I served it one weekend morning. Not only did the herbs emit a fragrant, woodsy smell, but visually, the plate lit up with a beautiful bright green color. Serve with a simple salad on the side and, color-wise, the plate will be as un-brown and un-gray as it gets.

- This is certainly in the spirit of Alice Waters, who told me that she eats salad three times a day, basically at every meal. ("You must have wonderful digestion," I remarked.)

- Waters uses a combination of fennel fronds, arugula, chives, and chervil. I use parsley, thyme, and sage.

- When Waters makes this, she uses at least ¼ cup, possibly even ½ cup of fresh herbs.

A combination of herbs and greens, whatever you have on hand	Kosher salt and freshly ground black pepper
6 large organic eggs, preferably from the farmer's market	Good-quality sourdough or whole wheat bread, sliced
Olive oil	1 clove garlic, peeled

Chop the greens and herbs with a sharp knife until they're fragrant little flecks (you want at least ¼ cup). Set them aside.

Crack all the eggs into a bowl, being careful not to break the yolks.

Pour out enough olive oil to coat the bottom of a 9-inch cast-iron skillet (a nonstick pan will work here too). You want a good layer of oil (about ¼ cup). Turn up the heat to medium and when the oil starts to feel hot, pour in the eggs. Sprinkle on salt and pepper and then crown all the eggs with the herbs.

While the eggs are cooking, toast the bread in a toaster, in a toaster oven, or under the broiler. When it's good and toasty, rub each piece with the garlic.

When the eggs are just starting to firm up on top but the yolks are still soft, after 1 to 2 minutes, turn off the heat and cover the pan. The residual heat will finish cooking the whites on top.

To serve, top each piece of garlic-rubbed bread with an egg and some of the oil from the pan. Don't eat it with a knife and fork; use your hands! Just don't get yolk on your shirt.

Bobby Hellen

Executive chef, Resto
New York, New York

Hacking the head off a goat isn't as gruesome as you'd think, especially when chef Bobby Hellen's at your side coaching you through it.

Hellen, the executive chef of Resto in New York's Murray Hill neighborhood, doesn't use a saw when cutting up a goat or a pig. He uses a sharp knife.

"You've just got to find where it moves," he explains as he shifts a leg back and forth. "The place where the joint goes in is where you put your knife."

When he passes me the knife and has me cut the goat apart in all the places he tells me to cut, it seems like I'm cutting through butter. This is the mark of a chef who understands the way animals are put together. It's also the mark of a chef who understands what to do when he takes the animals apart: in Hellen's kitchen, nothing goes to waste.

So, for example, the heart and liver and kidneys? They'll go into charcuterie. The ribs will be made into chops, the scuddle (loin ends) will be seared, and all the other parts that don't make it into an entrée or an appetizer will be used for stock.

Using all the parts of an animal like this is good on many levels. In economic terms, coming up with multiple dishes from one animal makes it possible to cook on a budget without sacrificing quality. It also induces creativity: Hellen, who designs tasting menus for tables who order one of his whole animal dinners, constantly develops new dishes to keep things interesting. "I like to do something unique," he tells me. (His walk-in is a vegetarian's chamber of horrors: shelves piled with lamb's brains, twelve kinds of house-made charcuterie, a pig's head, and so on.)

Most important, though, stretching an animal is good on an ethical level. It's a way of honoring the animal by using all of its parts. And ethics is something that Hellen thinks about when buying meat for the restaurant. "Emotionally, if an animal is stressed when it dies," he explains, "the muscles tighten. Plus there's so much other stuff in industrial meat, it's really bad for you. You should only buy meat that's raised ethically."

As ethical as he is when it comes to buying his meat, he's hardly a well-behaved schoolboy when it comes to what he does with it. Never mind the competitions he has with his fellow chefs to see who can eat the grossest part of the animal (he's eaten pig's eyeballs); Hellen can whip leftover meat into something so decadent, you'd never know it was made with kitchen scraps.

Take, for example, his Leftover Lamb BLT (page 42), made with lamb left over from the leg. He compresses the meat overnight so that it stays together when he sears it, then he places it on bread slathered with homemade mayo and topped with lamb bacon and the obligatory lettuce and tomato. He presses it all in a waffle maker, a quirky touch, slathering the outside of the bread with mayo too: "It'll toast up, you'll see."

I saw. And I ate. And it was so good, I didn't even think about the severed goat head staring at me while I devoured it.

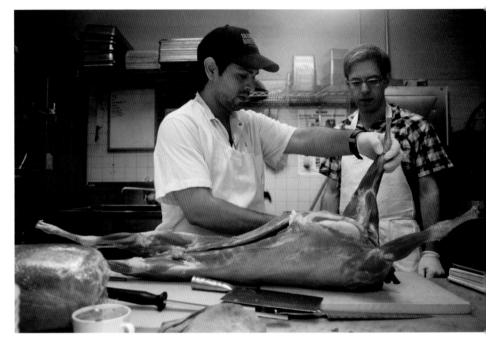

"I never take it easy on the mayo."

Yogurt-Marinated Leg of Lamb

Serves 4

A leg of lamb is a wonderful thing. You can do very little and it will taste good; and when it comes out of the oven, all golden and fragrant, you'll have enough meat to feed an army. But don't invite an army over to eat *this* leg of lamb: you want to save the leftovers to make a Leftover Lamb BLT (page 42). The yogurt here helps tenderize the meat, and as far as flavors go, you can take it in a variety of directions: for example, try cutting little slits all over the lamb and inserting slivers of garlic before roasting. Also, try toasting about a tablespoon of coriander seeds in a dry skillet until you start to smell them, then grind them in a spice grinder and sprinkle all over the lamb. Or you can keep it simple and follow this straightforward recipe; serve it with tsatsiki, a Greek salad, and a big, bold red wine and you'll be a very happy camper.

2 cups plain Greek yogurt (Fage is good)

1 tablespoon olive oil

1 tablespoon dried oregano

Juice of 1 lemon

1 tablespoon kosher salt, plus more to taste

One 5- to 7-pound leg of lamb, bone-in, silver skin removed (ask your butcher to do this)

Sea salt, for garnish

The night before you want to cook the lamb, make a marinade by whisking together the yogurt, olive oil, oregano, lemon juice, and kosher salt. Place the lamb in a container large enough to hold it and coat it completely in the marinade. Cover and refrigerate overnight.

Two hours before you're ready to cook it, remove the lamb from the refrigerator and let it come to room temperature.

Preheat the oven to 325°F. Place the lamb on a roasting rack in a large roasting pan. Roast until the thickest part of the lamb reaches an internal temperature of 135°F, about 2 hours.

Remove the lamb to a cutting board, cover with aluminum foil, and allow to rest for at least 20 minutes. To carve, lift the leg up so the bone is facing upward and hold it to stabilize it. Slice down, making thin slices.

Place the slices on a large platter and serve with a small bowl of sea salt for sprinkling on top. For an extra kick of flavor, serve with a bowl of tsatsiki, if desired. Don't throw out the bone or the leftover meat! (See the next two recipes.)

● To make a simple tsatsiki, start by peeling, seeding, and chopping a cucumber. Salt it well and leave it in a strainer for 1 hour. Place it in cheesecloth, squeeze out all the liquid, and fold it into 1 cup Greek yogurt with the juice and zest of 1 lemon, 1 clove garlic, minced, 1 teaspoon salt, and ½ teaspoon pepper. Allow to sit for 30 minutes before using.

● If you want a garlicky lamb, chop up a few cloves of garlic and throw them in there too.

● This is a case where it pays to own a probe thermometer. Place the probe in the thickest part of the lamb and allow the wire to trail out of the oven to the digital display on the counter. Simply monitor the display until the temperature reaches 135°F; you'll get perfectly pink lamb.

Lamb Stock

Makes 1 quart

A leftover lamb bone is a precious kitchen commodity; gelatin-filled and meaty, it's all you need—plus a few vegetables—to make a good, unusual stock. The directions are so simple, it's just a matter of taking the time to do it. But once you do, you can use your lamb stock for everything from soups (try it in Gina DePalma's lentil soup, page 90, instead of water) to risotto (see Michel Richard's Potato Risotto, page 183).

1 leftover leg of lamb, meat removed (just the bone)

1 whole onion, skin on

1 whole carrot, unpeeled

1 head of garlic

Enough ice or very cold water to cover everything

- Use ice so that the temperature comes up extra slowly, allowing for better flavor extraction (if you don't want to bother, just use very cold water).

This is a very easy recipe. Throw everything into a big pot. Put it on low heat and let it come to a bare simmer. Cook for 4 to 6 hours, skimming the surface every so often, until the stock is a dark color, and then strain. You can use it right away or freeze it in plastic soup containers. It will keep in the freezer for several months.

Leftover
Lamb BLT

Makes 1 sandwich

Lamb isn't the first thing that comes to mind when you think BLT, but somehow the combination of leftover lamb, crispy bacon, and homemade mayonnaise makes for a very satisfying sandwich. Hellen has you press the leftover meat in a pan the night before to help it come together into one uniform piece (see the first step), but if you're lazy, you can skip that step and just sear leftover lamb pieces in a hot pan; this warms up the lamb and gives it a little color. If you're a glutton like me, you can sear the lamb in the bacon fat after you cook the bacon. Pigs and baby sheep have never been better friends.

1 leftover leg of lamb with a decent
amount of meat still attached (see page 40)

1 egg yolk

½ cup plus 1 tablespoon canola oil

¼ cup extra virgin olive oil

Kosher salt

1 lemon, halved

2 slices good-quality sandwich bread,
sliced thick

2 to 4 pieces bacon, cooked until crisp

A small handful of arugula

2 to 4 slices of fresh tomato

● Hellen uses lamb bacon on his BLT, but seeing as it's unlikely that you'll find lamb bacon, regular bacon works very well.

The day before you want to make this sandwich, pull off all the extra meat from the leg of lamb. Place the meat in a pan or on a plate, then top the meat with another pan or plate of a similar size and weigh it down with heavy cans. Cover the exposed areas with plastic wrap or aluminum foil and place in the refrigerator overnight.

Make the mayo. Place the egg yolk in a bowl and combine the ½ cup canola oil and the olive oil in a measuring cup. Add a single drop of the combined oil to the yolk and whisk it in; repeat with another drop of oil. Keep doing that, drop by drop, and pay attention to what's happening in the bowl: you want the yolk to absorb each drop of oil. It should get thicker each time. Once you've added several drops, you can start including a stream of oil. Keep whisking and watching. If at any point you see oil separated from the thickened yolk, stop the stream and whisk vigorously until it's incorporated. Keep going—you can pour a thicker stream the further along you get—until the yolk has absorbed all the oil. Congrats; you just made mayonnaise! Now season with salt and add a squeeze of lemon.

Cut off squares of the reserved meat; they should be large enough to fit on the sandwich bread. Heat a skillet on medium, add the tablespoon of canola oil, and then add the meat, searing it until it's crusty and golden brown on both sides.

Place the meat on the sandwich bread (which you can toast first, if you're not pressing it) and top it with bacon, arugula, tomato, and a good amount of homemade mayo. If you're planning to press the sandwich in a panini press, shmear the outside of the sandwich with mayo too. Press the sandwich until it's toasty on the outside and eat right away.

● When I tried this the first time, my mayonnaise broke toward the end. You'll know you have a broken mayo when the liquids and solids aren't homogeneous. Even though there are ways to try to fix it, your best bet is to start again. If the oil is separated at any point, make sure to whisk it vigorously into the yolk. That's the best way to recover.

Lidia Bastianich

Television host, author,
and restaurateur
Queens, New York

Roots are important to chef Lidia Bastianich. In the summer, at her home in Queens, New York, Bastianich grows basil, peppers, eggplant, and tomatoes right in front of her house. The roots of these plants echo the roots of the plants her grandmother cultivated in Italy. "Everyone in Italy has a garden," she tells me. "You feel naked without it."

Family, and the rootedness it provides, is also important to Bastianich. On her TV show, you can regularly see her children and grandchildren assisting her in the kitchen. On the day that we cook together, we're joined by Bastianich's mother (whom everyone calls Nona); her daughter, Tanya; and her grandchildren, Lorenzo and Julia. Everyone congregates in the kitchen, where Bastianich holds court.

"I love what I do," she tells me as we begin prepping the first dish. "I have fun."

That first dish, Mussels and Clams Triestina, illustrates quite clearly how Bastianich's roots inform her cooking. "I've been eating mussels ever since I can remember," she tells me. "I'd go to the sea as a child, and mussels would grow on the rocks or the wood right there in the Adriatic."

She takes a big bowl of cleaned mussels and feels them. "If they feel light in your hands, don't buy them," she instructs. "If they feel like a rock in your hands, do." Why? A lighter-feeling mussel might be filled with sand.

To a hot pot Bastianich adds onions and red pepper flakes. When the onions soften, she adds two dozen littleneck clams. "The clams take longer," she explains as she covers the pan and allows them to open.

As we cook, Bastianich recounts the story of how her family came to America—a story that involves escaping communist Yugoslavia (her father was shot at as he made his way over the border) and surviving a refugee camp in Trieste, Italy. "Life there was rigid," she tells me as she adds the mussels to the pot. "I remember we stood in line for food."

Bastianich and her family made it to America courtesy of Dwight Eisenhower (who changed the quota for immigrants escaping communism) and the Catholic Church. "When you come here with fresh eyes," she tells me, "only then do you realize what America has to offer."

The bounty that surrounds her now is clearly something that Bastianich doesn't take for granted. As she plates the mussels and clams and proceeds through two more dishes—Ziti with Broccoli Rabe and Sausage and Frico with Potato (a fried cheese dish)—she tastes and expresses her pleasure with loud "mmm"s and "yum yum yum"s.

She reserves her biggest enthusiasm, though, for her children and grandchildren. When she offers a bowl of mussels and clams to Tanya, she seems genuinely amused when Tanya looks at her watch—it's 8:30 a.m.—and snaps: "No!"

Standing there washing dishes, with Tanya and the kids prepping ingredients, Bastianich couldn't seem more content. Here in Queens, Bastianich proves the value in planting your roots most deeply in the kitchen.

"You have to be open to creativity; you have to change things. That's the beauty of being a chef: you can make the recipe your own."

Ziti with Broccoli Rabe and Sausage

Serves 4

Pasta is my favorite food (above all others), and my fascination with it and love for it is very much due to the techniques I learned watching Bastianich make it on TV. Standing by her side as she made this (and as she let me break up the sausage with a spoon) was a treat beyond words. It was also very useful: when she finishes cooking a recipe on TV, you can't taste it. So I was careful to observe, while tasting this in her kitchen, that her pasta is way more unified than mine usually is: the sauce is almost fully absorbed by the pasta, and the proportions of cheese, broccoli rabe, and sausage are completely in balance. Getting that balance right is the hardest part, and the best way to learn it is by doing.

- Don't be lazy and waste the stems. Trimming them down with a paring knife makes them tender enough to enjoy.

- Bastianich prefers peperoncino, the Italian red pepper flakes often used as a garnish for pizza.

- Pecorino, a sheep's-milk cheese, is the most appropriate cheese to use here because there aren't any cows in the region this dish comes from (in southern Italy), just sheep.

Kosher salt

¼ cup olive oil, plus more for drizzling

3 large cloves garlic, crushed

½ pound sweet Italian sausage, out of the casing

1 pound ziti

2 pounds broccoli rabe (*broccoli di rape*), washed and drained, stems peeled with a paring knife, leaves roughly chopped

Crushed red pepper flakes

½ cup grated Pecorino cheese (or Grana Padano or Parmesan)

Bring a large pot of water to a boil and season it well with salt.

Place the ¼ cup olive oil and the garlic in a large sauté pan and cook on medium heat until the garlic starts to turn golden. Add the sausage, breaking it up with a spoon until you have bite-size pieces, and cook, stirring occasionally, until the sausage begins to caramelize.

Add the ziti to the pot of water, give it a stir, and half-cover it to allow it to come back to a rapid boil, then remove the lid (or it may boil over).

Add the broccoli rabe to the pan with the sausage and garlic and stir it with a pinch of salt and as much of the red pepper flakes as you like.

Now the secret ingredient: the pasta cooking water. Add a few ladlefuls (about 2 cups) to the pan with the garlic, sausage, and broccoli rabe. You want it to look relatively soupy. Cover that pan with a lid and lower the heat; allow it to cook together for a few minutes.

As the ziti reaches the end of its cooking time (look at the box to know that), taste a noodle in time to stop the cooking process while the ziti is still al dente. If it's still toothsome but mostly cooked, use a spider and transfer the pasta to the pan with the garlic, sausage, and broccoli rabe.

Stir and turn up the heat until most of the liquid has been absorbed by the pasta. Drizzle with olive oil and, off the heat, add the cheese. Give the pasta a final toss and serve immediately.

Frico with Potato

Serves 4 to 6

Rib-sticking comfort food usually involves something starchy with something gooey inside (think grilled cheese, lasagna, a calzone). This dish, which comes from the Friuli region in Italy, inverts the equation: you have something starchy (fried potatoes) inside something gooey (melted Montasio cheese). The result, which in Italian is called *formaggio fuso con patate,* may be the world's greatest hangover cure. Yes, it's greasy (though you can dab it with paper towels); yes, it's unhealthy (Bastianich says you can top it with a salad, if you'd like); but in terms of a crowd-pleaser, you can't do much better.

1 large baking potato, whole

Kosher salt

Enough olive oil to coat the bottom of a skillet

1 onion, sliced into half-moons

Freshly ground black pepper to taste

½ cup sliced scallions

½ pound Montasio cheese, shredded

● You can substitute a white cheddar, though Montasio is ideal.

Place the potato in a pot of cold water and turn up the heat to high. Bring to a boil, salt the water, and cook until a knife goes through the potato easily (15 minutes). Remove to a cutting board and wait until the potato is cool enough for you to peel it with a knife. Once peeled, slice it into ¼-inch disks. Set aside.

Coat the bottom of a nonstick skillet with olive oil and heat on medium until adding a bit of onion makes it sizzle. Add all of the onion, toss to coat with oil, and let the onion color a little, seasoning with salt and pepper as it does. It should take a few minutes to get good color.

Add the potato and let it cook directly on the heat for a few minutes, tossing occasionally, allowing it to develop color too (it's sort of like making hash browns). Add the scallions and season with more salt and pepper.

● Heating a traditional nonstick pan without oil can release carcinogens, so research the pan before doing so. A better bet is to use a well-seasoned cast-iron pan. (If it's not well seasoned, add a splash of oil.)

Heat a cast-iron skillet and when it's just warm enough to melt cheese but not scalding hot, add half of the cheese to it in an even layer. As it begins to melt, scoop the potato mixture on top and press it into another even layer. Sprinkle with the other half of the cheese.

Cook on medium-low heat, scraping around the sides, until the cheese forms a solid crust and shaking the pan causes the whole frico to shift.

● You can skip this step, if it makes you nervous. Just eat the frico with one side crusty and the other side melted.

When it detaches easily, slide the frico onto a plate, mop with a paper towel, and invert back into the hot pan to crisp on the other side.

Cook until the other side is crisp (a few minutes more) and flip back onto a plate. Serve warm with a salad on top or let it cool and eat it later. It'll still taste good.

Mussels and Clams Triestina

Serves 4 to 6

I don't know about you, but when I cook mussels or clams at home, the flavor is never big enough and the sauce is never rich enough to justify the effort. This recipe is the solution. The secret is lots of garlic, a good drinkable wine, and—the really unusual touch—bread crumbs to enrich the sauce. The result is big and bold and, with a side of grilled bread, makes a very satisfying lunch or first course. Though Bastianich prefers the mussels she ate growing up in Italy, she says, "If you get them fresh, they're just as delicious here."

- Make sure the mussels are alive: check by squeezing them shut. If they stay shut, they're alive; if they won't close, throw them out.

- Bastianich has a bay leaf tree outside her house and recommends that you keep one yourself.

- Try the Molino Bianco brand from Italy, which Bastianich's assistant, Amy, found in Bensonhurst in Brooklyn, New York.

Enough extra virgin olive oil to coat the bottom of a wide pot (approximately ¼ cup), plus more for drizzling

5 cloves garlic, peeled and crushed (for a stronger garlic taste, chop them)

2 small onions, sliced into half-moons

Kosher salt

A pinch of crushed red pepper flakes

2 dozen littleneck clams, washed and scrubbed

1 cup (or more) dry white wine (try Sauvignon Blanc or Tocai Friulano; it's important to use good wine because it's such a prominent part of the dish)

2 pounds mussels, washed, scrubbed, and debearded

4 fresh bay leaves

¼ cup to ½ cup dry, plain bread crumbs (or more)

3 tablespoons (or more) chopped fresh Italian parsley

Coat the bottom of a wide pot (one that has a well-fitting lid) with olive oil and add the crushed garlic cloves.

Turn up the heat to medium and allow the garlic to toast and turn golden. Once the garlic is golden, add the onions.

Let the onions cook slightly, 2 to 3 minutes (don't let them soften too much). Add a pinch of salt and a pinch of red pepper flakes (the size of the pinch depending on how spicy you like it), then add the clams, turn up the heat, and cover.

After 3 minutes, add the wine, bring to a boil, and cover again.

A few minutes later, check the clams: when they're just starting to open, add the mussels and bay leaves and cover again. Shake the pan every so often.

Wait another few minutes and check: when the mussels start to open, sprinkle in the bread crumbs and toss to distribute evenly. The sauce should thicken, though don't go crazy with bread crumbs or the sauce will be muddy. Taste and adjust the salt.

When the clams and mussels are open and the sauce is thick, drizzle olive oil over everything and add lots of chopped parsley. Serve in a big bowl with grilled bread on the side.

Grace Young

Cookbook author, *The Breath of a Wok*
and *Stir-Frying to the Sky's Edge*
New York, New York

Young's Kitchen Know-How

USE A fourteen-inch wok because of the surface area; use carbon steel because you can get it very hot before adding the fat. You can tell if a wok is carbon steel by studying the wok metal; if you see concentric circles—the result of the wok-shaping process—it's the real deal.

THE BIGGEST rookie mistake in wok cooking is getting the pan too hot. To reach the perfect temperature, use the water test. Put the wok on high heat and, after 30 seconds or so, begin flicking water into it. If the water evaporates right away, the wok is ready to go.

BEFORE USING A NEW WOK, scrub it several times with a stainless-steel scouring pad using hot soapy water to get the factory coating off. Then rinse the wok with hot water and follow the instructions on page 52 to season it.

Rarely is a bite of food so revelatory that it changes the way you think about an entire cuisine. Such was the case, though, when renowned Chinese cookbook author Grace Young offered me, straight from the wok, a spoonful of her fried rice.

"Chinese restaurant food is horrific," she tells me as I eat spoonful after spoonful of her rice. "They oil-blanch their meat and use MSG to camouflage funky flavors. Chinese home cooking is all about *pure* flavors."

And that's precisely what's so remarkable about this rice: the flavors are crystal clear. There's dried scallop, shiitake mushrooms, and Chinese sausage, each like a buried treasure of flavor. And the rice itself is perfectly cooked, the grains firm and not at all gummy or greasy, the whole thing light as air and yet wonderfully filling.

Credit goes to Young, of course, but more important, credit goes to her instrument of choice: the wok.

Young's wok is not expensive: it costs twelve dollars at K. K. Discount on Mulberry Street in New York. It's a fourteen-inch carbon-steel flat-bottomed wok, and those are details you should memorize. The last time I bought a wok I accidentally bought one with a nonstick surface: as I scraped the food around with a metal spatula (a tool Young recommends), the nonstick coating got all scratched and came off in the food. With a carbon-steel wok, that won't happen.

The wok, for Young, is the vehicle through which she channels her food philosophy, one that comes from her parents, Cantonese immigrants whose cooking Young adored from a young age.

"The Cantonese are snobs about food; they think they're the best cooks in all of China," she tells me as we slice beef for the next dish. "They have year-round seasonal produce and they honor it by cooking it super fast in a super-hot wok. It intensifies the flavor and aroma. They don't have to add a lot of seasoning."

Illustrating this, she peels a few bright red ripe tomatoes that she's boiled in hot water for just a few seconds to loosen the skins. She cuts them into wedges and then adds oil to her wok, which has been heating on the stove. She adds beef—flank steak that has been marinated with sherry, soy sauce, ginger, and garlic—and leaves it alone for a minute as it develops color. She removes the beef, adds the tomatoes, oyster sauce, chicken stock, a pinch of sugar, and scallions, covers it briefly "to intensify flavor," then returns the beef for 30 more seconds.

The resulting dish is remarkable, once again, for its purity of flavor. As Young promised, the flavor is intense, concentrated, and robust.

"The technique is so simple," says Young matter-of-factly.

"Fast food" is a dirty phrase for many people, but there's no shame in making food fast when the ingredients are this fresh and the technique is so sound. Trust me and the revelation of Grace Young's kitchen: to eat truly transporting Chinese food, get yourself a wok.

"Nothing will hurt this pan."

Beef with Tomato Stir-Fry

Serves 4

It may take work for me to convince you that this dish is both easier and cheaper than picking up the phone and ordering Chinese food delivered to your house, but once you have your <u>seasoned wok</u> and all the Chinese cooking staples ready to go—the soy sauce, the oyster sauce, the ginger—you'll make this and never want to pick up that phone for delivery again. Just make sure to serve it piping hot: as Young will tell you, food straight from the wok has a purity of flavor (the Chinese call it *wok hay*) that only lasts a few minutes. I have a hunch that devouring this quickly won't be a problem.

12 ounces flank steak

2 teaspoons cornstarch

1 teaspoon dry sherry

2 teaspoons <u>soy sauce</u>

1 tablespoon minced peeled ginger

1 tablespoon minced garlic

¼ teaspoon plus ½ teaspoon sugar

A pinch of kosher salt

1 teaspoon toasted sesame oil, peanut oil, or canola oil

2 to 3 very ripe tomatoes, blanched, skins removed, cored and cut into bite-size wedges, or 4 whole canned tomatoes cut into quarters

2 tablespoons <u>oyster sauce</u>

2 tablespoons chicken stock

¼ cup chopped scallions

Begin by cutting the meat into three equal portions. Slice each portion <u>against the grain</u> into 2-inch-long slices, ½ inch thick. Set aside.

In a bowl, make a marinade by combining the cornstarch, sherry, soy sauce, ginger, garlic, the ¼ teaspoon sugar, and the salt. Stir until the cornstarch is no longer visible and then stir in the meat. (Do this just before you stir-fry; no need to let it sit for long.)

Heat the wok and flick water in to see if it's ready: the water will evaporate instantly if it's hot enough. Swirl in the oil and then add the beef, spreading it out so it all gets a sear. Don't touch it for 1 minute. Give the meat a stir to sear the other side, and when it's just brown but not fully cooked, remove it to a plate.

Add the tomatoes, oyster sauce, chicken stock, the ½ teaspoon sugar, and the scallions. Cover the pan for 20 seconds to intensify the flavor.

Lift the lid, add the beef, and cook for another 30 seconds to a minute. When the beef is cooked through and the tomatoes are still somewhat firm but have released all their juices, remove to a platter and serve.

- To season your wok, put it on low heat and heat for 1 to 2 minutes, until the water has evaporated. The wok may change color. Turn off the heat and let the wok cool. Then, as a final step, turn up the heat to high (test the heat by flicking in water; when it evaporates, it's ready), swirl in 2 tablespoons of peanut oil, and add ½ cup of sliced unpeeled ginger and 1 bunch of scallions cut into 2-inch pieces. Reduce the heat to medium and stir-fry for several minutes (as much as 15 minutes), pushing the mixture all around the wok with a metal spatula. When the scallions are brown and crusty, remove the wok to a cold burner and throw out everything. When the wok is cool, wash it with hot water and a sponge, this time without soap. Finally, place the rinsed wok on low heat and heat for 1 to 2 minutes or until all the rinse water has evaporated. Now you have a seasoned wok that you can maintain by using it and by washing it, like a cast-iron skillet, without soap (unless truly necessary).

- Avoid generic soy sauce, which contains sodium benzoate, and use organic (Kikkoman makes a good one). As for oyster sauce, use Lee Kum Kee. Look for the one with the mother and child on the label (Young prefers this), not the panda.

- To understand why you cut against the grain, imagine a bunch of rubber tubes lying on top of each other. If you were to cut them the long way (with the grain), you'd get a bunch of long strings in each bite; if you cut them the other way (against the grain), you get a bunch of little bites that are more manageable.

Fried Rice with Dried Scallops and Shiitake Mushrooms

Serves 4

Forget everything you thought you knew about fried rice. This version is so ethereal, so otherworldly, it deserves another name. Take note: Young insists that this dish only works if you cook the rice the day before you fry it, so plan accordingly. Also, the three specialty ingredients this dish requires—dried scallops, dried shiitakes, and Chinese sausage—are worth seeking out. However, Young says you can replace the dried scallops with an equal amount of diced ham and, in place of the dried mushrooms, you can use fresh mushrooms and carrots that have been diced to ¼ inch.

2 cups sushi rice (Young recommends Premium Grade Nishiki rice)

2 tablespoons peanut oil (or other oil with a high smoking point, like canola or grapeseed)

1-inch piece of ginger, peeled and cut into very thin matchsticks

1 clove garlic, minced

½ cup dried scallops, soaked in water for an hour or two until very soft, then shredded

½ cup dried shiitake mushrooms, soaked for 25 to 30 minutes, stemmed, and cut into slices

1 or 2 pieces of Chinese sausage (buy in a Chinese butcher shop), cut into small pieces

1 to 2 tablespoons soy sauce

Kosher salt

¼ cup shredded scallions

¼ cup chopped cilantro

White pepper

The day before you plan to make the fried rice, place the 2 cups sushi rice in 2 cups water and soak for 30 minutes. Strain the rice, rinse under cold running water, and place in a small pot with 2 cups fresh water (or chicken broth for a richer rice). Bring to a boil, lower the heat, cover, and simmer for 10 minutes. Remove from the heat and keep the lid on for another 10 minutes. Fluff with a fork (this is important so the rice will separate easily in the wok the next day), cover, and refrigerate.

Place the wok on the stove and turn the heat to high. After a few moments, begin flicking water into the wok: you're looking for the moment when the water evaporates immediately. When it does, you're ready to go.

Swirl the peanut oil into the wok around the perimeter of the interior in one fluid motion. Add the ginger, garlic, scallops, mushrooms, and sausage and let cook for 1 minute, moving it all around with a metal spatula until the sausage looks cooked.

Add the cooked rice and swiftly break it up with the metal spatula, incorporating all the elements into the rice. Attack the clumps with the metal spatula, add the soy sauce, stir well, and, when everything looks to be incorporated, add salt to taste, the scallions, the cilantro, and white pepper to taste. Remove to a serving dish and eat right away.

Stir-Fried Bok Choy with Ginger

Serves 4

Chefs and home cooks often make statements about cooking that sound good when you hear them but, secretly, make you question their veracity. I have to confess that's how I felt, at first, when Young told me that the heat of a wok intensifies a vegetable's flavor. I mean, sure, cooking something does make it taste better; I especially like my vegetables roasted. But while roasting vegetables fundamentally changes them, wok-cooking just seems to make them softer. How intense could a vegetable taste after being tossed around a hot wok? Well, all my doubts imploded when I tasted this bok choy straight from Young's wok. In just a few seconds, this firm, grassy vegetable was positively exploding with flavor. It still tasted like itself, only it was infused with ginger and soy sauce—a magical combo that tastes especially good piping hot. I shall never doubt the power of the wok again.

1 tablespoon soy sauce

1 tablespoon sherry

1 tablespoon chicken stock

1 tablespoon peanut oil (or other oil with a high smoking point, like canola or grapeseed)

1 tablespoon shredded peeled ginger

12 ounces baby bok choy, cut into 2-inch pieces and patted very, very dry (any moisture will cause it to steam), stems and leaves separated

¼ teaspoon sugar

A pinch of kosher salt

In a small bowl, mix together the soy sauce, sherry, and chicken stock.

Heat the wok until a flick of water on the surface evaporates right away. Swirl the oil in down the side and add the ginger. When the ginger starts to crackle, add the bok choy stems. Stir with a metal spatula for 10 seconds, then add the bok choy leaves.

Cook, stirring, for 45 seconds to 1 minute, just until the bok choy starts to go limp. Add the sugar and salt and swirl the soy sauce mixture down the side of the wok.

Toss the bok choy in the sauce and taste for seasoning. Serve immediately.

If you poured the liquid directly onto the bottom, the temperature would drop too quickly.

Peter Dale

Chef, The National
Athens, Georgia

A self-described "small-town chef," Peter Dale—whose sophisticated interpretations of Southern food have been fêted by *The New York Times, Bon Appétit,* and the *Atlanta Journal-Constitution*—is a world traveler who still works and resides in the town where he grew up: Athens, Georgia.

"I like being in a small town," he tells me at his restaurant, The National. "I have a lot of freedom."

As a small-town chef, however, Dale must walk a tightrope, serving the food that he wants to make—much of it influenced by his time in Spain—while still catering to his audience of mostly Southerners. "People in the South eat shrimp and grits," he tells me as we enter his laid-back kitchen. "This is my interpretation of that."

He pours olive oil into a pan and adds diced chorizo. "I love Spanish chorizo," he says. "There's a great fattiness that coats your mouth and the paprika turns the oil orange."

Sure enough, as he turns up the heat, the air becomes fragrant with spice and the oil begins to tint red. "In the South, we normally use bacon for this dish, but I like it better this way."

His customers like it too. He uses sweet Georgia shrimp, a hat-tip to the South, while serving it all on polenta, a hat-tip to Italy. The finished dish marries the food of his childhood with the food he discovered in his travels, and it's all the better for it.

Other interesting parallels abound between the food here in the South and the food he's discovered in other parts of the world. "I love Middle Eastern and North African food," he tells me. "You find okra in those areas, but also here."

Okra, which is much maligned by those who find it slimy (count me among them!), is prized by Dale. "We love it down here," he tells me as he begins prepping his next dish, a fast sauté of okra and chickpeas. "Okra can be fried or stewed with tomatoes or pickled."

Dale's technique for cooking it is ingenious in the way that he avoids the slime factor. He gets a pan very hot, adds a splash of olive oil, and adds the okra, which he's sliced in half vertically. "If you cook it on high heat," he explains, "you sear it and lock in the gumminess."

The finished dish, which looks pretty Southern at first, gets topped with house-made harissa and a yogurt sauce made with lemon juice. Once again, it's a tribute to Dale's two primary influences, his childhood and his travels.

Dale's final dish, which is an homage to a dish he ate at Albert Adrià's Inopia, in Barcelona, is simply a pineapple dressed with lime sugar and pomegranate seeds. At Inopia, the dish got a drizzle of molasses from the Canary Islands, but here Dale uses cane syrup that his friend Jocelyn's dad has been making in his retirement. "They don't sell it," he says. "They just give it away."

A very Southern touch in a very Spanish dish; that's the way Dale likes to cook and the way his customers like to eat here in Athens.

"In Spain, they keep the shell on the shrimp and suck the head. We met with a little resistance to that here."

Shrimp and Polenta with Chorizo

Serves 2

Chorizo is a magical ingredient, the kind of thing that makes your food taste way more accomplished without asking anything of you beyond just buying it. D'Artagnan sells a good-quality chorizo that is readily available (see Resources, page 371); just make sure you're buying Spanish chorizo, which is already cooked, and not Mexican chorizo, which is raw. You can expand or contract this dish based on your needs: Feeding a bigger crowd? Double the amounts. Feeding just yourself? Cook as much chorizo and shrimp as you'd like to eat. It's really that simple.

2 cups water

2 cups whole milk

A pinch of kosher salt

1 cup polenta (not the quick-cooking kind)

½ cup small-diced Spanish chorizo

1 tablespoon olive oil

8 to 12 fresh uncooked shrimp, peeled and deveined, patted dry with paper towels

¼ cup white wine

¼ cup chopped fresh tomatoes

¼ cup chopped roasted red peppers

A big pinch of chopped Italian flat-leaf parsley

A handful of arugula

2 tablespoons unsalted butter

¼ cup freshly grated Parmesan

To make the polenta, bring the water and milk to a boil, add a pinch of salt, and then turn off the heat. Sift the polenta into the hot liquid, whisking all the while (this prevents lumps). Turn the heat back to low and cook, whisking every so often, for 30 minutes, or until the polenta gets really thick (you may need to switch to a wooden spoon).

Meanwhile, add the chorizo to a medium skillet (not nonstick) with the olive oil. Slowly bring up the heat to low and render the fat. You don't want too much color or for the chorizo to get crisp.

When the oil has turned orange and most of the fat has been rendered, push all the chorizo to the side and turn up the heat to medium high. Add all the shrimp: they should sizzle. You want the shrimp to get some color, so make sure the pan is hot enough.

Once the shrimp have some color, add the wine to deglaze the pan. Use a spoon to work up any brown bits and then add the tomatoes and the red peppers. Turn up the heat to reduce the sauce.

Feel the shrimp: they should be relatively firm and should look opaque. Add the parsley and arugula. Taste for seasoning; you may not need any salt because the chorizo is salted.

Stir the butter and Parmesan into the polenta and spoon the polenta onto serving dishes. Top with the shrimp and chorizo mixture and serve right away.

● Dale uses Red Mule polenta (see Resources, page 371); the mill's products are named for Luke, a red mule that powers the grist mill.

● You don't want to overcook the shrimp or they'll taste awful, so err on the side of undercooking.

Chickpeas and Okra with Harissa and Yogurt

Serves 4

Fire is your friend in the kitchen, and never more so than when you're cooking okra. Get your pan hot—hotter than you normally heat your pans—and watch as that slime-monster of a vegetable gets seared and golden brown on the outside. Make sure the chickpeas are dry so they get some color too. The finished dish, which gets topped with a harissa vinaigrette and a yogurt sauce, looks a bit like *patatas bravas,* Spain's famous fried potato dish, which is often topped with a spicy red sauce and white mayo. Here everything is a bit more wholesome but no less tasty.

FOR THE HARISSA VINAIGRETTE

4 tablespoons harissa (either homemade or store-bought)

2 tablespoons olive oil

2 tablespoons white wine vinegar

FOR THE YOGURT SAUCE

½ cup plain yogurt

Fresh lemon juice

Kosher salt and freshly ground black pepper

FOR THE REST OF THE DISH

Olive oil

2 cups fresh okra, tops cut off, sliced in half vertically

1 cup canned chickpeas, drained and patted dry

Make the harissa vinaigrette by whisking together the harissa, olive oil, and white wine vinegar. Taste to adjust.

Next, make the yogurt sauce by mixing together the yogurt, lemon juice to taste, and pinches of salt and pepper to taste.

In a small to medium sauté pan (not nonstick), heat the olive oil until almost smoking. When the oil is seriously hot, add the okra. Allow the okra to cook for a few moments and then flip it with a confident thrust of the pan (as one would flip an omelet) or, if that scares you, turn it with a spoon.

When the okra is nicely browned all over, add the chickpeas. Make sure the chickpeas are dry or everything will steam. Cook, tossing occasionally with tongs, until the chickpeas get a little color too. Season with a pinch of salt.

Spoon the okra and chickpeas onto plates and top with a generous amount of both the harissa vinaigrette and the yogurt sauce.

Dale makes his harissa by soaking ½ pound dried red chili peppers (he prefers guajillo) in warm water for 30 minutes. Then he drains them, removes the stems and seeds, and purees them with 15 peeled cloves garlic, 4 teaspoons freshly ground caraway seeds, 4 teaspoons freshly ground coriander seeds, and 2 teaspoons salt. He slowly adds extra virgin olive oil until the mixture becomes a paste. He stores it in a container covered with more oil, until ready to use.

If you can't find okra, you can use an equal amount of zucchini, unpeeled, cut into spears. The zucchini won't get as crisp but has a similar vegetable presence as okra, plus it's easier to find.

Dale is a fan of canned chickpeas at home but uses dried chickpeas at The National. To cook your own dried chickpeas, start the day before and soak the beans overnight with a teaspoon of baking soda. The next day, strain the chickpeas and place in cold water along with a cheesecloth sachet filled with diced onion, garlic, carrot, celery, thyme, bay leaves, peppercorns, coriander seeds, and cumin seeds. Bring the water to a simmer and cook until the chickpeas are tender, about 1 hour. After they're cooked, season them with salt.

Pineapple with Lime Sugar, Cane Syrup, and Pomegranate Seeds

Serves 4

For those big heavy dinners after which you don't want to serve a big heavy dessert, consider this simple dish of pineapple—beautifully presented in its natural container—topped with a few choice ingredients, namely, lime sugar, pomegranate seeds, and cane syrup. If you can't find cane syrup, use something similar from where you live. Good maple syrup purchased from a farmer's market works well; you can also try molasses. The lime sugar, which sounds fancy but takes just thirty seconds to make, is a great ingredient to keep around. Sprinkle it on other fruits (nectarines, orange slices) or, better yet, use it to coat the rims of the glasses the next time you make margaritas.

¼ cup sugar

1 whole lime

1 whole pineapple

Cane syrup (no set amount; judge it visually) or good maple syrup

½ cup fresh pomegranate seeds

First make the lime sugar. Over a bowl filled with the sugar, zest the lime aggressively, making sure to get only the green part (the white part, or pith, is bitter-tasting). Stir the lime zest and sugar together until well combined.

Prepare the pineapple by slicing it vertically through the stem and leaves, leaving everything intact. Slice each half vertically again so the pineapple is quartered. With a boning knife, cut out the core on top of each pineapple segment. Then slide the boning knife between the pineapple and the skin in one fluid motion, so you can easily lift the pineapple meat out. Finally, cut the pineapple into 10 even pieces and, keeping them all together, place them back in the pineapple skin. Place each quarter on its own plate.

Sprinkle the pineapple quarters with the lime sugar (you probably won't use all of it). Pour the syrup over the parts that aren't dressed with lime sugar. Sprinkle with pomegranate seeds and serve.

● I found it much more effective to pinch it together with my fingers instead of using a spoon.

Einat Admony

Chef-owner, Taïm and Balaboosta
New York, New York

Admony's Kitchen Know-How

Admony's Kitchen Know-How

USE VEGETABLE OIL or canola oil as a base for making a flavored oil. Olive oil can overpower a lot of flavors and it's more expensive and therefore wasteful to use it when you want a different flavor to dominate.

TO STOP food from scattering on a plate, and also to improve the presentation of it, use the back of a spoon to create an indentation to hold the featured item. For example, with the fried olive dish (see page 64), spoon the labneh into a bowl and place the back of a spoon at the center, circling outward until the labneh forms a ring and there's a hole in the middle for the olives.

ZAATAR, an herb that looks like oregano but has its own unique flavor, is great sprinkled on toasted pita that has been brushed with olive oil. Nigella seeds, which look like poppy seeds, are a good topping if you're serving baba ghanouj by itself.

Chef Einat Admony named her restaurant Balaboosta for a reason.

"*Balaboosta* is Yiddish for 'perfect housewife,'" she explains to me on a March morning at the restaurant. "It reflects a woman who can multitask, raise kids. It's a woman who can deal; she can raise her family, she cooks all the time. It's a hard-core woman."

Admony herself is a hard-core woman. She wears an army cap (she served in the Israeli army for two years and then in the Israeli air force) as she commands her way around the kitchen. And when it comes to one particular subject, Admony is more than hard-core; she's positively fierce. That subject is *flavor.*

"I hate when restaurant food is too fancy," she says as she begins wrapping eggplant in aluminum foil for her wildly flavorful baba ghanouj. "I don't get that. The most important thing is the flavor!"

She places the wrapped eggplant in a skillet and places another skillet on top. "Did you wrap the foil all the way around the eggplant?" I ask, trying to figure out the method behind the madness.

"You look like a smart guy," she says. "You can figure it out."

She turns up the heat and the eggplant cooks like that—wrapped in foil, sandwiched between two pans. When it's unwrapped, Admony scoops the insides into a blender with lemon juice, garlic confit, raw tahini,

honey, salt, and pepper. Needless to say, the resulting baba ghanouj is big on flavor, just the way Admony likes it.

When she plates it, she spreads it on toasted bread and tops it with a citrus herb salad with oranges, lemons, mint, scallions, and parsley. Despite the visual appeal, Admony shrugs it off.

"I put a lot more effort on the taste than on the presentation; it's not as important to me," she says.

So ignore the fact that her shakshouka—a traditional dish of eggs cooked in a tomato–red pepper sauce—is vividly red with flecks of dark green from Swiss chard, and focus on the big, bold flavors.

"I used to pass my sauces through a food mill," she says as we dig in with toasted pita brushed with zaatar. "Fuck that! Some food is too labor-intensive."

I ask if I can substitute a different tomato sauce to cook the eggs, maybe something with fewer ingredients.

"You can do anything," she says. "Just don't call it shakshouka."

For the finale, Admony coats olives in flour, egg, and panko bread crumbs and deep-fries them. She serves them in a bowl with labneh cheese and a harissa oil, made simply by blending harissa with canola oil. The bowl is a sea of white with a ring of fiery red surrounding it, the fried olives at the center.

"It's tasty," says Admony. "Not pretty. It's simple, and nobody cares if there's a flower on top."

We may eat with our eyes first, but in Chef Admony's kitchen the eyes are second-class citizens behind the taste buds. It's how food tastes that counts the most.

"I cook a lot at home. Most chefs never cook at home, but for me, I go home and I like to cook. It's something I never get tired of."

Fried Olives with Labneh and Harissa Oil

Serves 4

Frying doesn't have to be an ordeal. In the case of these olives, it's a simple matter of filling a pot one quarter of the way with oil, heating it until it's at frying temperature (350°F), and then carefully lowering in the olives, which you've coated in flour, egg, and two layers of ground panko. A minute later you'll have crunchy orbs of briny complexity that pair smashingly with the creamy labneh and fiery harissa oil. You can coat the olives ahead of time, store them in the refrigerator, and pop them into the fryer just when your guests arrive. Serve them with toothpicks so your guests don't burn their hands.

FOR THE LABNEH

1 quart organic plain yogurt

½ tablespoon kosher salt

FOR THE HARISSA OIL

**¼ cup harissa
(either store-bought or homemade)**

**¾ cup neutral oil
(either canola or vegetable)**

FOR THE OLIVES

1 cup all-purpose flour

3 eggs, beaten

Panko bread crumbs ground in a food processor (approximately 2 cups)

A mix of kalamata and manzanilla olives, pitted (about 2 cups)

Canola oil

Kosher salt

- For a homemade harissa, see Peter Dale's recipe, page 60.

- If you don't have cheesecloth, you can use a double layer of paper towels.

- It's a good idea, during this process, to have one "clean" hand and one "dirty" hand. The dirty hand is the one that'll drag the olive through the egg; the clean hand is the one that'll apply the flour and the panko. Otherwise you'll end up with two hands covered in eggy panko.

The night before you want to serve this, combine the yogurt and salt and place in a colander lined with cheesecloth set over a bowl in the refrigerator. As the liquid drains out, the yogurt will thicken, and 24 hours later you'll have labneh.

To make the harissa oil, blend together the harissa and the oil. That's it!

Prep the olives by setting up three pie plates (or other shallow pans): in the first, place the flour; in the second, the beaten eggs; and in the third, the panko. Olive by olive, roll each one in the flour, then in the egg, then in the panko, then back in the egg, then in the panko one more time. Set aside and continue until you've coated all the olives.

Now set up the frying station. Fill a small pot one quarter of the way with canola oil. Begin heating it to 350°F (you'll need a deep-fry thermometer).

Carefully lower the olives into the hot oil (you may want to use a spider for this) and fry until deep golden brown, moving them around a bit as they cook. Use the spider to lift them onto a plate lined with paper towels and sprinkle gently with salt.

Meanwhile, pile some labneh in a bowl. Place the olives in the middle and spoon the harissa oil around the edges of the bowl. Serve right away; the olives won't taste good cold.

Shakshouka

Serves 2 to 4

Most of us don't think about making eggs for dinner, but a dish like this is a godsend, especially when you're feeling tired and lazy and don't want to go to the store (assuming you already have a can of tomatoes, a red bell pepper, a jalapeño, and a carton of eggs on hand). Even if you do have to shop for this, it's a cheap and healthy dinner you can whip up at a moment's notice. Just make sure to have some good bread handy at the table for mopping up the sauce.

FOR THE SAUCE

¼ cup olive oil

1 onion, diced

½ jalapeño, seeds and membrane removed, cut into a small dice

1 red bell pepper, seeded and diced small

1 cup Swiss chard stems, sliced thin (optional)

Kosher salt

3 cloves garlic, crushed

1 tablespoon tomato paste

1 (28-ounce) can peeled tomatoes, crushed by hand

1 teaspoon black pepper

1 teaspoon paprika

½ teaspoon ground turmeric

1 teaspoon ground cumin

1 teaspoon crushed caraway seeds

1 bay leaf

1 tablespoon sugar

TO FINISH

¼ cup olive oil, plus more for drizzling

3 links of Merguez sausage, cut into rings

⅓ cup washed and shredded kale or Swiss chard

Kosher salt

6 to 8 eggs

Crusty bread

If you make this after making the baba ghanouj on page 66, you can use the leftover garlic oil from the garlic confit.

Whatever sauce you don't use you can freeze for your next shakshouka.

Start by making the sauce. In a pot, heat the olive oil on medium heat. Add the onion and cook until it gets a little color. Add the jalapeño, the bell pepper, and the chard stems, if using, with a big pinch of salt, and sauté until the peppers and stems soften. Add the garlic and tomato paste, cook for a minute more, then add the tomatoes and the rest of the spices, the bay leaf, and the sugar, plus another pinch of salt. Bring to a boil, reduce to a simmer, and cook for about 30 minutes, or until you have a smooth, flavorful sauce. Adjust for seasoning and remove the bay leaf.

To finish the dish, in a wide skillet with a lid, heat about ¼ cup olive oil. Add the sausage and cook until it starts to brown, 3 to 4 minutes. Add a good amount of the sauce—enough to cover the sausage. Bring to a simmer, add the kale or chard, and season with salt. Crack the eggs into the pan, season them with salt, and put a lid on the skillet. Lower the heat and cook until the egg whites are just cooked through but the yolks are still soft.

You can serve this dish right in its skillet with crusty bread on the side. Or scoop individual portions into warm bowls with a final drizzle of olive oil.

Baba Ghanouj Bruschetta with Citrus Herb Salad

Serves 4

There's an aura of mystery about this recipe: How does wrapping eggplant in aluminum foil and cooking it in a skillet with another pan on top get it so smoky? We can leave that for the food scientists to answer. In the meantime, you can certainly serve the baba ghanouj by itself, but serving it on toasted bread with a citrus herb salad on top is a great way to bring color and vibrancy to the dish.

FOR THE BABA GHANOUJ

2 cloves garlic, peeled

Canola oil

2 regular eggplants, stems removed, sliced in half vertically

Juice of 1 lemon

⅓ cup raw tahini, well stirred

1 teaspoon honey

Kosher salt and freshly ground black pepper

FOR THE BRUSCHETTA AND SALAD

4 slices of good sourdough bread

Olive oil

1 orange, supremed

2 lemons, 1 supremed and 1 reserved for juice

1 small fresh red chili, minced

¼ cup parsley leaves

¼ cup shredded mint leaves

¼ cup sliced scallions

Kosher salt

Date molasses (optional)

- To supreme citrus fruit, slice the top and bottom off the fruit so it stands neatly on a cutting board. Slide the blade of a very sharp knife between the flesh and the white pith and move the knife downward along the body of the fruit until the pith and the peel fall away. Continue until all the flesh is exposed and then, working over a bowl to catch the juices, separate the fruit sections from the membranes. These sections are known as "supremes."

- If the garlic turns too brown too quickly, you may want to turn off the heat and just watch the garlic to monitor the color. You'll still see bubbles around it; when the bubbles stop, turn the heat back to low and cook for several minutes, until a knife goes through the garlic easily.

- You'll probably only be able to do one eggplant at a time this way. Be patient!

- Don't freak out if your eggplant is totally charred black. It's a lot like roasting a red pepper; just scrape the black part away. You can even keep a little black in there for extra smokiness.

To make the baba ghanouj, start by making a garlic confit. Drop the garlic cloves in a small pot and cover with enough oil to submerge. Cook on low for about 30 minutes, until the garlic is tender and slightly brown. Remove from the oil and save the oil for another use.

Meanwhile, lay a sheet of aluminum foil in a cold skillet and place the eggplant, cut side down, on top of the foil. Wrap the foil around the eggplant and then place another heavy pan on top. Turn the heat on to medium and cook for approximately 15 minutes, until the eggplant is tender to the touch. Remove from the pan and allow to cool slightly.

Unwrap the eggplant and rub the exposed skin with some lemon juice. Now scoop out the flesh into a food processor or a blender and add the garlic confit, another squeeze of lemon juice, the tahini, the honey, and a pinch of salt and pepper. Blend until you have a smooth puree. There you have it: baba ghanouj.

To fancy it up, grill the bread on a grill or under the broiler. Brush with some olive oil, then top with a good helping of the baba ghanouj. In a separate bowl, combine the citrus supremes, chili, herbs, and scallions with a splash of olive oil and lemon juice and salt to taste. When it tastes great, pile on top of the bruschettas and, if you have it, drizzle with date molasses.

Nancy Silverton

Cookbook author; co-founder, La Brea Bakery; and chef, Pizzeria Mozza and Osteria Mozza
Los Angeles, California

With her mop of curly hair piled high on her head, it's impossible not to notice chef Nancy Silverton behind the bar at Osteria Mozza, the restaurant she co-owns with Mario Batali, in Los Angeles. The chef best known for making some of the greatest bread in the United States and the author of countless cookbooks, including *Breads from the La Brea Bakery* (which I've used to make sourdough bread with a natural yeast starter), is a quirky, dramatic presence.

"I'm not one of those chefs who likes to wander around the dining room chatting with customers," she tells me. "I need to be behind the counter handling food."

Handling food is what Silverton does best; whether she's prepping a focaccia for the oven or a simple plate of Prosciutto San Daniele with Warren Pear and Pomegranate Seeds (page 70), her hands are her primary tools.

"My mom always told me that I was terrific with my hands," she says. "For years, I took art classes and didn't believe her. It was only after I started cooking that I understood what she meant."

Silverton uses her hands to build plates of food that are as notable for their visual beauty as they are for their deceptive simplicity.

On one white plate, for example, she sets down three perfectly thin slices of Meyer lemon. When I say "perfectly thin" I mean these are technical wonders, Platonic circles that would stun the likes of Leonardo da Vinci. On top, she piles a salad of sliced celery ("I slice it on the *extreme* bias"), scallions, tarragon, chervil, "pale green" celery leaves, chives, and tiny basil leaves dressed in a lemon vinaigrette.

To that she adds three chunks of fresh mozzarella, and on top of each chunk, she lays a single anchovy. "*Alici di menaica,*" she says. "You can get them from Buon Italia in New York. They're much fresher than normal anchovies, and they're the only sustainably caught ones you can buy" (see Resources, page 371).

Silverton, who clearly surrounds herself with the best ingredients, wasn't always so particular about her food. "As a little girl," she says, "I had three favorite meals: frozen Salisbury steaks with butter, Swanson TV dinners, and creamed tuna on toast."

Everything changed when she got to college. "It was a fluke how I got into food," she recalls. "I went to Sonoma State and when I moved into the dorms, I noticed a handsome guy in the kitchen. So I told him that I loved to cook [a lie] and he hired me."

It may have been a fluke at the time, but Silverton's career—a storied one that is still growing—proves that her mother was right: her hands were built for this profession. But it's not all about her hands.

"I always cook from my heart," she tells me before I go. "Never from my head. I cook from my senses and follow my instincts."

Her instincts make her restaurants very popular (both Osteria Mozza and Pizzeria Mozza were packed the night I cooked with her), but it's her hands that keep the customers coming back. She's got something all of us should strive for in the kitchen: the magic touch.

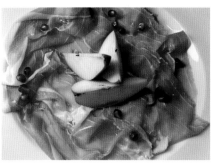

"I love stoves,
I love knives,
I love beautiful
wooden spoons.
I don't care about
pumps and beakers
and petri dishes."

Prosciutto San Daniele with Warren Pear and Pomegranate Seeds

Serves 2 to 4

This recipe is 100 percent shopping and 0 percent cooking. Instead of thinking of it as an assembly project, though, think of it more as an opportunity to craft a still life. The arrangement of the three primary ingredients—the prosciutto, the pear, and the pomegranate seeds—requires a certain amount of finesse. Play around, and remember: once you set this out, you have a totally simple first course that people will love. And all you had to do was shop for it.

½ pound prosciutto San Daniele (or other high-quality prosciutto), sliced thin

1 Warren pear or any other pear that's in season, cut into quarters (don't core it; leave the seeds intact)

Seeds from ½ pomegranate (see page 56 for seed removal tips)

Good-quality olive oil

Silverton's reason for this is simple: it makes the pear more beautiful to keep the quarters intact. Make sure to cut it right before you serve it, though, or it will oxidize.

Lay the prosciutto on your nicest white platter and crinkle it a little bit to give it texture. Place the pear quarters in the center of the plate. Scatter the pomegranate seeds all around. Drizzle very lightly with olive oil and serve.

Mozzarella with Meyer Lemon, Celery Salad, and Alici di Menaica

Serves 2 to 3

Once again, Silverton proves that if you find the right ingredients, it's just a question of putting them together properly on the plate. Here, three perfect circles of Meyer lemon—use a mandoline to achieve that—form the base of a plate that includes fresh mozzarella, a crunchy, acidic celery salad, and special anchovies that Silverton gets from the Buon Italia store in New York's Chelsea Market (see Resources, page 371; or use the best anchovies you can find).

FOR THE DRESSING

1 tablespoon minced shallots

¼ cup fresh lemon juice

1 tablespoon champagne vinegar

Freshly cracked black pepper

¼ cup olive oil

FOR THE SALAD

1 celery stalk, sliced thick on the extreme bias

2 scallions, sliced thin on the extreme bias

4 or 5 chives, cut into pieces

Leaves from 1 celery stalk (6 or 7 leaves)

Tiny basil leaves

Kosher salt

FOR ASSEMBLY

3 very thin slices of Meyer lemon

3 chunks of fresh mozzarella (from one round ball)

3 anchovies (preferably *alici di menaica*; see Resources, page 371)

1 hard-boiled egg

- Soak first, drain, and then filet off the bone.

- To perfectly hard-boil an egg, place it in a pan of cold water. Bring the water to a boil, and as soon as it gets there, remove from the heat and cover. Let the egg sit for 15 minutes, then drain; place the egg in an ice-water bath and then peel.

- For a more elegant look, press the whites first through a grater, clean it, and then press the yolks through.

First, make the dressing by whisking together the shallots, lemon juice, champagne vinegar, and black pepper. Gradually add the olive oil, whisking all the while, to create an emulsification. Set aside.

In a bowl, gently toss the salad ingredients and a pinch of salt with some of the dressing. Taste to see if it needs more dressing; adjust accordingly.

To plate, lay the slices of Meyer lemon on a platter. Surround with some of the salad and then set down the chunks of mozzarella, one on top of each lemon slice. Lay an anchovy on top of each mozzarella chunk.

Pile more salad in the middle and, with a Microplane grater, grate the hard-boiled egg on top, just before serving.

Mozzarella in Panna
with Pesto and
Slow-Roasted Tomatoes

Serves 2 to 4

Most of the time, when fresh mozzarella is made, it's stored in water. But *mozzarella in panna,* as Silverton explained to me, is different because it's stored in *cream.* "You can fake it," she says, "by pouring some cream on regular mozzarella." I've taken it one step further by warming the mozzarella directly in the cream, a step that allows the mozzarella to absorb some of the cream and makes this whole dish even sultrier. As for the tomatoes, roasting them on a rack is a subtle change from roasting them directly on a cookie sheet, but the tomatoes intensify even more this way (it prevents them from steaming). And when they are combined with the pesto, the warm mozzarella, and the cream? Watch out. You may witness fits of ecstasy at your table.

- Germ freaks may scold me for saying this, but if the tomatoes look clean enough to you, don't wash them. The heat from the oven should kill any germs, and the lack of any moisture on the tomatoes will ensure that they slow-roast (as opposed to steam).

- You can make this dish with a combination of cream and milk or, if you really don't want to use cream, just plain whole milk. It won't taste as decadent, though.

- If you can find *mozzarella in panna* at your local Italian market, use it (and skip the 1 cup cream). This recipe assumes that you don't have it.

A few bunches of cherry tomatoes, still on the vine

Olive oil

1 cup heavy cream

1 whole fresh mozzarella

¼ cup pesto (use Melissa Clark's recipe, page 97, minus the cilantro, or store-bought)

Baby basil, still on the vine

Small sourdough croutons (see Anne Quatrano's recipe, page 266), optional

Preheat the oven to 250°F. Set the whole tomatoes, still on the vine, on a rack on a cookie sheet and drizzle with olive oil. Cook them for about 2 hours, until they're slightly shriveled and the skins are just starting to fall off. Remove from the oven and allow to cool slightly.

In a small pot, heat the cream until warm but not boiling (you'll see a few bubbles around the edges and if you stick your finger in, it should feel just a bit warmer than body temperature). Turn off the heat and add the mozzarella in a few big chunks. Allow the mozzarella to steep for at least 15 minutes, soaking up the cream and warming up as it does.

Spoon the pesto onto a large serving plate or into a shallow bowl. Cube the warmed mozzarella and plate it with some of the cream on top. Place the slow-roasted tomatoes, still on the vine, alongside the mozzarella. Top with the baby basil and the croutons (if you're using them) and serve.

Harold Dieterle

**Winner, *Top Chef,* Season One;
and chef-owner, Perilla and Kin Shop
New York, New York**

**Dieterle's Kitchen
Know-How**

MINCED CHIVES, shallots, and
parsley work together to form
Dieterle's "holy trinity" that
can improve various dishes,
especially salads.

USE SEA SALT (Dieterle
prefers La Baleine) for
seasoning most foods except
for red meat; for that, use
kosher salt.

GOOD MUSHROOMS are like
expensive jewelry and should
be treated as such; seek out
the best you can find, when
you can afford it.

When you're standing in a kitchen with cameras jammed in your face and world-class chefs waiting to judge your food, you've got to be able to think on your feet. Actually, "think" is the wrong word for it. You've got to act, and act quickly. In that moment between knowing the challenge and acting on that challenge, how do you get inspired? How do you know what to make?

Meet chef Harold Dieterle, winner of Season One of Bravo's hit show *Top Chef.* Dieterle, as anyone who watched that season knows, is calm, cool, and collected in the kitchen. He keeps his cards close to his chest; you never really know what he's thinking while he cooks, and if you ask him he's often surprised by the question.

For example, when I join him in the kitchen of his West Village restaurant Perilla, I ask him how he came up with his new dish of fettuccine with lobster, cauliflower, lychees, and bone marrow. "How did you think to put all of those things together?"

He looks at me blankly for a second. Then he shrugs: "I've done a lot of traveling in Thailand," he says. "And lychees are in season right now."

"But how did you think to pair the lychees with the lobster and the cauliflower and the bone marrow?"

Again, he looks a little blank for a second. Then he says, "Well, I know lychees go well with lobster and lobster goes well with cauliflower."

"And the bone marrow?"

"It's a good substitute for butter," he explains. "That way I can put less butter in the dish and it'll still taste rich."

That explains one dish, but what about the other dishes on the menu? What about the creamed corn so popular that, according to Dieterle, "people freak out over it"?

This time Dieterle has a quick answer. "It's my mom's recipe," he explains. "We ate it growing up; only she used frozen corn and I use all fresh ingredients."

I know this is true because I've been assigned the task of cutting the kernels off the cobs. Dieterle suggests I do this directly into a plastic tub, so the kernels don't fly everywhere. He also has me slice garlic and shallots, and when I ask him if I'm doing a good job he shrugs. "You want to hold the knife more from the handle," he says.

Dieterle doesn't overthink things. He just does. When we've cooked the shallots and garlic and added the corn and the cream, he tells me to season it. I do so, gingerly, shaking some salt in.

"Taste it," he says.

I do and it tastes pretty good. But then I doubt myself—I overthink everything—and, nervous that this corn won't be great if it's underseasoned, I ask Dieterle to taste it to confirm that I seasoned it well enough.

He does taste it, pauses, and then grabs the salt canister and spins the top from the sprinkle holes to the giant hole. And then he dumps a giant stream of salt into the corn and cream, stirs, and smiles.

We both laugh and I don't even bother asking him how he knew it needed that much more salt. He'd probably just shrug and smirk and say, "It just did."

"I don't want guests to say, 'I could've made that myself.'"

Hearts of Palm Salad
with Mango
and Macadamia Nuts

Serves 2 to 4

According to Dieterle, this salad isn't worth making if you can't get fresh hearts of palm. ("I don't used canned foods, except for tomatoes," he told me.) Unfortunately, fresh hearts of palm aren't so easy to find. So, don't tell him I said this, but I think this salad is still worth making if all you can find is the canned stuff. With the slightly sour hearts of palm, the sweet mango (Harold uses a Champagne mango), and the crunchy-sweet macadamia nuts, it's a salad I go back to again and again.

● The best way to wash the lettuce is to submerge it in a bowl full of cold water and swish it, changing the water several times until no dirt is on the bottom.

FOR THE DRESSING

¼ cup white wine or champagne vinegar

1 shallot, finely chopped

½ to ¾ cup neutral oil (such as vegetable or grapeseed)

Salt and pepper

FOR THE SALAD

1 head Bibb lettuce, leaves separated, washed, and spun dry in a salad spinner

½ cup hearts of palm (from a can, unless you can find them fresh), sliced into thin coins

1 mango, peeled, sliced from the pit, and cut into small chunks

½ cup macadamia nuts, toasted in a dry skillet and then coarsely chopped

¼ cup Dieterle's holy trinity (a mixture of minced chives, shallots, and parsley)

First, make the dressing. In a measuring cup, measure out the white wine vinegar, add the shallots, and then whisk in ½ cup of the oil in a steady stream until it emulsifies. Adjust with salt, pepper, and up to ¼ cup more oil, tasting as you go. (Use a lettuce leaf to taste it.)

Place the lettuce, hearts of palm, mango, and macadamia nuts in a large salad bowl. Drizzle on some dressing, tossing as you do and tasting to see how much dressing it needs. Stop when everything is lightly coated.

Add Dieterle's holy trinity and taste again. Adjust for salt and pepper and serve.

Chicken with Rosemary, Fennel Pollen, and Balsamic-Braised Radicchio

Serves 4

This dish is my interpretation of one that Dieterle serves at Perilla. The restaurant dish is a poussin roasted on a bed of rosemary, brushed with fennel pollen oil, and served with balsamic-glazed radicchio and peaches tossed in a bagna cauda. This riff pairs chicken and radicchio in the same pan, making use of all the wonderful chicken bits that collect on the bottom. The fennel pollen oil is sheer indulgence—certainly not necessary, but a nice subtle note if you can find fennel pollen.

1 whole chicken, approximately 4 pounds, organs removed, washed, and patted dry with paper towels

1 tablespoon canola oil

Kosher salt and freshly ground black pepper

4 fresh rosemary sprigs

1 teaspoon olive oil, plus more if needed

½ teaspoon fennel pollen (optional)

2 heads radicchio (preferably Treviso), sliced in half vertically, core mostly removed (but not entirely, so it stays together), limp outer leaves discarded

¼ cup balsamic vinegar

¾ cup chicken stock (preferably homemade), plus more if needed

Flaky sea salt (optional)

1 tablespoon unsalted butter (optional)

Two hours before you start cooking, remove the chicken from the refrigerator and allow it to come to room temperature.

Preheat the oven to 475°F.

Place the chicken breast-side up in a cast-iron skillet. Rub the chicken all over with the canola oil and then sprinkle it all over, inside and out, with kosher salt and pepper. Stuff the cavity with the fresh rosemary, tuck the wings under the bird, and, if you want, tie the legs together with kitchen twine.

Roast in the oven for 15 minutes, or until the skin starts to darken. Then lower the temperature to 425°F and roast for another 45 minutes, or until the chicken is golden brown all over and the juices run clear when you cut between the leg and the thigh.

While the chicken is roasting, mix together the olive oil and fennel pollen (if using) in a small bowl.

Remove the chicken from the oven and lift it onto a cutting board. Brush the chicken all over with the fennel pollen oil and then tent it with aluminum foil and allow it to rest.

If there's a lot of fat in the skillet, pour it out until you have approximately 2 tablespoons left. If there's not enough fat, add 2 tablespoons olive oil. Place the pan on medium-high heat until the oil and/or fat is very hot and then add the radicchio, cut side down. Cook until the

Be aggressive. Use at least a tablespoon of salt for a 4-pound bird.

radicchio is deeply golden brown, about 1 minute. Flip the radicchio over and allow it to brown on the other side, 1 minute, and then remove the radicchio to a plate.

Add the balsamic vinegar and chicken stock to the pan. Bring to a boil and use a wooden spoon to dislodge the brown bits (those have lots of flavor!), then return the radicchio to the pan, cut side down.

Cover the pan and reduce the heat to low, allowing the liquid to simmer and the radicchio to cook for 10 to 15 minutes until a knife goes through it easily. If the liquid evaporates, add more chicken stock.

To serve, carve the chicken and serve with the braised radicchio, sprinkled with flaky sea salt, if desired. If you want, you can make a sauce with the liquid left in the pan by bringing it to a boil, adding the butter, and whisking until it's nice and thick. Spoon over the radicchio but not the chicken; you don't want to lose the delicate flavor of the fennel pollen oil. You can also serve the chicken with spicy French mustard or bagna cauda (see page 91), which is how Dieterle serves his.

Creamed Corn

Serves 4

The secret to this dish, the one Dieterle says people freak out over, is a very simple technique. You cook fresh corn (and this works best with fresh corn in summer, but you can do like Harold's mom and use frozen corn if you want—though Dieterle wouldn't) in cream and then blend it when it's soft. To that corn puree you add more fresh corn kernels and continue cooking; what you end up with is a creamy, corny (the good kind of corny) mixture that has both the depth of flavor of cooked corn and the freshness of corn straight from the cob. No wonder it's so popular.

3 tablespoons vegetable oil

2 shallots, thinly sliced

2 cloves garlic, thinly sliced

Kernels from 6 ears of corn, cut straight off the cob (make sure to scrape to get all the goodness off there), half reserved

Kosher salt and freshly ground black pepper

3 cups heavy cream

1 tablespoon chopped chives, for sprinkling

● That "goodness" is the starch, which will help thicken the corn puree.

Heat the oil in a medium pot for 30 seconds and then add the shallots and garlic. Cook until fragrant but not brown.

Add half of the corn and a generous pinch of salt and pepper.

Add the cream and stir. Cook on medium heat until the corn is cooked (careful that the cream doesn't boil too much), 5 to 10 minutes.

Pour the corn and cream mixture into a blender and blend until it's a smooth puree.

● Be careful when blending anything hot; leave a hole at the top for ventilation.

Pour the puree back into the same pot (no need to clean it) and add the rest of the corn. Add another generous pinch of salt and pepper and cook over medium heat until the new addition of corn softens a little. Taste for seasoning and texture and sprinkle in the chives. Serve immediately.

Vinny Dotolo & Jon Shook

Chefs, Animal and Son of a Gun
Los Angeles, California

Dotolo & Shook's Kitchen Know-How

IF YOU WANT to make up a salad, think about color, think about freshness, and think about acidity. "Ultimately, though," says Dotolo, "texture is what it's all about."

PEOPLE FUSS SO MUCH about knives, but a particular knife doesn't matter as much as you think it does. Any knife can be made sharp; the key is making sure that when you hold it, it feels comfortable. "The knife is an extension of your hand," says Shook. "So hold it and then decide whether to buy it."

A LARGE, HEAVY MORTAR and pestle are great for making anything that needs to be pasty (Shook and Dotolo use a medicinal version that Dotolo found at a flea market). Salsa verde, chimichurri, and aioli benefit from being made this way; the texture—especially with the salsa verde—is far more complex than if you use a food processor or a blender.

It's not easy to categorize the food that comes out of the kitchen of Animal, the must-visit Los Angeles restaurant co-owned by chefs Vinny Dotolo and Jon Shook, and that's the way the chefs like it.

"Sometimes chefs box themselves in by saying 'I do X,' or 'I do Y,'" Dotolo tells me from a table in the front of the restaurant early on a February morning. "Years later they're saying, 'I wish I could use soy sauce.'"

Dotolo and Shook use soy sauce. They produce dishes as disparate as bone marrow with chimichurri, lamb neck with daikon and black vinegar jus, and rabbit loin spring rolls. Their menu is strewn with ingredients from all over the world—chili, lime, mint, anchovies, buttermilk, sumac, vadouvan—and it's all there to help them achieve a very specific goal. "We want to make something that tastes good," says Shook.

With all of these ingredients at their disposal, it's possible that Dotolo and Shook might produce food that's muddled or over-wrought. But they avoid this by applying a specific set of values to their idiosyncratic brand of cuisine.

Dotolo explains: "I like to find a balance of things that might seem odd or interesting wrapped back into something that's accessible."

Shook adds, "It's not about the wow factor. It's translating what we love into something customers will love."

That's a great formula not just for restaurant cooking but also for cooking at home. Oftentimes, we who are food lovers try to foist uncommon or intimidating ingredients on our guests, only to have them politely spit their food into their napkins. The trick is to fuse challenging ingredients with elements that are comforting and familiar.

Look, for example, at the salad that Shook and Dotolo make with lettuces from the Santa Monica farmer's market. Those lettuces—with names like "freckle lettuce," "lola rosa," "black seed simpson," and "red perilla"—are a far cry from iceberg and romaine. But Dotolo and Shook don't dress these eclectic lettuces with exotic cheeses and oils you can barely pronounce, let alone eat. Instead, they make a dressing with sour cream and Meyer lemon juice and toss that with the lettuces, feta cheese, pita chips, beets (both raw and cooked), and avocado. The end result, piled up on the plate, looks like an iconic California salad that partied all night in Vegas. And the taste—which is both bold and refreshing—reflects that too.

Though it may seem like anything goes in the kitchen of Animal (where stocks and braises and pig ears simmer away), there's a method to the madness. With their P'tit Basque—a gratin of onions and leeks cooked in wine with thinly sliced chorizo and huge hunks of P'tit Basque cheese that gets blasted under the broiler and comes out bubbling and brown (so much so that Dotolo calls it "a decapitated French onion soup")—the flavors make sense, thanks to the acidity of the wine, the meatiness of the chorizo, and the creaminess of the cheese.

As for their ribs, which are slicked with a house-made balsamic barbecue sauce and blasted under the broiler ("There's so much sugar in that sauce," says Dotolo, "you can burn the *shit* out of them"), words fail. They're just that good—maybe the best I've ever had.

And that's pretty much the point at Animal, where the food has definition without having limitations. By pulling from all of the world's great cuisines, Dotolo and Shook have created a cuisine that's entirely their own. They stick to their guns but care about their audience. The results—with crowds lining up night after night—speak for themselves.

"A mango in California isn't as good as a mango in Florida, so why would we use them?"
—Vinny Dotolo

P'tit Basque with Chorizo and Grilled Garlic Bread

Serves 2 to 4

You can hear the collective "ooooooh" as you set this bubbling cauldron of melted cheese down on the table. Meet P'tit Basque, the most popular appetizer you're ever going to serve—and for good reason. Take all the things you love about French onion soup—the deeply caramelized onions, the gooey brown cheese—add chorizo, and subtract the actual soup and you'll have a good idea of what this dish is about. Serve with grilled bread rubbed with garlic.

Olive oil

1 onion, chopped

1 leek, <u>cleaned</u> and chopped

1 cup dry white wine

⅓ cup thinly sliced Spanish chorizo (from 1 medium-size link)

One big chunk of <u>P'tit Basque cheese</u>, broken into pieces (about a 1-inch-thick ring of cheese 6 inches in diameter)

A few thick slices of sourdough bread

1 clove garlic

- To clean a leek, slice it in half vertically and hold it under running water; this gets the sand out of each layer.

- Though you could probably substitute more traditional French onion soup cheeses—Gruyère, Emmentaler—it's worth seeking out P'tit Basque, a French sheep's-milk cheese, for this dish. Its presence here is notable (and gives the dish its name).

- If you don't have a gratin dish, use a glass pie plate.

Set two sauté pans over medium heat and add enough olive oil to coat the bottoms. When they're hot, add the onion to one and the leek to the other. Lower the heat slightly and allow both to cook. The onion should cook low and slow for 45 minutes, or until deep golden brown, like the onions in a French onion soup (see page 338). The leeks should cook just until translucent (about 10 minutes); then add the wine. Bring to a boil, lower to a simmer, and keep cooking until all the wine has evaporated and the leeks are "sec," which is a fancy way of saying "dry." When both the onions and leeks are ready, set them aside.

Preheat the oven to 450°F. Spoon a layer of the onions into a <u>gratin dish</u> and top with a layer of the leeks. Lay the sliced chorizo on top and then finish by covering everything evenly with the pieces of cheese. Bake until the cheese is melted and slightly brown on top, 3 to 5 minutes.

While that's baking, grill the bread on a grill or in a grill pan. You can also use the broiler; you want the bread toasty and golden brown. When it gets there, remove it from the heat and rub it all over with the garlic clove. Start at the edge to help break the clove up a little; then rub the clove across and drizzle with olive oil.

Carefully remove the gratin from the oven and serve right away with the bread. It's best when it's bubbly and gooey and hot.

Funky Lettuce Salad with Beets, Feta, and Creamy Meyer Lemon Dressing

Serves 2 to 4

A battle of good versus evil is waged on the plate when you serve up this salad, which gets its name from all the "funky" lettuces from the Santa Monica farmer's market Dotolo used when he made this with me at Animal (Vulcan lettuce, red oak, deer tongue, gem). The good comes from all the wholesome elements—the lettuce, the beets, the avocado—and the evil comes from all the naughty, fatty elements (sour cream, feta cheese, fried pita chips). What you wind up with is a big pile of colorful *stuff,* covered in white, and if evil wins out (as it often does), it's decadent enough to convert even the most ardent salad-hater.

FOR THE DRESSING

1 shallot, minced

½ cup fresh Meyer lemon juice (or regular lemon juice will do)

1 cup sour cream

½ tablespoon kosher salt

1 teaspoon sumac (see Resources, page 371), optional

FOR THE BEETS

2 cooked red beets, cut into bite-size chunks

2 cooked golden beets, cut into bite-size chunks

1 raw candy-striped beet, peeled and shaved on a mandoline

1 raw golden beet, peeled and shaved on a mandoline

8 or 9 big leaves of lettuce from the farmer's market (freckle lettuce, lola rosa, black seed simpson, red perilla) or an equal amount of romaine or escarole

Kosher salt

½ pound French feta

1 avocado, sliced

Pita chips (optional)

1 tablespoon minced chives

To make the dressing, whisk together all of the ingredients. Taste and adjust the seasoning.

Place the cooked beets, the shaved beets, all of the lettuce, and a pinch of salt in a large bowl and toss well. Add a few spoonfuls of dressing, crumble in the feta, drop in the avocado, and continue to toss until everything is coated (the best tool for this is your hands).

To serve, pull out the larger pieces of lettuce and lay them on a plate. Spoon on some of the beets and lay in some of the pita chips, if using, and avocado, sprinkling the avocado with a little salt when you do. Continue building the salad with lettuce, beets, avocado, and pita chips, until you've used everything up. Spoon on some more dressing and top everything with minced chives.

- To cook the beets, keep the red and golden ones separate and roast them in baking dishes or pans with a little water, covered with foil, at 350°F for 45 minutes to an hour, until a knife easily goes through them. They'll peel more easily once cooked. If you're feeling lazy or need to make this salad in a hurry, you can skip the cooked beets and just use the raw ones.

- A neat trick for slicing avocado is to cut the whole avocado in half vertically, then, once you remove the pit, make horizontal slits in the soft green part without going through the skin. Use a spoon to remove the flesh and fan out on the plate.

- To make pita chips, cut a pita into wedges and fry in a shallow layer of hot oil until crisp and brown. Blot on paper towels and sprinkle with salt.

Sweet-and-Sour Balsamic-Glazed Spareribs

Serves 4

I love a recipe like this, in which one familiar item (balsamic vinegar) combines with something else very familiar (in this case, the elements of a homemade barbecue sauce) to form something entirely new. The end result, which gets slathered all over spareribs that have been slow-roasted in the oven and baked at a high temperature until the two entities combine, makes for a sticky, tangy, unforgettable take on good old-fashioned ribs. If you're feeding a crowd, the oven is your best bet for that final step; if you have the time, though, try broiling the ribs with the glaze on top. The rib and the glaze fuse together and, if you take it far enough (just before it turns black), you get a crispy, sweet, and succulent rib that'll be your new standard from now on.

● The recipe for the glaze makes enough for up to four racks, so if you have a hungry crew, double the meat.

FOR THE RIBS

2 racks spareribs

Kosher salt

4 to 6 sprigs of fresh thyme

FOR THE GLAZE

2½ cups balsamic vinegar (don't waste your best balsamic here)

½ cup honey

2 cups ketchup

1 can beer (preferably dry)

1 tablespoon minced garlic

1 red onion, diced

½ cup dark brown sugar

1 tablespoon molasses

¼ cup grainy mustard

1 or 2 teaspoons Tabasco (depending on how spicy you like it)

1 tablespoon Worcestershire sauce

½ cup water

Preheat the oven to 250°F and place each rack of ribs on a square of aluminum foil. Sprinkle the ribs generously with salt, add a few sprigs of thyme to each, and then wrap well. Place the rib packets on a cookie sheet and bake for 3 to 4 hours, until the ribs are extremely tender. Allow the ribs to cool slightly in their packets before opening.

● Keep an eye on the sauce; it has a tendency to bubble up.

To make the glaze, combine all of the ingredients in a large pot on medium-low heat. Allow to simmer, stirring every so often, for a few hours, until the sauce is nice and thick. Set aside.

To bring the ribs and glaze together, do the following. Turn on the broiler (if you don't have a broiler, get the oven up to 450°F). Cut the rib racks into individual ribs, place them on a foil-lined cookie sheet or broiler tray, and brush them aggressively with the glaze. Pop them under the broiler and watch them carefully: all that sugar makes them burn very easily! You want the glaze to fuse with the ribs; it takes 3 to 4 minutes. If you're cooking the ribs in the oven, do so just until the glaze begins to bubble, 4 to 5 minutes. Serve the ribs hot with lots of napkins—trust me, you'll need them.

Gina DePalma

Author, *Dolce Italiano;* and pastry chef, Babbo
New York, New York

James Beard Award–winning pastry chef Gina DePalma, of Mario Batali's flagship restaurant, Babbo (where she's celebrated for putting her own unique spin on classic Italian desserts), was in Rome doing research for her next cookbook when she started to feel ill.

"I thought I wasn't adjusting to the water, the food," she tells me in her living room, where we're sipping iced tea. "So when I came back to accept my James Beard Award in 2008, I told my mother to make me a doctor's appointment."

The doctor listened to her symptoms and ran tests. On June 12, 2008, the results came back: DePalma had stage-four ovarian cancer.

Soon after, DePalma underwent surgery. "They cut my entire trunk open," she says, dragging her finger down the length of her body. "The time it took me to recover afterward was unbelievable."

DePalma spent the next few months undergoing chemotherapy, which made her very tired. "I watched a lot of food TV. I'd lie on the couch and watch Lidia four times a day."

The other element of her recovery came from her mother's kitchen. "My mother is a big believer in soup," she explains. When DePalma was growing up, her mother kept up the Italian tradition of having *primi* (a first course, usually a pasta) at every meal. "Two or three days a week, there'd be soup. You never got away from soup; it could be a hundred degrees outside, and Mom would serve a hundred-fifty-degree boiling soup."

As DePalma dealt with the aftereffects of her chemo, her mother "would shovel soup down [her] throat." One of these soups was her mother's lentil soup, which her mother would make on Friday nights, even after Vatican II and the Congress of Cardinals in the 1960s declared that Catholics didn't have to abstain from eating meat on Fridays. "According to my mother, we still can't have meat on Fridays," she says, laughing.

It's a riff on that very soup that DePalma makes for me in her kitchen when we start cooking together. Her version isn't one she could serve to her mother on a Friday, given that it contains Italian sausage. It also includes the classic Italian trifecta—onions, carrots, and celery—and Swiss chard. At the end, DePalma employs a fascinating technique: she slivers garlic, sizzles it in oil, and adds that to the finished soup, along with some grated Pecorino, to give it an extra kick of flavor.

This is a wonderfully rich and comforting soup, the kind you'd want to hover over on a freezing-cold day or, as intended, while recovering from an illness. The other dishes DePalma makes—a pungent bagna cauda (with lots of garlic and anchovies) and a lemon semifreddo with blackberries—are foods to eat when you're well, when you're surrounded by people and feeling jovial. DePalma clearly relishes making the latter foods; and after what she's been through, who can blame her?

But life isn't all happy moments, and sometimes we get sick. And when we get sick, it's good to know that even at our lowest moments, there will be soup. And the soup will make us feel better.

"Food isn't exciting without people. You can't take that out of the equation."

Lentil Soup with Sausage, Chard, and Garlic

Serves 6

This is a nourishing, healing soup with intense, surprising flavor that sneaks up on you as you eat it. You can certainly leave out the sausage (though the sausage fat adds character) and the greens, but those touches—plus the addition of sizzling hot garlic at the end—are what make this soup so unique. That final step, the addition of hot garlic and oil, is a great technique in general: try it any time you make a soup that would benefit from a hit of garlic. (I'm thinking tomato soup, for example.) This soup freezes very well, so make more than you think you'll need and save the rest for a miserable and damp winter's night.

- You can also make this with an equal amount of pancetta or use hot Italian sausage, if you like a hint of spice.

- DePalma uses Luigi Vitelli canned tomatoes.

½ cup olive oil, plus more for drizzling

4 large links of sweet Italian sausage, removed from the casing

1 medium onion, diced

2 celery stalks, cut into crescents

2 medium carrots, peeled and cut into crescents

4 cloves garlic, sliced (reserve half for later in the recipe)

Kosher salt

A pinch of crushed red pepper flakes (optional)

1 cup brown lentils, sorted

2 bay leaves

1 (28-ounce) can crushed tomatoes

6 cups water

Freshly ground black pepper

3 to 4 cups shredded red Swiss chard leaves or kale

Grated Pecorino Romano cheese

Heat ¼ cup of the olive oil (enough to coat the bottom of the pot) in a large pot on medium heat and, when it's hot, add the sausage. Break up the sausage with a wooden spoon until it starts to brown, about 5 minutes.

Add the onion, celery, carrots, the first two garlic cloves, a pinch of salt, and, if you like your soup spicy, a pinch of red pepper flakes. Stir, then add the lentils, bay leaves, tomatoes, water, and salt and black pepper to taste. Bring to a simmer and allow to cook until the lentils are tender, about 40 minutes. (It may be necessary to add more water if the soup gets too thick.)

When the lentils are cooked, add the Swiss chard and cook until the leaves are tender, just a few minutes more. Discard the bay leaves.

To finish (and don't skip this step!), add the remaining ¼ cup of olive oil to a small pan along with the remaining garlic; cook on medium heat just until the garlic turns soft (1 to 2 minutes) and then stir that, oil and all, into the soup. Drizzle the soup with more fresh olive oil and Pecorino Romano cheese and pass more cheese at the table. Serve the soup hot. Leftovers will keep for several days in the refrigerator.

- Oil and water are enemies, so it may sizzle and spurt. Stand slightly back when transferring the oil to the soup.

Bagna Cauda
with Vegetables

Serves 6 or more

Bagna cauda is a loud and flavorful emulsion of butter, olive oil, garlic, and anchovies that works like a hot, pungent dip for vegetables. DePalma achieves maximum impact by grinding the garlic and the anchovies each into a paste with the blade of her knife, breaking down all the cell walls and exposing the maximum amount of surface area so that when the pastes hit that fat, everything explodes into a bad-breath-causing symphony. You can serve this with a variety of vegetables, but I agree with DePalma that endive is the best for scooping up the maximum amount of bagna cauda in each bite.

4 to 6 medium cloves garlic

Kosher salt

4 tablespoons (½ stick) butter (salted or unsalted, doesn't matter)

6 to 7 anchovies, packed in olive oil

½ cup olive oil

¼ cup chopped parsley (optional)

A variety of vegetables cut for dipping: endive (separated into scoopy leaves), red and orange bell peppers (traditional for this dish), quartered radishes, and young carrots

● I learned from DePalma that bagna cauda originates from the Piedmont region of Italy, where peppers are prevalent.

Begin by grinding the garlic into a paste. First chop the cloves roughly, then chop again into finer pieces. Sprinkle salt over everything and keep chopping, occasionally pressing the garlic with the flat side of the knife, smearing it across the cutting board, and working it—chopping and smearing—until it forms a paste.

Drop the garlic into a pot with the butter and heat on very low heat.

While that's heating, make a similar paste with the anchovies: chop them and smear them against the board until you have a paste. Add that to the pan with the garlic and the butter and cook, on low heat, just until the anchovies melt away (3 to 4 minutes). You don't want the garlic to color at all.

Once the anchovies are melted, whisk in the olive oil. Remove from the heat and, if you like, add parsley.

Place in a serving bowl on a platter with all the vegetables arranged around it. Serve hot.

Lemon Semifreddo with Blackberries and Honey

Serves 6

For anyone who loves ice cream but doesn't own an ice cream maker, this is the recipe for you. The steps are very similar to those involved in making ice cream: you heat egg yolks (here, with a boiling sugar mixture) and then incorporate cream. Only in normal ice cream, the cream isn't whipped first; here, you fold in whipped cream, which gives the semifreddo (which means "half frozen" in Italian) a light-as-air fluffiness, resulting in something that's like the secret love child of gelato and a marshmallow. The only step that's tricky is adding the hot sugar mixture. Make sure it's at the right temperature (use a candy thermometer) or the eggs might coagulate. If you do screw up, take heart; it takes just a few more eggs to start again.

1¼ cups heavy cream

5 large egg yolks

¾ cup sugar, plus more for topping

Zest and juice of 1 lemon

½ cup fresh blackberries

1 or 2 tablespoons honey

¼ cup toasted sliced almonds

● That means when you lift up the whisk, the cream stays pointy.

Whip the cream, either by hand or in a stand mixer with a whisk attachment, until it holds stiff peaks. Cover with plastic and refrigerate.

Begin beating the egg yolks in a clean bowl in a stand mixer with a clean whisk attachment on medium-low speed. While you do that, place the ¾ cup sugar in a pot fitted with a candy thermometer. Add about ⅛ cup water or more until the sugar is just covered with water. Heat until the sugar reaches the soft ball stage on the candy thermometer, 235°F.

Very carefully, with the mixer on low speed, pour the hot sugar mixture into the egg yolks; make sure to pour down the side of the mixer bowl in a very thin stream so the hot mixture doesn't splash up. Once the sugar is added, turn up the speed and continue mixing for several minutes until the mixture is cool. (You'll know when you touch the mixer bowl and it's no longer piping hot.) When that happens, beat in the lemon zest and juice.

To fold the egg mixture into the cream, first gently whisk some cream into the eggs. Then pour the eggs back into the rest of the cream and fold, still working gently so the mixture doesn't lose air. With a rubber spatula, guide the mixture into six 6-ounce ramekins. Cover the ramekins and place in the freezer for at least several hours.

To serve, run a knife around the perimeter of the semifreddos and dip the bottom of each ramekin in a small pan of boiling water. This will loosen it enough to unmold. Wipe each ramekin dry, place a serving plate on top, and invert to release the semifreddo.

Make a garnish by mixing the blackberries, honey, a pinch or two of sugar, and the sliced almonds. Spoon the garnish over the semifreddo and serve.

Melissa Clark

Author, *In the Kitchen with a Good Appetite*
and *Cook This Now;* **and recipe columnist,**
The New York Times
New York, New York

Clark's Kitchen Know-How

KEEP A KITCHEN JOURNAL to record what you bring home from the farmer's market each time you go and what you made with it. That way you know what to expect and what you can make the same time next year when you return to the market.

KEEP A SALT PIG next to the stove so a pinch of salt is just a reach away; a darkroom timer is good to have, too, and is a visually interesting tool to keep track of what you have in the oven.

ALEPPO PEPPER from Turkey is a great condiment to keep on your kitchen table; it's fruity, smoky, and a little bit spicy. If your dinner turns out not-so-good, you can save it with a drizzle of olive oil and a sprinkling of Aleppo pepper.

How do you come up with original, publishable recipes?

Meet Melissa Clark. Clark has her original recipes published in *The New York Times* on an almost weekly basis. Her column, "A Good Appetite," is a reader-friendly, food-savvy dispatch that offers a straightforward yet creative approach to seasonal food. Week after week she churns out recipes that make their way into homes across America.

The place where it all starts is the place where I first meet her: the Union Square Greenmarket in Manhattan. Clark, like many other accomplished cooks, begins with great ingredients.

"Oohhh, we have to get some of this ricotta," she says at a stand that's selling fresh sheep's-milk ricotta. She leads us to another stand for half a loaf of rye bread and then to another stand for handfuls of sugar snap peas.

As soon as we get to her apartment in Brooklyn, those three ingredients are put to use as Clark begins to test various crostini combinations.

The bread gets sliced and popped into a toaster; the sugar snap peas are slivered and tossed with olive oil, lemon juice, a chopped clove of green garlic, and two minced anchovies. The toasted bread is spread with the sheep's-milk ricotta and topped with the sugar snap mixture. She cuts it into four pieces and asks me and her assistant, Jaimee, what we think.

We think it's great.

Clark isn't satisfied. She continues trying different combinations—one with English peas, one with just the ricotta—all while scurrying around the kitchen prepping other dishes (pesto, pasta, duck) and cooing over her toddler, Dahlia. Her strategy seems to be MOMENTUM, in all caps.

In a quiet moment, I ask Clark about her process: "How do you come up with these recipes? How do you know they're good and ready to print?"

"I've always created my own recipes," she tells me. "I just don't think about it."

She's been doing this since she was a child. "When I was eleven, I remember I wanted a purple cake. So I tried to make one without looking at a recipe. I mixed together the flour, the sugar, the butter, and the eggs and added lots of red and blue food coloring."

The cake, when it came out of the oven, was "a flat marble brick."

But that failure didn't discourage her; in fact, failure is simply a part of the routine of a top-tier recipe creator.

For example, once Clark tested an eggplant recipe only to find that the eggplant was bitter. Instead of throwing out the baby with the bathwater, Clark employed a clever tactic: "If it comes out and it's not what you want, change the name." That dish became "Bitter Eggplant Salad."

After eating her crostini, her trofie with pesto and ricotta, and an amazing seared duck breast with cherries, I reach the following conclusion: to create accomplished, publishable recipes, you must (1) know a few basic techniques and (2) let ingredients inspire you. Wander around the farmer's market, buy what looks good, take it home, and experiment. You may fail, but as long as you keep moving, it shouldn't matter.

"Don't be afraid," says Clark as I get ready to go. After watching her at work, it's clear that fear has no place in a recipe creator's kitchen. The essential ingredient is gumption.

"If you fail a lot, just call it 'recipe developing.'"

Crostini with Sugar Snap Peas, Radishes, and Anchovies

Serves 4

Think of this as a blueprint more than as a recipe. When Clark tested crostini after crostini in her kitchen, she tried toppings as various as English peas with garlic and lemon and lightly dressed pea shoots. In my own kitchen, I play around with toppings such as sweet pitted cherries (in season) tossed with olive oil, balsamic vinegar, and toasted walnuts and, in summer, raw zucchini sliced on a mandoline, drizzled with olive oil and balsamic, and sprinkled with sea salt. Use good toasted bread and ricotta, keep it seasonal, and let your imagination run wild. You'll be surprised at how many variations on crostini you can create.

4 slices country bread, cut in half (if large)

Extra virgin olive oil

1 clove green garlic kept whole, plus 1 clove finely chopped (regular garlic will work too)

1 to 2 cups sugar snap peas, strings removed and sliced extra thin on the diagonal

3 breakfast radishes, sliced extra thin

5 chopped anchovies

Zest and juice of 1 lemon

Kosher salt and freshly ground black pepper

1 to 2 cups fresh sheep's-milk ricotta

● If you want to make it extra special, you can whip the ricotta in a stand mixer with a splash of milk. Whipped ricotta is airy and smooth and worth the extra effort.

Brush the bread with olive oil. In a toaster, under the broiler, or in a cast-iron skillet, toast the bread until it's a deep golden brown on both sides.

Rub the bread with the whole garlic.

In a bowl, toss together the sugar snap peas, radishes, anchovies, chopped garlic, a splash of olive oil, and the lemon zest and juice and season with salt and pepper to taste.

Top each crostini with a spoonful of ricotta and then a big spoonful of the sugar snap mixture. Drizzle with more olive oil before serving.

Trofie with Basil and Cilantro Pesto

Serves 4

- If you use the garlic scapes, skip the basil and garlic cloves. Add two cups garlic scapes, chopped slightly on a cutting board first to get them started, after the pine nuts, and follow the rest of the recipe.

- Pine nuts are pricey; you can use walnuts as an alternative.

- The garlic will finish in the blender, but you need to chop it roughly to get it started.

Substitutions are tricky things. Mess with a recipe too much, and you lose the initial spark that makes it great. So I offer one substitution here: instead of the garlic scapes Clark uses when she makes this pesto (which only come around a few months out of the year), try basil and garlic cloves. As for the pasta, stick to Clark's suggested trofie, a tightly wound corkscrew of a pasta that catches the pesto in a really glorious way. If you want to substitute something else, choose another pasta with lots of nooks to catch the garlicky green pesto (orecchiette will work). Whatever you do, don't skip the cilantro: its presence is what makes this dish truly unique.

FOR THE PESTO

½ cup pine nuts, toasted in a dry pan until golden and fragrant

6 cloves garlic, roughly chopped

4 to 6 cups basil leaves, washed, dried, and loosely packed

1 cup cilantro leaves, washed and dried

Kosher salt

About 1 cup olive oil

Juice of ½ lemon

½ cup grated Parmesan cheese

FOR THE PASTA

1 pound trofie (or orecchiette)

Fresh ricotta cheese (ideally sheep's-milk)

Cilantro leaves, for garnish

Bring a large pot of water to a boil.

In a blender or a food processor, combine the pine nuts and the garlic. Add the basil and cilantro and a big pinch of salt and blend until it forms a paste. With the motor running, slowly pour in the olive oil until the pesto comes together to your liking (you may not need all the olive oil or you may need more). Add the lemon juice and the Parmesan and adjust for seasoning.

Salt the boiling water well (it should taste like seawater) and add the pasta, cooking it according to package directions (don't undercook; this dish doesn't finish in a hot sauce). When ready, remove the pasta to a bowl, add half the pesto, and stir to coat well. Taste and add more pesto based on your preference.

To serve, spoon the pasta into serving bowls and top each with a big spoonful of ricotta and a few cilantro leaves to garnish.

Seared Duck Breast
with Garam Masala
and Grapes

Clark

Serves 2 to 4

This recipe is a masterpiece. When I first made this at home, I stared at the plate dumb-founded. Did I really just make that? And was it really that easy? The secret lies in the technique: to cook a duck breast, you score the fat with a paring knife, sear it in a hot skillet until all the fat is rendered, flip it over, and finish it in the oven. Then, as it rests, you can make a sauce in the same pan. (Friendly tip: don't burn your hand on the handle!) This dish is going to blow you away, especially if you've never cooked duck breast at home.

- If cherries are in season—as they were when I cooked with Clark—by all means use them instead. Be sure to pit them first.

- Clark used this classic Indian spice blend, but you can use any spice mixture you like. Try playing with combinations of ground cumin, cayenne pepper, ground coriander seeds, ground fennel seeds, or ground cardamom.

1 whole duck breast
(approximately 2 pounds)

¾ tablespoon kosher salt

1 teaspoon pepper

1 teaspoon garam masala
(see Resources, page 371)

2 tablespoons unsalted butter

1 cup red seedless grapes, sliced in half

1 teaspoon ground cinnamon

¼ cup balsamic vinegar

1 teaspoon honey

Using a paring knife, score the duck breast by cutting a crosshatch pattern into the fat. Make sure you cut all the way through the fat but not through the meat itself. The point is to expose as much of the fat's surface area to the heat as possible so it renders quickly. Season the duck on both sides with the salt, pepper, and garam masala. Let sit, at room temperature, for 45 to 60 minutes.

Preheat the oven to 350°F.

Heat an ovenproof skillet (do not use nonstick) on medium-high heat for a minute or two. Place the duck in the skillet, fat side down (it should immediately sizzle), and don't touch it. Let it cook like this for 4 minutes. Lots of fat will melt out—that's a good thing. Use tongs to turn the meat over. The skin should be a deep, chestnut brown and the fat should almost all be melted away. If you still see white, continue cooking on the fat side until it's gone (but without letting the skin burn).

Place the skillet in the oven. Cook for 3 to 4 minutes and then take the temperature of the duck breast. It should be 120°F for rare and 130°F for medium rare (shoot for 125°F). Remove the duck to a cutting board to rest.

Pour off the duck fat for another use (it's great for frying potatoes). In that same skillet, melt the butter on medium heat. Add the grapes and cinnamon and stir for a minute. Deglaze with the balsamic vinegar and honey, stirring and cooking until the sauce is syrupy, about 1 minute.

Thinly slice the duck, on the bias, and fan it out on a platter. Spoon the grape sauce on top and serve.

98

Tim Artz

Engineer and extreme do-it-yourselfer
Oakton, Virginia

When the Cub Scouts asked Tim Artz, an electrical engineer in Oakton, Virginia, to make s'mores at his seven-year-old son's Cub Scout cookout, Artz responded like a grizzled action movie hero: "I'm not making s'mores."

Instead, Artz smoked eighty pounds of chicken legs and eighteen pounds of sausage in his Porkulator (a smoker he built himself from an oil drum), finishing them on a charcoal grill at the campground. He also served a four-gallon batch of homemade beans, an equal amount of potato salad with homemade mayo, and, for dessert, root beer floats with root beer that he brewed and carbonated himself.

Artz, you see, is a bit of an obsessive when it comes to making things himself. He makes his own honey (with three beehives outside his home) and then makes his own mead using what's left over. He makes his own soap using rendered beef fat the way his mother taught him to in Lancaster, Pennsylvania. He makes six kinds of hot sauce, which he puts in his own bottles with labels he also makes himself. He makes pickles, beer, you name it.

Artz grows things, too. He grows figs, Meyer lemons, kaffir lime leaves, two kinds of grapes, arugula, and San Marzano tomatoes.

Within those projects are more projects. For example, in his herb garden (where he grows thyme, sage, epazote, tarragon, and wormwood for making absinthe mead), there's a jar of liquid. When I ask about it, he says he's making *nochino*, a walnut liqueur he first tried at a friend's house in Milan. "It's a hilarious recipe," he tells me. "You have to pick twenty-four walnuts on the twenty-fourth of June."

"You didn't actually do that, did you?"

"Yes, I did," he says.

Of course he did.

How does Artz do all this? Why does Artz do all this? What's the point of doing all this? Should we be doing this ourselves?

The point becomes clearer when we start cooking. Artz heats milk (high-quality milk that he has delivered from South Mountain Creamery; see Resources, page 371) in a pot to which he adds a spoonful of citric acid. A few moments later, the milk's coagulated, and, after straining it, we have homemade ricotta. "It's that easy," says Artz.

With that homemade ricotta, Artz fashions a calzone using his homemade sourdough, his homemade mozzarella, his homegrown spinach, garlic, and parsley, and his self-manufactured hot sauce. The result is a hot, oozing loaf of comfort, remarkable for the fact that every element was produced right here. Local food doesn't get any more local.

In our remaining time together, we make a batch of his West Indies–style hot sauce, chicken croquettes, a loaf of plain sourdough, and sausage. (Artz even comes up with his own nickname: "You can call me the Sultan of Scratch," he tells me.)

The Sultan of Scratch may be obsessive, but the result of that obsession is a frugal, practical, earth-friendly approach to feeding himself and his family.

> ## "The things I grow are shaped by the things I want to make."

West Indies–Style Hot Sauce

Makes 6 cups

If you or someone you know loves hot sauce, you've got to try this recipe. It's a simple matter of simmering carrots, onions, and garlic, adding French's mustard, honey, and vinegar, blending it up, and then adding as many habaneros as you can handle. I can only handle six—any more, and my face will burst into flames—but if you're one of those "pain is good" kind of people, do it up! Wear gloves or use a sheet of plastic wrap to protect your hands when handling the habaneros. If you have the time and the know-how, this finished sauce can be placed in sterilized bottles. It makes a great gift.

● Artz says he's tried this with fancier mustards but that French's works the best.

5 carrots, washed, peeled, and cut into 1-inch pieces

1 medium yellow onion, peeled and cut into 1-inch dice

10 cloves garlic, whole, peeled

2 cups water

Kosher salt

12 ounces French's yellow mustard

½ cup honey

1 cup apple cider vinegar

6 to 12 assorted habanero peppers, cut in half, stems, seeds, and cores removed

Place the carrots, onion, and garlic into a Dutch oven. Add the water and a large pinch of salt to the pot. Cover and bring to a boil. Lower to a simmer and cook until all the vegetables are very soft (a knife should go through the thickest carrot easily), about 15 minutes.

Add the mustard, honey, and vinegar to the pot. Blend well with an immersion (stick) blender to make a puree. Taste and adjust the honey, vinegar, or salt for balance. Add the peppers, as many as you can handle. Pulse the mixture with the immersion blender again to break up the peppers into tiny flecks. Don't puree too much: the idea is to leave visible bits of pepper in the sauce, not to make a homogeneous puree.

● Be careful that you blend *all* the peppers, though. You don't want to leave big chunks of habanero in the sauce.

Seal in sanitized bottles or keep refrigerated. The sauce keeps for a year in bottles stored in a cool, dry location. If stored unsealed in a refrigerator, use within a month.

Spinach Calzone
with Two Cheeses

Serves 4 to 6

Even though Artz constructs this calzone to feature his homemade sourdough, ricotta, mozzarella, and hot sauce, as well as his homegrown spinach and garlic, make things easier on yourself. The dough can be made from scratch using the recipe on page 24 (which Artz contributed to), but it works equally well with store-bought pizza dough. As for the cheese and spinach and garlic, use store-bought and you will still be very satisfied. This is a monster of a calzone—humongous!—that can easily feed a family of four on a weeknight. In the spirit of Artz, serve a bit of homemade hot sauce (see his recipe, opposite) on the side. And if you want to make all the other elements by yourself, too, by all means do so.

8 ounces fresh baby spinach leaves (or an equal amount of frozen spinach, defrosted)

1 cup fresh ricotta cheese

½ cup fresh mozzarella, torn into pieces

6 cloves garlic, coarsely chopped

1 egg

2 teaspoons West Indies–style Hot Sauce (see opposite)

2 teaspoons chopped flat-leaf parsley

1 round of pizza dough, preferably homemade (see recipe, page 24)

1½ cups tomato sauce, for serving (optional)

If using fresh spinach, rinse it without drying it, then either place it in a microwave-safe bowl, cover it, and zap it until it's soft, or cook it in a steamer basket just until wilted. Squeeze out extra moisture and then roughly chop.

Preheat the oven to 400°F.

In a large bowl, stir together the spinach, both cheeses, the garlic, egg, hot sauce, and parsley.

On an oil-lined baking sheet, flatten the dough and work it into a large oval (about 9 inches across). Spread the filling inside it, leaving a 1-inch border all the way around.

Fold the dough over itself and pinch the edges to make a seal. Then roll the edges up and over to form a nice elevated crust. Slash the top of the calzone a few times with a very sharp knife to create air vents.

Bake for 25 minutes, or until the top is golden brown and the cheese has melted. Allow to cool slightly on the baking sheet and then cut into 1-inch wedges and serve with more of the hot sauce or, if you'd prefer it, warm tomato sauce.

Chicken Croquettes

Serves 4

"It's fried meat," said my friend Jimmy when I served this one summer night. "How could that be bad?" The answer is that it can't be bad; it is, in fact, very good. Think of these as elevated chicken nuggets and you'll get the idea. Artz makes his with chicken he smokes himself in his self-built industrial smoker, but since most of us don't have that (or a meat grinder), you can (and should) make this with ground chicken or turkey. It works very well; you just have to make sure you cook the croquettes all the way through when you fry them in the oil. Serve with a bright, acidic salad, such as Jonathan Waxman's Arugula Salad with Heirloom Tomatoes (page 12).

1½ pounds ground smoked chicken or turkey or plain chicken (ask your butcher to grind it for you)

½ pound fresh shiitake mushrooms, stems removed, cut into ¼-inch strips, sautéed in 4 tablespoons unsalted butter until brown, set aside, and cooled

2 tablespoons chopped sun-dried tomatoes

¼ cup fresh bread crumbs

2 cloves garlic, finely chopped

3 tablespoons grated Grana Padano or Parmesan cheese

2 tablespoons pine nuts, toasted in a dry pan until golden

2 large eggs

1 tablespoon chopped flat-leaf parsley

2 teaspoons white truffle oil (optional)

Kosher salt and freshly ground black pepper

1 cup panko bread crumbs

Grapeseed oil, for frying (or, if you can't find grapeseed oil, use canola or vegetable oil)

West Indies–Style Hot Sauce (page 102; optional)

In a large bowl, mix together the chicken, cooked shiitakes, sun-dried tomatoes, bread crumbs, garlic, cheese, pine nuts, eggs, parsley, white truffle oil (if you're using it), and salt and pepper to taste. Fold until well combined.

Pour the panko into a shallow pie plate. Form the meat mixture into small patties and coat the patties on both sides with the panko. Set the patties aside. (You can do this several hours ahead, covering and refrigerating the patties until ready to fry.)

Heat a ½-inch layer of grapeseed oil in a frying pan until it's hot when you hold your hand over it. Lower a few croquettes at a time and cook until brown and crispy on both sides and heated through the middle, 3 to 4 minutes per side. (If you aren't using smoked chicken, which is already cooked, make sure the patty is no longer pink in the middle before serving. The best way to know is to cut in.)

Serve with the hot sauce, if desired.

If you're using smoked chicken, it's fine to taste here (unless you're raw-egg squeamish); otherwise, make a spicy meatball (page 158).

Rebecca Charles

Chef-owner, Pearl Oyster Bar
New York, New York

Upon leaving chef Rebecca Charles's New York City apartment, I marched straight to Bed Bath and Beyond and purchased two eight-inch All-Clad stainless-steel sauté pans and a pair of metal tongs. Each pan cost fifty dollars and the tongs were ten dollars, which might seem like an indulgence, but after spending four hours cooking with Charles in her kitchen I knew the investment was sound: with these simple tools, you can make restaurant-quality seafood dishes at home.

Take, for example, the cod that Charles serves at her beloved New York City restaurant, Pearl Oyster Bar. She heats the two sauté pans simultaneously, and once they're hot, she ladles canola oil or clarified butter into one (coating the bottom) and fills the other halfway with water. Into the pan with the oil, she lowers a thick fillet of cod that's been soaked in milk, seasoned, and then dredged in a mixture of cracker meal (basically, pulverized saltines) and flour.

To the pan with the bubbling water, she adds corn that she cuts off the cob with a sharp knife, and seasons it with salt. "You could, of course, cook the corn in a separate pot of water, but then I think you lose some of the flavor when you strain it. Here, all the flavor stays in the dish."

And sure enough, as the water evaporates, a concentrated corn broth coats the bottom of the pan. To that she adds sugar snap peas, a few small heirloom tomatoes cut in half, chives, and "a big honker" of butter. She

"If you can't make something good out of salt, pepper, and protein, you have no business in the kitchen."

uses her tongs to add the butter (which she keeps, a pound of it, in a bowl next to the stove). With those same tongs she turns the cod over and cooks it on the other side. When she's finished, she spoons the corn mixture onto a plate and tops it with the cod, and there is a summery dish that'd put a smile on even the most jaded customer's face.

This two-pan method—which Charles repeats for me with soft-shell crab and again with skate—is part of the secret that makes Pearl such a success. Each night, no matter how crowded, two cooks on the line use this two-pan method to cook all of the hot food that goes out to the hungry throngs. This style of cooking—called *à la minute*—is unusual for a restaurant. "Most restaurants cook their food ahead and keep it warm," Charles explains. "I don't like to cook like that."

Cooking like this is all about rhythm. Sponge-wipe here, pan-toss there. It's not about following rules; it's about feeling your way through a dish. With two pans and a pair of tongs, you have the tools to make piping-hot restaurant food any time you want it: a worthy investment indeed.

Scallop Chowder

Serves 6

Sometimes you really don't want to know what makes restaurant food taste so good. I've eaten the scallop chowder at Pearl Oyster Bar for years, declaring it one of the best chowders I've ever had, and then the curtain was pulled back in Charles's kitchen when I saw that the main ingredient was a quart of cream. I e-mailed Charles before making this at home to ask if I could substitute milk; but because milk doesn't thicken the way cream does when it reduces, the answer was no. So I made the chowder the way it's meant to be made—with butter and cream and a shot of Pernod at the end—and my dinner guests swooned. Of course, I didn't tell them why it tasted so good. When it comes to good chowder, ignorance is bliss.

- Feel the scallops as you cut them up; sometimes there's a hard bit ("the boot") still attached that you should remove.

- Cut the potatoes and scallops into similar-size pieces.

4 tablespoons (½ stick) unsalted butter

1 large Spanish onion, chopped

Kosher salt and freshly ground black pepper

2 large white Idaho potatoes, peeled and cut into ½-inch dice (submerge in water until ready to use)

1½ pounds sea scallops, cut into ½-inch chunks

1 quart heavy cream

¼ to ½ cup Pernod

1 teaspoon chopped fresh thyme

Minced fresh chives

Begin by melting the butter in a large pot over medium heat. Add the onions, season with salt and pepper, and cook, lowering the heat a little, until the onions soften. Take your time here (about 10 minutes or so); this is where the onions develop flavor. Just don't let them brown.

Add the potatoes to the onions, season, and cook, again, slowly, for 5 more minutes.

Add the scallops, season again, stir, and add enough cream until everything is covered. Bring to a simmer and cook, slowly, until the liquid reduces substantially, approximately 45 minutes.

- When Charles made this, there was lots of bubbling going on. Keep it at an aggressive simmer, just short of a boil.

Add the Pernod—which gives everything a lovely anise flavor—and the thyme and cook a few minutes longer.

- Charles recommends that you make the chowder a day ahead and allow it to "cure" overnight.

Remove from the heat and either serve right away, with chives sprinkled on top, or allow the chowder to come to room temperature and refrigerate overnight. The flavors will develop if you allow for this extra step, but once you taste the chowder, you won't be able to wait. Keeps for 3 to 4 days, covered, in the refrigerator.

Smoked
Fish Salad

Serves 4

The Semitic side of me thinks you could rename this salad "Jewish salad." After all, there's sour cream, dill, and smoked fish, three flavors that conjure, for me, memories of post–bar mitzvah brunches. But even if you're not Jewish, there's much to enjoy here in this zesty dressing combo (it would even work without the smoked fish). Charles's method for making dressing is improvisational: "I encourage people to make up their own salad dressings," she told me. So play around with the herbs you use (try tarragon or basil), the fats (different oils, for example), and the acid (different vinegars or citrus juices) and see what you dream up.

FOR THE DRESSING

¼ cup white wine vinegar

1 minced shallot

¼ cup sour cream

½ cup olive oil

¼ cup chopped fresh dill

A pinch of sugar

A pinch of kosher salt

1 pound butter lettuce, washed

1 cucumber, sliced thin

½ pound smoked trout (or sable, sturgeon, or white fish), deboned

For the dressing, whisk together all the ingredients and then taste to adjust. For a more acidic flavor, add more vinegar. To thin out the consistency, add a splash of water.

Toss the lettuce with some of the dressing and put on a plate. Fan the cucumber around it and place the smoked fish on top. Spoon more dressing over everything; use just enough without going overboard. Serve immediately.

Cracker-Crusted Cod with Corn, Sugar Snap Peas, and Tomatoes

Serves 4

Here's the recipe to try out Charles's signature two-pans-and-a-pair-of-tongs technique. You can use this same technique with different fish (a cleaned soft-shell crab, skate) and a variety of vegetables (sugar snap peas with toasted almonds, garden peas). In all cases, soak the fish first in milk and get the pans very hot before cooking. The only issue is if you're feeding more than one. How many pans does it take to cook this dish for a family of four? I see your point. Try this: use two larger pans, one of which is ovenproof, and cook all four fillets in that and the corn in the other pan all at once. Finish the fish in the oven and it will all work out the same.

2 cups whole milk

4 equally thick fillets of cod

⅓ cup cracker meal

⅔ cup all-purpose flour

Kosher salt and freshly ground black pepper

Vegetable oil or clarified butter

1 to 2 cups fresh corn, cut off the cob with a sharp knife

½ cup stringed sugar snap peas, cut in half

½ cup heirloom cherry tomatoes, cut in half

1 tablespoon minced chives

2 tablespoons unsalted butter, softened

- You can buy cracker meal in the store or, to make your own, pulverize saltines in a blender or food processor until fine.

- See Kevin Davis's technique for making clarified butter, page 232.

- This simply means the more attractive side. You'll get a better sear on this side and this is the side that'll be faceup when you serve it.

Preheat the oven to 450°F.

Place the milk in a shallow pan and soak the cod for 20 minutes at room temperature. In another shallow pan, stir together the cracker meal and flour.

Place two large sauté pans on the stove (one should be ovenproof) and turn up the heat to medium-high. Remove the fish from the milk, pat dry with paper towels, and season well with salt and pepper. Dredge the fish in the cracker meal–flour mixture.

Add oil or clarified butter to coat the bottom of the ovenproof pan and place the fish, presentation side down, in the pan. It should sizzle immediately. At the same time, add about 1 cup water to the second pan, followed by a big pinch of salt and all the corn. Let it boil and cook for 30 seconds, then add the sugar snaps and cook for another 30 seconds. Meanwhile, check the fish: when it's brown and crusty on the presentation side, use tongs or a fish spatula to flip it over. Place the pan in the oven and cook just until the fish is cooked through (it will go from tranclucent to opaque), 2 to 3 minutes.

Add the tomatoes, chives, and butter to the pan with the corn and snap peas. Toss until everything is emulsified and coated, seasoning with more salt and pepper.

Ideally, the fish should finish cooking when the vegetables are ready. Remove from the oven and put the vegetables on the plate first and the fish on top, presentation side up. Serve immediately.

Gary Danko

Chef-owner, Restaurant Gary Danko
San Francisco, California

Though many of us can talk about cookbook authors who've influenced our cooking, few of us can say that we tracked down those cookbook authors and insisted that they become our mentors. But such was the case with chef Gary Danko and his hero, French cooking teacher Madeleine Kamman.

"At the CIA, I came across Madeleine's book *The Making of a Cook*," he tells me from the kitchen island in his San Francisco apartment. "Her book sang to me. What she was writing about, I had the same ideas about. It was a whole new style of cooking."

When Kamman came to the States to teach a class in New Hampshire, Danko immediately called her to enroll. He imitates her thick French accent: "Oh, I'm sorry, Gary; we are full, full, full."

When Danko persisted, Kamman moaned, "Gary, will you please give me the dignity!"

When he asked if it was because he was a man (Kamman was a noted feminist), she snapped, "You are full of shit!"

Eventually, though, not only did he win a seat in her class, he also became her assistant and traveled with her to France. Her lessons still inform his cooking to this day. "Madeleine was meticulous," Danko recalls. "She'd look at a plate and ask, 'Why is this component there? What role is it playing?'"

Danko himself is also meticulous, a fact that becomes very clear when we start cooking.

We begin with a blueberry crostada, and Danko has a unique method for making the crust. After using the food processor to combine the butter and flour and adding only the smallest amount of water, he dumps the pebbly mixture onto a sheet of parchment paper and then begins squeezing clumps, stacking them on top of each other. He uses the parchment to shape those clumps into a log that he slices in half, making two pristine disks.

After refrigerating the dough for one hour, and after rolling it out (he uses a bench scraper to fix any cracks in the perimeter), filling it with blueberries, and popping it in the oven, Danko begins making one of his signature dishes: buckwheat blinis with crème fraîche, smoked salmon, and caviar.

He coats a nonstick pan with clarified butter—"You need enough fat to float the blinis or they won't curl"—then uses a pancake dispenser to drop wet blini batter into the hot pan. The dispenser ensures circles as precise as the disks of crostada dough.

Pretty soon, the hot blinis are transferred to a plate and Danko uses a bag to pipe on crème fraîche. He lays on salmon and then pipes osetra caviar on top. "Eat it hot!" he instructs. I do and it is *good*.

Danko's precision and meticulousness is evident in everything he does, including the way he warms a bowl before adding the soup. ("There's nothing worse than hearing 'This soup's not hot enough,'" he says.) Danko may have once been an eager student, desperate to learn from his chef hero, but now the tables have turned and he's the teacher. And his high standards are enough to make a sloppy cook like me think twice before sloshing soup into an unwarmed bowl.

"The correct tool can save you a lot of time."

Buckwheat Blinis with Smoked Salmon and Caviar

Makes 12 blinis

If you want to impress guests, next time you throw a dinner party, present them with a tray of hot buckwheat blinis, straight from the frying pan, topped with crème fraîche, smoked salmon, and—if you feel like splurging—caviar. The key here is timing: you want to serve these piping hot, so don't start cooking until your friends ring the doorbell.

FOR THE FIRST BOWL

1 cup all-purpose flour

1 tablespoon sugar

1 tablespoon active dry yeast

1 cup milk, heated to body temperature (like a baby bottle, to 98°F)

FOR THE SECOND BOWL

1 cup buckwheat flour

2 teaspoons kosher salt

2 egg yolks

¾ cup milk, heated to body temperature (98°F)

TO FINISH

2 egg whites

¼ cup heavy cream

Clarified butter (see page 232) or vegetable oil

Crème fraîche

Several extra-thin slices of smoked salmon

Caviar (as nice as you want; optional)

Minced chives (optional)

- Clarified butter will add more flavor to the finished blinis.

- Be careful that the milk is not too hot (you might kill the yeast). Better to err on the side of the milk being too cool than too hot.

- It's easier to beat egg whites in a bowl that's room temperature; it's easier to whisk cream in a bowl that's very cold.

- Danko points out that "the first pancake is the sacrificial pancake," the one you make to test the temperature: it's for you to snack on.

- Danko piped his crème fraîche and caviar using plastic bags with the corners cut off. This makes the process slightly neater.

In the first bowl, combine the dry ingredients with a whisk and slowly add the warm milk. Do the same in the second bowl with the buckwheat flour, salt, yolks, and warm milk. Cover both and allow them to rest for 1 to 2 hours at room temperature.

Combine both batters in one large bowl, folding them together with a rubber spatula. In a separate bowl (ideally a copper bowl), beat the egg whites with a large whisk until soft peaks form. Fold the egg whites into the flour mixture. In another bowl, whisk the heavy cream until soft peaks form. Fold into the flour mixture, cover, and allow to rest one more hour at room temperature.

To cook, add enough clarified butter or vegetable oil to a nonstick skillet to make a thick layer (about ½ inch). Heat on medium high until hot and then add the blini batter either using a pancake dispenser or pouring from a liquid measuring cup. The blinis should be small, about 1 inch in diameter. Cook on one side, and when bubbles form on the surface and the perimeter starts to brown, flip them over. The second side will cook faster.

Remove the blinis to a paper-towel-lined plate and *immediately* top with some crème fraîche, a curl of smoked salmon, and, if you're using it, ½ teaspoon caviar. Garnish with the chives, if desired, and serve.

Asparagus Soup with Spinach and Tarragon

Serves 4 to 6

Water-based soups are a challenge for any cook. Whereas stock provides richness and depth, a water-based soup requires that you coax as much flavor as you can from every element. So here, in this vividly green asparagus soup, you let the onions soften for a while in butter. Then you enhance the flavor with garlic, tarragon, and a pinch of nutmeg. By the time you blend the mix with big handfuls of spinach, you won't believe how much nuance and complexity you've created in a soup that's basically asparagus, onions, and water. Of course this tastes a thousand times better if you make it when asparagus is in season (that would be spring).

● Danko uses dried tarragon; I prefer fresh. The choice is yours.

Kosher salt

1¼ pounds asparagus, bottoms discarded, tops set aside for garnish, the rest cut into ½-inch rounds

2 tablespoons unsalted butter

½ cup diced onion

1 clove garlic, grated on a Microplane

1½ teaspoons dried tarragon or 1 tablespoon fresh tarragon, finely chopped

A pinch of freshly grated nutmeg

6-ounce bag fresh spinach leaves, cleaned

Crème fraîche (optional)

Minced chives (optional)

Fill a pot halfway with water and bring it to a simmer. Season with salt and quickly blanch the asparagus tips until just cooked through (a fast minute or two). Shock in ice water (this stops the cooking and sets the color) and set aside.

Pour out the water from the first pot, wipe it dry (no need to scrub it), and melt the butter on medium heat. Add the onions and a pinch of salt and lower the heat. Cook, very gently, stirring the onions every so often to avoid browning.

When the onions are translucent and soft (about 20 minutes), add the garlic, the rest of the asparagus, the tarragon, and the nutmeg. Add enough water to cover everything but not too much water (you can always add more later). Season with salt, tasting the water to make sure it has flavor (the water is what will flavor the asparagus). Bring to a full boil, lower to a simmer, and cook until the asparagus is extra tender (you should be able to easily mash it against the side of the pot with a wooden spoon). Add the spinach and remove from the heat.

● You could also use an immersion (stick) blender here.

When the soup has cooled slightly, add to a blender and puree until you no longer see the dark green flecks from the spinach. (Be careful when blending anything hot! Leave an opening at the top of the blender, covering with a dish towel.)

Strain through a fine-mesh strainer into a separate pot (or into the same pot, but clean it first). You can chill the soup at this point and serve it cold later on or, if you'd prefer to serve it hot, you can reheat it with a little water. To serve hot, ladle the soup into warm bowls and garnish with the asparagus tips and with some crème fraîche and chives, if desired.

Blueberry Crostada

● Simply wrap the second crust tightly in plastic wrap and place in the freezer. When you're craving crostada, defrost it in the refrigerator the night before you want to bake it.

● Danko thinks you should use a kitchen scale for measuring. Scales are very cheap and you can buy them easily on amazon.com or at any kitchen supply store.

● Out of season, I make this with frozen blueberries straight out of the freezer and it works quite well. You can also make crostadas with all kinds of fresh fruit: try nectarines, apricots, and cherries in the summer, when fruit is at its best.

Makes 1 crostada plus 1 extra crust for later

If you're anything like me, pie dough is the bane of your existence. You've read all the advice and you're aware of all that you're supposed to do. (Keep everything cold! Keep the pie dough moving on the counter so it doesn't stick!) But it doesn't matter—you get the same hopeless pie dough as a result. That is, until you try this recipe: Danko's method, which involves a scale, a food processor, and a big sheet of parchment paper, is foolproof. Don't worry if you don't roll the dough in a perfect circle. And even if the filling leaks while it cooks, you can just cut those leaky parts away later. What you end up with is a crostada so gorgeous and so delicious, no one will believe you made it yourself!

FOR THE CRUST(S)

10 ounces all-purpose flour, sifted (about 2 cups)

1 teaspoon kosher salt

¼ cup sugar

6 ounces very cold unsalted butter, cut into ½-inch cubes (about 12 tablespoons, or 1½ sticks)

¼ cup ice water (or more)

FOR THE FILLING

4 cups blueberries, washed and dried

¼ cup plus 1 tablespoon sugar

A pinch of kosher salt

5 teaspoons cornstarch

Ice water

Vanilla ice cream (optional)

To make the crust, combine the flour, salt, and sugar in a food processor. Pulse one time. Add the cold butter and pulse 15 times (each pulse should last 1 second). You should end up with a bowlful of pea-size pieces. Through the hole at the top of the food processor, add the ice water and allow the processor to run for 10 seconds. Grab a clump of dough in your fist: if it just holds together, you're ready. If not, put the lid back on and add another tablespoon or two of ice water until the dough does hold together.

Lay a large sheet of parchment paper on the counter. Dump the contents of the food processor onto one side of the parchment. Pick up a handful of dough, squeeze it together with your fist until it forms a tight clump, and then lay that clump on the other side of the parchment. Continue doing this until you have a pile of squeezed-together dough clumps.

Move the pile to the center of the parchment and use the paper itself to shape that pile into a log. Wrap the parchment around it and push and press and roll until it has formed a smooth uniform shape. Cut the log in half and shape each half into a disk. Wrap each disk in plastic wrap, refrigerating one (for the crostada) and freezing the other (for another crostada down the road). Refrigerate the crostada dough for 1 hour.

Preheat the oven to 400°F. Remove the dough from the refrigerator, unwrap it, and dip the entire disk in flour. Place the dough in the center of another piece of parchment dusted with flour. Use a rolling pin to whack it a few times to relax the gluten. Begin rolling from the center outward, monitoring the edges: if they start to crack, squeeze them back together using a pastry scraper (also called a bench scraper), pressing the flat side of the metal against the cracking exterior of the circle until it's whole again. Continue to roll out until you have a 12-inch circle. (If it seems to be sticking to the parchment, lift the parchment a bit and sprinkle some flour beneath the dough.) Slide the parchment with the dough on it onto a cookie sheet. Set aside.

To make the filling, combine the blueberries, the ¼ cup sugar, the salt, and the cornstarch in a large bowl. Stir with a rubber spatula.

Add the fruit to the center of the dough. Use the parchment to bring the outside of the circle of dough up all around the fruit, leaving the fruit at the center exposed. The final diameter of the shaped crostada should be about 7 inches.

Brush the entire crostada with ice water and sprinkle with the remaining tablespoon of sugar. Bake for 45 to 50 minutes, until the center of the filling is bubbling.

● The reason for this, according to Danko, is that cornstarch doesn't fully dissolve until the liquid is at a boil. So if you don't let the filling bubble in the center, you may have some residual starch in your crostada.

Allow the crostada to cool slightly and then flip it over onto the back of another cookie sheet to remove the parchment. Flip it right side up again and cut with a serrated knife. Serve, while still warm, with scoops of good vanilla ice cream.

● This is utterly terrifying, but it works. The fruit doesn't fall out because of all that cornstarch (it's almost like a jam at this point) and the parchment comes off easily.

Alex Raij &
Eder Montero

Chef-owners, Txikito and El Quinto Pino
New York, New York

Many a couple has broken up after attempting that most dangerous of romantic pursuits: cooking together.

One partner doesn't get the pan hot enough; the other partner adds too much salt. Three days later boxes are packed, DVDs are being divvied up, and friends are picking sides. Does it always have to be this way?

Welcome to Txikito, a Basque restaurant in Manhattan that's run and owned (along with another restaurant, El Quinto Pino) by a married couple, chefs Alexandra Raij and Eder Montero.

"We get into really big fights almost every day," Raij says as she and Montero explain how they work together without destroying their marriage. "But five minutes later, we've moved on."

In their large kitchen (which is underneath the restaurant), Raij and Montero work apart as much as they work together. Montero will prep vegetables while Raij cooks chickpeas in a pressure cooker. When they do work together on a task, careful negotiations ensue.

Raij takes the lid off the pressure cooker and ladles the cooked chickpeas into a blender with some of the cooking liquid and the onion and carrot that also cooked in there. Montero adds a mixture of hot olive oil, garlic, and smoked paprika that sizzles as it hits the liquid. As Montero puts a lid on the blender and prepares to turn it on, Raij interjects,

"Eder, use a towel to cover the opening at the top. I don't want that to explode."

Montero smirks mischievously and turns the blender on anyway. Raij recoils for a second and then, when she sees all is okay, rolls her eyes. To many a couple, a scene like this rings totally familiar.

But perhaps because running two restaurants requires so much of them, Raij and Montero don't have time to quibble. Raij gets busy brining the eggplant for a dish that features a technique that Montero, who grew up in Bilbao, Spain, learned while working at a Japanese restaurant.

"When Eder worked at Nobu, in New York, he learned this technique," she says as she cuts slits into exposed eggplant flesh. "We'll do cooking demonstrations in Spain and everyone will be blown away by this. And they'll have no idea it's Japanese."

The enthusiasm and pride Raij shows about her husband's eggplant trick (a trick, as you'll see in the recipe on page 123, that involves coating the eggplant with cornstarch before frying it) reveals something about how they're able to work so well together: they're big fans of each other's work.

And because they each bring different areas of expertise to the table—Raij attended the Culinary Institute of America in Hyde Park, New York; Montero attended La Escuela Superior de Cocina de Donosti in San Sebastián, Spain—they each have arenas in which they can be more authoritative than the other. This is a good formula for couples cooking at home: know your strengths and your weaknesses and delegate jobs based on those strengths and weaknesses.

"We know pretty clearly who's who," says Montero. "She gives me so much pressure and I give it to her. I don't let her do something that's not her best."

The look on Raij's face as he says this is both amused and defensive. ("What does he consider not my best?" I can imagine her thinking.) But clearly they find each other amusing and, more important, their two voices fuse together seamlessly on the plate.

"No one else can make our food," says Raij. "It's our story."

And the story, quite clearly, is a romance.

"Sometimes you have to give yourself permission to figure out something quietly alone: like how to peel an artichoke."

—Alex Raij

Fried Eggplant with Honey

Serves 4 to 6

The challenge of frying eggplant is that the outside cooks faster than the inside and so the exposed surfaces get too dark before the eggplant is cooked through. This recipe solves the problem by using a trick Montero picked up at Nobu: coat the eggplant (which gets brined, first, in salty water) in cornstarch. The cornstarch prevents the eggplant from turning brown right away and that buys time, so at the end you wind up with custardy eggplant, properly cooked, and a crackling crust. Finish with the honey-vinegar glaze and a sprinkling of fleur de sel, and you have a sweet, sour, salty bite of heaven to start out any meal.

Kosher salt

3 skinny Japanese eggplants, sliced in half vertically, left unpeeled; or 2 regular eggplants, peeled and cut into ¼-inch rounds

1 cup cornstarch

Canola oil

½ cup honey

A few lemon thyme or regular thyme leaves (optional)

A splash of sherry vinegar

Fleur de sel, for sprinkling (optional)

Fill a large bowl with cold water and add kosher salt until the water tastes salty. Score the cut surface of the eggplant in a crosshatch pattern with a sharp knife, not cutting all the way through, to allow it to absorb a good amount of the brine. Drop the eggplant into the brine, weight it down with a plate, if necessary, and allow it to soak for 1 hour.

Set up a fry station: Pour the cornstarch into a pie plate. Set up another plate with paper towels to drain the eggplant on when it comes out of the oil. Finally, fill a wide, deep pot at least one quarter of the way but no more than halfway with canola oil. Heat the oil to 350°F.

Meanwhile, make the glaze. In a small pot, heat the honey over medium-low heat with the thyme leaves, if you're using them, until just simmering, 1 to 2 minutes. Add enough vinegar to thin it out and taste to adjust for balance. The glaze should be sticky but somewhat loose. Set aside at room temperature.

Drain the eggplant from the brine and pat it very dry with paper towels. Dredge the eggplant in the cornstarch, shaking off any excess, and carefully lower into the hot oil. (Don't crowd the pan; you may need to do this in batches.) Fry the eggplant for 3 to 4 minutes, until it's crisp on the outside and thoroughly cooked on the inside. (If you're not sure, take a piece out and cut into it: the eggplant should be soft all the way through, with no hard spots.)

Drain the fried eggplant on paper towels and then place on a serving plate. Drizzle with the glaze and a small sprinkling of fleur de sel, if desired. Serve piping hot.

● Taste the eggplant first; you may not need the extra salt at the end.

Spring Vegetable Confit

Serves 4 to 6

How do you turn something wholesome into something sinful? The answer is a three-letter word: *fat*. In this case, applying a classic Spanish technique, a healthy amount of spring vegetables—artichokes, leeks, scallions, and fava beans—are cooked slowly in olive oil. It's an easy do-ahead, and it's easy to adjust based on what you find at the farmer's market: try it with shallots, asparagus, sugar snap peas, or Jerusalem artichokes.

4 globe artichokes

2 lemons, halved

2 bunches of scallions, cleaned and sliced into ½-inch rounds

1 leek, cleaned well and sliced into ½-inch rings

1 clove garlic, sliced thin

6 rosemary leaves, chopped very fine

Kosher salt

Extra virgin olive oil

½ to 1 cup fava beans, podded and peeled, or an equal amount of frozen lima beans straight from the freezer

A few fresh mint leaves

Smoked Basque sheep's-milk cheese (Idiazábal), soft goat cheese, or Parmesan

First cut off and discard the dark green parts of the leek, then slice the leek vertically through the top. Hold it under running water to get all the sand out of the layers. Leeks can be very sandy, so rinse them a few times.

When you buy fresh fava beans, they'll come in pods. Taking them out of the pods is easy; taking them out of their second skin, however, requires some work. (You have to dig your thumbnail in to really get it off.)

A serrated knife works well for slicing off the top of the artichoke.

Prepare the artichokes by peeling away the tough outer leaves first. Slice off the top of the artichoke (about an inch from the top) and slice off the bottom part of the stem. Continue to pull back leaves until you get to the pale green part. Now slice the artichoke in half vertically and use a paring knife to trim the exterior of the stem and the hard parts surrounding the base of the artichoke. Use a spoon to scoop out the choke (that's the hairy, red bit in the center; it's inedible). As you do this, rub the surface of the artichoke with a lemon half to stop it from turning brown. Place the prepped artichokes in a bowl of cold water acidulated with the juice of another lemon half.

Place the artichokes, scallions, leeks, garlic, rosemary, and a good sprinkling of salt in a wide shallow pot. Pour in enough olive oil to come up just halfway (once you turn on the heat, the vegetables will release enough liquid to cover themselves).

Turn the heat up to high, and when the oil just starts to bubble, reduce the heat to low. Cook at a very gentle simmer for about 20 minutes, uncovered, until the artichokes are completely tender (a knife should go through one easily).

When the vegetables are cooked, discard half of the liquid (you can just pour it off) and then stir in the favas (or limas) and some torn mint, being careful not to break up the other vegetables.

To serve, find a wide plate and spoon some of the vegetables across it. Squeeze the remaining lemon halves over everything and then shave the cheese on top. The remaining vegetables will keep for at least a week submerged in their liquid in the refrigerator.

Chickpea and Salt Cod Stew

Serves 4 to 6

In the summer of 2008, I spent a week in Barcelona, eating myself silly. When the smoked paprika hit the pan with the olive oil and garlic in this dish, I was instantly transported back. This dish has a lot going for it: it's a protein-rich one-pot meal and, with the addition of the cod, an entrée for anyone who doesn't eat meat or chicken. Go easy on the salt at the beginning: the chickpeas suck in all the liquid as they cook, and if you oversalt too early, that's hard to fix (trust me!).

● Frozen cod is a fine option here because you're going to cure it anyway. Defrost it before salting.

● Raij suggests buying chickpeas from a store that sells a lot of beans because dry beans that sit on the shelf for a long time get "desiccated." Indian markets or Latin American markets are the best choices.

FOR THE COD AND CHICKPEAS

12 ounces <u>cod</u>, or salt cod (*bacalao*) soaked for 24 hours in several changes of water

Kosher salt

1 pound <u>dried chickpeas</u> (garbanzo beans)

1 whole yellow onion, unpeeled

1 peeled carrot

1 bay leaf

1 whole head of garlic (unpeeled)

FOR THE REST OF THE DISH

⅓ cup olive oil

2 cloves garlic, sliced

1 tablespoon paprika or smoked paprika

¼ teaspoon cayenne pepper (or more if you like it spicy)

½ cup black kale or regular kale leaves cut into ribbons (you can use spinach too)

Extra virgin olive oil, for drizzling

Remove any skin from the cod fillet, then cut into ½-inch cubes. Toss the cubes with lots of salt, place on a plate, cover with plastic, and refrigerate for 2 hours. After 2 hours, rinse off the salt and set the cod aside. If you're using salt cod (*bacalao*) that you've soaked, skip this step.

To a large pot or a pressure cooker, add the chickpeas, onion, carrot, bay leaf, and garlic. Cover with at least 1 inch cold water (no need to cover the onion all the way, just the chickpeas) and add enough salt to flavor the water, but not too much because you'll be adding the salted cod later. Turn the heat up to high. Bring to a boil, reduce to a simmer, and cover. In a pressure cooker, cook for 55 minutes; in the pot, cook for 2½ hours.

When the chickpeas are tender and cooked all the way through, set the pan aside. Discard the garlic and bay leaf.

Place the whole onion (remove the skin first), the carrot, and about 2 cups of the chickpeas in a blender with enough liquid from the pan to cover. In a skillet, add the olive oil and sliced garlic and cook over high heat until the garlic turns golden, 1 to 2 minutes. Add the paprika and the cayenne and remove from the heat. Pour into the blender with the vegetables, chickpeas, and liquid.

Place the lid on the blender but remove the cap and cover the hole at the top with a dish towel to let steam out. Turn the blender on and blend until the mixture is creamy. Pour the mixture back into the pot of cooked chickpeas and stir. You want it to be brothy.

Put the pot back on medium heat, allow the mixture to warm up (5 minutes or so), then flake the cod pieces into the hot chickpeas (feel for bones as you do this, just in case). Add the kale and stir, cooking just until the kale is wilted and the fish is cooked through, 3 to 4 minutes more. Taste for seasoning (you may also want to add more cayenne pepper). Ladle the stew into warm bowls and drizzle on some extra virgin olive oil before serving.

Alain Allegretti

Chef-owner, La Promenade des Anglais
New York, New York

When, at the ripe young age of seventeen, Alain Allegretti decided to become a chef, he had a slew of options. Having grown up in Nice with an Italian father and an Italian grandmother, he certainly could have embraced those Italian roots and gone to work in Rome. His grandmother had taught him how to make her signature cavatelli—a dense noodle made with ricotta cheese—but then again, being in Nice, she also taught him how to make pot-au-feu and clafoutis, undoubtedly French dishes.

To complicate things, Allegretti's mother is Vietnamese. She would make her signature *bam bou,* a dish with angel hair, crispy beef, cucumber, soja, and peanuts that the young Alain loved. But Allegretti, the burgeoning chef, didn't tap into his Asian roots either.

Instead, he forged his own path, fusing all of these influences into a cuisine of his own. As we cooked together in the kitchen of his former restaurant, Allegretti, the dishes he cooked—cavatelli with spring vegetables, seared fish with fennel salad, and a chocolate cherry clafoutis—feature his own idiosyncratic approach to food and cooking while celebrating the influence of his mentors.

From his grandmother, he learned not to waste: vegetables from leftover pot-au-feu make their way into the next day's cassoulet. From Jacques Maximin, the great French chef, he learned to go to the market and to be inspired by ingredients. "He went to the market every day at eleven o'clock," Allegretti recalls fondly. "And he'd come back and say, 'We're going to make this, this, this, and this.'" From Alain Ducasse, another mentor, he learned to be very, very picky. "Everything he bought had to be top quality," Allegretti tells me.

With so many legendary mentors and so many influences, how did Allegretti find his own way?

"You see all these different teachings," he tells me, "and you pick what you like the most."

You also incorporate your own passions and prejudices into the mix. For example, Allegretti makes it a point to stay in good shape, so health is an important component of his cooking. His food isn't too heavy, too buttery, or too salty. "Everything is balanced," he explains. "Nothing comes up first in your mouth."

He also filters other cuisines through his own perspective. When he once saw a taco on the cover of *Food and Wine*, it upset him, he says. "This is *Food and Wine* magazine and they put a Mexican taco on the cover?" (Hearing this with his thick French accent is pretty funny.)

So Allegretti devised his own version of a taco; he made a taco shell out of a tuille flavored with lavender and then he filled it with tuna tartare. An authentic taco? Hardly. But a dish by a man whose own culinary path might've gone in any direction but which led him to New York, cooking the food of his childhood and the food of his teachers in his own personalized way?

Absolutely.

"Every chef
will try a dish
from childhood.
If you have a
great memory,
share that . . .
that's the idea."

Cavatelli with Pesto, Peas, and Ricotta Salata

Serves 2 to 4

It can't always be springtime; so even though Allegretti makes this dish using peas, fava beans, and sugar snap peas from the farmer's market, I came up with my own version that can be made year-round using frozen peas, one of the few vegetables that actually hold up to and sometimes—because they're sweeter—improve upon the fresh version. The key technique to this dish is the creation of a liaison, an emulsion of chicken stock and butter. It enrobes the cavatelli in a satiny coating that helps marry the pesto, the peas, and the pasta. Even though fresh cavatelli isn't absolutely essential here (substitute a small dried pasta, if you must), it certainly makes a big impact when you use it. If you can't find it fresh, try making it yourself.

● There's a lot of pesto in this; make sure you have enough to get everything coated.

Kosher salt

4 tablespoons (½ stick) unsalted butter

1 cup chicken stock

1 pound fresh cavatelli (if you can find it at your local Italian store) or 1 pound dried orecchiette

1 10-ounce bag frozen peas

½ to 1 cup pesto (store-bought, or use Melissa Clark's recipe, page 97, without the cilantro)

Freshly ground black pepper

¼ pound ricotta salata

● The wide pan helps with evaporation; otherwise, you'll have cavatelli soup!

Bring a large pot of water to a boil and add salt.

In a wide sauté pan, bring the butter and the chicken stock to a boil, stirring to create an emulsion. Season with salt and let it reduce until it becomes creamy and smooth, about 3 minutes (there should be about 1 cup of liquid still in the pan). Set aside.

Drop the cavatelli into the boiling water and cook for several minutes. When they start to float, add the frozen peas to the pot with the cavatelli. Cook for just a minute more, or until the cavatelli are toothsome but cooked through.

Use a spider to lift the cavatelli and peas into the pan with the butter and stock. Turn up the heat and give everything a toss, adding the pesto and continuing to toss until the pasta and peas are coated and there's no more liquid on the bottom of the pan. Taste for salt and season with pepper to taste.

Spoon into bowls and shave ricotta salata over the top. Serve right away.

Pan-Seared Branzino with Fennel Salad

Serves 4

When a dish is as simple as this one—seared fish with a bright, crunchy salad—you have to get every element right for it to be successful. So focus, as you make this, on the two primary elements: make sure to cut the fennel evenly and dress it so that it's balanced. And for nice, crispy skin on the fish, get the pan and the oil smoking hot and then lay the fish in carefully (away from you, so the oil doesn't splatter). Approach the dish confidently and the results will speak for themselves.

1 fennel bulb, sliced in half and cored

Juice of 1 lemon, plus more lemon for serving

¼ cup extra virgin olive oil, plus more for the fish

¼ cup chopped parsley

Kosher salt and freshly ground black pepper

4 fillets of branzino (or you can substitute red snapper or black sea bass), skin on, scaled and deboned

4 tablespoons (½ stick) unsalted butter, cut into 4 pieces

8 to 12 fresh thyme sprigs

4 cloves garlic

Make the fennel salad: Using a mandoline slicer, shave the fennel into thin pieces and toss in a bowl with the lemon juice, olive oil, parsley, and salt and pepper to taste. Adjust for acid and salt.

Preheat the oven to 400°F.

Add enough olive oil to coat the bottom of a large ovenproof sauté pan (large enough to hold 4 fish fillets; or use 2 pans), set it on the stove, and bring the heat up to high. Season both sides of the fish with salt and pepper. When the oil is smoking, carefully lay the fish skin side down into the oil away from you, and press down with a spatula so that the skin touches the pan evenly. (The fish will curl as it cooks, so keep pressing.)

Put the pan in the oven for 2 to 3 minutes, just until the fish is cooked through (it will go from translucent to opaque), and then return it to the burner over medium heat. Add the butter (1 tablespoon per fillet), thyme (a few sprigs per fillet), and garlic (1 clove per fish) and baste the fillets with the juices.

Plate the fennel salad on 4 plates and place the fish alongside, spooning the sauce on top. Serve with more lemon juice.

Chocolate Cherry Clafoutis

Serves 4

With a consistency somewhere between that of a pancake, a moist chocolate chip cookie, and a custard, this dessert comes from Allegretti's grandmother. It's a simple combination of almond flour (which you can buy or make yourself in a food processor), crème fraîche, vanilla bean, kirsch or almond extract, and eggs. The key is baking this in a water bath so that it stays moist. You can make it ahead and just leave it out until it's dessert time and then prepare for it to vanish in thirty seconds.

● To make almond flour, grind blanched, slivered almonds in a food processor until powdery. Be careful, though, not to blend too much or you'll have almond butter!

6 tablespoons sugar, plus more for coating the soufflé dish or ramekins

6 tablespoons almond flour (purchased or homemade)

6 tablespoons crème fraîche

2 whole eggs

2 egg yolks

1 vanilla bean, sliced in half and seeds scraped out with a paring knife

½ tablespoon kirsch or 1 teaspoon almond extract

10 fresh dark cherries, pitted and sliced in half

2 ounces bittersweet chocolate (such as Ghirardelli), broken into small pieces

Spray a large (4-cup) soufflé dish or 4 individual (6-ounce) ramekins with cooking spray. Pour in some sugar and swirl around so it sticks to the sides; pour out any excess.

Whisk together the 6 tablespoons sugar, the almond flour, crème fraîche, whole eggs, egg yolks, the seeds from the vanilla bean, and the kirsch or almond extract. Allow to sit for 1 hour at room temperature.

Preheat the oven to 350°F.

Place the cherry halves on the bottom of the soufflé dish or ramekins along with the chocolate. Pour the batter over evenly and place the soufflé dish or ramekins in a roasting pan. Fill the roasting pan carefully with hot water so it comes up to the level of the batter in the soufflé dish or ramekins.

Bake for 30 minutes (it may take longer), until the filling is just set. Wiggle the dish, and if the filling doesn't wiggle, it's ready.

Allow to cool (if you can wait), 30 minutes or so. The clafoutis is best served at room temperature.

Samin Nosrat

**Teacher, chef, and co-creator
of the Pop-Up General Store
Berkeley, California**

Nosrat's Kitchen Know-How

CANNING HAS its rules (see Linton Hopkins, page 294), but here's an easy method: Clean the jars with very hot water and preheat the oven to 250°F. Heat the jars in the oven, put the lids in boiling water for a minute or two, and when you finish the jam, ladle it into the hot jars, seal with the hot lids (tighten all the way and then loosen a quarter turn), and let them sit. You should hear the "pop" that means there's a vacuum seal. If you don't hear it, put the jars into the 250°F oven until they pop.

SINCE THE BACK corners of an oven get the hottest, and since the legs of the chicken take the longest to cook, push the roasting pan toward one back corner with the legs pointing toward it for the first half of cooking; then move the pan so the legs point to the other back corner for the second half of cooking. (Nosrat got this tip from watching Jacques Pépin!)

THOUGH THEY'RE EXPENSIVE, copper pots are worthwhile because they conduct and distribute heat really well and evenly. For jam-making they're ideal, and if the pan is shallow, it allows steam to escape and cooks the fruit more quickly.

When the buttermilk-marinated chicken comes out of the oven, it's golden brown and fragrant, but that doesn't mean there's room to leave the pan on the stove. So chef Samin Nosrat, who has a sunny but small kitchen in Berkeley, California, lifts the chicken onto a plate and moves the hot cast-iron pan to her rain-slicked patio to cool off, making room for the pot of water into which she'll drop the butternut squash tortellini that we just hand-rolled on her rolling wooden kitchen island.

This is a lesson in making it work at home: Nosrat doesn't make excuses, she makes food. Lots and lots of food that feeds her friends (including Michael Pollan, from whose tree she gets her Meyer lemons), employers (like Alice Waters, who hires Nosrat to make butternut squash tortellini at events), and customers (with chef Chris Lee, Nosrat runs the Pop-Up General Store, where they sell prepared foods).

Nosrat doesn't skimp on ingredients: she uses excellent olive oil (one local, one from Italy) and beautiful farm-fresh eggs (both blue and brown). Her cooking equipment is also impressive, including a large copper pot that she fills with Meyer lemons, grapefruit, and blood oranges for her citrus marmalade.

"Paying attention to little details makes you a good cook," she explains as she hands me a stone mortar and pestle and asks me to mash some roasted butternut squash.

This is the filling for her famous tortellini, and it's all about the little details. To this mixture, Nosrat adds chopped sage, grated Parmesan, brown butter, and crushed amaretti cookies. She tastes and announces, "I'm going to take it a little further: a little saltier, a little sweeter."

Once the filling is done she has to make room for the pasta machine. Bowls and plates are moved to her counter, dishes are shifted around in the sink, and soon we're rolling pasta. Everything happens in one fluid motion, which is the secret to making things work in a small kitchen: keep it moving, keep it shifting, and food will be made.

When it comes to making her pasta dough, Nosrat is a master. To a large bowl, she adds double-zero flour from Italy ("It has an incredible softness," she explains) and applies her general ratio (really just a starting point): one cup flour to one egg to one yolk. There's no olive oil, no salt; she likes her pasta pure, like they make it in Italy.

Using her hands, she brings the dough together. "I already know I'm going to make this wetter," she says and asks me to separate another yolk. We continue to add yolks until the dough comes together into a beautiful golden ball.

"Wetter is better," she says. "If it's too dry, it will crack."

From there, Nosrat feeds the dough through her machine, and by the time we're finished, we've made about twenty-five tortellini. They sit there on a cookie sheet, ready to be boiled, and I look at them and think about people with much larger kitchens who've never produced anything this good.

The lesson is clear: a small kitchen's no excuse. When it comes to making great food at home, where there's a will, there's a way.

"Every chicken
is different; every
oven is different.
You have to learn
how to be present."

Buttermilk-Marinated Roast Chicken

Serves 2 to 4

When you make fried chicken, sometimes you soak it in buttermilk the night before to tenderize it. The same concept applies here, except instead of frying the chicken, you're going to roast it whole. And the finished chicken—which before it was soaked in buttermilk, was seasoned aggressively with salt—will be delectably tender and moist and packed with flavor. Take heed, though: because of all that buttermilk, the chicken will bronze in patches at first (places where the buttermilk soaked in more thoroughly) and then turn a deep brown color, almost like a Thanksgiving turkey. If that happens too fast or it gets too dark, simply cover the darkest spots with foil. It will still taste wonderful.

1 whole 4-pound chicken, cleaned (organs removed) and patted very dry

Kosher salt

1 quart buttermilk, well shaken

Any mixture of sliced green garlic, onions, parsnips, carrots, or other root vegetables (just to put at the bottom of the pan), cut into ¼-inch pieces

Olive oil

2 bay leaves

Spicy French mustard such as Roland (optional)

- Nosrat says, "I am *maniacal* about salting chicken."

- You can salt the chicken only a few hours before adding the buttermilk, but it won't taste as good.

Forty-eight hours before you want to eat this chicken, salt it aggressively. That means using at least a few tablespoons, if not more. The reason is that much of the salt will get washed off by the buttermilk, so here you're helping the inside of the chicken get seasoned. Put the chicken in a covered container and refrigerate overnight.

Twenty-four hours later, place the chicken in a resealable plastic bag and fill the bag with the buttermilk. Seal it, squish the buttermilk all around the chicken, place on a rimmed plate, and refrigerate. If you're so inclined, over the next 24 hours you can turn the bag so each part of the chicken gets marinated, but that's not essential.

When you're ready to roast, preheat the oven to 475°F. Add a layer of vegetables to a large cast-iron skillet and coat them with about ¼ cup olive oil and sprinkle with salt.

Remove the chicken from the plastic bag and scrape off as much buttermilk as you can without being obsessive. Place the bay leaves in the chicken's cavity. Truss the chicken by placing a 12-inch length of butcher's twine with its center in the small of the chicken's back. Tie the twine around each wing tightly and then flip the chicken over and use the remaining twine to tie the legs together as tight as you can.

Place the chicken on top of the vegetables and drizzle it with a little more olive oil. Place the pan in the oven with the legs pointing toward the back left corner and close the door. You should hear the chicken sizzling pretty quickly.

Roast for 15 to 20 minutes. When the chicken starts to brown, lower the heat to 425°F and continue roasting for 30 minutes and then move the pan so the legs are facing the back right corner of the oven. Continue cooking for another 30 minutes or so, until the chicken is brown all over and the juices run clear when you cut between the leg and the thigh.

When the chicken's done, remove it to a platter and let it rest for 10 to 15 minutes before carving it. Serve with the roasted vegetables and, if you like it, spicy French mustard.

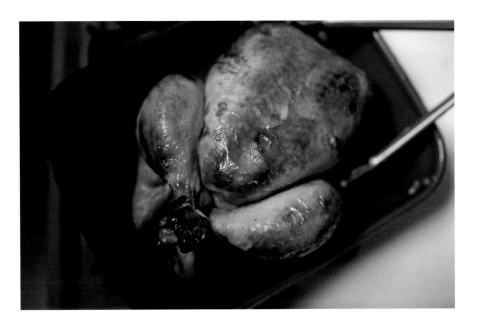

Pasta Dough

Makes several sheets of pasta dough

This method for making pasta dough is so sensible and so specific, it'll become your go-to recipe for fresh pasta. What I love about it is that it's all about intuition and your sense of touch: add eggs or egg yolks (depending on how rich you want your dough) until the dough comes together. Then use the pasta machine to knead it, carefully monitoring the shape, until you have a smooth, thin sheet of pasta dough that you can cut and shape into tagliatelle, garganelli (see page 280), or, as in the next recipe, tortellini. Just make sure that your pasta machine clamps well to your counter: it makes the entire job much easier.

2 cups double-zero flour from Italy (see Resources, page 371), plus more, as necessary

2 eggs plus 2 egg yolks (plus more, as necessary; have at least 4 ready to go)

- This isn't absolutely essential—all-purpose flour will work fine—but if you can find double-zero, use it. It makes a silkier dough.

- If you want a less luxurious pasta (and one that wastes fewer egg whites), you can use whole eggs too; the dough just won't be as rich or yellow.

Place the flour in a large bowl and make a well in the middle. Add the eggs and yolks and beat them together, at first, with a fork. Slowly work in the flour from around the well and then switch to your hands, pulling bits of dough from the fork tongs and working the dough with your fingers, pinching and kneading, as it comes together. If it doesn't come together (and chances are it won't), add another yolk and continue to work it, collecting everything at the bottom of the bowl. Continue adding yolks and working until the dough comes together into a sticky ball. If the ball is dry and crumbly, add another yolk and work that in: you want a wetter dough. (Don't worry if it's not homogeneous; it'll get kneaded together in the pasta machine.)

When you have a ball of dough, remove it to a sheet of plastic wrap, sprinkle it lightly with flour, and cover it tightly, allowing it to rest for 20 to 30 minutes at room temperature.

Set up the pasta machine by clamping it to a counter. (If you have a pasta-making attachment for your mixer, even better!) Flatten the dough as much as you can and, with the pasta machine at its widest setting, feed it through.

Now here's the thing: the first time it goes through, it'll come out looking like Swiss cheese. That's okay! This step, with the pasta machine at the widest setting, is totally forgiving: you can't screw up. You can put it through this setting again and again, and each time you do, the dough will get smoother and flatter (you're essentially kneading it). The goal is to create a smooth rectangular sheet that is the same width as the machine itself: to achieve this you can fold the dough in half or you can lay pieces of dough on top of each other and feed that through until you get a smooth sheet. Continue folding and feeding (sprinkling with flour if it's too sticky) until you do.

When you have a smooth, rectangular flat sheet, lower the machine to the second setting and run the dough through once. Pay attention to the dough as it goes in: you don't want it to fold upon itself as it goes through, or your dough won't be a smooth sheet anymore.

Run it one time through the third, fourth, and fifth settings. If the dough is sticking, sprinkle it with a little more flour.

● You may want to cut the sheet in half, if it becomes difficult to manage, then feed each half through separately. (It helps to have a pasta-making partner.)

Run it through the second-to-thinnest setting three times. At this point, the dough should be thin enough for tortellini and certain other pasta shapes. (If you made it too thin, it wouldn't hold the filling or its shape.) If you're making linguine or tagliatelle, take it thinner, running it three times through the final (and thinnest) setting.

When you're finished, cut the dough into 3 or 4 sheets, flour slightly so they don't stick to one another, and cover with a damp towel until ready to use. (It's best to shape the dough right away; it can dry out easily.) Once the dough is shaped, you can refrigerate or freeze it until ready to use.

Butternut Squash Tortellini

Makes 24 tortellini

When you make this recipe for the first time, you're going to serve up these little pillows of fresh pasta dough filled with brown buttery butternut squash puree and everyone's going to stare at you. They're going to look from you back to the plate and back to you and they're going to be thinking, "How in the world did [insert your name here] make this?" What you'll know that they won't is, really, once you get the pasta-making technique down, the rest is shockingly easy. I suggest making the filling first and the pasta dough second so the dough doesn't dry out. And make lots and lots of pasta, more than you think you'll need, because whatever you don't boil now, you can freeze for later. Then, whenever you want to awe dinner guests with your culinary prowess, you just have to open your freezer and boil some water. The rest takes care of itself.

FOR THE FILLING

1 butternut squash (½ pound to 1 pound)

4 tablespoons (½ stick) unsalted butter

3 or 4 amaretti cookies, crushed with a rolling pin or in a mortar with a pestle

½ cup grated Parmesan cheese, plus more to taste

1 whole nutmeg

A few sage leaves, finely minced

Kosher salt (if necessary)

TO FINISH

1 recipe Pasta Dough (page 138)

4 tablespoons (½ stick) unsalted butter

4 to 6 sage leaves

Grated Parmesan cheese, for garnish

Preheat the oven to 400°F. Halve the butternut squash lengthwise, scoop out the seeds, and place the squash facedown on a parchment-lined cookie sheet. Bake until the squash is very tender (a knife goes through the skin easily), 45 minutes to an hour. The squash should be somewhat browned and extra squishy.

Allow the squash to cool a bit and then scrape the flesh into a large bowl, discarding the skin. In a small pot, cook the butter on medium-high heat until it's deep brown and smells toasty and nutty. Pour into a clean heat-proof bowl so it stops cooking.

Now's the fun part: flavor the squash to your own personal taste. Add some of the brown butter, some of the crushed amaretti cookies, a generous sprinkling of Parmesan cheese, a good grating of nutmeg, and a pinch of the sage. Give it a stir and taste: you want it to be intensely sweet and salty (only a little bit will go into each tortellini, so make it count). Add more butter, cookies, cheese, nutmeg, sage, and salt until you can't imagine it tasting any better. Then set it aside.

- If it's a large butternut squash, you may wind up with too much filling. Make lots of pasta dough so you have tortellini to freeze. Problem solved.

- Nosrat takes the butter right to the edge; it almost looks black. But burnt butter won't make the tortellini taste good, so proceed cautiously.

continued

Butternut Squash
Tortellini (continued)

Place a sheet of pasta dough on a floured surface and, using a 2½-inch round cookie cutter, cut out circles. Make sure to cut them close together because you're not going to reroll the dough you don't use.

With either a piping bag or a small pair of spoons, put a tiny dollop (about 1 teaspoon) of filling at the center of each round. You don't want too much filling or it will ooze out. Continue doing this until you have a table full of circle shapes with filling in the middle.

With a spray bottle, mist everything lightly with water (or, if you don't have a spray bottle, dip your fingers in tepid water and flick it all over the pasta): this will keep the pasta pliable and will help it stick. To make the tortellini, fold a circle of dough in half. Squeeze out all the air that surrounds the filling and pinch the edges tightly to make a seal. It should look a bit like a calzone. Now, along the straight edge where the filling is, make a dent with your finger. Fold this dent in on itself, bringing the edges together and pinching them. That's it: you've made a tortellini.

Continue doing this until you've used all the dough and most of the filling, tossing the tortellini on a plate with some flour so they don't stick. You have two choices now: you can cook the tortellini right away or freeze them for later. If you want to freeze them, plop them onto a parchment-lined cookie sheet with some flour and place them in the freezer for an hour. Then pluck them off the sheet and put them in a freezer bag; they'll keep that way for at least a month. When you cook them from the freezer, drop them straight into boiling water—no need to defrost.

To serve the tortellini immediately, bring a pot of water to a boil. Season aggressively with salt (it should taste salty) and drop in the tortellini. They take longer to cook than most fresh pasta because they're folded twice; even when they float, you'll need to cook them several minutes longer (3 to 5 minutes of cooking, total).

In a separate pan, heat the butter and the sage leaves together until the butter is foamy and the sage leaves are sizzling. (If the butter starts to brown, add a ladleful of pasta cooking water to stop the cooking.) When the tortellini are ready (the best way to know is to taste one), use a spider to lift them into the pan with the butter and sage. Toss them gently on medium heat, allowing the pasta to absorb the butter, and then spoon onto plates. Sprinkle with more Parmesan cheese and serve right away.

Anthony Martin

Chef, Tru
Chicago, Illinois

When you think "fine dining," you probably don't think "NASCAR."

But chef Anthony Martin, who's the executive chef of Tru—the legendary Chicago restaurant where chefs Rick Tramonto and Gale Gand made their names—is the son of a race-car driver. His father works as a mechanic by day and races cars at night. Clearly it's genetic because Martin has racing in his bones too.

"If I didn't cook, I'd be involved in motor sports in some way," he tells me matter-of-factly in the kitchen of his Chicago apartment.

As it stands, he keeps a race car at his family home in Ohio and owns a Jeep Grand Cherokee SRT8 (the fastest Jeep you can own, apparently). He rides a race bike to work every day and says that he never takes it out of first gear.

You'd think a cook with a racer's soul like Martin's would have trouble fitting into the sophisticated world of fine dining, but that's not the case. Despite his speedy inclinations, watching Martin in the kitchen is like watching a painter rather than a racer. And art, not speed, is what got him started in the first place.

"I've been drawing since I was three," he tells me. "When I create a dish, I start by drawing it in my notebook." He finds his notebook and shows me a few examples.

Martin's painterly side comes through quite clearly when we start working on his

> **"Before service, I get everyone amped up, like we're going into a championship football game. By the time the first ticket comes in, everyone's bouncing up and down."**

beet salad. The elements are fairly simple: oven-roasted red and yellow beets, toasted pecans, herbs, and a cumin oil. On a lark, I ask if I can try plating it first to see how far off I am from the way he would plate it.

"Sure," he says, a skeptical look on his face.

I study the white plate for a moment. Martin has red beets in one bowl and yellow beets in another so the red don't stain the yellow. With a spoon I lift a red beet and plop it in the center of the plate. Then with another spoon I lift a yellow beet and place it next to the red one. I continue this way until all the beets are in a line.

"That's one way to do it," he says, placing the beets back in their bowls and wiping off the plate. "But I would've gone more organic, separating them at different points on the plate so we appreciate them all. Then we can add the green."

The delicacy with which Martin plates his version is remarkable considering that

back when he worked in Las Vegas (at Joël Robuchon), he used to race cars through canyons in the desert. But his finished plate is masterly, a still life of beets and apples that belongs as much on a gallery wall as it does on a dinner table.

"Is there any correlation between the work you do at the restaurant and racing?" I ask, after we've devoured his lamb shanks roasted in a clay pot and while we're prepping peaches poached in Grand Marnier and orange juice.

"It's a lot more work than people think. My dad used to come home at one in the morning from a race and then fix a drive shaft until eight and then go to work as a mechanic. And working as a cook in a restaurant, so much work goes into every plate of food, most people don't have any idea."

The fast-paced nature of a restaurant kitchen suits Martin well, but it's his ability to slow down that makes him a great chef.

Beet Salad with Pecans, Herbs, and Apple

Serves 4

I learned a lesson re-creating this recipe at home. Don't throw everything into a big bowl and toss it all around. An aggressive toss will affect not only the way the salad looks, but the way it tastes too. Use restraint when plating and you shall be rewarded. The goal here is to emphasize the beets in all their natural red and gold glory.

6 red beets, rinsed and scrubbed clean	Sherry vinegar
6 golden beets, rinsed and scrubbed clean	½ cup pecans
⅓ cup olive oil, plus more for drizzling	1 tablespoon melted unsalted butter
Kosher salt and freshly ground black pepper	1 cup various herbs (parsley, tarragon, chives, chervil), chopped
Cumin seeds	1 Granny Smith apple, unpeeled, cut into 2-inch-long matchsticks

Preheat the oven to 325°F.

Create packets of beets—2 beets of the same color per packet—using squares of aluminum foil. Drizzle the beets with olive oil, sprinkle with salt and pepper and a few cumin seeds, and seal the packets tight. Place the packets on a cookie sheet lined with aluminum foil (just in case the beets bleed) and roast for 1 hour, testing the beets with a paring knife toward the end. If the knife goes through them very easily, they're done.

When the beets are done, allow them to cool until you can handle them and, using paper towels, wipe the skin off. Place all the red beets in one bowl with more olive oil, sherry vinegar, and salt and pepper to taste; do the same with the golden beets in a different bowl.

Raise the oven temperature to 400°F. On a separate cookie sheet, toss the pecans with the melted butter and more salt and pepper. Bake and allow them to toast, approximately 8 to 9 minutes. Allow to cool slightly, chop the nuts coarsely, and set aside.

While the pecans are toasting, pour the ⅓ cup of olive oil into a small pan and add 1 tablespoon of cumin seeds. Turn up the heat, and as soon as the oil begins to bubble, remove from the heat and allow to cool. That's the cumin oil.

To plate, keep the small beets whole and place them at various points on the serving dish (or dishes). Cut the larger beets into disks and do the same, staggering red and gold. Drizzle a drop of cumin oil onto each beet and sprinkle with the pecans. Combine the juices left over in the two bowls and toss the herbs in that dressing. Scatter the herbs around the beets and top the beets with the matchsticks of apple. Evaluate with a painter's eye and rearrange to make it as pretty as possible.

● Martin says you know a pecan is toasted properly when you break it open and the inside is no longer white (it'll turn brown too).

● You could do as Martin does and pour this mixture into a coffee grinder to better incorporate the seeds into the oil, but when I first did this it made a huge mess. If you do try it, I'd suggest blending a little at a time.

Lamb Shanks Roasted with Root Vegetables

Serves 4

Simplicity itself, this dish seems at first as if it might be underwhelming. You brown lamb shanks and put them in a Dutch oven (or, if you have it, a clay pot) with a bunch of vegetables and bake for two hours. Where's the thrill? The exotic spices? The unexpected chef-y twist? Well, the twist is that what comes out of your oven is comfort food at its most delectable. The meat literally falls off the bone and the vegetables are enriched by all the fat from the lamb. Just remember to season the meat well before you brown it and, when you do brown it, make sure to brown it well (that's where most of the flavor originates). On a cold winter's night, with a glass of strong red wine, this is a dinner that'll warm you back up, both body and soul.

Olive oil

2 to 4 lamb shanks, depending on the size, silver skin removed

Kosher salt and freshly ground black pepper

3 tablespoons melted unsalted butter

2 cloves garlic, peeled

A few rosemary branches

A few thyme sprigs

½ pound fingerling potatoes

A few small carrots, scraped with a knife to keep them rustic

4 whole peeled shallots

1 celery root (celeriac), peeled and cubed

1 cup chicken stock

Preheat the oven to 325°F.

Heat a Dutch oven or, if using a clay pot, start with a skillet on medium-high heat. Add a splash of olive oil, season the lamb shanks well with salt and pepper, and sear on all sides. Don't move the meat too much as it's browning; you want to develop a golden crust (about 5 minutes per side). When the lamb shanks are seared, turn off the heat, remove the lamb to a plate, and brush butter on the meat.

Off the heat, drop the garlic, herbs, potatoes, carrots, shallots, and celery root into the Dutch oven or the clay pot and season with salt and pepper. Pour the chicken stock in just to create a layer on the bottom and place the shanks on top.

Cover the pot and roast for 2 hours, or until the meat begins to pull away from the bone.

Spoon out the vegetables onto a platter and top with the cooked shanks. Let the meat rest for 10 minutes before serving.

Orange-Poached Peaches with a Graham Cracker Crust

Serves 4

This dessert is a study in contrasts: the crispy graham crackers and the soft peaches, the hot orange-peach sauce and the cold freshly whipped cream. Make sure not to overpoach the peaches; you want them to still have some bite. You can make this ahead; just heat up the sauce before you serve it.

6 tablespoons water

¼ cup granulated sugar

¼ cup Grand Marnier

2 cups freshly squeezed orange juice, plus more to cover the peaches

4 peaches, peeled with a peeler

4 tablespoons (½ stick) cold unsalted butter, cut into cubes

6 graham crackers, crushed in a resealable plastic bag with a rolling pin

½ cup cold heavy cream

2 to 3 tablespoons powdered sugar

1 teaspoon vanilla extract or ½ teaspoon vanilla paste

● You might doubt that it's possible to peel a raw peach with a peeler (the skin is so thin), but Martin said if you wiggle the peeler from side to side as you peel, it'll work. And sure enough, it does. It's easier to start peeling at the bottom of the peach.

● If the caramel seizes and you see a hard plastic-like piece at the bottom, don't worry: it'll melt as you bring the liquid back to a boil.

Place the water and granulated sugar in a heavy medium saucepan and cook on medium heat until it turns a light caramel color (it'll take 3 to 5 minutes). Remove from the heat, add the Grand Marnier (be careful, it's flammable), and then stir in the 2 cups of orange juice. Return to medium-high heat, whisking all the while, until it's smooth and hot, about 3 more minutes.

Carefully add the peaches and make sure they're fully submerged. Lower the heat to a very gentle simmer and cook for 30 minutes, covered. You don't want the peaches mushy, so check them every so often: they should be just cooked inside (a knife should go in easily).

Remove the peaches to a platter (reserve the juices in the pan) and see where they split. When they're cool enough to handle, cut around the seam of the split—separating the peach in half—and remove the pits.

Whisk the butter into the leftover cooking juices in the saucepan over medium heat and reduce until the mixture forms a thick sauce, 5 minutes or so.

Coat the exterior of the peaches with the crushed graham crackers and then carefully slice the peaches into wedges, wiping off the knife after every slice so you don't get crumbs on the inside of the peach.

In a chilled medium bowl, whisk the cream, 2 tablespoons of the powdered sugar, and the vanilla until the cream holds its shape but is still somewhat soft. If it's not sweet enough for you, whisk in an extra tablespoon of powdered sugar.

When you're ready to serve, place a few peach wedges on each plate, spoon the peach sauce over, and then top with the whipped cream.

Ana Jovancicevic

**Entrepreneur and celebrated dinner party hostess
Brooklyn, New York**

Jovancicevic's Kitchen Know-How

SALTED RED CHILIES are terrific on chicken, meat, fish, you name it. To make them, simply slice a few chilies (try Thai chilies or jalapeños), sprinkle them heavily with salt, and let them sit at room temperature for 2 hours. Then rinse them off, place them in a small pot, and cover with olive oil. Cook at a very low temperature for 20 minutes, turn off the heat, and allow them to cool before storing with the oil in clean jars.

A SILVER PLATTER may be a symbol of wealth and entitlement, but it's also a lovely tool for entertaining. When I arrived at Jovancicevic's, she used a simple silver platter to present a bowl of cut-up fruit and a glass of water. It's a small gesture that goes a long way.

WHEN THROWING a dinner party, it's not essential to make everything yourself. Make what you can and buy everything else—meat, cheese, breads, even dessert—from your favorite providers. The key is *abundance*.

In New York City, a place with so many talented chefs, it's pretty rare for a home cook to stand out. Ana Jovancicevic (pronounced *yo-van-chich-ev-ich*) is the exception. An invitation to one of her famous dinner parties is sought after by chefs and food critics (*Village Voice* food critic Robert Sietsema is a frequent guest). James Beard Award–winning food writer Rachel Wharton says of Jovancicevic, "She is an amazing thrower of parties—she goes all the way: whole lambs, trays of stuffed peppers, and big bowls of couscous."

At her home in Clinton Hill, Brooklyn, Jovancicevic describes the party she threw the previous Christmas. "I had seventy-five people," she says. "I roasted a baby lamb and a baby pig—I had to cut them in half to make them fit in my oven—and piled every surface in my apartment with food." Tables were covered with twenty-foot-long pizza biancas, assorted meats and cheeses, and five kinds of punch.

How did she pull it off?

"I'm very organized. I start planning three weeks ahead; I call the meat guy and order the pig and the lamb. Whatever I don't make, I buy."

Abundance, more than anything else, is a key component of Jovancicevic's strategy, not just in entertaining but in cooking at home as well. ("I relate to the Romans in that way," she says.) Her refrigerator positively overflows with fruits and vegetables, and the dishes that she teaches me wouldn't be out of place in Brobdingnag from *Gulliver's Travels.*

Her *gibanica,* a Serbian specialty that involves dipping phyllo dough in a bowl full of eggs, feta cheese, goat cheese, and a Serbian cheese called *kajmak,* then piling it up in a springform pan and baking until it emerges golden brown from the oven, is an absolute spectacle.

Her braised rabbit with carrots and mushrooms is hearty enough to sate you for days, and her plum dumplings are a meal in themselves. Clearly, no one leaves hungry when they come to visit Jovancicevic. "I don't know how to do a small amount," she says.

Yet, despite her knack for abundance, Jovancicevic isn't impractical when she entertains. At her Christmas party, she served the food on heavy-duty, biodegradable paper plates. She bought her flowers from the flower district in New York. The key is to create a feeling of abundance without breaking the bank: "At my parties, it just *feels* over the top."

At an engagement party that she threw, she brought a whole smoked pig's head from Fatty 'Cue, the restaurant of her ex-husband, Zak Pelaccio. "I love the visual effect," she explains. "You eat it off the cheek."

Less may be more in some circles, but at Jovancicevic's more is definitely more. And the many happy dinner guests who pass through her doors just can't get enough.

"In order to be a good cook, you have to love to eat."

Braised Rabbit with Carrots and Mushrooms

Serves at least 6

My friend Morgan likens this finished stew to the rabbit stew Sam and Frodo made while journeying into Mordor in *The Lord of the Rings*—yes, we're nerds!—a stew that filled them with comfort and a sense of home. That's what this is: instant winter-night comfort. You don't have to use a rabbit—in fact, Jovancicevic told me the original recipe calls for a chicken—but the rabbit certainly makes it special. As for the dumplings, they not only add substance to the stew, but they also thicken the liquid. Just be careful not to stir too much once you make the dumplings or they'll break up and create a muddy mess. Serve this with a bright salad, some bread, and a light red wine.

- If the carrots are smaller, you can cut them into thirds.

- To clean the mushrooms, don't run them under water (they'll suck up the water like a sponge). Just wipe them off with a damp paper towel.

FOR THE STEW

1 rabbit, cut up into pieces (ask your butcher to do this)

Kosher salt and freshly ground black pepper

1 cup all-purpose flour

Olive oil

1 large onion, chopped

3 fresh bay leaves or 1 dry

6 cloves garlic, chopped

½ cup dry white wine, plus a splash more

6 carrots, peeled and quartered

1 (10-ounce) carton button or cremini mushrooms, quartered

6 cups chicken stock (plus more, if necessary, to cover)

FOR THE DUMPLINGS

2 cups all-purpose flour

A pinch of kosher salt

3 eggs

¼ cup canola oil

Pat the rabbit dry with paper towels and season it well with salt and pepper. Fill a pie plate with the flour and toss the rabbit pieces until they're coated.

In a Dutch oven, heat ¼ cup olive oil on high heat until hot. Shake excess flour off the rabbit pieces and add them to the oil without crowding the pan (you may need to do this in batches). Allow them to sit and sizzle in the hot oil until thoroughly brown on one side, about 5 minutes; then, with tongs, turn them and brown thoroughly on the other side, another 5 minutes. When they're fully brown, use the tongs to lift them to a plate. Set aside.

In the same pan, add the onions and bay leaves. Season with a little salt, and when the onions start to soften, add the garlic. Continue to cook until the garlic is fragrant (a minute or so), then add the ½ cup of wine. Allow that to reduce and then taste the mixture for salt. Add the carrots and mushrooms with a pinch of salt, continuing to cook until the carrots start to soften, 3 to 5 minutes. Return the rabbit to the pan along with another splash of wine. Cover the rabbit and vegetables with chicken stock (you want everything submerged). Bring to a boil, reduce to a simmer, and cover partially.

Cook, stirring occasionally, for 1 hour and 30 minutes, or until the rabbit meat is falling off the bone. Occasionally taste the liquid and adjust for seasoning, but don't be too aggressive too early on: as it reduces, the flavor will intensify.

While the rabbit is cooking, make the dumpling batter. Stir together the flour, salt, eggs, and oil and then add a small trickle of water, stirring all the time, until the mixture resembles pancake batter. Cover with plastic wrap and refrigerate for at least an hour.

To make the dumplings, dip a soupspoon into the hot rabbit liquid and then into the bowl with the dumpling batter, scooping some batter up onto the spoon. Lower the spoon back into the hot liquid, allowing the dumpling to detach by itself. Continue with the rest of the dumpling batter, dropping dumplings randomly into the pot. Allow the dumplings to cook for an additional 20 minutes, with the pot half covered.

To serve, ladle the rabbit, vegetables, and dumplings into bowls with a good amount of liquid. Serve hot.

Gibanica with Feta, Goat Cheese, and Kajmak Cheese

Serves at least 6

This *gibanica* is created simply by dipping sheets of phyllo into a cheesy custard and crumpling them into a greased cake pan with removable sides. Putting it in the oven, you'll be suspicious: it doesn't look very pretty. But when it comes out? You'll be patting yourself proudly on the back. Make this for breakfast, brunch, a cheese course, or just to keep around for snacking. And though a deep springform pan is ideal to create a towering *gibanica,* you can use a regular 2-inch deep, 9-inch round springform pan. You want to be able to remove the sides, though, so a regular cake pan won't do.

1 to 2 packages of phyllo dough (preferably a thicker phyllo, if you can find it, though regular will work), defrosted

Canola oil

6 eggs

1 pound feta cheese, broken up

1 cup *kajmak* cheese (if you can find it) or cream cheese, at room temperature

1 cup sour cream

5 ounces goat cheese

¼ cup seltzer, plus more if necessary

● Try to find Bulgarian feta.

Preheat the oven to 375°F. Unwrap the phyllo on a work surface and cover with a damp kitchen towel.

Brush a deep 9-inch springform pan with lots of canola oil.

In a large bowl, combine the eggs, feta, *kajmak,* sour cream, goat cheese, the ¼ cup of seltzer, and ¾ cup canola oil. Don't overstir: you want chunks of all the different cheeses to show up in the finished dish.

Place a sheet of phyllo in the bottom of the prepared pan, crumpling it slightly like a tissue so it fits. Brush with oil. Put another layer on top and brush again with oil.

Take another sheet of phyllo, dip it in the egg-cheese mixture, and crumple it slightly while it's submerged. You don't want it totally saturated in egg and cheese, so do this fast and then lift the phyllo into the cake pan. Repeat with the next sheet of phyllo. Repeat again and again until either you've used up all the egg-cheese mixture or you've reached the top of the pan. When that happens, add a layer of undipped phyllo on top, brush with oil, and then break some phyllo up on top of that for decorative purposes. Brush with a little more oil and then place the pan on a cookie sheet lined with aluminum foil or in a larger baking pan (it may leak slightly).

● If it's browning faster than the inside is cooking, you can lower the oven temperature to 325°F or cover the top with aluminum foil.

Bake for approximately 1 hour, until the *gibanica* is golden brown all over and mostly firm with just a slight spring when you press down in the center.

Remove to a cooling rack, and when it's just cool enough to handle, push the bottom up through the sides of the pan. Place the *gibanica* on a cake stand and cut big slices to serve.

Plum Dumplings with a Brown Sugar Crust

Makes 20 large dumplings

Imagine a doughnut. Now imagine a dumpling. Combine the two in your head, add a plum, and you'll have a sense of what this dessert tastes like. It's a dessert so rich and dense, you'll want to serve it after a light dinner. The trickiest aspect of this dish is getting the dough to a consistency that allows you to stretch it out enough to hold a wedge of plum and a sugar cube. Doing this requires lots of flour. Whatever you do, don't skip the brown-sugar bread crumbs at the end! They're what give the dumplings their doughnut-like appearance and also contribute necessary sweetness and texture.

5 or 6 medium to large Yukon Gold potatoes, peeled and quartered

2 large eggs

2½ cups all-purpose flour, plus quite a bit more (you'll see)

2 pinches of kosher salt

20 small Italian plums, pitted, or 5 regular plums, pitted and quartered

20 sugar cubes

4 tablespoons (½ stick) unsalted butter

¼ cup dark brown sugar

A pinch of cinnamon (optional)

1½ cups store-bought unseasoned bread crumbs

In a large pot, cover the potatoes with an inch or two of cold water. Bring the pot to a boil on high heat, lower to a simmer, and cook until the potatoes are very tender (you want to be able to rice them easily), about 20 minutes.

Strain the potatoes in a colander and cover them with a dish towel for a minute or two, which will steam them a bit more. Using a ricer, rice them into a large bowl.

To the potatoes, add the eggs, the 2½ cups of flour, and the salt. Stir together and then turn the dough out onto a floured board. Place a cup or two of flour in another bowl; you'll be using that as you work the dough and it's best not to contaminate the whole bag as you grab. Sprinkle the dough with flour from the bowl and knead the dough, working in as much of the flour as you need and flipping the dough occasionally, until the dough is no longer sticky (10 minutes or so). When you have a smooth dough, shape it into a large loaf.

Cut off a chunk of dough (½ cup or so) and, with your hands and some more flour, flatten it into a disk. Pull and stretch the dough until it is wide enough to hold a plum wedge and a sugar cube. Pack those in there and wrap the dough around it, being careful not to tear the dough. When the plum and sugar cube are completely wrapped in dough, twist it to cinch it together, and set it aside. There's your first dumpling! Repeat until you use up all the dough.

A ricer is an inexpensive tool that allows you to press the potato through small holes to produce a soft and airy texture. If you don't have a ricer but you have a food mill, you can use that instead.

Bring a large pot of water to a boil. Drop the dumplings in carefully (as many as you can get to fit in one layer) and allow them to cook. They'll float when they're done (depending on the size of the dumplings, 5 to 10 minutes).

In a large skillet, melt the butter, then add the brown sugar. Allow the brown sugar to melt into the butter a bit, add the cinnamon (if you're using it), and then add the bread crumbs. Stir and cook until the bread crumbs are toasted and the sugar is well incorporated, about 3 minutes.

Lift the cooked dumplings one by one into the pan with the bread crumbs and roll them around to coat. Serve them hot. Any dumplings you don't boil can be frozen on a cookie sheet (this takes a few hours), stored in a resealable plastic bag, and boiled later. The uncooked frozen dumplings will keep for a month.

Sara Moulton

Television host and author, *Sara's Weeknight Meals*
and *Sara Moulton's Everyday Family Dinners*
New York, New York

Moulton's Kitchen Know-How

IT'S IMPORTANT to have good, fresh butter on hand for cooking and baking. You can tell if your butter is fresh by studying the color once you cut into it. If the color on the outside is different from the color on the inside, the butter is no longer fresh.

STEELING is an essential process to get the fine grains on a knife's edge aligned. To do this properly, hold the steel straight out (it should have a rubber handle) and rest the bottom of the knife's blade at a 20-degree angle on the far end, then drag the knife toward the rubber handle. Do the same thing at the same angle on the other side of the knife over and over again until the knife slices through a tomato without any pressure.

TO DEBONE a chicken breast, first feel for the bones with your fingers. Lay the breast on the work surface and slide a boning knife between the flesh and the bones (most likely, the rib cage) until the bones detach. Use your fingers to feel for any other bones and use the knife to detach them.

In 1975, Sara Moulton attended the Culinary Institute of America. The ratio of men to women was six to one; and out of a class of 452, Moulton graduated second. "I showed those assholes," she tells me in her New York City apartment, a devilish grin on her face.

On television, where she inspired me to start cooking in the first place, Moulton comes across as a gentle, nurturing, mothering type. (And, indeed, she is the mother of two twentysomethings.) But in real life, Moulton is irreverent (she has a wicked sense of humor), and, more important, she's a force to be reckoned with in the kitchen. That becomes abundantly clear when I arrive and she stands, in a samurai-like pose, steeling her knife. "Hold your arm out like this," she says, dragging her knife back and forth across the steel. The rapid-fire slashing sounds make her seem like a character straight out of *Kill Bill.*

I'm here to learn how Moulton filters her classic French training through the sensibility of the everyday, average American home cook—something for which she's famous. The answer, I learn from watching her in action, is to be *practical.*

For example, when Moulton prepares the filling for a stuffed chicken breast (a filling that contains raw chicken), she advises that you make a "spicy meatball" so that you can taste it for seasoning without eating raw chicken. She heats a small pan, adds a splash of grapeseed oil (her favorite neutral oil), rolls the filling into a ball, places it in the pan, and flattens it like a pancake. Sixty seconds later, we're tasting and determining whether the filling needs more salt. "Just a pinch," she concludes.

Her practicality spills over into all areas: she grows her own herbs on the windowsill (rosemary, thyme, sage); she doesn't believe in prepping too much before you cook; she advises packing smelly food remains into the refrigerator until garbage day ("so they don't smell up your house"); and when she gives me a turn at chopping an onion, she instructs me to "keep it attached at the root end so it doesn't all fall apart."

She also maintains genuine enthusiasm for learning new practical tricks. "I took a class at King Arthur Flour," she tells me, "and everyone in the class measured out flour the way we normally do and then we weighed it, and the difference between each of ours was between ten and sixteen ounces." The best way to measure flour, she shows me, is to rest the measuring cup on a piece of aluminum foil and shake flour from a spoon into it. "You never stop learning," she tells me cheerfully.

By the time we're finished, we've stuffed a chicken liver mousse we've made into prunes soaked in Armagnac, roasted those stuffed chicken breasts until they're golden brown, and crafted an apple tart so beautiful I can't believe I was involved in its creation. (As I sliced the apples for it, Moulton rooted me on: "You've really got the hang of it!")

Moulton is easy to underestimate when she's in mom mode; it's when she breaks out the sharpening steel that you'd better snap to attention. This CIA salutatorian means business.

"We should be cooking the onions while cleaning the chicken. Why waste time?"

Chicken Liver Mousse

Serves 6

At first I was nervous that my dinner guests would be squeamish when they heard the *L* word (that word being *liver*), but with all the butter in here, and the addition of sweet, grapy port, this has the power to convert even the most offal-averse into a Hannibal Lecter.

9 tablespoons unsalted butter, at room temperature	1½ teaspoons minced fresh sage or ½ teaspoon dried (optional)
1 large onion, finely chopped	1 cup tawny port
Kosher salt	2 teaspoons fresh lemon juice
1 pound chicken livers, cleaned (cut out all the white stringy bits) and cut in half	Breton crackers, for serving
Freshly ground black pepper	12 prunes (optional)
1½ tablespoons fresh thyme leaves or 1½ teaspoons dried	1 cup Cognac (optional)

● Warning: the chicken livers may spit as they cook.

● Seriously, don't overcook the livers (I've learned from experience). The mousse will be chalky and unpleasant.

Melt 3 tablespoons of the butter in a large skillet (do not use nonstick) over medium heat. Add the onions and sauté, with a sprinkle of salt, until the onions are soft but not brown, about 4 minutes. Scrape into a food processor (make sure the pan is left clean).

Increase the heat to medium high and add another 3 tablespoons of the butter and all of the chicken livers to the skillet. Sauté until the exteriors are brown—3 to 4 minutes—and then season with salt, pepper, the thyme, and, if you're using it, the sage. Cook for another minute until the livers are lightly caramelized but still pink inside.

Remove the skillet from the heat and add the port. Return the skillet to medium-high heat and deglaze it by scraping up the brown bits with a wooden spoon. Bring the liquid to a boil and continue to cook until it has reduced to 2 tablespoons. Pour into the food processor. Process the mixture until it's very smooth and then scrape the mixture into a fine-mesh sieve. Using a rubber spatula, push the puree through the sieve into a separate bowl.

● It'll look soupy, but fear not... it'll firm up in the fridge.

Let the mixture cool almost to room temperature, and then whisk in the final 3 tablespoons of butter and the lemon juice; taste and season with salt and pepper.

Line a bowl with plastic wrap and transfer the liver puree to that bowl. Cover and chill for at least 3 hours or overnight.

● This idea came to Moulton on a lark when we took the mousse out of her refrigerator; it's a classically French combo.

The next day, you can unmold it and serve it with Breton crackers or, if you'd like, you can stuff it into Cognac-soaked prunes. To do that, place the Cognac in a small pan, bring to a simmer, and add the prunes. Cook for 15 to 20 minutes, until the prunes have absorbed the liquid. Turn off the heat, allow to cool, and then cut open each prune and fill it with some mousse. Try not to eat them all before serving.

Stuffed Chicken Breasts

Serves 4

No one wants to eat a boring skinless chicken breast. Here is a remedy. Buy chicken breasts with the skin on and stuff the space between the skin and the breast with a mixture that contains lots of flavor: spinach, fennel seeds, nutmeg, and lemon zest. You can be aggressive with those spices, too; they'll really amp up your dinner. Don't worry if you can't get the skin all the way around the filling—it'll still taste good!

Two 1-pound whole chicken breasts, deboned but not skinned

1½ tablespoons crushed ice

3 tablespoons well-chilled heavy cream

¼ cup firmly packed chopped cooked spinach (about ½ pound fresh)

¾ teaspoon kosher salt, plus more for seasoning

¼ teaspoon crushed fennel seeds

¼ teaspoon freshly grated lemon zest

⅛ teaspoon freshly grated nutmeg

⅛ teaspoon freshly ground black pepper, plus more for seasoning

1 tablespoon vegetable oil

- Your best bet is to buy bone-in, skin-on chicken breasts and do the boning yourself (you can't make this without the skin, so don't even try). For advice on deboning a chicken breast, see Kitchen Know-How, page 158.

- You can use frozen spinach here; just defrost it first.

- This is the point at which you should make a spicy meatball (see page 158) to taste for seasoning.

Arrange the chicken breasts skin side down on a cutting board, making sure the skin is evenly stretched over the breasts, and halve them. Remove the fillet strip from each breast, discard the white tendon, and grind the fillet strips only in a food processor. Add the ice, blend the mixture until the ice is absorbed, and, with the motor running, add the cream.

Add the spinach, ¾ teaspoon salt, fennel seeds, lemon zest, nutmeg, and ⅛ teaspoon pepper and blend the filling well, scraping down the sides. Turn the breasts skin side up and, beginning at the pointed end, pull the skin back carefully, leaving the thin transparent membranes attached at the opposite end.

Spread 3 tablespoons of the spinach filling evenly over each breast, smoothing it and stretching the skin over the filling to cover it.

Chill the chicken, wrapped tightly in plastic wrap, for at least 1 hour. (You can even do this a day ahead.)

Preheat the oven to 400°F.

In a large ovenproof skillet, heat the oil over moderately high heat until it is hot but not smoking. Season the skin side of the chicken with salt and pepper, add the chicken to the skillet skin side down, and then season the other side. Sauté the chicken for 1 to 2 minutes, or until the skin is golden brown. Turn the chicken skin side up, place the skillet in the oven, and bake until cooked through, around 10 minutes (start checking for doneness after 8 minutes). Transfer the chicken to a plate and let it stand, loosely covered with foil, for 5 minutes. Serve with roasted potatoes and a salad.

French Apple Tart

Serves 6

This stunning pinwheel of a dessert might intimidate you at first. Don't let it. Essentially, you're just making a piecrust (and if Moulton's technique, which is very user-friendly, doesn't do it for you, try Gary Danko's on page 118), laying the crust in a tart pan, and piling thinly sliced apples on top. Well, not piling: placing each apple slice in a big circle within a circle within a circle, which means this is more of an assembly project. But, I assure you, even the most unskilled among us can make this tart happen.

Here's a fun, irrelevant fact: Gary Danko, Sara Moulton, and Susan Feniger all graduated from the same CIA class in 1977.

This is one of the few places where table salt is preferable to kosher salt, because it dissolves more easily into the dough.

FOR THE PASTRY

8 tablespoons (1 stick) cold unsalted butter, cut into ½-inch cubes

1¼ cups all-purpose flour, plus more as needed

¼ teaspoon table salt

2 to 4 tablespoons ice water

FOR THE TART

6 Golden Delicious apples, peeled, cored, halved, and sliced ⅛ inch thick

¼ cup sugar

4 tablespoons (½ stick) cold unsalted butter, sliced thin

½ cup apricot jam, heated and strained

Vanilla ice cream or sweetened whipped cream (optional)

To make the pastry, blend the butter with the flour and salt in a cold bowl, using your fingertips to pinch the ingredients together until they resemble coarse meal, with a few lumps. Drizzle in 2 tablespoons of the ice water and incorporate with a fork. Test the mixture by squeezing a handful: if it holds together without crumbling apart, it's ready. If not, add more ice water 1 tablespoon at a time and work in gently (don't overwork or the pastry will be tough).

Turn the dough onto a floured work surface and divide it into 4 portions. With the heel of your hand, smear each portion once in a forward motion to help distribute the fat. Use a bench scraper to bring the dough back together and form it into a disk. Wrap in plastic wrap and chill in the refrigerator for at least 1 hour.

Remove the dough from the refrigerator. If it's rock solid, let it warm up for a few minutes (though not too much).

On a lightly floured surface with a rolling pin, roll out the dough into a 13-inch round. To ensure it stays round, push out from the center with the rolling pin and turn a little bit clockwise each time.

Place the dough over the rolling pin to transfer it to a 10-inch tart pan with a removable fluted rim. Trim the excess dough by rolling the pin across the top. Don't force the dough into the nooks and crannies because it'll shrink; just urge the dough in the right direction. Cover and refrigerate for 1 hour.

If this part is a disaster, don't re-roll! That'll make your dough tough. Just continue to roll the dough out, even if it's not a perfect circle or it tears or you just have a big heap of dough scraps. Press the scraps into the tart pan, fill it up with more scraps, and press them in. When you bake it, no one will know the difference and it will still taste great.

Preheat the oven to 375°F.

Remove the cold tart shell and arrange the apples on it like a wheel with a rose at the center (see photograph below). That means you want spokes of apples going toward the center, and then, in the center, a ring of apples that gets tighter and tighter as it blossoms into a flower. (Again, use the picture for reference.)

Sprinkle the sugar on top of the apples, top with the butter slices, and bake for 45 minutes, or until the crust is cooked and the apples are golden. Brush with the warmed apricot jam while the tart is still hot. Serve with ice cream or a spoonful of whipped cream, if desired.

Marco Canora

Chef-owner, Hearth
New York, New York

Canora's Kitchen Know-How

GARLIC AND PARSLEY together is one of the most classic Italian combinations. Chop the parsley first, then smash the garlic, place the smashed garlic on top of the pile of parsley, and resume chopping. The garlic flavors the parsley and the parsley flavors the garlic. Chop for a good 5 minutes for the two to unify. When you're finished, you can use the mixture with the braciola (see page 170), or you can use it with sautéed mushrooms, fried eggs, shrimp, and many other dishes.

PASSATA is the Italian name for tomatoes passed through a food mill. You can purchase authentic Italian *passata* from a company called La Valle (it's labeled "Passata di Pomodoro"; see Resources, page 371). Otherwise, find a good can of tomato puree.

SOFFRITO, a mixture of aromatic vegetables cooked at a low temperature, forms the basis of many classic Italian dishes. It can be cooked to various degrees to achieve various effects. A darker soffrito is appropriate for more intensely flavored dishes (such as meat); a lighter soffrito works better with more delicate dishes, such as fish.

Ladies and gentlemen, please take your seats; chef Marco Canora is ready to make his signature gnocchi—a gnocchi so good that William Grimes of *The New York Times* once referred to a bowl of it as "lightweight and butter-laden, each dollop an eye-rolling pleasure bomb."

Please be advised that there are no tricks up Canora's sleeve; everything that you're about to see is 100 percent real. "All you need to make great gnocchi is potatoes and flour," explains Canora in the kitchen of his New York apartment, wielding a tray of Idaho potatoes hot from the oven.

When asked where he got his gnocchi recipe—from his grandmother? a trip to Italy?—Canora will answer, matter-of-factly, "I just came up with it. I knew the less liquid I had, the less flour I'd have to use and the lighter the gnocchi would be."

How does he extract the liquid from the potatoes? Observe as he takes the extremely hot potatoes (they baked for more than an hour at 350°F) and slices them in half to expose the maximum amount of surface area. Watch as he scoops out the insides into a ricer and then rices the potato all over his kitchen counter. Pay attention as he spreads it out with a spoon and then stabs, stabs, stabs it with that same spoon, spreading out the potato shreds and fanning them with a bench scraper (an essential gnocchi-making tool, as you'll find out).

Why is he doing this? "To allow steam to escape." Steam equals water. Water equals the need for more flour. More flour equals heavy gnocchi.

This commonsense approach applies to every dish Canora cooks. His beef braciola is cooked in a sauce that begins with a soffrito. ("I live for soffrito," he tells me. "It's the starting point for everything in Italian food.") In a food processor he combines 50 percent onion, 25 percent celery, and 25 percent carrot. "Do it by eye," he says. "This isn't technical. If the ratio's a little bit off, it's not the end of the world."

After adding garlic, thyme, parsley, and basil, he whirs the mixture up with a little olive oil and adds it to the pan in which he just browned the meat. "All cooking starts with fat," he says. "You add flavor to fat," he continues, pointing to the soffrito in the pan, "and then you add that flavored fat to something. And that's your dish."

The other dish he teaches me—a salad made with dandelion greens, white anchovies, and hard-boiled egg—is one that his mother used to make. "She'd say, 'You have to eat this because it cleans your blood!'" he tells me.

But, ladies and gentlemen, you didn't pay good money for witty personal anecdotes or soffrito lessons. You paid to watch the master make his gnocchi. Watch as he sprinkles the now-cooled potato with flour. ("Like a dusting of snow," he says. "A single fine layer.") Lean closer as he works that flour into the potato with a bench scraper until "the potatoes suck it all in and it just looks like potato again."

Two more additions of flour (see the recipe, page 168) and Canora is rolling

"I'm not trying to reinvent the wheel."

the dough into logs, then cutting the logs into gnocchi. He boils the gnocchi until they float, spoons some of the tomato sauce infused with the beef and soffrito into a pan, and brings it all together until everything's coated. He plates the gnocchi and tops it all with Parmesan and parsley.

Which is your cue to rise and give the chef his standing ovation. He'll be humble, though, and bow his head: making gnocchi's not rocket science, it just takes good common sense.

Light-as-Air Potato Gnocchi

- Use what you want right away; freeze the rest on a cookie sheet until hard, then pluck them off and store them in freezer bags or containers for up to a month.

- You want to keep the potatoes dry, so don't rinse.

- Err on the side of overbaking; the potatoes should be really tender.

- As much as I wish I had asbestos hands like the chefs in this book, I found it easier to do this wearing an oven mitt.

- Don't get lazy here: this is how you get rid of all that steam (i.e., water).

Makes 3 or 4 dozen gnocchi

Rarely does the word "delicate" come into play when describing gnocchi, but if you follow this recipe—and, by all means, you should—the resulting gnocchi will be so light and airy, you'll be nervous to toss them in a pan with sauce for fear that they will fall apart. (I suggest lifting the gnocchi out of the boiling water with a spider straight into serving bowls and then topping with either melted butter and Parmesan cheese or the sauce from the braciola on page 170). This recipe isn't so much a recipe as it is a technique, and the technique is all about getting the steam out of the gnocchi. The cooler you get it, the less flour it'll take and the lighter it'll be. Feel your way through it and you'll create what may very well be the best gnocchi of your life.

6 large baking potatoes (older potatoes are better; they have less water), skin on, wiped clean

3 to 4 cups all-purpose flour

ESSENTIAL TOOLS

Food mill or ricer

Bench scraper (also called a pastry scraper)

Preheat the oven to 350°F. Place the potatoes on a cookie sheet, poke each several times with a fork or knife, and bake until easily pierced with a knife, 1 to 1½ hours.

Immediately slice the potatoes in half lengthwise to expose the maximum amount of surface area. Quickly scoop the steaming-hot insides into a food mill or a ricer. Pass the potato flesh through the mill (on its finest setting) or the ricer onto a clean, wide work surface (marble, granite, or metal work best). Do not use a cutting board.

Stab the pile of potatoes with a small metal spoon, spreading it out into an even, shallow layer but being careful not to drag the spoon (that works the starch); stab downward and evenly across for up to 10 minutes, until the potatoes are broken down into very small bits and cool to the touch.

Use a bench scraper to flip over the middle portion of potato, which will still be hot underneath. Stab this again and again with the spoon until cool.

Sprinkle the entire mass of potato with an even blanket of flour (about 1 cup). Incorporate it by stabbing with the bench scraper for several minutes until you can no longer see flour, only potato. Fold in the outer edges and stab again; the mass should get smaller.

Add another portion of flour, sprinkling it evenly over the whole mass again. Stab again with the bench scraper, but this time, as you do it, slowly bring the mixture together into a mound. It should begin to look like a cohesive dough: press it tightly together with the bench scraper so you can flip it over.

Make a pile of flour on the work surface and flip the mound of potato and flour onto it. Sprinkle with another layer of flour and, using the bench scraper, press the flour in, fold over, press again—don't knead!—until you no longer see any trace of flour. When the dough sticks to the counter, you're finished.

Form the dough into a large loaf; bang it, roll it, hit every side, and push it together to get rid of any air inside. Sprinkle flour onto a clean part of the work surface and flip the loaf onto it. Generously coat the outside of the loaf in flour. Let rest for 3 to 4 minutes.

Use the bench scraper to take a 1-inch-thick slice from the loaf. The cross-section should look aerated and not wet. Roll the slice into a snake, the diameter of which will determine the size of the gnocchi. (Aim for ½ inch in diameter.)

Continue rolling snakes from slices of the loaf, coating them in flour, and when you have a few, use the bench scraper to cut them into individual ½-inch gnocchi. Toss the gnocchi on a cookie sheet coated with flour.

To cook, bring a pot of water to a rapid boil and season aggressively with salt. Boil the gnocchi just until they float (about 3 minutes) and serve them either with melted butter, sage, and Parmesan or with the red sauce from the recipe for braciola (see photograph below). Top with more Parmesan and parsley.

Braciola (Rolled Beef with Garlic and Parsley Braised in Tomato Sauce)

Serves 4

Here's a rustic, familiar "Sunday gravy" kind of dish: sirloin that's sliced thin and pounded (you can ask your butcher to do this; tell him you're making *braciola*, pronounced "bra-zhule") and cooked with soffrito and tomato puree until fork tender. The meat is certainly a high point, but the sauce (which gets infused with the meaty brown bits) is the real star—you can spoon it, as Canora does, over gnocchi. Or it works equally well on pasta or polenta or sopped up with crusty bread.

FOR THE BEEF

½ cup flat-leaf parsley

3 small cloves garlic, peeled

2 pounds beef sirloin (well marbled)

Kosher salt and freshly ground black pepper

¼ pound thinly sliced pancetta

FOR THE REST OF THE DISH

½ medium red onion, peeled and diced

1 celery stalk, roughly chopped

1 carrot, roughly chopped

1 clove garlic, peeled and roughly chopped

1 tablespoon chopped thyme leaves

1 tablespoon chopped parsley

1 tablespoon chopped basil

Olive oil

Kosher salt

½ cup dry Italian red wine (such as Grumello, Chianti, or Barbera)

24-ounce bottle of La Valle Passata di Pomodoro (see Resources, page 371)

1 bay leaf

Freshly ground black pepper

> If you can't find this or any other *passata*, use tomato puree.

Begin by chopping the parsley and smashing the garlic. Then place the garlic on top of the parsley and chop them together, integrating the two (see Kitchen Know-How), for a good 5 minutes until the mixture looks like a paste.

Thinly slice the beef against the grain. Lay each slice down on a piece of plastic wrap, cover with more plastic wrap, and pound with a meat hammer until it's an even thin slice.

Lightly season each piece of meat with salt and pepper, sprinkle some of the garlic-parsley mixture on top, and then top with a piece of pancetta. With the meat lying lengthwise in front of you, roll it from the bottom toward the top. Use a toothpick to cinch the rolled meat together. Repeat with the rest of the slices and then season the outsides with salt and pepper.

Make a soffrito by combining the onion, celery, and carrot in a food processor. Pulse a few times and then add the garlic, thyme, parsley, and basil. Continue to pulse until everything is nicely minced but not liquefied: you want to see little flecks of the ingredients. Set aside.

continued

Braciola
(Rolled Beef with
Garlic and Parsley
Braised in Tomato Sauce) (continued)

● Careful, it spits. Do this on the back burner.

In a large Dutch oven, heat a few tablespoons of olive oil on medium heat until it feels hot when you hold your hand over it. <u>Lay the beef rolls in the oil and cook</u>, turning, until brown on all sides. (Don't overcrowd the pan; you don't want the beef to steam. If necessary, do this in batches.)

When the meat is brown all over, use tongs to remove it to a plate. Add another splash of olive oil to the pan and add the soffrito with a pinch of salt. Cook for a while, stirring to pick up brown bits from the bottom of the pan, until the soffrito just starts to color (2 to 3 minutes). When it does, return the beef to the pan.

Add the wine and use it to scrape up any brown bits left on the bottom of the pan. Add the *passata,* the bay leaf, and a gentle sprinkling of salt and pepper (not too much because the flavors will intensify as the sauce reduces). Bring to a boil, lower to a simmer, place a cover halfway over the pan, and cook for 40 minutes, or until the beef is tender (a knife will go in easily). If the sauce becomes too thick, add a little water. Remove the bay leaf.

To serve, remove the beef from the pan and remove the toothpicks. Dress with the sauce and save the remaining sauce for the gnocchi or another type of pasta. Eat hot. Leftovers will keep for several days in the fridge.

Raw Dandelion Salad with Hard-Boiled Eggs and Pickled White Anchovies

Serves 4

Normally, salad dressings are emulsified with a raw egg yolk, but in this recipe hard-boiled eggs play the role of emulsifier and help marry the few but disparate elements: the olive oil, balsamic, bread crumbs, pickled white anchovies, and dandelion greens. And though the greens in this salad are replaceable—you can try escarole or romaine hearts—the pickled white anchovies really make this salad special. They're sweet and tangy and have a visually dramatic presence; the jarred gray type just won't be the same.

A few handfuls of dandelion greens, washed and spun dry in a salad spinner

4 hard-boiled eggs (see page 71), peeled and chopped

Toasted bread crumbs (optional; see page 197)

8 pickled white anchovies (*boquerones*; see Resources, page 371)

Good-quality olive oil

Balsamic vinegar

Kosher salt and freshly ground black pepper

Cut the bottoms off the dandelion greens and discard. Chop the rest of the greens a few times so each green is bite-size. Add a layer of greens to a large salad bowl.

Sprinkle the chopped egg and the toasted bread crumbs (if you're using them) over the greens, and then lay the anchovies on top.

Take the salad to the table, and when you're ready to serve, drizzle on olive oil, balsamic vinegar, and salt and pepper to taste. Toss with salad tongs and taste for balance. Serve right away, before the greens start to wilt.

Roy Choi

Chef and co-creator, Kogi Truck, Chego, and A-Frame
Los Angeles, California

To a hot wok sizzling with oil, I add a handful of sliced onions, chef Roy Choi at my side. In my left hand, I'm holding a large ladle-like spatula, and my instinct is to move the onions around. Choi stops me.

"The most important thing," he scolds me, "is not to be impatient. You have to let things happen."

I set the ladle-spatula down, but Choi isn't finished.

"You have to let go of all the fucking bullshit," he continues as the onions soften. "You have to feel what's going on."

He leans toward the wok. "I can feel everything about this wok right now," he says. "I can hear it. I can feel the heat."

Is it time to move the onions? Choi says, "The biggest thing for a home cook to learn is: we haven't touched this pan once. We're allowing it to happen." He gives me a knowing glance. "You probably would've touched them to the point of *molestation*."

Choi, the chef behind L.A.'s super-popular Kogi Truck and Chego, the rice-bowl restaurant where we meet, is an intense guy, and his intensity has a history. Earlier in the day, before stepping into the kitchen, he had talked about growing up *extremely* poor. "This shit really happened," he told me. "I remember sewing an alligator onto my Le Tigre shirt. I remember wearing my shoes inside out."

As his parents filed for bankruptcy again and again and moved Choi and his sister from place to place—Englewood, West L.A., Koreatown, La Cienega, Norwalk, Anaheim, Mission Viejo—Choi didn't realize how poor they really were because he was always so well fed.

"Every day my mom would wake up at four a.m. and cook a feast like Americans cook for Thanksgiving. But she would do it every day."

Choi would regularly wake up to the smells of stews simmering, fish frying, and cabbages fermenting. When I ask if he got teased for taking smelly food to school, Choi says, "The people who poke fun at that kind of food were probably eating shit. The food my mom made was full of vitamins and protein and love and care."

Love and care are precisely what matters most to Choi when cooking in his own kitchen. As we coax the onions out of the wok (we're cooking Chego's Chicken Henhouse Bowl in stages because a home stove doesn't get hot enough), Choi watches me add the greens and, finally, the rice.

"Does rice play a prominent part in your cooking?" I ask.

"Um," he replies, "this is a rice-bowl restaurant."

Rice, it turns out, isn't just a prominent part of Choi's cooking, it's a central component to an entire way of life. "You have to wash your rice thoroughly *five times*," he tells me.

"Why?"

"To get rid of the starch, to clean it, and because of the *spirituality* of it. You won't understand it, because you didn't grow up with it like me, but rice is everything to our existence. It's like a temple. That's why we wash it five times."

Choi cooks with his heart on his sleeve and with a deep spiritual connection to his food. He may have been poor, but he never went hungry, and the significance of that fact has never left him. Food is more than just a meal. It makes us who we are; it builds us up as people.

Which is why, in Choi's kitchen, you respect your rice and you don't fuck with your onions. These things matter.

"You have to fall in love with the process."

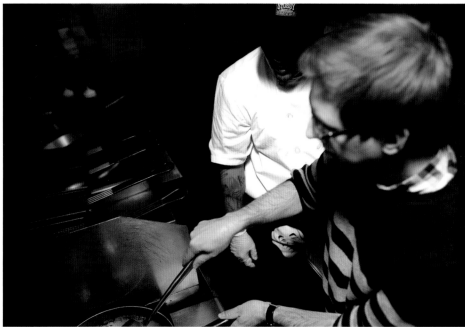

Choi's Favorite
Banana
Milk Shake

Serves 2 people or 1 greedy bastard

During my time with Choi, I asked him about something I had read in *Food and Wine:* he loves milk shakes. "It's true," he said. "I do." So I asked him for his favorite milk shake recipe and this is what he dictated. After making this at home, I can see why it's his favorite. It all comes down to one unexpected ingredient: a handful of crushed ice. Usually milk shakes are so heavy and dense, you nearly rupture a blood vessel sucking them up through a straw. The crushed ice here lightens the mixture and makes the shake refreshing rather than heavy. Make sure the banana is dark, though; an unripe banana won't have nearly as much flavor.

Vanilla ice cream (Häagen-Dazs or another quality brand)

Cold whole milk

A handful of crushed ice

2 teaspoons sugar

1 very ripe banana

A squeeze of honey or a squeeze of lemon juice or both

Place a few scoops of vanilla ice cream in a blender. You want to go heavy on the ice cream.

Add the milk so it comes up halfway to the level of the ice cream. Add the ice, sugar, banana, and honey and/or lemon juice.

Blend the mixture and try to find a perfect balance between thick and thin, creamy and viscous. You may need to add more milk to thin it out. Taste a spoonful and adjust the honey and lemon juice.

Pour into tall glasses and serve with straws.

Sweet Chili Sauce

Makes 4 to 6 cups

This is a fantastic sauce and the key ingredient to Choi's Stir-Fried Chicken Henhouse Bowl (page 178). Without this sauce, the Henhouse Bowl would be a sad stir-fry of vegetables, chicken, and rice. With this sauce, it skyrockets into the stratosphere. But this very spicy, slightly sweet sauce works wonders for anything: chicken, fish, scallops, shrimp, even just a plain bowl of rice. You don't need to incorporate all these ingredients to make it work. The key ingredients are the chili sauce, citrus, herbs, onion, garlic, and ginger. Everything else just makes it that much more intense.

● You can substitute a different brand of chili sauce and it'll work, but it won't be exactly the same, obviously, as Choi's. Mae Ploy is available at specialty markets and online at amazon.com and others.

1 (10-ounce) bottle <u>Mae Ploy sweet chili sauce</u>

⅔ cup loosely packed Thai basil leaves

⅔ cup loosely packed cilantro leaves

½ cup freshly squeezed lime juice (from about 5 medium limes)

⅓ cup freshly squeezed orange juice (from 1 medium orange)

1 medium yellow onion, peeled and coarsely chopped

½ bunch scallions (white and light green parts), coarsely chopped

8 medium cloves garlic, peeled and slightly chopped (to get them started; the blender will do the rest)

3 tablespoons sriracha hot sauce (see Resources, page 371)

2 tablespoons Korean crushed red pepper (see Resources)

2 tablespoons toasted sesame seeds (also called *geh;* see Resources)

2-inch piece of fresh ginger, peeled and coarsely chopped

1 dried Anaheim chili, stemmed and coarsely chopped (optional)

1 serrano chili, stemmed and coarsely chopped (optional)

4 teaspoons kosher salt

4 teaspoons Korean chili paste (see Resources; optional)

1 teaspoon freshly ground black pepper

Add all of the ingredients to a blender.

Blend for about 1 minute, until you have a smooth puree. Taste to adjust for citrus, heat, and salt. Use immediately or refrigerate in a jar for later use. The sauce will last about a week in the refrigerator.

Stir-Fried Chicken Henhouse Bowl

Serves 2

A wok is such a good tool to have (see Grace Young, page 50), especially if the thought of spending hours on making dinner after a hard day of work fills you with angst. This dinner, which is as simple as stir-frying some chicken, onions, and rice and adding a sauce, can be ready in a jiffy if you have the ingredients ready to go. The herbs and fried shallots amp up the flavor, but if you're tired, skip them. The point is: you can make a hot, satisfying dinner in a matter of minutes.

Canola oil

½ yellow onion, peeled and thinly sliced

1 cup cooked chicken, diced

½ cup cleaned and sliced Chinese broccoli or whole spinach leaves or a combination

2 cups cooked white rice

½ cup Sweet Chili Sauce (page 177), plus more to taste

A big handful of cilantro leaves, plus more for later

A big handful of Thai basil leaves, plus more for later

1 or 2 red Fresno chilies, thinly sliced

A few tablespoons of toasted sesame seeds (also called *geh;* see Resources, page 371)

A three-finger pinch of fried shallots (see Kitchen Know-How, page 174)

2 fried eggs (optional)

- This is a great way to use leftover chicken, but if you want to use fresh chicken, buy 1½ pounds boneless, skinless chicken thighs, cut them into manageable pieces, and marinate them in a resealable plastic bag for 30 minutes in the refrigerator with ½ cup lime juice, ½ cup soy sauce, ¼ cup toasted sesame oil, 1 medium Asian pear (grated), and 1 teaspoon freshly ground black pepper. Pat very dry with paper towels and cook the chicken in the first step instead of the second step, before cooking the onions.

- Choi uses a Japanese short-grain rice called Calrose Asia (see Resources, page 371). After washing it (see Kitchen Know-How, page 174), he cooks the rice in a rice cooker. If you don't have a rice cooker, use Grace Young's method from page 54.

Set a wok on high heat. Swirl about 3 tablespoons canola oil along the rim, and when it's good and hot, add the onions. Lower the heat a bit and wait for the onions to develop some flavor. When they just start to brown, scrape them into a bowl and set them aside.

Swirl in a little more oil and add the chicken. Stir the chicken a bit, and when it's warm, scrape into the same bowl with the onions.

Now add another squirt of oil—make sure the wok is still hot—and add the greens. Stir, allow them to wilt slightly, and then scrape into the bowl with the onions and the chicken.

Add another squirt of oil and then add all the rice at once, flattening it like a pancake. Allow it to sit for a bit, lower the heat, and after it's sizzled for a minute, start moving it around, scraping the bottom of the wok. You don't want a film on the bottom; you want the rice to be in direct contact with the heat. Slowly cook and warm the rice, without adding color. When it's ready, return the onions, chicken, and greens to the wok and stir.

Turn up the heat and add the chili sauce. Stir and taste: it will probably need more sauce, so add more until it tastes great. When it does, add the cilantro, the Thai basil, some of the Fresno chilies, some of the toasted sesame seeds, and some of the fried shallots.

Spoon the stir-fry into bowls and top with more herbs, chilies, sesame seeds, fried shallots, and, if you're up for it, a fried egg. Eat it hot.

Michel Richard

Chef-owner, Citronelle and Central Washington, D.C.

Chef Michel Richard has an eggshell on his nose.

He's just shown me his contraption for cutting the top off of an egg—a weird metal skullcap with a lever that you snap—and now that the egg's been hollowed out, he's turned it into a clown nose. "My kids love this," he says, laughing.

A clown, though, he is not. Richard is one of our nation's greatest chefs; as the proprietor and owner of both Citronelle and Central in Washington, D.C., Richard has cooked for presidents (a fact that he shrugs off, casually) and some of the greatest names in the history of gastronomy, including the founder of nouvelle cuisine, Paul Bocuse.

You'd think a chef of his stature would be an egotistical monstrosity, but Richard is the absolute opposite: he is humble and kind, and he exudes such a natural warmth that anyone who comes near him is instantly charmed.

I'm here because Richard's warmth and whimsy aren't just character traits, they're an integral part of his cooking. His playfulness and joie de vivre are evident in such dishes as "fake scrambled eggs," in which he cooks a scallop mousse in a bain-marie and serves it in that cut-open eggshell, or potato risotto, a dish that he teaches me to make after first showing me how to make his signature mushroom stock.

Step one: put mushrooms in the food processor. Blitz. Step two: add the chopped mushrooms to a pot, turn on the heat, and wait. Eventually, the mushrooms will release their liquid. Strain it through a chinois. (Says Richard: "Without a chinois, you are a bad cook.") And that's it. You have mushroom stock.

What's remarkable is that both that stock and the mushrooms left behind after straining will be fodder for several dishes: We'll use the stock to make potato risotto, and we'll also use it to make a mushroom sauce with butter and cream. The mushrooms we'll wrap around chicken and bake until we have mushroom-crusted chicken breasts.

As we cook, Richard is constantly tasting, constantly adjusting. For example, toward the end of cooking the risotto he decides he doesn't like the color and adds squid ink, turning the risotto black. Then he decides he doesn't like the texture ("Too liquid," he says), so he strains it. By the time the dish is plated, however, you would have no idea how much of it was improvised: it looks like the work of a master chef (which, in fact, it is).

The secret of cooking whimsically, it turns out, is to be constantly in the moment, to react immediately to what's happening around you. It also helps to have a solid foundation of techniques from which you can pull. And, most of all, to have a sense of humor about yourself and the food you're cooking, which Richard certainly does.

"I like big butts!" he raps to me as I get ready to go. "You know this song?"

I nod.

"No," he corrects himself. "I like *beef* butts."

His laugh fills the room, and the rest of the kitchen laughs right along with him.

"Button mushrooms are my favorite mushrooms. Even the old, tired ones have flavor."

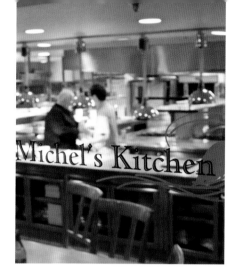

Mushroom
Stock

Makes 2 to 4 cups

You will be astonished at the ease and usefulness of this recipe. Actually, it's not so much a recipe as it is a technique: a way to extract two primary ingredients from a box of button mushrooms. You can use the mushrooms and stock in Richard's Mushroom-Crusted Chicken Breasts with Mushroom Jus (page 184) and Potato Risotto (opposite), respectively; and, according to Richard, the stock works equally well, reduced, in soups, vinaigrettes, and other sauces (such as a sauce for steak au poivre). Just watch the mushrooms carefully: once they've released all the liquid they're going to release, strain right away or the precious mushroom stock will evaporate.

**8 cups button or cremini mushrooms,
cleaned with a damp paper towel**

Begin by pulverizing the mushrooms in a food processor. This is tricky: you don't want to overdo it; just shred them enough so they're still in somewhat solid pieces, like mushroom confetti.

Add the mushroom confetti to a large pot and heat over medium heat. Stir occasionally and wait for the liquid to come out; you want to capture the moment when the maximum liquid is in the pot, before it starts reducing again. Watch it carefully, and when it looks as liquidy as it's going to get (a few minutes from when you started), strain the liquid through a chinois into a separate pot.

Use right away or refrigerate (it will last a week) or freeze (it will last a few months). Don't throw the cooked mushrooms away! Use them in Richard's Mushroom-Crusted Chicken Breasts with Mushroom Jus.

Potato
Risotto

Serves 2

I'm not going to lie: this recipe takes work. It requires that you slice potatoes very thin, then hold the slices together as you drag them over a Japanese mandoline to produce uniform flecks of potato rice. If you get past that challenging step (even Richard cut his finger doing it), the rest is easy. The result is something really unusual: a surprisingly light dish that combines the best elements of risotto and mashed potatoes and turns them on their head. By itself, this makes a nice first course; as an entrée, it should be paired with something more substantial, such as seared scallops.

1 pound large Yukon Gold potatoes, washed and peeled

1 quart chicken stock or Mushroom Stock (opposite)

Kosher salt

3 tablespoons olive oil (or enough to coat the bottom of the pan)

½ large yellow onion, finely chopped

Freshly ground black pepper

2 tablespoons unsalted butter

½ cup grated Parmesan cheese

1 tablespoon minced <u>chives</u>

Richard added squid ink to turn his risotto black, but I like keeping it its natural color and adding chives to emphasize the dish's mashed potato–like qualities.

Begin by cutting the potatoes into rice. First, slice each potato along the length into ⅛-inch-thick disks, only don't cut all the way through (this'll help keep the potatoes together as you do the next step). Using a mandoline (and really, that's the only way to do this) fitted with the fine-julienne blade, slide the potato sliced side down so it begins to produce little flecks like rice. You'll have to work hard to hold the potato together while you do this, so watch your fingers. By the end you should have between ½ and 1 cup potato rice; submerge it in water until you're ready to cook or it'll turn brown.

In a medium pot, bring the stock to a simmer and season lightly with salt (make sure it tastes good).

Heat the olive oil in a separate pot and add the onions over medium heat. Sauté for several minutes until translucent and then add the potato and stir. (If you'd been storing the potato in water, make sure to strain it well first.)

As if you were making regular risotto, add a few ladlefuls of stock to the pot with the potato rice until it's covered and cook at a low simmer (gentle bubbles), stirring every so often, for 20 minutes, adding more stock as it depletes.

After 20 minutes, begin tasting for texture: does it need more time? Only you can know. If it's ready, season with salt and pepper and, off the heat, add the butter, Parmesan, and chives. If the potato risotto is extra soupy (and this is normal) you can strain it. Serve it in bowls while still hot.

Mushroom-Crusted Chicken Breasts with Mushroom Jus

Serves 4

Boneless chicken breasts and button mushrooms come together here via a magical formula that combines humdrum ingredients into something sublime. The only thing that might give you pause is wrapping the chicken in plastic wrap and baking it in the oven. If you don't have heavy-duty restaurant-grade plastic wrap, use aluminum foil. Either way, make sure to slice the chicken before you serve it; it'll look prettier than serving it whole.

4 large boneless, skinless chicken breasts

Mushroom stock (about 2 cups) and cooked mushrooms (about 4 cups) from the Mushroom Stock recipe (page 182)

Kosher salt and freshly ground black pepper

A sprinkle of curry powder

1 teaspoon cornstarch

2 tablespoons unsalted butter

½ cup heavy cream

Juice and zest of 1 lemon

Fresh oregano leaves (optional, for garnish)

Preheat the oven to 325°F.

Trim the chicken breasts so they're relatively oval-shaped. Place the bits you trimmed off (about ½ cup of raw chicken) in the food processor and pulverize. Add the ground chicken to a bowl with the cooked mushrooms and stir together with salt, pepper, and curry powder. To taste it, make a "spicy meatball" (see page 158).

For each chicken breast, lay a piece of restaurant-grade plastic wrap (or foil) on the counter; it should be twice the size of the breast. Wet it slightly. Spoon a large mound of the mushroom mixture onto the plastic and flatten it by folding the plastic wrap over and pressing. Unfold and you should have a base larger than the chicken breast itself. Place the chicken on top of the mushroom mound and quickly fold all the plastic around it so the chicken is now almost entirely covered by the mushroom mixture. Make sure the packet is tight. Repeat with the other breasts and then place the plastic-wrapped chicken on a cookie sheet. Bake for 20 to 25 minutes until touching the chicken reveals it to be firm all over. Remove from the oven, carefully take off the plastic wrap, and set the chicken aside.

Place the mushroom stock in a pot and turn up the heat. Add the cornstarch, butter, and cream and salt, pepper, and curry powder to taste and whisk, whisk, whisk until it thickens. When it's a rich, creamy consistency, squeeze in some lemon juice and continue whisking. Taste for salt and acid.

To serve, slice the chicken into ½-inch slices and spoon the sauce on top. Garnish with lemon zest and fresh oregano leaves, if using.

● Chef Richard tasted it raw! Unless you enjoy salmonella or have the constitution of a legendary French chef, I don't recommend doing the same.

● If you don't keep whisking, the mixture might curdle.

Susan Feniger

Chef-owner, Street; co-owner, Border Grill
Los Angeles, California

Flames erupt out of chef Susan Feniger's scalding-hot pan, a pan filled with Manila clams, and Feniger doesn't flinch. "One thing people don't do at home is get their pans hot enough," she informs me.

Flames suit Feniger, a chef who's positively fearless in the kitchen. While making one of her favorite dishes, kaya toast (a Singaporean street sandwich of homemade coconut curd and salted butter that's served with a fried egg drenched in black soy sauce), she steeps pandan leaves—a grassy-smelling green available in Asian markets—in a pot of boiling coconut milk. The fearless part comes when, after she whisks the hot milk into a bowl of eggs and yolks, she wrings out the boiling-hot pandan leaves with her hands. "Make sure to squeeze it out like this," she says, no sign of pain on her face. "You'll get all this amazing flavor."

The fearlessness goes hand in hand with the energy Feniger brings to everything she does. The woman who, along with her business partner, Mary Sue Milliken, changed the Los Angeles culinary landscape with City Café and Border Grill in the 1980s and '90s, and who helped build the burgeoning Food Network with the show *Too Hot Tamales,* is a born adventurer.

Her hunger for bold, exciting flavors started in her mother's kitchen, where her mom, "a great cook," would make comfort-food classics like lasagna, brisket, cheese dreams, fudge, and icebox cake. In high school, Feniger traveled to Israel, where she ate baba ghanouj, falafel, and halvah for the first time. Eventually, she attended the Culinary Institute of America in New York and got a job working at the original Quilted Giraffe upstate. "It wasn't enough for me, though," she says, "because I wasn't learning enough."

After working in Kansas, she moved to Chicago, where she met Milliken at Le Perroquet. "Nothing got thrown out there," she tells me. "We'd use butter wrappers like wax paper, to cover the pastry cream; we'd use the fat from chicken stock, clarify it, and use it to sauté; we'd use the stems from broccoli to make mousse."

She exhibits the same enthusiasm for her latest obsession: street food, which she features at her restaurant, Street.

Those Manila clams, made fiery with a strong dose of black pepper and joined by garlic, ginger, soy sauce, brown sugar, and lime, are poured into a bowl and then covered with a handful of fresh herbs. "Oh my God," says Feniger, stirring it all around. "It's so fantastic when it's mixed in there."

The flavor is explosive. "It's that sweet salty thing that I love," she cheers.

The intensity is matched by the intensity of her kafta—lamb meatballs—served with baked feta cheese and drizzled with pomegranate molasses. And it's matched by the kaya, which is also sweet and salty and complex from those pandan leaves. The smile on Feniger's face as I eat speaks volumes: as much as she loves to discover new tastes and techniques, she loves to share them even more.

"I love what food does with bringing people together."

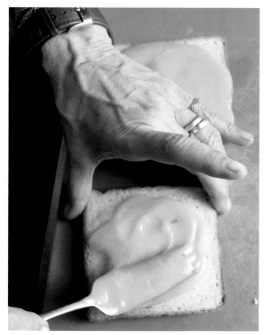

Kaya Toast

Serves 4 (with a good amount of coconut curd for later)

This is a make-ahead dish and a perfect thing to serve at brunch (it is, after all, a Singaporean hangover cure, not to be confused with frico, the Italian hangover cure on page 47). The sweet coconut curd on the toasted bread is almost like a pastry; but dipped into the soy-sauced egg, it goes in a whole new direction. Ninety percent of the work here involves making the curd in a double boiler. Make sure, while whisking, that you don't whisk feverishly: you're not trying to beat air into it. You're just trying to keep the eggs from scrambling. Also, watch the water temperature: you don't want it boiling, just simmering. If you think the curd is getting too hot, take it off the heat for thirty seconds or so. The end result, if you follow all the steps, is something totally unusual and highly enjoyable.

FOR THE CURD

1 cup coconut milk, well stirred

1 cup sugar

8 pandan leaves, carefully washed, or 2 tablespoons grated peeled ginger

3 eggs

3 egg yolks

A pinch of kosher salt

TO ASSEMBLE

8 slices pain de mie, pullman, or Pepperidge Farm white bread

4 tablespoons (½ stick) cold salted butter, thinly sliced

4 eggs

Black soy sauce (also called siew dam)

- Pandan leaves are available in Asian markets. If you don't want to bother finding them, make this dish with the ginger. It's still very much worth it.

- This is a thicker, more syrupy soy sauce. But you can use high-quality regular soy sauce here too.

- If you're using ginger, it's a good idea to taste here to see if you've added enough. You can always grate in a little more.

Place the coconut milk in a small pot with the sugar and either the pandan leaves or the ginger. Bring to a boil on medium-high heat, making sure the pandan leaves are completely coated, and cook for 1 minute. Turn off the heat and let steep for 10 minutes.

Depending on how much of a masochist you are, either wring out the hot leaves into the pot right away or wait until they're cool enough to handle. You want to extract as much flavor from them as you can. Once you wring them out, discard them.

Set up a double boiler by bringing a pot of water to a gentle simmer and finding a stainless-steel bowl that fits neatly on top. Place the eggs, yolks, and salt in the bowl and whisk, and then carefully whisk in the hot infused coconut milk.

Set the bowl over the pan of simmering water and whisk, gently, for the next 15 to 20 minutes (you don't have to do it constantly; just keep it moving around). The goal is to keep the eggs from scrambling, so if you think the mixture's getting too hot, take it off the heat for a bit.

- Keep in mind that the bowl acts as a lid and makes the water hotter than if it were uncovered. Once it's at a simmer, keep the temperature dial somewhere between low and medium-low.

After 15 minutes, the mixture should start to thicken (you may switch to a rubber spatula at this point). You know it's done when you can make a line in the curd with your spatula and the line stays visible for a second. When that happens, remove the curd from the heat and allow to cool. You can either use it right away or refrigerate it, covered, for later use.

To finish the dish, put 2 slices of pain de mie into one toaster slot at the same time. This will brown the outsides but keep the insides uncooked. When they're toasty, spread the uncooked part of one slice with the coconut curd. Lay on a few slices of cold salted butter and top with the other piece of bread. Cut the sandwich into quarters and set aside. Repeat with the remaining slices of pain de mie.

Using a little bit of that same salted butter, cook the eggs slowly, sunny-side up, in a small nonstick pan. Slide the eggs onto plates next to the sandwich quarters and douse them with a good splash of black soy sauce. To eat, dunk the sandwich into the egg yolk and the soy sauce.

● For those of us who don't have toasters (count me in your number), lay the bread in a broiler pan and just broil one side until it's toasty.

Black Pepper Clams

Serves 2 to 4

Here's a dish that comes with a warning: look out! When Feniger makes this, the pan is so hot there is an eruption of flames when she adds the clams. It's all very cool and very dramatic, though it nearly gave me a heart attack the first time I made it at home. If you're a wimpy cook, this may not be the dish for you. If you're brave, though, you'll be rewarded with smoky clams infused with ginger, garlic, soy sauce, brown sugar, lime juice, and herbs. The biggest crime would be to not have rice or bread at the ready to soak up the sauce; it's the best part.

¼ cup water

1 tablespoon soy sauce

1 teaspoon Lee Kum Kee oyster sauce (see page 52)

1 teaspoon light brown sugar, plus more to taste

2 tablespoons canola oil

8 to 12 Manila clams (other clams will work too), cleaned

1 tablespoon minced garlic

1 tablespoon grated peeled ginger

2 teaspoons freshly ground black pepper

1 tablespoon unsalted butter

1 to 2 limes, cut in half

A mix of cilantro leaves, mint leaves, and slivered scallions (about ½ cup)

Whisk together the water, soy sauce, oyster sauce, and sugar and set aside.

Get a wide skillet very, very hot (don't use a nonstick pan: high heat can cause it to release carcinogens). How hot you get the pan depends on you, but if you hover your hand over the pan you should feel some serious heat.

Carefully add the oil and then add the clams, shaking the pan. Step back! Did flames shoot up? They might still, especially when you toss the clams and the oil spits in a gas flame. Don't be scared; this is fun.

Once the clams have cooked for 30 seconds, add the garlic to the pan. Cook for 10 seconds or so (you don't want the garlic to burn, but you want to cook out the raw taste), then add the ginger and black pepper. Toss and then add the soy sauce mixture. Raise the heat and, if the clams aren't opening yet, cover the pan. Cook until the clams start to open, 3 to 4 minutes. (Discard any clams that don't open.)

To finish, add the butter, a big squeeze of lime juice, and a handful of the herbs. Stir, and taste the liquid. You want a great balance of sweetness and acidity, so adjust with more sugar and/or lime juice, if necessary.

To serve, pour everything into a large serving bowl and scatter the rest of the herbs on top. This is great served with grilled bread or a bowl of white rice.

Here's a trick to use when you need a lot of pepper for a recipe: instead of grinding it by hand, put a teaspoon or two of whole peppercorns into a spice grinder (or clean coffee grinder) and zap until it's coarsely ground.

When Feniger makes this, she adds an extra spoonful or two of brown sugar and lots of lime juice at the end. You really want to play up the contrast of sweet, savory, and tart, so do the same.

Lamb Meatballs (Kafta) with Baked Feta and Pomegranate Molasses

Serves 4

These are oh so easy to make and oh so satisfying. Whereas meatballs made with ground beef are semi-reminiscent of meat loaf, these lamb meatballs—or *kafta*—are way more dynamic. Because there aren't any bread crumbs in the mixture, these meatballs have a tendency to fall apart in the pan: make sure to pack them tight when you shape them. They are great make-aheads: brown the outsides, set them on a rimmed cookie sheet lined with aluminum foil, and when you're ready to serve them, pop them into a 425°F oven.

- If you can't find the chili powder, use cayenne pepper.

- You can easily make your own pomegranate molasses (see the recipe on page 367).

2 tablespoons canola oil, plus more for later

2 cups diced white onion (from 1 large onion)

1 tablespoon chopped garlic (from 2 cloves)

1 pound ground lamb

⅓ cup chopped parsley

1 teaspoon kosher salt, plus more to taste

1 teaspoon freshly ground black pepper, plus more to taste

1½ teaspoons paprika

½ teaspoon Reshampatti chili powder (see Resources, page 371)

1 egg, mixed with a fork

½ pound feta, cut into 1-inch-thick slices

A drizzle of either pomegranate molasses or date syrup

Preheat a large skillet, and when it is hot, add the oil. Add the onions and cook over high heat so the onions caramelize quickly (see Kitchen Know-How, page 186). When the onions start to soften and brown, add the garlic and cook for another minute, until the garlic is just cooked but not at all brown. Set aside and allow to cool before adding the mixture to the meat.

In a large bowl, using your hands, combine the lamb, parsley, salt, pepper, paprika, chili powder, egg, and the cooked onions and garlic. You can be aggressive here; you want to work it a little so the meatballs hold together. It's essential now, for seasoning's sake, to make a "spicy meatball" (see page 158). Adjust the seasoning and shape the meat into ¼-cup meatballs. Set aside on a large plate.

Preheat the oven to 425°F. In a large clean skillet (you can wipe out the one you used to fry the onions and garlic), heat another splash of canola oil until hot. Add the meatballs (though don't crowd the pan). Cook the meatballs until brown on all sides and then remove them to a rimmed cookie sheet lined with aluminum foil. Pop the meatballs into the oven for 3 to 5 minutes and then test one by cutting into it: if it's cooked all the way through, they're ready.

Meanwhile, in a small ovenproof pan, add another splash of the oil and lay in the feta cheese. Bake until the cheese starts to melt a bit. Scoop the cheese onto the serving dishes, top with some of the meatballs, and drizzle with pomegranate molasses. Serve everything hot.

Christopher Israel

Chef-owner, Grüner
Portland, Oregon

Israel's Kitchen Know-How

IF YOU CAN'T FIND crème fraîche, it's easy to make your own. Just add a few tablespoons of buttermilk to a container of heavy cream, stir it, and leave it out for 12 hours or more, covered loosely with plastic wrap. Refrigerate after it has thickened. It will keep, covered, for a week.

FOR EXTRA-SMOKY BACON, order online from Nueske's in Wittenberg, Wisconsin (see Resources, page 371).

WHEN USING NUTMEG (as you will in the Swiss Chard and Ricotta Dumplings, page 198), you don't want to taste it. You just want enough to add depth of flavor. The key, though, is using freshly grated nutmeg, which tastes entirely different from the preground stuff.

Having grown up in San Diego, California, eating the traditional American food that his parents cooked and the traditional Mexican food that his grandmother cooked, and after helping to jump-start the Portland food scene in the 1990s with his Mediterranean restaurant Zefiro and then tackling the Far East with the Chinese restaurant Saucebox, chef Chris Israel sought a new frontier. And that frontier is Germany.

"People don't have a positive concept of German food," he tells me at Grüner, his Portland, Oregon, restaurant, which *GQ* magazine named one of the best new restaurants in the United States in 2011. "Even though so many American dishes have roots in Germany—hamburgers, hot dogs—Americans have a hard time with Germany."

But peek into the Grüner kitchen for a moment, and you'll start to wonder why: hot pretzels are carried steaming out of the oven; containers overflow with sauerkraut, spicy mustard, speck, and buckwheat spaetzle; strips of smoky bacon are cooked and ready to sit atop crème fraîche on tarte flambée (an Alsatian pizza).

"People think all German food is heavy," Israel tells me as we proceed to a long wooden table to make our first dish, a radish salad. "But it doesn't have to be."

Israel brings all of his life experience, not just his travels through Germany, to the table when he cooks. Featuring radishes in a salad, for example, is as much a function of honoring Germany (radishes are big in Bavaria) as it is an homage to his time in San Francisco, where he ran the front of the house at the ingredient-driven Zuni Café.

The plating, too, taps into Israel's background: he spent years as an art director for *Vanity Fair*. As he shaves the bright red radishes on a mandoline slicer he tells me: "You have to ask yourself, 'How does each dish look and how does that relate to every other dish?'"

Flavor matters too. Over the radishes, he drizzles an esoteric ingredient from Austria: pumpkin seed oil. I put a bit on my finger to taste it and the flavor is toasty and nutty, a flavor echoed by the toasted pumpkin seeds that Israel sprinkles over the salad.

We continue on to a mushroom dish—chanterelles and creminis sautéed with caraway seeds (another signature German ingredient) and placed in a gratin topped with bread crumbs—and then we conclude with Swiss chard dumplings, made with ricotta and based on an Italian technique.

"Alpine cuisine includes food from France and Italy," says Israel by way of explanation.

The blurry lines between the various food cultures melded here echo a time when Europe's borders themselves were fluid. "Modern Europe is all about borders," he says, "but it wasn't always that way."

It's the blending in of German cuisine that's won Israel so much attention and acclaim. Americans may be suspicious, but Israel is doing his part to remind us that great food in Europe doesn't come exclusively from Italy, France, or Spain.

"Cooking is
a journey;
it's a way to
experience the
world without
leaving home."

Radish Salad with Toasted Pumpkin Seeds and Pumpkin Seed Oil

Serves 2 to 4

This is a very subtle salad and one that benefits from restraint. So go easy on the dressing, the salt, the pepper, and that one main specialty ingredient: the pumpkin seed oil. I'd like to tell you that you can leave it out, but then, really, what do you have: a plate of shaved radishes? The pumpkin seed oil is what makes this dish special (see Resources, page 371).

1 bunch of red radishes (or, if you can find them, black radishes or icicle radishes; any variety will do), rinsed and blotted very dry on a kitchen towel

¼ cup cider vinegar

¼ cup canola oil

Kosher salt and freshly ground black pepper

A variety of herbs, finely chopped: any combination of dill, chives, parsley, savory, chervil (about ⅛ cup)

¼ cup pumpkin seeds, toasted

Pumpkin seed oil

Microgreens, azuna, or any small green (about 2 cups)

To toast raw pumpkin seeds (sometimes called pepitas), place them on a rimmed baking sheet and cook in a 350°F oven. When they look toasted and slightly brown (5 to 10 minutes), toss with a small amount of canola oil and salt. Use right away.

Carefully slice the radishes on a mandoline to create an array of perfectly round and perfectly thin disks.

Make a quick dressing by whisking together the cider vinegar and the canola oil with salt and pepper to taste.

Dress the radishes in a mixing bowl very delicately. Arrange them artfully on a serving dish or on individual plates.

Top with the various herbs and toasted pumpkin seeds. Swizzle some pumpkin seed oil over the radishes.

Toss the microgreens with the remaining dressing and pile in the middle of the plate.

Chanterelle and Cremini Mushroom Gratin

Serves 4 (or more)

Mushrooms get the deluxe treatment here in this elegant side dish. First they're sautéed with butter, a shallot, some onion, parsley, and caraway seeds (an ingredient you probably best know from rye bread). Once they release their liquid and start to brown, they get bathed with a generous addition of crème fraîche—which makes the whole thing creamy and tangy—and an extra hit of vinegar. Poured into a gratin dish (you can also use a glass pie plate) and topped with slightly toasted bread crumbs (they finish up in the oven), you have a dish that's rich, satisfying, crunchy, and meaty—a great side for chicken or steak or just by itself with a salad and bread.

● If you can't find chanterelles (a prized mushroom, and correspondingly expensive), use any combination of exotic mushrooms or just creminis exclusively. This recipe works with all mushroom combinations.

2 tablespoons plus 1 teaspoon unsalted butter

½ to 1 cup fresh bread crumbs, ground relatively fine

1 shallot, minced

¼ yellow onion, chopped fine

¼ cup finely chopped parsley, plus 1 or 2 pinches for later

2 cups chanterelle and cremini mushrooms, wiped clean with a damp paper towel and sliced thick

Kosher salt

½ to 1 teaspoon caraway seeds

½ cup crème fraîche

1 tablespoon champagne vinegar, plus more as needed

1 or 2 pinches of all-purpose flour

Preheat the oven to 400°F.

In a small sauté pan, melt the 1 teaspoon of butter. Add the bread crumbs and toast until they get just a little color (they'll finish toasting in the oven). Set aside.

Melt the 2 tablespoons of butter in a large sauté pan on medium heat and then add the shallots and onions. Cook for a minute until slightly translucent, then add the parsley. Cook for an additional 30 seconds (the mixture should give off a sweet aroma).

Add the chanterelles and cremini. Season with salt and caraway seeds. Give everything a toss and then cover the pan, letting the mushrooms cook for about 10 minutes on low heat, stirring every now and then.

When the mushrooms are soft, add the crème fraîche, vinegar, and a pinch or two of flour (depending on how thick you want it). Cook until the mixture thickens, another minute or so. Taste and adjust with more salt and/or vinegar.

Pour the mushroom mixture into a gratin dish or a glass pie plate and top with the bread crumbs. Bake for 5 to 10 minutes, until the top is golden brown.

Remove from the oven and sprinkle with the final pinch or two of chopped parsley. Serve hot.

Swiss Chard and Ricotta Dumplings

Serves 4 or more

Don't let the Swiss chard fool you; there's very little that's healthy about this dish. But who cares about healthy? What you get if you make this is a bowlful of green-flecked, cheesy dumplings swimming in a pool of butter. It's also a fun dish to make because so much of it is based on your own sense of touch. You want to add just enough flour so that you can easily roll the dough and cut it up into dumplings. Using a bench scraper to do that cutting is smart because then you can use the flat side of the scraper to scoop everything up straight into the pot of boiling water. Be sure to drain the ricotta cheese overnight before you start the dumplings (if you don't, the dumplings will require more flour, and they'll be heavier).

2 cups ricotta cheese, set over a strainer lined with cheesecloth and drained overnight in the refrigerator

1 cup blanched Swiss chard, squeezed dry and chopped

2 cups grated Parmesan cheese

Kosher salt

A pinch of freshly grated nutmeg

2 eggs, plus 3 egg yolks

1 cup all-purpose flour, plus more for rolling

3 to 4 tablespoons unsalted butter

- To blanch the chard, first take the leaves off the ribs and then drop the leaves into unsalted boiling water for 3 minutes. Shock them immediately in an ice-water bath to stop the cooking.

- Do a taste test here: it should have a bold flavor.

- The best way to know if it's rollable is to remove a small ball of dough from the bowl and try to roll it into a snake between your hands. If that works, it's ready to go.

In a large bowl, combine the ricotta, chard, Parmesan, 2 tablespoons salt, the nutmeg, eggs, and yolks with a large rubber spatula. Mix as thoroughly as possible before adding the flour: once you add the flour you want to mix it as little as possible or the dumplings will be tough and gluey.

Add the flour ¼ cup at a time and work it in gently with the rubber spatula. Study the dough as you go: is it very sticky? You don't want it super dry but you want to be able to roll it later to form the dumplings. Stop adding flour when the dough reaches a rollable texture.

Allow the dough to rest for 30 minutes at room temperature (during which time it will continue to stiffen).

When you're ready to roll the dumplings, flour a board and your hands. Remove the dough to the board and sprinkle some flour on it. Roll the dough into a long rod, approximately ½ inch thick. Cut the rod into 1-inch-long dumplings.

Bring a large pot of water to a boil and season lightly with salt. Drop the dumplings in and cook for 3 to 4 minutes, until they float.

Melt the butter in a medium-size pan and lift the dumplings from the boiling water into the pan to finish, tossing them gently. Serve immediately.

Tony Mantuano

Chef-owner, Spiaggia
Chicago, Illinois

When chef Tony Mantuano opened Spiaggia in Chicago in 1984, a customer told him: "You're never going to make it if you don't put a meatball on the menu."

At the time, the kind of food Mantuano was cooking—ingredient-driven regional Italian food—hadn't been seen before in Chicago or, for that matter, most of the United States. Instead of spaghetti with the obligatory meatballs, Mantuano was serving squid-ink pasta. People were perplexed. But Mantuano, a large man with a large presence, kept calm. And calm, I observe in my time with him in his kitchen, is what allowed Mantuano to steer the ship through those initial choppy waters, to help build Spiaggia into a world-renowned dining destination, and to achieve a status few others can claim: he's President Obama's favorite chef.

Unlike the chefs on TV who scream and shout, Mantuano stands towering over the kitchen space and surveys it all with a kindness and grace that seems out of place on a man of his stature. He's almost always grinning; he seems to regard the people and activity around him with detached amusement.

That's certainly the case with Spiaggia's executive chef, Sarah Grueneberg, who joins us when we get started in the kitchen. The first dish requires the use of a contraption called a *bigolaro*. "It's Venetian in origin," Mantuano explains. "They call it the burro because it looks like a donkey."

Indeed, this machine with a small bench for a body and a metal contraption for a head does look like a donkey. As Grueneberg and Mantuano discuss who's going to operate it, I ask if I can. Mantuano grins his signature grin. "Sure you can."

I sit on the bench, and Grueneberg presses the pasta dough into the metal apparatus. Then I pull down on the lever and start turning a wheel, which extrudes the dough through several large holes.

"This is hard work," I say when the going gets tough.

Mantuano grins.

Grueneberg has placed a bowl of double-zero semolina flour beneath the extruder to catch the fat strands of pasta (so they don't stick), and when we're finished, she shows me how the *bigolaro* gave the pasta a rough exterior that will catch the sauce better.

As for the sauce, Grueneberg and Mantuano have set out on the counter a beautiful array of small purple, yellow, and red heirloom cherry tomatoes. They start by salting a big pot of boiling water: "The most important thing is to salt the water," says Mantuano.

"The lighter the sauce, the thinner the pasta should be. It's a texture thing: flavors and textures have to match."

To a pan, Mantuano adds slivered garlic that's been soaking in oil, along with more olive oil to coat the rest of the pan, and then he cranks up the heat. When the garlic is sizzling, he adds a bunch of the tomatoes and shakes the pan vigorously. "You really want these tomatoes to fry so their flavor comes out."

When oil spills out of the pan, flames shoot up, but, as expected, Mantuano remains calm.

He also remains calm later as we're rolling focaccia dough through a pasta machine to flatten it (we'll stuff it with mozzarella, olives, and basil) and when we plate a Pantesca salad made with calamari, peewee potatoes, more cherry tomatoes, and capers.

This food is a far cry from spaghetti and meatballs, but that's the point. "It tastes like Italy," Mantuano says.

As we stand there eating calmly, I have to agree.

Tagliatelle with Cherry Tomatoes

Serves 4

Pasta that is forced through a die—as is bigoli, Mantuano's original choice for this recipe—can't be made without a pasta extruder. And since most of us don't have a pasta extruder, this recipe would seem, at first, to be out of reach. (I once tried extruding pasta with a Play-Doh Fun Factory. It doesn't work!) Bigoli has a thick, rough texture that catches sauce well, but it's really not that different from fresh pasta rolled through a pasta machine. So, my suggestion: if you don't have a pasta extruder, make this recipe using fresh pasta that you cut into tagliatelle. It'll do just as good a job soaking up this bright, acidic summery sauce. (But if you can get your hands on fresh bigoli, by all means use that.)

Kosher salt

Extra virgin olive oil

4 cloves garlic, sliced extra-thin

2 cups assorted cherry tomatoes (red, yellow, and purple heirlooms are best), patted dry

Fresh pasta dough (see page 138), rolled through a pasta machine to the thinnest setting and then cut into tagliatelle

Freshly ground black pepper

8 whole basil leaves

Ricotta salata (about ¼ pound)

● You need to be aggressive here because this salted water is also going to season the tomatoes down the road.

Bring a very large pot of water to a boil and salt it aggressively. If you dip your finger in (be brave!), it should taste like the sea.

Coat a large sauté pan (not nonstick) with about ¼ cup olive oil and add the garlic. Cook over medium heat, stirring the garlic, just until it starts to brown.

Add all of the tomatoes (make sure they're dry so they fry). With the heat cranked up to high, let them cook for a minute, shaking the pan but being careful not to splash the oil.

As the tomatoes cook, add the fresh pasta to the boiling water. It'll cook pretty quickly; check for doneness after 3 or 4 minutes.

Add a ladleful of the pasta water to the tomatoes and garlic in the pan (warning: it will sizzle and splash) and add several grinds of black pepper. Stir. When the pasta's just al dente, lift it with tongs directly into the pan with the tomatoes.

Add one or two more ladlefuls of water and cook the pasta together with the tomatoes until everything comes together. The sauce itself should get thick as the starchy water, the olive oil, and the tomato juices emulsify.

At the very last second, add half of the basil leaves. Taste and check the seasoning (you may need to add some salt). Remove from the heat.

Using tongs, lift the finished pasta onto warmed plates, tangling the noodles into a nest. Top with more fresh basil and with shaved ricotta salata.

Stuffed
Focaccia

Serves 8

It sounds fancy, but this recipe is a cinch to put together. Mantuano puts his focaccia dough through a pasta machine to make it easy to layer, but, after trying that, I found it much easier to use a rolling pin. Make sure to sprinkle the work surface, the rolling pin, and the dough itself with flour to save yourself any trouble. And though this recipe specifies what to stuff in the focaccia—mozzarella, Parmesan, basil, and olives—you can use your imagination. Pesto would taste great, as would sun-dried tomatoes.

FOR THE DOUGH

2 packets active dry yeast

Pinch of sugar

2 cups lukewarm water

¼ cup plus 2 tablespoons extra virgin olive oil

5 cups all-purpose flour, plus more for rolling the dough

2 teaspoons sea salt

FOR ASSEMBLY

Olive oil, for coating the pan and the focaccia

2 tablespoons cornmeal

4 ounces fresh mozzarella, sliced

½ cup grated Parmesan cheese

1 cup loosely packed basil leaves

1 cup pitted taggiasca olives (if you can't find them, try kalamata)

Kosher salt and freshly ground black pepper

In a small bowl, combine the yeast, sugar, and water and let sit until the mixture is bubbly, about 5 minutes.

Stir in the 2 tablespoons of olive oil.

Combine the flour and sea salt in the bowl of a mixer fitted with a dough hook. Pour in the yeast mixture on low speed and mix until the dough peels away from the sides, 3 to 5 minutes.

Transfer the dough to a lightly floured bowl and cover with a towel. Let it rise for 1 hour, or until it doubles in size.

On a floured surface, knead the dough until it forms a smooth ball. Divide into two balls and allow to rest, covered, for another 15 minutes.

Preheat the oven to 300°F. Grease a 12-by-18-inch baking pan (like the kind you'd use to make lasagna) with olive oil and sprinkle in the cornmeal.

Using a pasta machine or a rolling pin, flour one ball of dough and roll it out to fit the length and width of the baking pan. Lower it into the pan and layer with the mozzarella, Parmesan, basil, and ¾ cup of the olives. Lightly sprinkle with kosher salt and pepper.

Roll out the second ball of dough and place it as a second layer on top of the filling, fitting it into the pan. No need to create a seal, but gently press the edges together.

Brush the top with more olive oil and garnish with the remaining ¼ cup of olives by pushing them half an inch down into the top layer at intervals.

Cover the pan with aluminum foil and bake for 30 minutes. Uncover and bake for another 15 minutes, or until the crust is golden.

To test for doneness, stick a paring knife into the middle of the focaccia; if the knife comes out clean, it's done.

Drizzle with more olive oil and allow to cool for 20 minutes before removing and slicing with a serrated knife.

Pantesca
Salad

Serves 4

You hear it often, but this time it's true: this salad is all about the ingredients. Because there are so few, seek out the best you can find. When Mantuano and Grueneberg assemble this salad in the Spiaggia kitchen (it's based on a salad Grueneberg ate on the island of Pantellena, off the southern coast of Sicily), they use such a colorful array of farmer's-market potatoes and tomatoes—reds, yellows, and purples exploding across the plate—that I can't imagine re-creating this salad without them. You can only really make this salad in summer, and when you do, make sure to shop with an eye for color. Be generous with the olive oil at the end. That's how they do it in Italy.

1 cup assorted peewee potatoes (baby Yukons, purple potatoes, fingerlings, German butterballs), boiled in salted water until cooked through, then sliced in half

1 cup assorted cherry tomatoes, preferably heirloom (purple, orange, yellow, etc.), sliced in half along the equator

½ red onion, slivered very thin

Extra virgin olive oil (the best you have)

Balsamic vinegar (the best you have; it should be syrupy)

Sea salt and freshly ground black pepper

5 pieces calamari, cleaned, purple skin removed

1 lemon

⅛ cup dried capers, reconstituted in water

Whole basil leaves

- Make sure to remove the big piece of plastic-like matter inside the calamari; you'll know it when you find it.

- You may not use all the onion. Try to keep an even ratio between the tomatoes, potatoes, and onion.

Arrange the potatoes in a single layer on a serving dish, then layer the tomatoes on top. Scatter some of the onion on top and then drizzle with olive oil and a few drops of balsamic vinegar. Sprinkle with sea salt and pepper.

In a sauté pan, heat ¼ cup olive oil until very hot. Season the calamari with salt and pepper and sear very quickly until slightly browned and just cooked inside.

Squeeze the lemon over the calamari. Cut the tubes into rings and place on top of the potatoes and tomatoes, pouring the pan juices over all.

Sprinkle the capers over the calamari, tomatoes, and potatoes; add a splash of olive oil, some basil leaves, more lemon juice, and salt and pepper to taste. Serve immediately.

Renee Erickson

**Chef-owner, Boat Street Cafe
and The Walrus and the Carpenter
Seattle, Washington**

Erickson's Kitchen Know-How

GRAY UNREFINED sea salt—
gros sel in French—has a
unique flavor that improves
whatever you're cooking. If
you go to France, you can buy
a big bag for just two euros.
To buy here, see Resources
(page 371).

THE LEAVES at the heart
of a bunch of celery are an
underappreciated ingredient;
they will perfume whatever
you're cooking with a subtle
celery flavor. Use in soups,
stocks, poaching liquids, or
anywhere else where you
want an extra vegetal note.

WHEN EATING mussels (see
recipe, page 213), use a
discarded half-shell to scoop
out the meat of your next
mussel. Or, perhaps even
better, use a whole discarded
shell like tongs to pull out
the mussel meat from the
next mussel and deliver it to
your mouth. (That's the way
Erickson eats hers.)

Many chefs care about quality ingredients, but chef Renee Erickson takes it one step further. In the bright and airy kitchen of her home in the Ballard neighborhood of Seattle, I tell Erickson that I want to wash my hands before we cook.

"One second," she says, walking into another room.

She returns moments later with a prettily wrapped bar of high-quality, milk-scented soap. And that's just the tip of the iceberg.

Looking around her personal kitchen, you can tell how much Erickson loves quality ingredients by the eclectic collection of bottles and jars that surrounds her.

A green bottle of fresh Trampetti olive oil comes straight from Italy. A jar of Ballard honey comes directly from the bees that she keeps in her backyard (the Ballard Bee Company cultivates it for her in exchange for some of her bees' honey). Meyer lemon oil is labeled Colline di Santa Cruz, from Valencia Creek Farms in California. In a bag, she keeps espelette chilies sent to her by a farmer friend in Oregon. "They're floral, not spicy," she tells me, "and for my last meal I'd want spot prawns roasted in garlic and butter and espelette with a little lemon juice."

In a different section are assorted jars of jams that Erickson makes herself: huckleberry, Cara Cara orange, and Meyer lemon. One of her restaurants, the Boat Street Cafe, sells jams around the country (her mother manages that business), but these jams are from Erickson's own personal collection.

In a bowl on her kitchen table is an exotic "hand of Buddha," a citrus fruit that looks like Medusa's head. "It makes the house smell so good this time of year," she explains.

It's one thing to buy a bunch of nice stuff to cook with and it's another thing to know how to use what you buy. Erickson illustrates the latter by preparing the simplest appetizer you're likely to ever encounter: dates sautéed in olive oil with salt.

The key, of course, is using the best ingredients. The dates are Medjool and they're unpitted because, Erickson asserts, "they're better. Dates get smashed when they're pitted." The olive oil is the freshest she has and the salt is Maldon sea salt.

When she brings these things together using a pan, high heat, and a few flips and tilts, the result is magic: sizzling, salty, and sweet. And to think that it's as much about shopping as it is about cooking.

This is not to diminish Erickson's skill. What she has that most of us don't is an exceptional palate: when we prepare the mussels with cider and cream, she creates a perfectly balanced mussel cooking liquid by tasting and adjusting according to her sense of what tastes right. And the same is true for the liquid we use to poach the halibut and to make the pistachio pesto that goes on top.

Few of us permit ourselves the luxury of buying the best ingredients when we shop for food. Most of us can't afford it. But Erickson, who's as down-to-earth as they come, makes a solid case for indulging when you stock your kitchen. Great ingredients make for great food; it's just that simple.

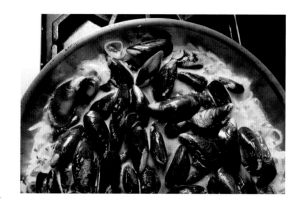

"I think people stress out about food and make it seem like a big deal when really, it's not. It's a lot simpler than they think."

Sautéed
Medjool Dates

Serves 4

A hot pan. Olive oil. Dates. Salt. That's all you need to make an appetizer that's as satisfying as one that might take hours of your time. Medjool dates, which are meatier than other varieties, soak up the oil and crisp up on the outside, resulting in a hot, salty, chewy treat. Just be careful: the dates, because of all their sugar, can burn easily, so take it right to the edge and then remove them from the pan. And be generous with the salt—the play between sweet and salty is the best part.

¼ cup good olive oil

2 cups Medjool dates, unpitted

1 tablespoon Maldon sea salt, plus more to taste

In a skillet large enough to hold the dates, heat the olive oil on high heat. When adding a date causes the oil to sizzle, add the rest.

Give the dates a few tosses while they heat up and soften, 1 to 2 minutes. Don't cook too long or they'll burn (a few dark brown spots here and there, though, won't hurt the flavor).

Pour the hot dates onto a plate with the olive oil from the pan and sprinkle with the salt. Serve immediately.

Poached Halibut with Pistachio–Meyer Lemon Pesto

Serves 2

There's a rustic elegance to this dish of gently poached halibut topped with a pistachio pesto. The elegance comes from the provenance of the ingredients: the Meyer lemon, the green pistachios (preferably from Sicily), the white Bordeaux, and the good olive oil you drizzle on at the end. The rusticity comes from the way it's presented; a simple fillet of fish with a few scoops of nutty, herby pesto on top. Of course, you can tone down the elegance by using a cheaper fish, a regular lemon, less fancy pistachios, and a cheaper white wine, but for a special occasion, go for elegance. It's a good time to light your candelabra.

2 cups (one 9-ounce container) unsalted green pistachios, shelled

2 cups Côtes de Gascogne or similarly un-oaked white Bordeaux

2 cups water

3 tablespoons unsalted butter

1 heart of a bunch of celery, with leaves, left whole

2 slices lemon

2 fresh bay leaves or 1 dried bay leaf

Kosher salt

1 large fillet of halibut, about 1 pound

1 cup cilantro leaves, loosely packed

½ cup parsley leaves, loosely packed

¾ cup good olive oil

Zest and juice of 1 Meyer lemon

Best-quality olive oil, for drizzling

Maldon sea salt

> Halibut can be very expensive, depending on where you live. If you want to make this but don't want to spend the money, try another firm white fish such as haddock or cod.

> Pistachios are also expensive, so make sure to monitor this process. You'll be angry if you burn them.

> There are a few ways to know that the fish is done; touch is probably the most effective. The second is visual: you can use a knife to poke into one of the fillets and see if the flesh is still translucent or pink.

Preheat the oven to 400°F.

Pour the pistachios into a cast-iron pan (or onto a cookie sheet) and toast in the oven for about 10 minutes, shaking every so often, until they're fragrant. Allow to cool.

Meanwhile, prepare the poaching liquid: In a pot large enough to hold the fish, add the wine, water, butter, celery heart, lemon slices, and bay leaves. Bring to a boil over high heat and reduce the liquid to a level that'll put it just over the top of the fish, 5 to 10 minutes.

Cover, reduce the heat to low, and allow the liquid to steep for 30 minutes longer.

Taste the poaching liquid—it'll have a funky, bitter taste—and season lightly with kosher salt. Adjust the heat so the liquid barely simmers and then place the fish into it.

Allow the fish to cook for 10 to 15 minutes, until it's just firm when you touch the top.

Meanwhile, prepare the pesto: In a food processor, combine the pistachios, cilantro, parsley, and a pinch of kosher salt. While it's spinning, slowly pour in the good olive oil and pulse until it forms a thick paste. Don't overpulse: you want it chunky. Stir in the Meyer lemon juice.

To plate, use a spatula and a spoon to remove the cooked fish to a platter. Pat with paper towels and drizzle the best olive oil you have over it. Top with a big mound of pesto and sprinkle with the Meyer lemon zest and Maldon sea salt. Serve right away.

Mussels with Cider, Cream, and Mustard

Serves 4

Cheap, versatile, and incredibly easy to cook, mussels are a busy cook's best friend in the kitchen: throw some garlic and wine into a pot, add the mussels, cover, and a few minutes later you have dinner. Erickson raises the bar and uses more eclectic ingredients—a dry cider, spicy mustard, and cream—but the essentials are still the same. The Domaine Dupont cider Erickson uses is notably bitter. When I make this I sometimes use a sweeter alcoholic cider, which she warned me against ("That's not what we're going for"), but truthfully I kind of like the play between the sweet cider, the briny mussels, and the spicy mustard. Proceed as you wish. Serve with crusty bread and a glass of leftover cider, and you're set.

1 pound mussels

All-purpose flour

2 tablespoons unsalted butter

2 shallots, thinly sliced

2 cups dry English cider

1 tablespoon spicy mustard (try Beaufor)

1 tablespoon fresh thyme leaves

Kosher salt and freshly ground black pepper

¼ cup heavy cream

Clean the mussels by placing them in a large bowl of cold water with a spoonful of flour. As they soak, examine them. Discard any mussels that are cracked or that won't close. After 15 minutes, drain the water and rinse one more time.

On medium-high heat, melt the butter in a wide pot or Dutch oven large enough to hold all the mussels. When the butter's hot and foaming, add the shallots and cook for 30 seconds to 1 minute, until the shallots start to brown.

Add a little bit of the cider and all of the mustard. Stir until combined, and then stir in the rest of the cider and the thyme. Bring to a boil and taste for flavor, adjusting with salt and pepper.

Add the mussels and cover. They cook very fast, so begin checking them after 1 minute. Remove to a platter any mussels that open. Re-cover and continue checking until all the mussels are opened and removed. Discard any that don't open.

To the liquid in the pan, add the cream and cook on high heat until the sauce is thickened. Taste to adjust.

You can serve this two ways: you can pour all of the sauce over the mussels on the platter, or you can remove the mussels from their shells and place them in the sauce and serve it as more of a soup. Either way, make sure to have bread handy to sop up that sauce: it's the best part.

● This is a wonderful technique that you should apply to all mussel dishes: remove them as soon as they open and they'll never taste rubbery or overcooked.

213

Omar Powell

Graduate of the Culinary Institute of America and professional chef Duluth, Georgia

At the Sugarloaf Country Club in Duluth, Georgia, chef Omar Powell runs the kitchen the same way that countless other chefs run country club kitchens. He makes what his customers want. Hamburgers. Cobb salads. Iced tea.

Only, a few of his customers know a secret. And that secret is that Powell is one of the *best* Jamaican cooks around, a chef who cut his teeth at the Culinary Institute of America and at Daniel on New York's Upper East Side, but whose truest talent is interpreting the food of his youth on Montego Bay.

"I had a colorful childhood there," he tells me from the kitchen of his Duluth home, where he lives with his wife, Nathalie, and his daughters, Jordan and Hailey. "We planned our summers based on what fruits were available. In June they have naseberries; in August, it's mango season."

Powell cooks authentic Jamaican food with both a deep sense of authority ("Our flavor profile includes thyme, allspice, green onions, and cloves") and a profound sense of enjoyment ("You have to like the subcutaneous gristle to really like oxtails").

His oxtails—which he seasons overnight with paprika, garlic powder, onion powder, and sugar—are a perfect example of how he filters his Jamaican food knowledge through the prism of the French culinary techniques he picked up at the CIA and Daniel; he uses them in a cassoulet.

"It's almost like an oxtail chili," he says as he stirs together the shredded oxtail meat, cannellini beans, beets, and carrots. "The French just put it in their language and charge a lot more for it."

The beet and the carrot are there for color—"We eat with our eyes first," he says—but their flavor contributes a great deal too. "Booyah!" he exclaims as he takes his first bite.

If Powell takes great pleasure in the Jamaican food that he cooks at home, he also cooks it with a measure of pride. "Rum cake is a staple in Jamaica," he says as he begins unwrapping a rum cake that's been curing for a few days wrapped in wax paper and plastic, seasoned every so often with more rum. "It's only had a few times of the year—Christmas and at weddings. Those are the only times you can spare the money."

This particular recipe comes from Nathalie's mother ("She would be so proud to have you share the recipe," Nathalie told me) and is an extravaganza of spices (cinnamon and nutmeg), molasses, and, of course, white rum. "The biggest secret of the cake is the rum," says Powell. "Use J. Wray and Nephew, if you can find it."

It's a shame that Powell's daily customers don't get to experience the accomplished Jamaican food that he makes at home (the smart ones know to ask for his specialties off the menu). The good news is that Powell is in the process of opening a restaurant in Atlanta where he'll cook Jamaican food with a French flair.

Trading in hamburgers for oxtails, Powell's ready to cook the food that he loves.

"It's never too early for the relationship to start between the meat and the vegetables."

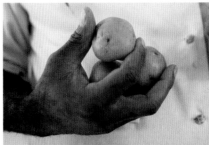

Oxtail
Cassoulet

Serves 4

When these oxtails come out of the oven, intensely brown and fragrant, I have to stop myself from tearing them apart and consuming them right then and there. Patience, it turns out, is a virtue when it comes to this dish; both in applying the dry rub a day before you cook the oxtails and then letting them refrigerate an extra day after you cook them to develop the flavors. If you do all that, on the third day, you'll be rewarded with a deeply satisfying meaty stew that's brightened with carrot and beet and hits of garlic, parsley, and thyme. Truth be told, you *can* make this all in one day (I've done it) and it will still be good, though just not as good. See how well you fare when you give it a go.

FOR THE OXTAILS

1 teaspoon paprika

1 tablespoon kosher salt

1 teaspoon freshly ground black pepper

1 teaspoon garlic powder

1 teaspoon onion powder

1 teaspoon sugar

6 large oxtails, on the bone

3 tablespoons olive oil

3 celery stalks, chopped

2 carrots, peeled and chopped

1 tablespoon tomato paste

FOR THE CASSOULET

1 golden or red beet, peeled and cut into ½-inch cubes

1 fat carrot, peeled and cut into ½-inch cubes

Kosher salt

3 hot Italian sausages, removed from the casings

Olive oil

2 cloves garlic, chopped

½ onion, chopped

1 celery stalk, chopped

1 tomato, chopped

½ cup canned cannellini beans, strained

1 tablespoon chopped fresh thyme

Freshly ground black pepper

¼ cup chopped parsley

Begin 2 days ahead by making a dry rub for the oxtails. In a small bowl, mix together the paprika, salt, pepper, garlic powder, onion powder, and sugar and rub all over the oxtails. Place the oxtails in a lidded container and refrigerate overnight (you can even do it for 2 nights).

The day before you want to serve the cassoulet, preheat the oven to 350°F. Bring the oxtails to room temperature. Cook them by heating the olive oil over medium-high heat in a Dutch oven or a lidded pan large enough to hold everything. When the oil is hot, add the oxtails and brown them thoroughly on each side without moving them around too much, to let them develop color. As the oxtails brown, bring 6 cups water to a boil in a separate pot.

When the oxtails are almost brown all over, add the celery and carrots to the pan. Stir and then add the tomato paste to an uncrowded spot in the pan, stirring it slightly. Lower the heat and allow the tomato paste to toast a bit, gently, along with the carrots and celery.

Add enough of the boiling water to the pan to cover the oxtails by three quarters. Cover the pan and place in the oven for 2½ to 3 hours, until the oxtails fall apart when pulled with a fork. When the oxtails are done, allow them to come to room temperature and then refrigerate them in their liquid to allow the flavor to develop overnight.

When you're ready to assemble the cassoulet, remove the oxtail pan from the refrigerator and warm it up a bit on the stove over low heat to reliquify the braising liquid. Meanwhile, bring a small pan of water to a boil. Drop in the beets and the carrots, along with a pinch of salt, and lower to a simmer. Cook just until the beets and carrots are cooked through but still somewhat toothsome, about 10 minutes; strain and set aside.

Place the oxtails on a large plate and remove all of the meat with your fingers, discarding the bones. Strain the braising liquid with a chinois or a strainer and set aside.

To make the cassoulet, add the sausage to a large pot or pan with a splash of olive oil. Raise the heat to medium high and cook, breaking it up with a spoon, until the sausage begins to brown. Add the garlic, onions, and celery and allow those to cook for a minute or two. Add the tomato, beans, all of the oxtail meat, the strained braising liquid, the thyme, and a few grinds of pepper. Stir, bring to a simmer, and taste to adjust for salt. Remove from the heat and add the strained beet and carrot and the chopped parsley. Serve hot.

- Because of the sugar in the rub, the meat will brown more quickly than it would by itself. Monitor carefully so the sugar doesn't burn.

- Check the oxtails after an hour or so to see how much liquid is left in the pan. If it's reduced too much, add another cup or two of boiling water.

- If you want to skip the cassoulet, you can certainly eat these just like this. Serve over rice with the strained braising liquid.

Jamaican Squash Soup with Chicken and "Spinners"

Serves 4

"We have this soup on Saturdays in Jamaica," Powell told me as he made it in his kitchen. "Pumpkin soup is big there. Sometimes, on weekends, you go from friend's house to friend's house to see who has the best pumpkin soup." What I love so much about this one is the way the raw chicken that goes in creates its own stock, enriching everything around it and leaving you with tender pieces of chicken that turn this simple soup into a satisfying dinner. The "spinners" are dumplings that get their name because of the way you shoot them spinning through the air into the soup.

- To peel the squash, Powell cuts the whole thing in half through the stem, then peels it all around with a very sharp knife. Make sure to scrape out the seeds before using.

- Use the legs, thighs, wings, and back (cut it into 3 pieces) with all the skin and bones attached (that'll give great body and flavor). Wrap the breast in plastic and refrigerate or freeze for another time.

- Powell uses dried habanero powder but suggests the fresh peppers as an alternative.

- You can also use taro root, says Powell. I use a regular yam and that works too. Powell warns that the skin of a white yam can irritate your hands, so proceed cautiously.

- If it displaces so much liquid that it looks like your pot is going to overflow, ladle out some of the water.

FOR THE THYME OIL

¼ cup olive oil

1 bunch of thyme

FOR THE SOUP

10 cups water

1 kabocha, butternut, or acorn squash, peeled, seeded, and cut into 1-inch chunks

A whole chicken (3 to 4 pounds), cut into parts, minus the breast

Kosher salt

2-inch knob of ginger, peeled and finely minced or grated

2 cloves garlic, minced

½ jalapeño or habanero pepper, seeded and chopped

1 white yam from Jamaica, peeled and cut into quarters

3 red potatoes, cut into quarters

½ white onion, chopped

1 celery stalk, chopped

1 carrot, peeled and chopped

A few sprigs of thyme, for garnish

FOR THE SPINNERS

1 cup all-purpose flour

1 tablespoon kosher salt

Enough water to form a dough

Start by making the thyme oil. Place the oil and thyme in a small pan and raise the heat to medium. When the thyme starts popping, remove the pan from the heat and allow the thyme to steep in the oil while you make the soup.

In a large pot or Dutch oven, bring the water to a boil on high heat. Add the squash and the chicken and a good pinch of salt, bring back to a boil, lower to a simmer, and cook for about 30 minutes, until the squash is tender; a knife should go through it easily when pierced. Skim off any scum that floats to the top.

When the pieces of squash are tender, use a large spoon to fish them out and place them in a blender. Blend until they're creamy and smooth and then return them to the soup, stirring to combine.

continued

Jamaican Squash
Soup with Chicken
and "Spinners" (continued)

Add the rest of the ingredients, except for the thyme, to the soup, along with some more salt, and continue to simmer.

To make the spinners, place the flour and salt in a bowl and take the bowl to the sink. Turn the faucet on to a slow, steady stream of lukewarm water and add it to the flour, stirring with your fingers. As soon as you have something that looks like a dough, knead the dough to develop the gluten. Grab a golf-ball-size knob of dough and roll it in your hands as if you're making a snake out of Play-Doh. On the final motion of rubbing your hands together to make the snake, launch the skinny snake (or "spinner") into the soup. Repeat until you've used up all the dough.

Continue to cook the soup until the yam and potatoes are cooked through and the spinners are no longer doughy, about 15 minutes. Taste the soup for salt and ladle it into bowls. Drizzle the thyme oil on top and garnish with a few more sprigs of thyme.

Jamaican Rum Cake

Makes one 9-inch cake

If gingerbread had a tipsy Jamaican cousin, this would be it. The flavors here are capital-B big (when was the last time you baked a cake with 1½ tablespoons of vanilla extract in it?), but the end result has an intense, spicy flavor and can easily handle all the rum that is added. Make sure to grease the pan well because the cake will rise a lot, almost like a muffin; it helps to use an offset spatula to detach it. Serve with a dollop of whipped cream or, better yet, a shot of rum.

FOR THE DRIED FRUIT

¼ cup raisins

½ cup pitted prunes

1 cup white rum (preferably J. Wray and Nephew brand), plus ¼ cup more for sprinkling on the finished cake

FOR THE CAKE

2¾ cups all-purpose flour, plus more for dusting the pan

1½ tablespoons baking powder

1½ teaspoons salt

1 tablespoon ground cinnamon

½ tablespoon freshly grated nutmeg

½ pound (2 sticks) unsalted butter, at room temperature

2½ cups dark brown sugar

4 large eggs, at room temperature

1½ tablespoons vanilla extract

¼ cup molasses

Powdered sugar (optional)

Place the raisins and prunes in a large heat-proof bowl and, in a small separate pot, bring the white rum to a boil over medium-high heat; be careful that it doesn't flambé. Pour the boiling rum over the fruit and cover with plastic wrap. Set aside.

When the fruit has absorbed most of the liquid and has cooled almost to room temperature, puree it in a blender until it's a fruity, rummy mash.

Preheat the oven to 350°F. Fill a baking pan halfway with water and place it on the oven's bottom shelf to create steam. Spray a 9-inch round cake pan with cooking spray, line it with parchment paper, and spray once again. Dust it with flour, tapping out any excess.

In a bowl, sift together the flour, baking powder, salt, cinnamon, and nutmeg. Set aside.

In a stand mixer fitted with the paddle attachment, cream the butter with the brown sugar until fluffy and light, about 3 minutes. Lower the speed and add the eggs, one at a time, until they're fully incorporated.

Add the vanilla, molasses, and blended fruit to the mixer and mix just until they're combined.

With the mixer on low, slowly add the dry ingredients to the wet ingredients, a little at a time. Finish by incorporating the final bit of flour mixture into the batter with a rubber spatula.

If this doesn't happen successfully, consider adding the fruit to the pot in which you warmed the rum and turning up the heat. Allow it to simmer until most of the liquid is absorbed, then turn off the heat and cover.

Pour the batter into the prepared cake pan and bake until the top is dark and firm, 45 minutes to 1 hour, or until a cake tester comes out clean.

Remove the cake pan to a cooling rack, wait 5 minutes, and then flip the cake down onto another cooling rack, remove the pan and the paper, and sprinkle with the reserved ¼ cup rum. Allow to cool completely. To serve, flip right side up onto a cake stand and, for a visual pop, sift on some powdered sugar. Wrapped in wax paper and then plastic wrap, this cake will keep, at room temperature, for up to 3 weeks. (You have to sprinkle it with rum every so often to keep it punchy.)

Jessamyn Waldman Rodriguez

Founder, Hot Bread Kitchen
New York, New York

Jessamyn Waldman Rodriguez did not enter the food world to get rich. She came to food by way of a graduate degree in public policy from Columbia University, a stint at the United Nations, and a year as program director of a human rights–focused high school in Crown Heights. It was from there that she found herself in the bread kitchen of one of New York's most storied restaurants, Daniel.

"I got there by pure benevolence and good luck," she tells me from the workroom of the nonprofit she started, Hot Bread Kitchen.

"I told the head baker there, Mark Fiorentino, about this idea I had and he took me under his wing."

The idea that she had is one she'd spent years developing: she wanted to create a place where low-income immigrant women, many of whom are excellent bakers, could learn to bake in a professional setting. "I wanted to help women gain capital so they can get hired," she tells me.

Since starting in 2008, Rodriguez has trained twenty-one bakers. Many of the women who come through Hot Bread Kitchen bring recipes of their own from their home countries—tortillas, lavash, focaccia, m'smen (a Moroccan flatbread), and challah—which Rodriguez incorporates into the menu of items that they, as a team, produce. These breads are then sold all over New York City, from the Union Square Greenmarket to Zabar's to Dean & Deluca.

Most of what Rodriguez knows about bread-making comes from her time at Daniel (where she was the first woman ever to work in the restaurant's bakery). "I didn't know if I'd love baking before I started there," she tells me. "But I loved the action, the hustle-bustle."

Turns out hustle-bustle is essential to running a business. "You don't realize how fast you have to work to make a bakery profitable. It's not how quickly you can do one baguette, it's how quickly you can do a hundred baguettes."

Efficiency of movement is the name of the game, and Rodriguez (who's nine months pregnant when we cook together) illustrates this as she begins demonstrating her signature country bread (or pain de campagne). "Our bread has two leavening agents in it," she tells me as she begins setting the scale. "A pre-ferment and a commercial yeast."

What's a pre-ferment? "A pre-ferment allows you to integrate whole wheat batter into a white-flour dough. It's a pretty classic French baking technique."

The pre-ferment—which has been refrigerated for twenty-four hours to develop the flavor—is added to a mixture of bread flour, yeast, and salt that's been mixed and allowed to sit for twenty minutes during a process called *autolysis*. "That allows you to develop gluten without beating the hell out of the bread."

Soon—after a few more rises—we're shaping the bread into *boules,* which themselves go through another rise before baking in a 500°F oven. After that, Rodriguez shows me how she uses day-old bread to make her quirky bread salad (her technique of flicking the toasted bread with a balsamic vinegar

solution is totally brilliant) and how she turns Hot Bread Kitchen tortillas (made, painstakingly, in-house) into chilaquiles, a fantastic Mexican breakfast.

All the while, Rodriguez is managing the office, the kitchen, and tour groups that come through to see how this all works. She's a woman whose charitable nature is not at odds with her extreme ambition. She's not here to conquer the food world; she's here to help other women get a leg up. And judging by the breads that come out of the Hot Bread Kitchen, these women are well on their way.

"Women have skills, and these recipes are valuable."

Country Bread
(Pain de Campagne)

Makes 4 medium-size boules

Attention, disciples of the famous no-knead bread that took the food world by storm after Jim Lahey revealed his recipe. Yes: that bread is remarkably easy and results in a truly accomplished bread for very little work. But this recipe? It takes the bread to the next level and doesn't ask you to do much more. In both cases you start the night before; here, you make a pre-ferment with whole wheat flour and yeast. The next day, you mix that in with bread flour, more yeast, and water and let the mixer do the work. True, there are two more rises, but the finished bread is really out of this world, reminiscent of the bread you get at the finest of fine restaurants. The next time you make bread, let this be your bread of choice.

FOR THE PRE-FERMENT

122 grams whole wheat flour

106 grams water, at room temperature

1 gram wet yeast or 3 grams dry yeast (dissolved in a tiny bit of water)

TO FINISH THE BREAD

1,046 grams King Arthur organic bread flour

712 grams cold water

6 grams wet yeast or 18 grams dry yeast (dissolved in a tiny bit of water)

25 grams kosher salt

Canola oil

Cornmeal

● You must use a kitchen scale to make this recipe work. Place a large bowl on the scale and reset the weight to zero. Set the measurement to "grams" and then spoon in the flour until it hits the right amount. Reset to zero again and add the next ingredient (the water) until you have the precise amount. Continue this way until you've completed the recipe.

The day before you want to bake this bread, make the pre-ferment. In a bowl, combine the whole wheat flour, water, and yeast. Mix it together with your hands and then place in a covered container in the refrigerator for 24 hours (this will develop lots of flavor and help the whole wheat flour integrate more seamlessly into the finished bread).

To make the bread, combine the bread flour and cold water in the bowl of a mixer using the dough hook. Mix on low speed for 4 minutes, or until you see complete integration of the flour and the water. Once that happens, allow the dough to rest in the mixer for 20 minutes (this is called *autolysis*).

After 20 minutes, add the yeast, the salt, and the pre-ferment from the refrigerator to the dough in the mixer. Mix for 2 to 3 minutes on low speed until the ingredients are incorporated and then raise the speed to medium (5 on most mixers), allowing the dough hook to work the dough for another 3 minutes. Listen for a slapping sound: that's good. After 3 minutes, the dough should have a sheen: that means the gluten's well developed. Be careful not to overmix.

Oil a large plastic container with a lid and place the dough in it. Cover and place in a warm spot for 1 hour or until it doubles in size.

Turn the dough out onto a floured work surface. Divide the dough into four 400-gram pieces, using the scale to weigh them. With your hands, roll each piece into a boule. To do this you want to find the smoothest part of the piece of dough and stretch that around the rest of the dough. Tug the dough and shape it into a round ball. Place the ball on the work surface seam side down and use the side of your hand, gliding it across the side of the boule as you rotate the boule, to pinch it even tighter. Place the finished boule on a cookie sheet sprinkled with cornmeal. Repeat with the other pieces of dough and then cover the sheet with plastic wrap and allow the dough to rise at room temperature for 1 more hour, or until it doubles in size. Reshape the boules (they'll deflate slightly) and score each with a straight razor or a serrated knife, making a crosshatch sign, with the lines closer to the edges of the bread. (This will help to control the way the bread expands in the oven.)

Preheat the oven to 500°F for at least 30 minutes. You have a choice here: If you have a baking stone, you can use that. If not, you can bake the bread right on that same cookie sheet (though it's best to bake only 2 loaves at a time). Either way, place a metal baking pan on the lowest rack in the oven to heat up and just before you add the bread, pour a cup of water into the pan: it should sizzle. (You're trying to create steam here.) Place the bread on the shelf above the pan (or onto the baking stone) and pour 1 more cup of water into the pan, quickly closing the door.

Bake the bread for 25 to 30 minutes. You'll know it's done when it's golden on the outside and if, when you tap the bottom of the loaf, it sounds hollow. Repeat with the other 2 loaves and allow them all to cool before eating. Those that you don't eat can be refrigerated, wrapped in plastic, for up to several days. Warm in the oven before serving.

Bread Salad with Tuna, Capers, and Olives

Serves 4

I've made bread salads before (most notably, the Italian bread salad known as panzanella), but I've never made one quite like this. And every step here—from slowly toasting the bread in the oven so it gets crisp through and through, to rubbing the bread with raw garlic for punchy garlic flavor, to dressing the bread first with a balsamic vinegar solution so that every piece gets an intense hit of tang—adds up to a pretty incredible final result. With the addition of the tuna, this is perfect for a picnic; take the tuna out and you can serve this as a side for lots of dishes, including Bobby Hellen's Yogurt-Marinated Leg of Lamb (page 40).

1 or 2 day-old loaves Country Bread (page 226) or ciabatta or another Italian bread

2 cloves garlic

⅓ cup balsamic vinegar, plus more to taste

One 8-ounce jar tuna packed in olive oil, drained and flaked into pieces

1 cup cherry tomatoes sliced in half vertically, or 3 large red tomatoes cut into wedges

½ cup kalamata olives, pitted and sliced in half vertically

¼ cup salt-packed capers, soaked in water and drained

¼ cup chopped parsley

Olive oil

Kosher salt

Slice the bread into 1-inch-thick slices and lay the slices on a cookie sheet.

Place in a cold oven and turn up the heat to 350°F, allowing the bread to come up to temperature along with the oven. Bake until the bread is just golden, flipping the bread over after 10 minutes so it toasts evenly. Be patient: it might take a little while (anywhere from 10 to 20 minutes, depending on how quickly the oven heats).

Allow the bread to cool so you can handle it. Then rub each piece with some garlic.

With your hands, break the bread into 1-inch chunks into a large bowl. In a separate bowl, dilute the ⅓ cup of balsamic vinegar with ⅔ cup cold water, stirring to combine. Drizzle the balsamic mixture over the bread, stirring the bread as you do that so all the pieces get evenly coated.

Add the tuna, tomatoes, olives, capers, and parsley to the bowl with the bread. Add a good glug of olive oil and a sprinkling of salt and stir. Taste the salad and, inevitably, you'll need to adjust it. Add more salt, balsamic, and/or oil until it tastes fantastic.

You can serve it right away or allow it to sit at room temperature for an hour or two (this gives time for the flavors to develop).

● Press down while you do this, so the rough bread exterior breaks down the garlic as you rub it. You get more garlic flavor that way.

Chilaquiles

Serves 4

¡Dios mio! How did I live so long without this recipe? A neophyte to Mexican cooking, I was intimidated, at first, about making this dish of tortillas cooked in a sauce made of poblano chilies (charred over a gas flame) and tomatillos (simmered with water until tender). But those chilies and tomatillos blend up quickly in a blender with an onion and cilantro, and suddenly you have this bright, acidic, subtly spicy base that gets sucked up by the crispy tortillas. Spoon it onto a plate, top it with a fried egg or two, onions, more cilantro, and sour cream, and you have a breakfast that is *muy bueno.*

FOR THE TOMATILLO SALSA

½ pound tomatillos, papery husks removed, washed

3 poblano chilies

3 tablespoons chopped cilantro or epazote

½ onion, chopped

Kosher salt

1 tablespoon olive oil

Several handfuls of the best corn tortilla chips you can find

4 eggs, fried

1 radish, sliced (optional)

½ red onion, chopped

¼ cup cilantro, chopped

4 ounces queso fresco or cotija cheese, grated

¼ cup sour cream or crema (Mexican sour cream)

• Rodriguez suggests—in fact, insists—that you fry your own tortillas for this recipe. To do so, cut up a bunch of fresh corn tortillas (look for "*tortillas de nixtamale,*" which means they're made with corn and not maseca, a genetically modified corn product) into 8 triangles and leave them out to dry for 1 hour. Once dry, add 1 inch vegetable oil to a deep skillet, heat to 350°F, and carefully lower in the tortillas. Fry until crispy but not brown. Use a spider to lift them onto paper-towel-lined plates and sprinkle with lots of salt.

Place the tomatillos in a pot and add just enough cold water to cover. Bring to a boil over high heat, lower to a simmer, and cook just until the tomatillos are soft. Drain.

Meanwhile, using a pair of tongs, char the poblano chilies directly over a gas flame until they are black all over and soft. Use paper towels to remove the skin, then cut in half and remove the seeds.

Place the tomatillos, roasted poblanos, cilantro, onions, and a pinch of salt in a blender and blend until smooth. Taste for salt.

In a large pot, heat the olive oil slightly over medium heat. Add the tomatillo salsa and ½ cup water and bring to a boil. Lower the heat, stir, and allow to reduce slightly.

Add the crispy tortilla pieces and cook over medium heat for a minute or two until the tortillas are soft. Most of the liquid should be absorbed.

• Measure the water using the blender that had the tomatillo salsa in it and pour it directly into the pot. It's a great way to use up what's left in the blender.

Pour the mixture onto a platter and top with the eggs and all of the toppings. Eat it hot.

231

Kevin Davis

**Chef-owner, Steelhead Diner
and Blueacre Seafood
Seattle, Washington**

The steelhead trout is called "the fish of ten thousand casts." According to chef Kevin Davis, who named his first restaurant the Steelhead Diner, to catch steelhead "you have to be out by yourself in nature. You have to know where to be and how to be there and how to present yourself to the fish."

In other words, it takes a certain amount of *intensity* to do it right. And *intense* is the word I'd use to describe Davis's food at both Steelhead and his newer restaurant, Blueacre Seafood. The flavors are big and bold and bright; the three dishes we prepare together are all cooked over very intense heat. Flames shoot out of the pans, they're so hot. As I said: it's intense.

Davis himself comes from a family of intense cooks in New Orleans. Family ritual dictated that each family member had his or her own dish and that they and only they could make it. "My grandmother made chicken stew or okra gumbo, and no one else would make it." His uncle David's signature dish—Pompano David—is one of the dishes we cook, renamed Trout David.

When he was eleven, Davis's mother died. His dad decided that Davis, his brother, and his sister would each cook dinner two nights every week. "It turned out," says Davis, "that by the time I graduated high school, I knew how to cook."

From those inauspicious beginnings, a chef was born.

When we start, he lays a wet rag under his fiberglass cutting board (he uses fiberglass because he can throw it into the dishwasher) to keep it from shifting around. And he does all his chopping, dicing, and mincing with a giant cleaver.

"Whoa," I say when I first see it. "Isn't that dangerous?"

"Not at all," says Davis. "It's an indispensable all-purpose kitchen tool. It's ergonomically designed, it fits right into your hand. It's great for chopping; you can break down chickens with it or fine herbs. In China, they're universal."

He finishes chopping the garlic that's going into the fish marinade, and then adds: "Cleavers make great scrapers, too."

When it comes to prepping fish—some might say it's Davis's forte—he is both aggressive and delicate. He uses a stiff boning knife to cut out the spine of the trout he's prepping. He uses it to cut out the bones, too (he leaves the skin intact), and then uses pliers to pull out the bones he couldn't get the first time around.

That fish will eventually get cooked on the grill while, on two very hot burners, we fry up salt-and-pepper Dungeness crab and, in a different pan, white asparagus with orange and Marcona almonds. The cooking is fiery and fast and the results are big. The whole time, though, Davis is focused and intense—much like I imagine he is when he gets a bite on the line while fishing for steelhead.

In both cases, immediate actions matter; split-second decisions result in either success or failure. Cooking in the moment, like this, can be exhilarating—and the results speak for themselves.

"I could live anywhere there's fishing, wine, and mushrooms."

Trout David

Serves 2

This is a magic trick of a recipe: place a fillet of trout coated in olive oil, shallots, garlic, and herbs in a pan, stick it under a broiler, and a few minutes later you have a perfectly cooked, deeply moist, and flavorful piece of fish ready to serve. Don't let the simplicity fool you. The best part is, you can expand or reduce the recipe based on how many people you're serving and how many trout fillets you can fit under your broiler. You could also use salmon, pompano, or redfish, as long as the fish still has its skin.

- Run your fingers over the fish to make sure there aren't bones; if you find any, use pliers or your fingers to remove them.

- Use any herbs that are in your garden: parsley, tarragon, mint, and so on.

1 large fillet of trout (about ½ pound), skin kept intact

1 shallot, minced

1 clove garlic, minced

Grated zest of 1 lemon, plus lemon wedges for garnish

2 tablespoons chopped fresh oregano, sage, and basil

¼ cup olive oil, plus more if needed

Kosher salt and freshly ground black pepper

Lay the trout on a dish that can go in the broiler, skin side down and flesh side up.

In a small bowl, combine the shallot, garlic, lemon zest, and herbs. Stir in the olive oil to create a kind of runny paste; use more oil if necessary. Season well with salt and pepper.

Rub the herb paste all over the fish and place it in the refrigerator to marinate for 10 minutes.

Heat the broiler and place the fish inside about 1 inch away from the flame. Cook for 5 minutes or so, until the fish is firm on top and bubbles rise up from the herb oil mixture in the middle of the fish: when it's bubbling, it's done.

Serve hot on a platter with lemon wedges.

Salt-and-Pepper Shrimp

Serves 4

The loud sizzle you should hear when you add the shrimp to the pan echoes the loud sizzle you'll feel in your mouth when you eat the finished product: a rollicking Asian-inspired dish of crispy shrimp infused with ginger, fresh herbs, and soy sauce. When Davis makes this at Blueacre Seafood, he uses a fresh, just-boiled Dungeness crab (and if you have crab on hand, by all means, use it here), but I like it best with shrimp. You must serve it with rice to soak up all the delicious sauce.

1 pound large shell-on shrimp, rinsed, deveined, and patted dry

Kosher salt and freshly ground black pepper

1 cup Wondra flour

¼ cup clarified butter (see Kitchen Know-How, page 232)

1 small onion, chopped

1-inch piece of ginger, peeled and minced

1 tablespoon turbinado sugar

5 or 6 whole Thai basil leaves

¼ cup slightly chopped cilantro

¼ to ½ cup soy sauce

Cooked white rice, to serve

● Wondra flour is a barley flour that doesn't get gummy when you sauté it, which is why Davis uses it here.

● This step is key. If you notice the butter starting to brown, that means you haven't clarified it properly and, therefore, won't be able to get it hot enough to really sear the shrimp. If that happens, start again and use canola oil or another oil with a high smoke point (vegetable, grapeseed) instead.

Toss the shrimp in a bowl with lots of salt and pepper and the Wondra flour. Set aside.

In a pan large enough to hold all the shrimp, heat the clarified butter until smoking hot. Tilt the pan away from you so the butter doesn't splash you, and add all the shrimp.

Don't touch the shrimp for the first 30 seconds or so and then peek underneath to see if they're browning. Give them a toss, make a clear spot in the middle of the pan, and add the onions there. Cook for another 30 seconds and add the ginger.

Stir, add another hit of salt and pepper, and add the sugar. Stir again, add the herbs, and toss to combine.

Finally, add the soy sauce. Cook for another 15 seconds and then serve immediately with rice.

Crispy White Asparagus with Orange and Marcona Almonds

Serves 4

Let's be honest: it's hard to get excited about white asparagus. But when it's cooked in a scorching hot pan with olive oil, garlic, and herbs, deglazed with orange juice, and then tossed with orange zest and toasted almonds, you have something to be *very* excited about. The key, as with Davis's shrimp, is to have the pan so hot that the asparagus gets caramelized and brown. This is also a good recipe to practice your flip, that chef-y technique of making food in a pan flip on top of itself like a wave. The key is confidence: forcefully thrust the pan out and up and watch as what's inside comes back toward you. Not only is it impressive, it keeps you from mashing up the asparagus with a spatula.

● Julia Child once advised practicing this flipping technique with dried beans in a rimmed skillet.

● If the white asparagus is especially tough, you may want to peel it.

● If you don't want to spend the money on Marcona almonds (which come from Spain and are sweeter than traditional almonds), you can use regular almonds or almond slivers. Just make sure to toast them first in a dry sauté pan over medium heat, tossing every so often, until brown and fragrant.

3 tablespoons extra virgin olive oil

1 bunch white asparagus, rinsed and patted dry, cut on the bias into 1-inch pieces (discarding any tough woody ends)

Kosher salt and white pepper

3 cloves garlic, sliced

5 whole basil leaves

Juice and zest of 1 orange

½ cup Marcona almonds, toasted and chopped

Finishing salt (such as Maldon sea salt)

In a pan large enough to hold all the asparagus, heat the olive oil on high heat until smoking hot. Tilt the pan away from you and add all the asparagus. Return the pan to high heat and don't move the asparagus for at least 30 seconds. Sprinkle with kosher salt and white pepper.

When the asparagus starts to brown, toss it and clear a hot spot in the middle of the pan. Add the garlic to the hot spot and allow it to cook until the garlic starts to brown. Add the basil and toss or stir.

Add the orange juice and another sprinkling of kosher salt. Wait for the asparagus to absorb the orange juice and the olive oil (taste one to see if it's tender enough to continue; if not, keep cooking until it is). When everything's absorbed and the asparagus is tender, add the orange zest and toasted Marcona almonds.

Pour onto a platter and sprinkle with finishing salt. Serve immediately.

Asha Gomez

Creator, Spice Route Supper Club; and chef, Cardamom Hill
Atlanta, Georgia

The sights, smells, and sounds in Asha Gomez's kitchen are so alluring, so mouth-watering, that when we finally sit down at the table to eat with her husband, Bobby, and her friend Bill, it takes me a moment to notice that there isn't any silverware.

"Utensils aren't big in Kerala," explains Gomez. "We eat with our hands."

When she sees my worried look she adds, "It makes the food taste better."

Let's rewind for a moment. Gomez is the proprietor of the Spice Route Supper Club, a tribute to the region where she and her husband are from: Kerala, a state in southwest India. When Gomez talks about Kerala, her big blue eyes light up. "The Arabian Sea is on one side, the Indian Ocean is on the other side. Everything there is lush and vibrant."

That includes the food, which Gomez re-creates with passion, inspired by her memories of the communal home where she grew up with her mother and her mother's sisters, who would prepare breakfast, lunch, tea, and dinner day in, day out.

"There was magic in that kitchen," says Gomez as she begins prepping the ingredients for the first dish she's going to teach me, Beef Ularthiyathu.

Magic implies fantasy, but the food Gomez makes is very real. She uses only fresh curry leaves, which she calls irreplaceable. "Curry leaves and curry powder have nothing in common," she tells me. "In India, we don't have curry powder. It doesn't exist."

As Gomez drags her fingers along the length of a curry stem, dropping the leaves into hot oil, the fragrance begins to fill the room, and Gomez tells me, "That's the smell of Kerala."

The senses have always been important to Gomez, who for years ran an ayurvedic spa in Atlanta. After massaging her clients, she would ask them if they were hungry (her apartment was right next door, so she always had food handy). It got to the point where clients would call to ask what Gomez was cooking that day before making their appointments. This pleased Gomez, who saw food as a natural extension of her job: "Food culminated the experience beautifully. We nourished their bodies."

In addition to touch, smell, and taste, the visual is important to Gomez. "I like things to be beautiful," she tells me. Her plates are all white and she uses different shapes for different dishes. When she makes her thoren, a stir-fry of carrots and green beans, she doesn't add turmeric because she doesn't want it to turn yellow.

At last, the food is cooked—in addition to the beef and the thoren, there's yogurt rice—and we're at the table, about to eat with our hands.

Bobby shows me how to compact the rice into a patty that can then be used to scoop up the beef and the thoren. At first, I must confess, I'm wishing I had a fork. But eventually, I get the hang of it: I scoop some rice, beef, and vegetables, and as the food travels from my fingers into my mouth, there's nothing getting in the way. This is what it means to be connected to your food—something that only happens when you engage all your senses, which is an easy feat in Asha Gomez's kitchen.

"It's all about connecting to your food."

Chai Tea

Serves 2

Upon my arrival at Gomez's home, she immediately offered me a glass of chai tea, which she poured from a beautiful silver tea service. The secret to a good chai (which means "tea" in Hindi; therefore "chai tea" is "tea tea") is very simple: you have to buy whole cardamom pods. It's their pure flavor and their flavor alone that makes chai taste like chai. Once you buy them (and they'll last for a while), you can use them to flavor other things too, such as oatmeal.

1 cup whole milk	4 tea bags of black Darjeeling tea
1 cup water	¼ cup honey, plus more to taste
8 cardamom pods, crushed	Freshly grated nutmeg

I like a strong cardamom flavor. If it's too intense for you, try using 4 to 6 crushed pods.

In a small pot, combine the milk, water, and cardamom. Heat over a low flame and simmer, gently, for several minutes until the liquid is infused with the cardamom.

Add the tea bags, bring to a boil, and then turn off the heat. Let the tea steep for several more minutes.

Strain the tea into mugs and add honey to taste. Grate fresh nutmeg on top and serve.

Beef Ularthiyathu

Serves 4

"It's our beef bourguignon," Gomez said about this dish when we first made it together. Yet there's a lot more going on here than with a traditional beef stew: you have the subtle perfume of the fresh curry leaves; the powerful punch of ginger, garlic, and chilies; and the nuanced shadings of the coriander, garam masala, and turmeric. When you first add the beef to the pan, it may all look a bit dry, but put the lid on and 5 to 10 minutes later you'll lift it to discover lots of liquid: the meat gets braised in its own juices. Serve with the yogurt rice (page 245) and thoren (page 242), and make sure to eat it with your hands!

2 tablespoons olive oil

2 tablespoons coconut oil, plus 2 more tablespoons for later

2 stems of fresh curry leaves (see Resources, page 371)

1 red onion, sliced along the length of the onion

Kosher salt

1 thick 2-inch-long piece of ginger, peeled and grated (¼ to ½ cup grated ginger)

6 cloves garlic

3 dried red chilies

½ large red tomato, sliced

1 heaping teaspoon mild cayenne pepper

2 heaping teaspoons ground coriander

1 heaping teaspoon garam masala (see Resources)

¼ teaspoon ground turmeric

3 pounds top round beef, cubed, rinsed and patted dry

There's really no substitute for this. If you can't find fresh curry leaves, leave them out; do not, by any means, use curry powder. It's not the same.

Sometimes you can find this labeled as "stewing beef." Cut into 1-inch cubes.

Place both oils in a large skillet and turn the heat to medium. When the oil is hot, stem the curry leaves right into the oil and add the stems too. Cook (they should sizzle) until they start to brown, 30 seconds to 1 minute.

Add the onions and a pinch of salt and cook until the onions soften, 2 to 3 more minutes. Then add the ginger, garlic, dried red chilies, and tomato. Season again and stir, then add the cayenne, coriander, garam masala, and turmeric. Taste and adjust; you may want to add more cayenne for color and heat. Cook for another 2 minutes, just until the tomato begins to release its juices.

Add the beef and turn up the heat. Stir until the beef is well coated and the liquid comes to a boil. Cover the pan, lower the heat to a simmer, and cook for 45 minutes to 1 hour.

Taste the beef: it should be tender. If not, keep cooking. When it's finished, turn up the heat to high and scrape up the brown bits from the bottom of the pan, incorporating them into the beef and the pan sauce. Add the final 2 tablespoons of coconut oil, stir, and serve immediately.

At this point, you can set the pan aside, leave it covered, and allow the flavors to develop before you serve it an hour or two later. You could even make it a day ahead, refrigerate it, and reheat it the next day.

Thoren with Carrots and Green Beans

Serves 4

When you don't have a frame of reference for a recipe, it can seem very exotic and even scary. That's how I felt about thoren—an unexpected combination of green beans, carrots, garlic, cumin seeds, and shredded coconut—until I made it and served it on a plate next to Gomez's beef and yogurt rice. In that context, suddenly its role on the plate became very clear; thoren is the "peas and carrots" portion of an Indian square meal! Except this recipe will flip any memory you have of waterlogged frozen peas and carrots on its head. Here everything is bright, flavorful, punchy, and crunchy too—peas and carrots with pizzazz.

3 big cloves garlic, peeled

1 teaspoon cumin seeds

½ cup shredded coconut (from the refrigerated section, not sweetened)

1 finger chili, sliced

2 tablespoons olive oil

2 tablespoons coconut oil

1 teaspoon mustard seeds

1 stem of curry leaves (see Resources, page 371)

15 long green beans (you can use haricots verts), stems discarded, chopped into ¼-inch pieces

3 large carrots, peeled and chopped the same size as the green beans

Kosher salt

● A finger chili is a long light-green chili you can find at ethnic markets. If you can't find it, you can substitute another chili here, such as a jalapeño.

With a mortar and pestle, pound together the garlic and cumin seeds. Add the coconut and the chili and continue to work until everything is relatively blended, though not mashed to pieces.

In a large skillet, heat the oils over high heat. Add the mustard seeds and wait for them to start popping. When they do, strip all the curry leaves from the stem into the oil and then add the stem too. Add the green beans and carrots and a big pinch of salt and stir.

● When you do this, you may want to step back. Those curry leaves can splatter.

Add the garlic mixture and stir. Add a pinch more salt and cook just until everything is flavored but the vegetables are still crunchy. The only way to know if the thoren has the texture you like is to taste it. Adjust for salt and serve it up.

Yogurt
Rice

Serves 4

Rice, by itself, is normally a vehicle for something else. Not so here, where rice is cooked, fluffed, and then added to a pan of olive oil, mustard seeds, curry leaves, and yogurt. Suddenly the rice is a perfumed, slightly sour event all on its own; and as a vehicle, it's a moist, tangy foil to the spicy beef it's meant to accompany. You can serve it hot right when you make it or serve it later at room temperature.

1 cup basmati rice

2 cups water

Kosher salt

3 tablespoons olive oil

1 tablespoon mustard seeds

**1 stem of curry leaves
(see note on page 241)**

1 cup plain yogurt

● You can make the rice ahead and refrigerate it until you're ready to make the yogurt rice.

In a large pot with a lid, add the rice to the water with a pinch of salt. Bring to a boil over high heat, lower the heat, and simmer, covered, for 12 minutes on the lowest flame.

Remove from the heat and fluff the rice with a fork.

Heat the olive oil in a large skillet until hot, and then add the mustard seeds and curry leaves, gliding them off the stem, and the stem itself.

When the seeds start popping, add the yogurt and turn off the heat. Remove the stem, add all of the rice, stir, and either serve right away or allow it to come to room temperature and serve. It's best to eat this the same day that you make it.

Chuy Valencia

Chef, Chilam Balam
Chicago, Illinois

Like most twenty-four-year-olds, chef Chuy Valencia is a scattered whirlwind of energy, impulsive (he got a skull tattooed on his neck the day that I cooked with him) and ever-so-slightly distracted. ("Shit," he says when my photographer and I arrive; he forgot we were coming.)

Unlike most twenty-four-year-olds, Valencia is the chef and part-owner of a restaurant, Chilam Balam in Chicago. When he gets behind the stove, he is as focused, knowledgeable, and driven as chefs twice his age.

When I first walk into his kitchen, Valencia is busy making a guajillo chili sauce, a sauce he takes pride in.

"Bitter's an underappreciated flavor," he explains to me as he gathers cinnamon sticks, dried Mexican oregano leaves, and whole black peppercorns onto a metal plate. He then takes a blowtorch and sprays them all with fire until they light up and fill the air with a charry, outdoorsy smell. He blends the mixture in a blender with chicken stock, strains it, and adds it to a guajillo chili puree.

When the sauce is done, he tastes it and adjusts it with sugar. ("It's a little rough," he says when he first tries it.) To showcase it for me, he grills up a chili-marinated flank steak and pours the sauce on top. He also makes a fast ceviche with Hawaiian blue marlin that he's marinated in lime juice for forty-five minutes.

These are both great, but Valencia's crowning achievement is his tamale. I confess to him early on that I've never really had a tamale (there wasn't a lot of great Mexican food where I grew up). Valencia makes his from memory: he starts with duck fat in a KitchenAid mixer, though he says you can also use lard.

He mixes it until it's creamy and foamy and then adds a spoonful and a half of baking powder and fresh masa ("Corn that's been nixtamalized," he explains) in a ratio of five parts masa to one part fat. He tests the resulting mixture to see if it's buoyant in a glass of water; when it floats, he knows he has it right.

We stuff the filling into corn husks and then we add chicken in a tomatillo sauce that we made earlier. He teaches me how to seal everything and how to place it in the steamer. The resulting tamale—which comes out hot and steamy thirty minutes later, and which he tops with tomatillo sauce, sour cream, queso fresco, cilantro, and radishes—is wildly delicious. "The problem now," he says sincerely, "is that if this is your first tamale, it'll spoil you for all others."

Valencia's hubris is matched in equal measure by his boyishness. While we're cooking, he gets a text from one of his suppliers, who saw Valencia's Facebook status update about drinking too much. The supplier wrote: "Slow down, Chuy."

This riles Valencia up. "I thoroughly enjoy drinking!" he announces to me and his sous-chef.

Then he sees me and my notepad and asks: "Are you writing this down?"

I nod.

"Oh God, my mom's going to kill me."

"If you can't find duck fat or lard, move from wherever you're living."

CUAJILLO SAUCE 8/9

Tomatillo Chicken Tamales

Serves 4

Forgive me, you who like shortcuts; I'm about to be uncompromising. To make extraordinary tamales at home, you're going to have to track down an ingredient that's hard to come by. The search took me all the way to the Corona neighborhood in Queens, New York—47th Avenue and 104th Street, to be exact—to a place called Tortilleria Nixtamal. That ingredient is fresh corn masa, as essential for authentic tamales as matzoh meal is for authentic matzoh ball soup. Can you make these tamales with masa that you find in the store? Yes, you can, but you'll miss out on the purity and unique texture that makes them so notably good. So do yourself a favor and find out where you can buy some fresh corn masa in your own neighborhood.

FOR THE HUSKS

8 dried corn husks, plus more for any leftover filling

FOR THE CHICKEN

8 chicken thighs, bone in, skin removed

1 onion, quartered

1 bay leaf

A pinch of kosher salt

FOR THE TOMATILLO SAUCE

12 medium tomatillos (or 3 cups small), stems and papery husks removed, rinsed and patted dry

A splash of vegetable oil

1 white onion, chopped

Kosher salt

1 or 2 habaneros, chopped (depending on how spicy you like it)

FOR THE TAMALES

4 cups fresh corn masa, ground for tamales

¾ cup duck fat or pork fat

2 tablespoons baking powder

A few pinches of kosher salt

FOR THE GARNISH

Sour cream (optional)

Habanero sauce (see Resources, page 371; optional)

Queso fresco (optional)

Cilantro leaves (optional)

1 radish, sliced thin (optional)

If you're pressed for time, you can also use the meat from a store-bought rotisserie chicken.

The night before you want to make this, place the corn husks in a lidded container and cover with hot water. Allow to soak overnight at room temperature.

To prepare the chicken, place the chicken thighs in a wide pot or Dutch oven with the onions, bay leaf, and salt and cover with cold water by 1 inch. Bring to a simmer, half-cover, and cook for 1 hour, or until the chicken comes apart easily with a fork. Remove the chicken to a plate, and when it's cool enough to handle, shred the meat. Discard the bay leaf.

Don't throw away the liquid; you've just made a very decent chicken stock. You can refrigerate it or freeze it for a later use.

continued

Tomatillo Chicken Tamales (continued)

To make the tomatillo sauce, heat the broiler. Place the tomatillos in a cast-iron skillet and put the skillet under the broiler. Broil until the tomatillos begin to char, and then flip them upside down and char the other side. Continue doing this for approximately 20 minutes, until the tomatillos are very soft and charred all over, then place in a blender and mix.

In a large skillet over medium heat, heat the vegetable oil until hot and cook the onions with a pinch of salt until soft. Add the habanero and continue to cook until it softens, then add the blended tomatillos. Simmer the sauce, with another pinch of salt, until slightly reduced, about 10 minutes. Taste for seasoning and then add the reserved chicken. Taste one more time for seasoning and set aside.

Now it's time to make the tamales. Set up a steamer and bring water to a simmer. Meanwhile, in a stand mixer with the whisk attachment, mix the masa and the fat together on high speed until the fat has worked itself into the masa and a smooth mixture has formed. Mix in the baking powder and salt.

To assemble the tamales, tear off a strip of the soaked corn husk (you'll use this to tie the tamale up in a moment). Lay the corn husk flat in your hand with the wide side to your left and the narrow side to your right. Spoon a layer of the masa mixture onto the husk, pressing it flat and keeping it more to the left side than the right. Top the masa with some of the tomatillo chicken mixture and then fold in the two sides and then the end, tying it all up with the reserved strip. Set aside and continue making tamales until you've used up all the masa, the chicken, and the corn husks.

Place the tamales in the steamer basket, cover with a lid, and steam for 20 minutes, or until the masa mixture is cooked and set (you should be able to see through the open end). To serve, open the tamales and, if desired, garnish with a zigzag line of sour cream. Top with habanero sauce, queso fresco, cilantro, and sliced radish, to taste.

Place sour cream in a squeeze bottle, add a splash of water, and shake gently to thin it out slightly.

Ceviche

Serves 4

Refreshing is the word that comes to mind when I think of this ceviche, a cooling, citrusy combination of fish, lime juice, onion, tomato, and cilantro. The balance of fish, vegetables, oil, salt, pepper, and hot sauce is entirely up to you and your preferences. Like it hot? Go heavy on the hot sauce. Like it a bit sweeter? Add a pinch of sugar. Just be sure to time it so the fish only marinates for the requisite forty-five minutes; if it sits too long in the acid, the fish will turn mealy. Serve with good tortilla chips and a cold Mexican beer.

- Other firm white fish, such as tilapia, work well here too.

- Some limes are juicier than others; don't worry if you don't get the full amount of juice. Take what you have, pour it over the fish, and stir it every 10 minutes or so.

- Valencia uses heirloom tomatoes that he buys at the farmer's market.

- He recommends the Yucateco brand of habanero sauce (see Resources, page 371).

1 pound **Hawaiian blue marlin, mahimahi, or halibut,** filleted by the fishmonger, cut into ½-inch cubes

1 to 2 cups fresh lime juice (enough to cover the fish; about 8 limes)

1 English cucumber, peeled, seeded, and diced

1 **tomato,** diced

½ red onion, diced

¼ cup chopped cilantro

A few hits of bottled **habanero sauce**

A pinch of Mexican oregano

Kosher salt and freshly ground black pepper

A splash of olive oil

Sugar (optional)

In a medium bowl, marinate the fish in the lime juice for 45 minutes.

Strain the fish and toss in a bowl with all of the other ingredients to taste. If it's too acidic, add a pinch of sugar. Serve by itself or with tortilla chips for scooping.

Flank Steak with Guajillo Chili Sauce

Serves 4

This dish was a revelation for me, especially since I'd never used dried chilies before. Who knew that simply soaking dark red and black guajillo and ancho chilies in hot water would reconstitute them so quickly? They mix up effortlessly in the blender, producing a fantastic base for both a marinade and a sauce. There are so many fascinating touches in this recipe—garlic cloves still in their skins toasted in a skillet, a whole cinnamon stick browned until fragrant and then blended with chicken stock—that by the time you eat everything together, you'll marvel at how dynamic and layered a dish it is, a smoky, soulful pairing of sauce and meat. Start the marinade a day ahead for maximum flavor.

FOR THE MARINADE

4 dried guajillo chilies

4 dried ancho chilies

4 cloves garlic, still in their skins

½ cinnamon stick

A pinch of cumin seeds

A pinch of dried Mexican oregano

A splash of apple cider vinegar

Kosher salt and freshly ground black pepper

4 flank steaks (6 to 8 ounces per person)

FOR THE SAUCE

1 (8-ounce) package guajillo chiles

8 cloves garlic, still in their skins

Vegetable or grapeseed oil

1 quart chicken stock

Kosher salt

1 white onion, sliced into half-moons

½ cinnamon stick

1 teaspoon whole black peppercorns

1 teaspoon dried Mexican oregano

A pinch of sugar (optional)

The night before or at least a few hours before you plan to serve this, marinate the steaks. To make the marinade, start by soaking the chilies in hot tap water for 30 minutes to an hour until they're rehydrated and mostly soft. Meanwhile, place the whole garlic cloves in their skins in a dry cast-iron skillet and turn the heat to medium. Slowly toast the garlic cloves, lowering the heat slightly and shaking the pan every so often, until they're slightly charred on the outside and begin to turn golden on the inside (it's okay if there are a few charry spots on the inside too). When a knife goes through the garlic easily, remove from the skillet, discard the skins, and add the garlic to a blender. Cut the stems off the softened chilies, slice them in half vertically, remove the seeds and membranes, and add them to the blender too. Finally, throw the cinnamon stick, cumin seeds, and oregano into the same skillet in which you toasted the garlic (no need to clean it). Cook quickly until they're fragrant—you don't want the seeds or the oregano to burn—and add them to the blender. Add a good splash of cider vinegar, a big pinch of salt, and a few grinds of pepper and blend. Taste! It should be very flavorful; if not, adjust with more salt and vinegar.

Place the steaks in a resealable plastic bag, pour in the marinade, and seal. Turn the bag a few times so the marinade distributes evenly. Place on a platter and refrigerate until an hour or two before you plan to cook them, then allow the steaks to come to room temperature.

To make the sauce, once again soak the guajillos until they're soft, about 30 minutes. Also, toast the garlic as you did for the marinade and, once toasted, discard the skins and set the garlic aside. When the chilies are soft, remove the stems, seeds, and membranes and add them to a blender with enough hot water to make a thick puree. Strain the puree into a separate bowl.

In a large skillet (don't use nonstick), heat a splash of oil on medium heat and then add a ladleful of the guajillo puree. Toast it until it begins to change color, then push it aside and add another ladleful of puree to the hot oil, adding more oil as necessary. Keep doing this until you've toasted the entire batch, being careful that the already cooked puree doesn't get too dark. When the whole puree has been toasted, add enough chicken stock to thin everything out and to start making a sauce. Add a big pinch of salt.

In a separate pan, heat another splash of oil over medium-high heat. When it's nice and hot, add the onions and cook quickly to caramelize them to a light golden color. Add the onions to the blender along with the garlic. Place the cinnamon stick, black peppercorns, and oregano in the cast-iron skillet in which you toasted the garlic and heat them until fragrant, 2 minutes or so; add them to the blender. Add about 1 cup chicken stock and blend until you get a smooth puree.

● This isn't a slow caramelization like you'd do for French onion soup; it's a fast caramelization.

Strain the puree into the guajillo chili sauce and stir, tasting and adjusting the salt. Allow this to simmer for 30 minutes over low heat, during which time the flavor will continue to develop.

When the sauce is ready, cook the steaks. Remove the steaks from the plastic bag, scraping off most of the marinade (no need to be meticulous about this), and heat a cast-iron skillet over very high heat. Sprinkle the steaks with a little more salt and add a splash of vegetable oil to the skillet. Sear the steaks, two at a time, on both sides until crusty and cooked to your preference (about a minute on each side for medium rare). Serve immediately with a big ladleful of the warm guajillo chili sauce on top.

● Because flank steaks are so thin, you can't really tell by touching if they're cooked properly. The best way to know for sure is just to cut right into the middle of a piece while it's still in the skillet.

Tom Douglas

**Chef-owner, Dahlia Lounge, Palace Kitchen,
Etta's, and nine other restaurants;
and cookbook author
Seattle, Washington**

Douglas's Kitchen Know-How

ALWAYS KEEP a rack of lamb in the freezer. Throw it into the refrigerator the night before you want to cook it and the next day let it come to room temperature, pat it very dry, and proceed with the lamb recipe on page 261. An elegant dinner is just a hot pan away.

COOKING RICH FOOD is easy: butter, olive oil, and bacon fat can't help but make food taste good, but they're cheats. So pull back when you can without compromising the overall taste: use vinegar and other acids instead of fats to pump up the flavor. Use salt smartly too.

IT'S DIFFICULT to get raw spinach leaves dressed properly because they're somewhat waxy and the dressing doesn't cling. Therefore, when making a raw spinach salad, use more dressing than you normally would.

On a typical night in Seattle, twelve hundred people eat at a Tom Douglas restaurant. This is not an accident. The man who may very well be Seattle's most famous chef ("You're cooking with Tom Douglas?!" was the awed reaction I'd get in the days leading up to my meeting him at Palace Kitchen) is a consummate businessman. "I'm as motivated by the business side of things as I am by the food side," he told me at the beginning of our time together.

It's rare to meet a chef so candid about his or her motivations. Most chefs these days prefer to think of themselves as tortured artists, hoping that their single scallop with truffle foam puts them on the level of a Picasso while simultaneously charging you thirty-two dollars. Douglas has no patience for this. "My taste gets simpler by the day. I don't need to go to a three-star Michelin restaurant ever again."

Yet make no mistake: Douglas takes his food seriously. He just doesn't put his ego before customer satisfaction; he wants to make people happy. And as we cook several dishes together, there's no doubt that the food we're cooking is the kind of food that puts smiles on faces and butts in chairs.

For example, the crab cake. Douglas recalls that when he moved to Seattle in 1977 from Delaware, "There wasn't one crab cake on one menu in this whole town." Celebrating one of Seattle's most precious ingredients—the Dungeness crab—Douglas handles the crab delicately. "You don't want to bust up the expensive parts," he explains as he feels for shell and adds the fresh meat to a bowl of mayonnaise, mustard, lemon zest and juice, salt, and Aleppo pepper.

As he fries up the cakes (after dipping them in panko bread crumbs), he explains that his restaurants are successful because they are so of their place. "We want you to know, when you eat here, that you're in the city of Seattle. No one else can do what we do here." Douglas serves up that Dungeness crab cake with wedges of lemon ("You want something acidic," he explains) and hands me a fork. One bite and I'm convinced.

The food that Douglas cooks is instantly familiar. Like the spinach salad he makes with bacon, pear, grapes, and curried cashews. That last bit, the curried cashews, shows his attention to detail. The red onion he adds shows his deference to customers: "I don't like it, but most people do."

For the big finale, he sautés lamb chops coated in his signature spice rub (which he sells online) and serves them with a celeriac-potato gratin plus some Brussels sprouts and mushrooms. "Think taste, think texture, think temperature," he tells me. "The creamy gratin, the chewy lamb chop, the crunchy Brussels sprouts and mushrooms."

Douglas may not consider it a work of art, but twelve hundred customers a night can't be wrong: he knows how to feed people well.

"I don't like to use a knife that's smaller than I am."

Spinach Salad with Pear, Curried Cashews, and Bacon

Serves 2 to 4

This is a salad of champions, a big plate of *stuff*—spinach, frisée, radicchio, red onion, pear, grapes, and homemade curried cashews—dressed in a comforting honey mustard dressing. To seal the deal, you sprinkle everything with freshly rendered bacon, crisp and hot from the pan. Pay attention to the visual here; you want to create a nice balance of red from the radicchio, green from the spinach, and then frizzy, tangly bits of frisée. Served with some bread, this could be a satisfying, filling, relatively nutritious (let's ignore the bacon) weeknight dinner.

> Douglas prefers using a combination of the outside leaves, which are bitter, and the inside leaves, which are less bitter, to using the whole thing.

FOR THE CURRIED CASHEWS

2 tablespoons unsalted butter

1 teaspoon chopped rosemary

1 teaspoon curry powder

¼ teaspoon cayenne pepper

1 tablespoon dark brown sugar

½ teaspoon kosher salt

¾ cup raw cashews

FOR THE DRESSING

2 tablespoons Dijon mustard

1 clove garlic, smashed and chopped

1 tablespoon honey

¼ cup white wine vinegar

1 tablespoon toasted sesame seeds (optional)

Kosher salt and freshly ground black pepper

¾ to 1 cup olive oil or canola oil or a combination of both (depending on how much it needs)

FOR THE SALAD

¼ pound slab bacon, cut into lardoons

Outside and inside leaves from 1 head of frisée, cut into bite-size pieces

½ head of radicchio, sliced into strips

1 cup fresh spinach leaves

¼ red onion, sliced thin (optional)

1 ripe Bosc pear, cut into wedges

A few seedless red grapes

Preheat the oven to 350°F.

Make the curried cashews: In a small ovenproof pan, melt the butter on medium heat and add the rosemary, curry powder, cayenne pepper, brown sugar, and salt. When it all melts together, add the cashews and give them a toss. Cook for a minute on the stovetop and then place the pan in the oven. Roast, stirring occasionally, until the cashews are a deep toasted color, glossy, and caramelized, about 10 minutes. Remove the cashews to a plate to cool.

In a bowl, whisk together the mustard, garlic, honey, vinegar, sesame seeds, and a pinch of salt and pepper. Slowly add the oil as you continue to whisk until it forms an emulsified dressing. Taste for balance.

Place the lardoons in a cold, dry skillet, turn the heat on to medium, and cook until the fat is rendered and the bacon is a deep golden brown, about 7 minutes. You may want to add a splash of oil to help it along. Drain the bacon on paper towels.

In a separate bowl, combine the frisée, radicchio, spinach, and, if you like it in your salad, the red onion. Add enough dressing to coat everything and taste to make sure you have enough.

Put the salad mixture on plates and garnish with the pear, grapes, and curried cashews; you may also want to spoon more dressing on top. Garnish each plate with spoonfuls of the hot bacon and serve right away.

Crab Cakes with Lemon and Dill

Makes 4 cakes

Even though it's an oft-touted item on restaurant menus, very little goes into making a good crab cake. It's simply a matter of making a flavorful mayonnaise-based sauce to flavor the crab, using the freshest crab you can get, and treating the crab gently as you combine it. Douglas doesn't serve his crab cake with tartar sauce or any other mayo-based sauce because there's already so much in the cake itself; instead, he recommends any acidic accent, such as tomatillo salsa, salsa verde, or, as suggested here, just lemon wedges and dill.

"If it's mock crab from the unrefrigerated section of your supermarket, don't make crab cakes," says Douglas.

To cook crabs yourself, only use crabs that are still alive. Fill the biggest pot you have (preferably a stockpot) with a few gallons of water, add sliced lemons, bay leaves, and a few tablespoons salt, and bring to a boil. Drop in the crabs, cover, and cook for 5 to 10 minutes for blue crabs and for 12 to 20 minutes for Dungeness crabs, until the shells are bright red. Remove the crabs to the sink and rinse with cold water.

You can use store-bought (I like Hellmann's) or, if you want to make your own, Tom Douglas recommends making an olive oil–based mayo; Bobby Hellen's recipe (see page 42) would work well here.

The fat really doesn't matter so much here. Clarified butter is ideal because you can get it really hot for a nice sear while also getting the flavor of butter; but regular butter or oil works well too.

2 cups fresh crabmeat, from either Dungeness or blue crabs, cooked and shelled

½ cup Dijon mustard (Maille is a good brand to use)

½ cup mayonnaise

A big pinch of Aleppo pepper (see Clark's Kitchen Know-How, page 94)

¼ cup chopped chives

1 whole egg

1 egg yolk

Zest and juice of 1 lemon, plus 1 lemon cut into wedges

A pinch of kosher salt (optional)

2 cups panko bread crumbs

Clarified butter (see Davis's Kitchen Know-How, page 232), regular, unsalted butter, or canola oil (enough to coat your pan)

¼ cup chopped fresh dill

Begin by squeezing any excess moisture out of the crabmeat (do this as gently as you can). Then, with your fingers, feel for shell as you place the crabmeat into a bowl without breaking it up. You want nice chunks of crab.

In a large bowl, combine the mustard, mayo, Aleppo pepper, chives, egg, egg yolk, lemon zest, and lemon juice with a big rubber spatula. Taste the crabmeat at this point: if it was cooked in a salty brine, you won't need to add salt to the dish. If the crab isn't particularly salty, though, add some salt to the mayo mixture. Taste for seasoning.

Add three quarters of the mayo mixture to the crabmeat and stir gently to combine. You want a good ratio of crab to mayo; if it looks too dry, add more mayo mixture.

Pour the panko bread crumbs into a shallow pie plate. Gently shape the crab into medium-size patties, coat each patty with the panko, and remove to a plate. Continue until you run out of crab.

continued

Crab Cakes
with Lemon
and Dill (continued)

● If the crab cakes do fall apart, that means you did something right, according to Douglas. "I'd rather have chunks of meat flaking apart than a crab paste," he explains.

Refrigerate the crab cakes for 4 hours; this will help them hold together.

Preheat the oven to 350°F.

Heat an ovenproof sauté pan (don't use nonstick) on medium heat. Add butter or a splash of canola oil and, when it's good and hot, add as many crab cakes as you can without crowding the pan or lowering the heat too much.

Cook until golden brown on one side, about 3 minutes, and then flip. Place the pan in the oven and bake for 5 minutes, or until the crab cake is set. If you want to use a thermometer, you know it's done when the crab cake registers 145°F in the middle.

Serve very hot with the fresh dill sprinkled on top and the lemon wedges alongside.

Porcini-Crusted Rack of Lamb with Celeriac-Potato Gratin

Serves 4

Earthiness is the name of the game here. You have the earthy porcini mushrooms, along with smoked paprika and herbes de Provence, that are rubbed on the lamb; then you have the earthy celeriac (or celery root) sliced thin with potatoes and gratinéed with cream, butter, and cheese. This is the kind of dinner you eat in front of a wood-burning fire in the winter.

- You can substitute other root vegetables such as turnips or rutabaga.

- If you can't find rosemary, sage, or thyme, use a single herb or any combination you like.

- If you want to save money and you're only serving yourself or yourself and one other person, ask the butcher to sell you individual chops. Simply coat the chops in the same rub and then, in a very hot cast-iron pan greased with a little vegetable oil, sear the chops on one side, flip them, and finish them in the hot oven along with the gratin. It'll only take a few minutes; use a thermometer to read the temperature of the inside of each chop. (You want it at 120°F for medium rare.)

- It's trendy to get the rack of lamb "frenched"—to have the meat shaved off the bones so it looks prettier—but Douglas is against this. "You lose the best part!" he insists.

- Don't skip this step: it allows the meat to finish cooking.

FOR THE LAMB

½ cup dried porcini mushrooms, ground to a powder in a spice grinder

½ cup smoked paprika

1 teaspoon freshly ground black pepper

2 teaspoons kosher salt

1 tablespoon herbes de Provence

1 rack of lamb, excess fat removed, at room temperature

Vegetable oil

FOR THE GRATIN

2 celeriac (celery roots), peeled and sliced into thin rounds on a mandoline

6 medium Yukon Gold potatoes, sliced into thin rounds on a mandoline

2 tablespoons chopped rosemary

2 tablespoons chopped sage

2 tablespoons chopped thyme

Kosher salt and freshly ground black pepper

½ cup grated Parmesan cheese

½ cup heavy cream

3 tablespoons unsalted butter, cut into cubes

Combine the porcini powder, smoked paprika, pepper, salt, and herbes de Provence in a bowl and then rub it all over the lamb.

Preheat the oven to 475°F.

In a gratin dish or a small ovenproof skillet, make a layer of celeriac and top with a layer of potato. Sprinkle with some of each herb, salt and pepper, and some of the Parmesan and drizzle in a little of the cream. Repeat with another layer of celeriac, potato, herbs, salt, pepper, and Parmesan and continue layering until you've used everything. Pour the rest of the cream on top and dot with the butter. Place the pan in the hot oven and bake until it's deep golden brown on top, 10 to 12 minutes.

Heat another ovenproof skillet on medium heat and add a splash of vegetable oil and the meat. Sear until brown on one side, flip the meat, and place it in the oven. Cook until an instant-read thermometer inserted into the lamb's center reads 120°F for medium rare, 5 to 10 minutes.

Remove to a plate and allow the meat to rest for 15 minutes.

When ready to serve, slice the rack into individual chops and place on a plate with a spoonful of the gratin.

Anne Quatrano

Chef-owner, Bacchanalia, Star Provisions,
Abbatoir, and Floataway Café
Atlanta, Georgia

My question is fairly innocent, as far as questions go: "How do you peel a grape?"

Chef Anne Quatrano is quick with her retort: "With your teeth."

That pretty much captures Quatrano: funny and brusque and slightly glib about what she's doing, which, at this moment, involves garnishing a deconstructed baba au rhum with a dollop of crème fraîche, cinnamon-infused sultanas, and the peeled grapes. The finished dish is a geometric work of art: round plate, rectangular brioche, and those ovoid grapes. In Quatrano's kitchen, you eat with your eyes first.

Which is why she insists that everything—the toasted brioche, the duck that we cook before that—get blotted with paper towels, both out of the pan and after it's sliced. "I refuse to have blood on the plate," she tells me, almost wincing at the thought of bloody duck. (She blots the brioche so it's not greasy.)

The visual extends to how she preps vegetables for a soup. When she makes her pasta fagioli, every ingredient is prepped to highlight its natural beauty. The baby turnips are kept whole, the baby fennel sliced in half, and the Yukon Gold potatoes are scooped with a melon baller to echo the other shapes. When the soup is finished, it's as stunning to behold as it is to eat.

"This is really good," I say as I begin devouring it.

"It *is* really good," Quatrano agrees.

Quatrano started cooking at an early age in Fairfield, Connecticut, because her mother didn't cook at all. "I cooked because I got hungry," she tells me. "And when I got older, I left as soon as I could. I wanted my autonomy."

Her quest for autonomy took her to San Francisco, where she begged for a job at the legendary Zuni Café. She went to cooking school in the mornings and worked at Zuni at night. It was in cooking school that she met her husband and future business partner, Clifford Harrison. They eventually moved to Atlanta to live in a double-wide trailer on a sixty-acre piece of property that her mother owned.

Together, Quatrano and her husband built a house, built a barn, built a fence, and turned the sixty acres into a working farm. In 1992 they opened their first restaurant, Bacchanalia, using the food from the farm to stock their kitchen.

"That's amazing," I say, in awe.

"I'm not sure it's that admirable," Quatrano counters. "There are wonderful farmers here in Atlanta."

The point, though, is that in her quest for autonomy, Quatrano rose to a stature unknown to most working chefs in America. She cooks the food that she loves and presents it in a way that meets her very exacting standards. Still, Quatrano doesn't see it that way: "I'm hugely responsible for lots of people, and that's not an autonomous kind of feeling. Everything I do directly affects them."

Try as I might to convince her that she achieved precisely what she set out to achieve, her unspoken message back to me is clear: Go peel a grape.

"I think food should be visual, don't you?"

Herb-Cured Duck Breast with Baby Turnips and Meyer Lemon

Serves 2

If Melissa Clark's duck breast with grapes (see page 98) is easy enough to be a weeknight dinner staple, this version is slightly fancier. It requires that you make a cure with herbs, salt, and sugar that you rub onto the duck a few hours before you cook it. Because of the sugar, though, you'll have to be careful; when the duck hits the pan, it will brown up quicker and you may not have time to render it all before it starts turning black. The best strategy is to trim the fat down to a quarter inch before you apply the cure. Don't trim too much, though, or you won't get that glorious crisp skin! As for the sauce, the milk might sound strange, but think of it as a lighter version of cream and then you'll get where it's going. The final combination of fiery bronzed duck in a mellow, perfumed herbal broth is an absolute knockout.

- There are a lot of herbs in this dish, which makes sense because Quatrano grows most of her herbs herself at her farm. If you don't have lots of herbs handy, no need to break the bank. Choose one or two that you like and leave the rest out. The recipe will still work very well.

FOR THE DUCK

½ cup sugar

⅓ cup kosher salt

½ cup basil leaves

¼ cup mint leaves

1 tablespoon fresh rosemary

1 teaspoon grated orange zest

1 clove garlic, peeled

1 large duck breast, with the fat trimmed down to ¼ inch and then cut into a crosshatch pattern, being careful not to cut through the flesh of the duck

FOR THE SAUCE

2 tablespoons high-fat unsalted butter, such as Plugra (see Kitchen Know-How, page 262)

½ onion, sliced thin

3 baby fennel, sliced in half, or ¼ large fennel, cored and sliced thin

4 baby turnips, cleaned and peeled with some of the green still attached

Peel and juice of 1 Meyer lemon (use a vegetable peeler to make thin strips of yellow skin)

1 cup chicken stock

¼ cup milk

¼ cup mixture of chopped chervil, parsley, and tarragon

Kosher salt and freshly ground black pepper

Fleur de sel or other finishing salt

Additional chopped chervil, for garnish (optional)

Blend the sugar, kosher salt, basil, mint, rosemary, orange zest, and garlic in a food processor until it's well incorporated. Place the duck in a covered container or a resealable plastic bag and rub it all over with the cure. Cover and refrigerate for 4 hours, but no longer or it will get too salty.

Rinse the cure off the duck completely and then pat it very dry.

To make the sauce, gently melt the butter over medium heat in a medium pot and add the onions. Cook until they start to soften and then add the fennel, turnips, and Meyer lemon peel. Stir, and then add the chicken stock and Meyer lemon juice. Bring to a gentle simmer and let the stock reduce by at least half (this may take 10 to 15 minutes on low heat). Once it has reduced, set aside.

To cook the duck, preheat the oven to 400°F. Get an ovenproof pan (do not use nonstick) very hot over high heat. Add the duck, fat side down, and allow the fat to render, 5 to 10 minutes. Monitor carefully; you don't want the sugar in the duck to burn. If it gets too dark too fast, lower the heat. When it's a beautiful golden brown and almost all the fat has rendered, flip the duck over and cook for a minute on the other side. Place the pan in the oven and roast for 2 to 3 minutes, until a thermometer placed in the center of the duck reads 125°F. Remove the duck to a plate and allow it to rest for at least 5 minutes.

While the duck is resting, finish the sauce. If it's reduced too much, add a bit of water. When the consistency is a bit soupy, add the milk and the herbs and adjust for kosher salt and pepper.

Blot the rested duck dry with paper towels and then slice it thin. Blot one more time with paper towels.

Spoon the sauce (mostly vegetables, a little liquid) into warmed bowls. Top with some of the sliced duck and a little more of the sauce. Sprinkle with fleur de sel and garnish with chervil, if using.

Pasta Fagioli

Serves 4

Think of this soup as more of a concept than a recipe. Quatrano throws in a handful of turnip greens while making hers and says: "This is the idea of a pasta fagioli. Use anything you've got." The garnishes for this soup—the dehydrated olive powder and the sourdough croutons—aren't necessary, but they sure make it great.

½ sourdough boule, crusts removed, cut into small cubes

¼ cup plus 3 tablespoons olive oil

Kosher salt and freshly ground black pepper

¼ cup finely chopped onion

¼ cup finely chopped celery

¼ cup finely chopped carrot

3 cloves garlic, peeled and thinly sliced

4 baby fennel, sliced in half, or ¼ large fennel, cored and sliced into thin strips

4 baby turnips, peeled, or 1 large turnip, peeled and cut into bite-size pieces

½ cup balls of peeled Yukon Gold potato, scooped with a melon baller

4 skinny baby carrots, peeled and quartered

¼ cup cooked cranberry beans (optional)

¼ cup cooked cannellini beans (you can use canned)

4 to 6 cups good-quality chicken stock

½ cup chopped turnip greens (optional)

½ pound elbow-shaped pasta

Crushed red pepper flakes

A sprinkling of kalamata olive powder (optional)

Preheat the oven to 400°F. Toss the cubed sourdough on a rimmed cookie sheet with ¼ cup of the olive oil and some salt and pepper. Bake, tossing every so often, until the croutons are golden on all sides. Remove from the oven and allow to cool.

For the soup, begin by heating the 3 tablespoons of olive oil on medium heat in a large pot, Dutch oven, or *saucier*. Add the onions, celery, and chopped carrot and cook, gently, for a minute. Add the garlic and cook for 30 seconds more. Nothing should brown; it should just soften.

Add the fennel, turnips, potatoes, baby carrots, and beans and stir. Season lightly with salt.

Add the chicken stock and bring the liquid to a boil. Add the turnip greens, if using, and the pasta; lower the heat and simmer until everything is cooked, 10 to 15 minutes. Taste for salt and pepper; for heat, add a pinch of red pepper flakes.

To serve, ladle the soup into bowls and top with the sourdough croutons and a sprinkling of the kalamata olive powder.

You can make the olive powder a few days ahead of the soup. Simply pat dry pitted kalamata olives (about 1 or 2 cups, depending on how much you want) and place them on a parchment-lined rimmed cookie sheet into a 220°F oven. Let them dehydrate for 6 hours, until totally dry to the touch. Once dry, allow them to cool and then grind them in a spice grinder. Store the olive powder in a covered container in the refrigerator.

Baba au Rhum with Grapes and Crème Fraîche

Serves 4

This is not a traditional baba au rhum, so purists, stand back. Instead, this is an elevated French toast infused with a syrup made with a whole orange, white rum, sugar, and a cinnamon stick and garnished with jewel-like golden raisins also infused with another cinnamony syrup. If you cut the brioche the right way—that is, into fat, rectangular spears—your guests won't recognize it as breakfast for dessert. And if you have any brioche left over, you can serve it for breakfast. In either case, this dish will leave you very satisfied.

FOR THE GOLDEN RAISINS

1 cup water

½ cup sugar

1 cinnamon stick

½ cup golden raisins

FOR THE RUM SYRUP

1 cup sugar

½ cup water

1 orange, cut into quarters

1 cinnamon stick

¼ cup white rum

FOR THE CUSTARD

½ cup heavy cream

½ cup milk

¼ cup sugar

1 egg

1 egg yolk

½ teaspoon vanilla extract

FOR THE BABA

4 tablespoons (½ stick) unsalted butter (1 tablespoon for each piece of brioche)

1 loaf of brioche, crusts removed, cut into wide rectangular sticks (about 1-by-1-by-5 inches)

¼ cup crème fraîche or sour cream

A handful of peeled grapes

Lemon mint (optional)

● Don't ask me how to peel them! I'm still trying to figure that out. I suspect you use your fingers or a small paring knife. If flustered, you can just leave them whole or cut them in half.

For the raisins, bring the water, sugar, and cinnamon stick to a boil in a small pan, then reduce the heat and allow to simmer for 3 minutes. Add the golden raisins, cover, and simmer until they're plump and most of the liquid is gone, then set aside.

For the rum syrup, combine the sugar, water, orange, and cinnamon stick in another small pot; bring to a boil, reduce the heat, and simmer for 8 minutes. Add the rum and set aside.

For the custard, in a medium bowl whisk all the ingredients together by hand until smooth. Set aside in the refrigerator until ready to use.

continued

Baba au Rhum
with Grapes and
Crème Fraîche (continued)

To finish the dish, put a sauté pan over medium heat and start melting the butter in it. Depending on the size of the pan and the size of the brioche sticks, you can cook them all at once or in batches. Distribute the butter accordingly.

Soak each piece of brioche in the custard for 1 full second (that's a "one Mississippi" kind of second) and then add to the hot pan. Fry on all sides until deep golden brown (2 to 3 minutes per side).

When the brioche is cooked, pat it dry with paper towels and place it on a serving plate. Spoon rum syrup onto each piece; use enough to soak the bread.

To finish, spoon a small dollop of crème fraîche onto each piece of toasted brioche. Sprinkle the golden raisins on top and garnish with the peeled grapes and the lemon mint, if using. You've got to serve this dish hot.

Hugue Dufour

Chef-owner, M. Wells
Queens, New York

Dufour's Kitchen Know-How

DON'T WASH your cast-iron pans (and especially not with soap!). Instead, wipe out the contents with paper towels and leave them greasy. If there's food stuck to one, you can scrub it with a wet sponge, but the point is that the more grease that's left on the surface, the more naturally nonstick the pan will become.

USE EBAY to find interesting serving vessels. For example, at M. Wells they serve Caesar salad (see recipe, page 273) in a vintage soup tureen that Dufour and his wife, Sarah, found online.

THERE'S NOTHING WRONG with drinking a glass of wine while you cook. "It helps your focus," argues Dufour.

In Spain, on a farm where he was helping slaughter pigs, chef Hugue Dufour encountered a woman who had peculiar ideas about feeding her children breakfast. "You know how when you have liver problem is good to have liver?" he asks me in his thick French accent while drinking a glass of red wine at his runaway success of a gourmet diner, M. Wells. "Well, this lady say, 'If you eat brain, you'll be more intelligent!'"

So every morning this woman would make a tortilla Española for her children using blood sausage (good for the blood, I suppose?) with brains hidden inside to make her kids smart. Which explains why on the counter before us, there's a cooked calf brain sitting on a spiral of blood sausage ready for us to use in Dufour's take on that same dish.

"I've never had brain," I say timidly.

Dufour cuts me off a piece. "Try it," he says and, unsure of how to react, I do.

It's creamy. It tastes vaguely of, well, chicken. Dufour laughs and tells me about a dish he once served called "rabbit oysters." "We took rabbit heads and we poached them for an hour; there's a natural seam that shows up on the skull. We'd cut them open with an oyster knife and serve them like oysters."

Dufour is as creative with animals and animal products as is a vegetarian chef who works exclusively with vegetables. For example, one of the dishes he teaches me is called Bone Marrow and Escargot.

From the butcher, Dufour gets bone marrow sliced vertically, so you get this long bone with the fat marrow inside. He scoops out the marrow with an offset spatula (one of his favorite tools), trying to keep it together in one big piece so that when it cooks, it will stay whole. (If it were in pieces, because it's pure fat, it would all melt.)

Onto the bone he slathers a shallot puree that contains garlic, peppercorns, and good red wine; on top of that, he lines up escargot from a can. He rests the marrow back on top and sprinkles everything with garlic, parsley, and bread crumbs. Into a hot oven it goes and when it comes out, it's impossible to stop eating: fatty, crusty orbs of marrow resting on garlicky, shallot-ensconced snails.

Dufour's meat infatuation started early. When he was eleven, growing up in Canada, his dad gave him a gun and took him hunting and Dufour shot everything in sight. "Squirrels, little birds," he recalls, somewhat solemnly. "It was never easy, though. I remember going home and crying."

Those tears would later inform his career as a chef. "It's like harvesting a carrot," he explains. "If you pick it, you care about preparing it properly. You know you should do something with it. It's the same process."

Which takes us back to that brain in the tortilla. As Dufour lays it in, I think, "This animal died and it's wasteful if we only eat the parts that don't look like animal parts. Using all the parts is the only real way to honor the animal."

And maybe I'm just saying this to further my point, but after eating the calf brain out of the hot pan with the potatoes, eggs, and blood sausage? I felt a tiny bit smarter.

"Spring is beautiful for testicles."

Bone Marrow and Escargot

Serves 6

This recipe begins at the butcher, where you'll buy marrow bones; it takes you to a gourmet shop, where you'll buy escargot in a can. There will be peeled shallots, a bottle of good red wine, and a blastingly hot oven. You'll wind up with one of the most astonishing dishes you'll ever produce in your kitchen.

FOR THE SHALLOT PUREE

10 whole shallots, peeled

1 small carrot, peeled and diced

4 stems of thyme

3 fresh bay leaves or 1 dried

1 teaspoon black peppercorns

1 head of garlic, cloves separated and peeled

1 bottle of good red wine (such as Pinot Noir)

8 tablespoons (1 stick) very cold unsalted butter, cubed

Red wine vinegar

Kosher salt

FOR THE PERSILLADE

2 cloves garlic, chopped

½ bunch of parsley, chopped

1 cup fresh bread crumbs

A pinch of kosher salt

FOR THE REST OF THE DISH

3 marrow bones, sliced in half vertically (ask the butcher to do this; you don't want rings of marrow bone)

One 7½-ounce can of escargot from Burgundy (see Resources, page 371)

Kosher salt

- Marrow bones can be Flintstone-size. Be sure to ask the butcher to cut off the ends to make them more manageable.

- If this is taking longer than you'd like, toward the end you can remove the lid, turn up the heat, and cook until almost all the liquid evaporates.

To make the shallot puree, combine the shallots, carrot, thyme, bay leaves, peppercorns, garlic, and wine in a large pot. Bring to a simmer, cover, and cook for 3 to 4 hours until the liquid is absorbed.

Remove the thyme and bay leaves and, in a food processor, puree the mixture. As it's whirring, slowly add the butter. Add a splash of red wine vinegar and taste to adjust for salt and acid. Set aside.

Make the persillade by combining the garlic, parsley, and bread crumbs in a food processor with a pinch of salt. Pulse just until it all comes together but the bread is still textured. Set aside.

Preheat the oven to 500°F. On a cookie sheet lined with aluminum foil, place the 6 bone marrow halves. With an offset spatula, and trying to keep the marrow intact, scoop out the insides and set aside.

Spread each empty bone half with the shallot puree and line up a few escargot on each bone. Sprinkle the escargot with salt and top with the reserved marrow. Sprinkle the marrow with salt and then sprinkle everything with the persillade–bread crumb mixture until covered.

Bake just until the bread crumbs are brown but before all the marrow has melted, 3 to 5 minutes. Serve right away with some crusty bread.

Smoked Herring Caesar Salad

Serves 2 to 4

What makes this salad so notably great is the smokiness from the herring; it's as if a regular Caesar salad dressing spent some time hanging around the bad kids at school. The Worcestershire also adds another layer of umami to the proceedings; give this a try and chances are, you won't go back to regular Caesar again.

1 fillet of smoked herring (with any bones removed)

1 cup red wine vinegar

2 cloves garlic, chopped

1 egg yolk

⅓ cup grated Parmesan cheese, plus more for later

1 tablespoon Worcestershire sauce

13 turns of black pepper, plus more to taste

1 cup extra virgin olive oil

Kosher salt

3 large heads of romaine lettuce, cleaned and sliced

Sourdough croutons (see page 266)

- This is a measurement based on how many times Dufour rotated his pepper grinder. It's probably about a good teaspoon of freshly ground pepper.

- We skipped this step when Dufour and I made this Caesar together and it tasted great; but he suggests that you do it if you have the time.

- Dufour recommends topping it with so much Parmesan you can no longer see the salad. Though that may be extreme, Sam Sifton, in his *New York Times* review of M. Wells, wrote that the Caesar is "showered in enough Parmesan to qualify as both crazy and just exactly the right amount."

To soften the herring a little, soak it in the red wine vinegar in a shallow plate for a few hours at room temperature before you use it. Discard the vinegar after soaking.

In a food processor, combine the herring, garlic, egg yolk, Parmesan, Worcestershire, and pepper until you have a paste. With the motor running, slowly drizzle in the olive oil until you have an emulsified dressing that looks like an aioli. Taste the dressing for salt and pepper and adjust.

In a large bowl, combine the romaine and the croutons. Add a big spoonful of the dressing and toss, adding more dressing as you see fit. When you're happy with the amount, transfer the salad to a soup tureen (see Kitchen Know-How, page 270) or cold individual salad bowls. Top each with lots of Parmesan grated on a Microplane grater and more freshly ground pepper.

Tortilla Española
with Chorizo

Serves 4

Yes, this recipe was originally taught to me with blood sausage and calf brain, but when I make it at home I apply the same technique to a more common ingredient that I usually have on hand: chorizo. If you want to be brave and try the blood sausage and the brain, the only important step is that you cook them both first (preferably, by poaching). Once cooked, simply sub in the blood sausage for the chorizo and add the calf brain just before you place the tortilla in the oven. Either way, it's a robust, filling breakfast.

3 large Yukon Gold potatoes, peeled and quartered

Kosher salt

½ cup olive oil, plus more for the pan

1 yellow onion, diced

Freshly ground black pepper

6 large eggs

2 to 3 links Spanish chorizo, sliced into fat rings

Prep the potatoes by boiling them in salted water until very tender. Meanwhile, in a sauté pan, heat the ½ cup olive oil slightly on medium-low heat and sweat the onions with a pinch of salt until they are just translucent but not brown, 8 minutes or so. When the potatoes are done, drain them very well and add them to a bowl with the onions and the olive oil from the pan. Mash everything and season with salt and pepper until it tastes great (like olive-oil mashed potatoes).

In a separate medium bowl, crack the eggs and whisk them with salt and pepper until the whites and yolks are homogeneous. Add enough of the potato mixture to achieve a ratio of three quarters potato and one quarter egg.

Preheat the oven to 450°F. Squirt olive oil all around a 10-inch cast-iron pan and heat it on medium heat, then add the chorizo. Cook just until it's slightly crusty, then add the egg-potato mixture. Stir and then allow it to set and cook for 30 seconds or so. The outside should cook to the point that when you shake the pan, the contents shift together. Finish in the oven until the egg mixture is just set on top, 10 to 15 minutes. Serve with crusty bread.

- The drier your potatoes are, the better the chance they won't collapse if you try to flip them out later.

- If you're not squeamish about tasting raw egg, you should taste here for salt and pepper.

- Flipping this out of the pan is risky—depending on how wet it is inside, it may collapse. If you're nervous, use a pie server to serve it out of the pan.

Michael White

Chef-owner, Marea, Osteria Morini, and Ai Fiori
New York, New York

In all caps, chef Michael White is yelling at me.

"IT'S PASTA, ADAM ROBERTS, NOT NOODLES! NOODLES ARE ASIAN!"

We are in the kitchen of White's latest New York City restaurant venture, the much-anticipated Osteria Morini, and the scene feels like something out of an Aaron Sorkin drama. Clusters of chefs congregate around tables in the dining room discussing dishes; groups of manager-types stand near the bar and debate the length of the cocktail stirrers. The excitement in the air is palpable, and White himself has been here at seven a.m. every day testing recipes ("Only one out of every ten makes it onto the final menu," he tells me). The fact that he takes the time out of his day—in the few short days leading up to the opening—to cook with me is nothing short of remarkable. As he leads me in, he says, "Adam Roberts, do you know how lucky you are to be here right now?"

Michael White likes to call me by my full name. Everything he says is both bombastic and slightly tongue-in-cheek, including the yelling about the pasta. In that moment, I was asking White about the importance of fresh noodles—I mean fresh pasta!—versus the dry stuff. White, quite clearly, has strong opinions on the subject: "People have a preconceived idea that Italian food is inexpensive. But I have ten to twelve pasta makers working for me; I spend a fortune making fresh pasta. And yes, it's entirely worth it."

Earlier, in fact, White's chef de cuisine, Bill Dorrier, toured me around the new restaurant facility, including a room downstairs where two men stood side by side constructing various pasta shapes. With them, Dorrier showed me how to roll my own garganelli using a dowel and a lined board. The care and intricacy it required comes back to me as White serves me that same garganelli, this time coated in a sauce made with cream and speck (a kind of smoked prosciutto).

"Boom!" cheers White as he adds grated Parmesan. We both take a taste and the next word he exclaims makes lots of sense in the moment: "SEX!"

The smokiness of the sauce is intense, but the star of the show is definitely the pasta itself. "With fresh pasta, you have something you really worked on," he says as he moves on to the next dish. "And it's that much more meaningful."

The next dish is a tortellini (house-made, of course) in a meaty ragù infused with cream. His final dish is made with mussels and beans using a pasta, *creste de gallo* (it means the crest of a rooster because it's shaped like a coxcomb), that he extrudes from a machine. He adds sliced garlic to a pan with olive oil. "Each piece of garlic is exactly the same thickness," he says, explaining how minced garlic doesn't give you any control over the end result. Here he's entirely in control (and recommends using a mandoline to achieve the same effect).

The finished dish is a glorious balancing act of flavors and textures. And, once again, the pasta is the star, this time chewy and texturally complex.

Leaving the restaurant, it's hard not to notice the enthusiasm with which everyone moves around me. It's clear that White has cultivated such devotion because he treats everything with as much intensity as he does a bowl of fresh pasta. It makes everyone around him care that much more too.

"All that cream gets sucked into the pasta and ... it's heaven."

Tortellini with Pork in Creamy Meat Ragù

Serves 4

This ragù is a meat lover's extravaganza. If you can't get the butcher to grind the mortadella, simply toss it into a food processor and pulse a few times until it's all chopped up (but don't overprocess or it'll get pasty). If you don't like chicken livers, you can leave them out of the ragù, but you'll be missing out on an extra dimension of flavor. And if you're really feeling lazy, you can just make the tortellini and skip the ragù (make a simple tomato sauce and add a big hit of cream at the end) or, vice versa, make the ragù and use rigatoni instead. In any combination, this is a winning dish.

FOR THE RAGÙ

½ cup extra virgin olive oil

½ cup diced yellow onion

¼ cup diced peeled carrot

¼ cup diced celery

¼ cup tomato paste

2 (28-ounce) cans whole peeled tomatoes and juices

Kosher salt and freshly ground black pepper

½ pound ground beef

½ pound ground pork

½ pound ground veal

½ pound ground chicken livers

1 sprig of fresh rosemary

1 sprig of fresh sage

2 bay leaves

2-inch rind from Parmesan cheese (optional)

½ cup heavy cream

FOR THE TORTELLINI

1 recipe Pasta Dough (page 138)

½ pound ground pork

½ pound minced prosciutto

½ pound ground mortadella

¼ cup freshly grated Parmesan cheese, plus more for garnish

1 egg, lightly beaten

A pinch of freshly grated nutmeg

● If your butcher won't grind these, you can—like the mortadella—grind them in a food processor.

First make the ragù by heating ¼ cup of the olive oil in a Dutch oven over medium heat and adding the onions, carrots, and celery. Cook until golden brown, 12 to 15 minutes. Stir in the tomato paste and cook for another minute. Add the tomatoes one at a time, crushing them as you add them. Season with salt and pepper and cover the pot, turning the heat to low.

Meanwhile, in a large skillet, heat the remaining ¼ cup olive oil over medium heat and add the beef, pork, veal, and chicken livers. Season with salt and pepper and cook until the meat is no longer pink, breaking it apart with a wooden spoon. With a slotted spoon, transfer the meat to the sauce; add the rosemary, sage, bay leaves, and Parmesan rind, if using. Simmer uncovered for 1½ to 2 hours on low heat, adjusting for salt and pepper, until the sauce is nicely unified and tastes intense and rich.

To make the tortellini, follow the instructions on page 142, but substitute a filling by combining in a bowl the pork, prosciutto, mortadella, Parmesan, egg, and nutmeg. To test the flavoring, make a small meatball (see page 158) and fry it in a pan to cook the raw pork. Taste it and adjust the filling accordingly.

Shape the tortellini according to the instructions and toss them on a cookie sheet with flour until ready to use.

Bring a large pot of water to a boil. Season well with salt. Drop the tortellini into the pot of boiling water and cook until they are just about cooked through, 2 to 3 minutes.

Meanwhile, add the cream to the hot sauce, remove the bay leaf, and adjust for salt and pepper. If you have more ragù than you think you'll need to sauce the pasta, set some aside for another time.

Use a spider to lift the tortellini into the pan with the ragù. Toss on low heat, allowing the tortellini to suck up some of the sauce. Spoon into hot bowls and sprinkle more Parmesan on top.

- If you're not going to use them right away, either cover with a damp towel or, for much later use, freeze right on the cookie sheet and then store the individual tortellini in a freezer bag.

- Whatever ragù you don't use, you can freeze. When ready to use, defrost it in the refrigerator overnight and warm it up in a pot with a little water.

Garganelli with Speck and Cream

Serves 4

This is a bowl of pure decadence: a sauce made of cream infused with speck (a type of smoked prosciutto) and bitter radicchio gets soaked up by fat tubes of homemade garganelli. Making the garganelli is really fun: just follow Samin Nosrat's recipe for fresh pasta (see page 138), cut up a sheet into 1-inch squares, and roll the squares on the back of a wooden spoon or dowel into thick tubes. Whatever pasta you don't use right away, you can freeze. I have a hunch, though, you'll eat this all in one swoop.

1 recipe Pasta Dough (page 138), rolled from the second to the thinnest setting

1½ to 2 cups heavy cream

¼ pound speck, julienned

1 cup sliced radicchio

½ cup freshly grated Parmesan cheeese, plus more for garnish

To make the garganelli, lay a sheet of the pasta dough on a floured work surface. With a pizza cutter or a sharp knife, cut the sheet into 1-inch squares. If you have a lined board for making ridges in the garganelli, great! If not, you can try rolling it on a clean new comb to get the ridges. But ridges aren't essential. What's essential is that you have something that resembles a dowel; a wooden spoon with a thick cylindrical handle would work best. Lay a square of pasta dough on the ridged board, comb, or work surface so that it looks like a diamond. Lay the dowel down so it rests horizontally on the bottom tip of the diamond and then roll the dowel, with the pasta dough on it, over itself, pressing down to get those ridges and forming a garganelli. When you reach the top of the diamond, push down tightly to make a seal and slide the garganelli off the dowel. Place the finished garganelli on a floured cookie sheet and repeat with the rest of the pasta dough.

Bring a large pot of water to a boil and add plenty of salt.

In another pot, bring the cream and speck to a simmer on medium-low heat, allowing the speck to infuse the cream with its smokiness. (Don't let the cream boil over.) After 5 to 6 minutes, add the radicchio to the cream and speck.

Add the garganelli to the boiling water. Because it's fresh-made, it will cook quickly. After 2 to 3 minutes, taste one to see if it's almost cooked through. When the pasta is al dente, lift all the garganelli with a spider into the pan with the cream, speck, and radicchio. Allow it to simmer until it's soaked up a lot of the cream and there isn't much liquid left in the pot, about 2 minutes.

Remove from the heat, stir in the Parmesan, and then scoop into warm bowls. Serve immediately with more fresh Parmesan sprinkled on top.

When I make it at home, I skip the ridges and the garganelli still does a great job of soaking up all the sauce.

Even though the speck is salty, you should taste the cream to see if it needs a pinch or two of salt.

Cavatappi with Mussels

Serves 4

As delicious as mussels are, served by themselves—even with a crusty bread and salad—they never quite fill you up the way you want them to. Enter this pasta. Here, cooked mussels are worked into a pasta sauce made with garlic, red pepper flakes, cannellini beans, and fresh tomatoes. And though White serves this with *creste de gallo*, a coxcomb-shaped pasta that he achieves with a pasta extruder, this also works quite well with a box of dried cavatappi (a coil-shaped pasta).

FOR THE MUSSELS

Extra virgin olive oil

3 cloves garlic, sliced thin

A pinch of crushed red pepper flakes

½ bottle of dry white wine

Kosher salt

1 pound mussels, cleaned and debearded

FOR THE PASTA

1 pound dried cavatappi

¼ cup extra virgin olive oil

3 cloves garlic, sliced thin

One 15-ounce can cannellini beans, drained and rinsed

A pinch of crushed red pepper flakes

2 large red tomatoes, diced

¼ cup chopped parsley

Best-quality olive oil, for drizzling

To a pot or a wide skillet with a lid, add a splash of olive oil, the garlic, and the red pepper flakes and turn up the heat. When the garlic starts to get toasty and fragrant, pour in the wine. As the wine starts to boil, add a pinch of salt and then add all the mussels. Cover the pan and shake periodically, checking every so often to see if the mussels open. As they open, transfer them to a bowl. When they're cool enough to handle, pull the meat out of each shell and set aside, discarding the shells. Pour any liquid from the pan into the bowl with the mussels.

Bring a large pot of water to a rapid boil and season well with salt. Drop in the dried cavatappi and cook for about 8 minutes.

Meanwhile, in a skillet, heat the ¼ cup of olive oil along with the garlic. When the garlic has started to soften but isn't yet brown, add the cannellini beans and stir. Add the mussels, the mussel cooking liquid, a pinch of red pepper flakes, and the tomatoes. Cook on medium heat, stirring gently, allowing the flavors to develop, seasoning with salt and tasting for balance.

When the pasta is ready, use a spider to lift it into the pan with the mussels. Stir. If the pan is too dry, ladle in a little pasta water; when the sauce is unified, remove the pan from the heat and add the parsley. Drizzle your best olive oil on top before serving in warmed bowls.

You can use the same skillet that you use to cook the mussels; just wipe it out first.

Parsley adds both color and an herbal freshness here, so don't be shy with it.

Amanda Cohen

Chef-owner, Dirt Candy
New York, New York

On the floor of her New York City restaurant, Dirt Candy, chef Amanda Cohen is laughing as she picks up containers. "This is what happens in a tiny kitchen," she explains, still reeling from the container avalanche that had hit moments earlier. "On a good day, only one thing goes wrong."

Dirt Candy's kitchen is seventy-five square feet. With regular customers packing the house almost every night, Cohen—who works alongside three others in the tiny space—is forced to be resourceful. ("A menu is dictated by the size of the kitchen," she tells me.) Her resourcefulness leads, in turn, to creativity, and Cohen's food is endlessly creative. That's why I'm here to cook with her. I'm here to answer the question: "How do constraints lead to innovation in the kitchen?"

Answer #1: You're forced to use everything because there's no room to store anything. When making her famous carrot buns (a riff on Chinese pork buns), Cohen buys bunches of purple, orange, and yellow carrots and puts them to immediate use. She juices them all separately, uses their pulp to make carrot powder, and then chops the remaining carrots for the carrot filling. Some of the juice goes into the bun dough and the remaining juice is used to roast the carrots. The end result is like a multicolored carrot extravaganza, and it's a function of being resourceful.

Answer #2: With only so much room for ingredients, you have to make them count. Cohen doesn't kid around when it comes to flavor: she shops regularly at Kalustyan's, the famous spice store in Curry Hill (as the Murray Hill neighborhood of Manhattan is informally known), and stocks up on such flavor enhancers as preserved lemons, Berber seasoning (an Ethiopian spice blend), and shoyu (a stronger version of soy sauce). In addition, she makes her own orange powder, carrot powder, and dried zucchini and keeps flavored oils (parsley, cilantro) and salts (celery, sea) on hand.

"Vegetables," Cohen says, explaining her crowded cabinets, "don't have a lot of flavor. You have to do a lot to make them taste good." (Cover your ears, Alice Waters.)

Cohen attacks her kitchen tasks with great force and bravado. She peels ginger aggressively with an ordinary metal spoon (the best way to peel ginger, it turns out); she proofs her yeast in a food processor because the processing heats it up and helps it activate; she measures out the dough for her carrot buns with a scale so each portion is exactly the same. When she preps her lemongrass, she peels away the outer stalk and then smashes the lemongrass with a knife, dragging the knife across, to release all the oils. Her attitude is can-do and adventurous. "When I came up with my carrot buns, I was like, 'Can we make a dough with carrot juice and flour?' And it turns out, we can!"

Despite the constraints of her tiny kitchen (or maybe because of them), Cohen produces complex, exciting food that's won her a devoted following. Turns out that it's not the size of your kitchen that matters; it's how you use it.

"People aren't as creative as they could be in the kitchen."

Carrot Dumplings

Serves 4 to 6

The first time I made Cohen's carrot buns, I loved the filling—a vibrant mixture of spice, sweetness, and acid—but felt the bun dough itself took too long to make, given that it requires several rises and setting up a steamer. I pitched the following question to Cohen: "What if I make carrot dumplings, instead?" The response: "I think that sounds like a great idea." This recipe is the result. It makes enough for many dumplings, which is a good thing: you can use what you want right away and freeze the rest for later.

FOR THE CARROT FILLING

4 medium carrots, cut into ¼-inch dice

2 cups (one 16-ounce bottle) carrot juice

¼ cup oyster sauce or vegetarian oyster sauce

1 teaspoon fresh lime juice

1 tablespoon toasted sesame oil

2 teaspoons shoyu or soy sauce

1 teaspoon kosher salt

2 tablespoons rice wine vinegar

1 tablespoon olive oil

1 teaspoon Tabasco sauce

2 tablespoons brown sugar

TO FINISH THE FILLING

1 teaspoon olive oil

1 teaspoon toasted sesame oil

1 teaspoon chopped peeled ginger

1 teaspoon chopped garlic

1 cup diced deseeded hothouse cucumbers

½ cup sliced scallions

¼ cup toasted sesame seeds (see Resources, page 371)

2 teaspoons cornstarch

FOR THE CARROT-HOISIN DIPPING SAUCE

1 cup carrot juice

1 teaspoon olive oil

1 teaspoon toasted sesame oil

1 teaspoon chopped garlic

1 teaspoon chopped peeled ginger

¼ teaspoon crushed red pepper flakes

¼ cup hoisin sauce

2 teaspoons cornstarch

FOR THE DUMPLINGS

1¾ cups all-purpose flour, plus more as needed

½ cup carrot juice

Preheat the oven to 400°F.

In a 9-by-13-inch baking dish, mix together all the ingredients for the carrot filling. Bake for at least 1 hour, stirring every 15 minutes. The carrots will get slightly crispy on the exterior, but the inside should be firm and moist. Taste after an hour to see if they're cooked. If not, continue cooking and check every 10 minutes until they're done.

To finish the filling, in a large pot, heat the olive oil and sesame oil over medium heat and add the ginger and garlic. Cook for a few seconds and then add the baked carrot filling and any juices from the baking dish and turn the heat to high. Once the mixture bubbles, 2 to 3 minutes, add the remaining ingredients except for the cornstarch. When the liquid starts to reduce, after 5 minutes or so, add the cornstarch and cook until there is very little liquid left in the pan, 5 to 10 minutes. Let cool.

Make the dipping sauce by reducing the carrot juice to ½ cup in a small pan over medium heat. In a separate pot, add the oils, garlic, ginger, and red pepper flakes and cook for 3 minutes. Add the hoisin and the reduced carrot juice and let come to a slight simmer. Add the cornstarch, and when the sauce returns to a simmer, remove from the heat, place in a blender, and mix thoroughly. Allow to cool.

Make the dumplings by stirring the flour and carrot juice together in a bowl. Remove to a floured surface, knead for a few minutes, and bring the dough together and shape into a ball. Allow to rest for 10 minutes and then divide the dough into 16 smaller balls. Flatten each ball and roll out with a rolling pin (you may need to sprinkle with more flour) to create a flat round circle. Fill each dumpling with 1 teaspoon of the carrot filling, and then pinch tightly closed. (If you have filling left over, either make more dumplings now or refrigerate the filling for up to a week and make dumplings later. Any dumplings you don't use right away can be frozen for up to 6 months.)

Bring a pot of salted water to a boil. Drop the dumplings in, a few at a time, and boil until they float and cutting into one reveals it to be cooked all the way through, 3 to 4 minutes. Serve on a platter with a bowl of the dipping sauce on the side.

● You can skip this step and just use wonton wrappers or white bread (see Kitchen Know-How, page 284), but the carrot juice in the dumpling dough does give the finished product extra carrot flavor and color.

● You can also pan-fry or steam these dumplings, but boiling is the easiest method.

Celery Salad with Mushrooms and Grapes in a Celery Leaf Pesto

Serves 4

"Who likes celery?" Amanda Cohen asked me gleefully when she taught me this salad. "Nobody!" Yet this recipe rescues celery from its lowly status on the vegetable totem pole. Strategy #1: Work celery into the dish in three forms (the leaves go into a pesto, the seeds go into the dressing, and then, of course, the celery itself is the salad). Strategy #2: Big flavors. Grilled mushrooms and grapes add earthiness and sweetness; garlic and lemon juice rev things up even more.

FOR THE PESTO

1 big bunch of Chinese celery leaves (about 1 cup), rinsed

¼ cup toasted sliced almonds

1 clove garlic, minced

Kosher salt

Olive oil (about ¾ cup; enough to make a pasty pesto)

FOR THE SALAD DRESSING

Zest and juice of 1 lemon

⅓ cup white wine vinegar

½ clove garlic, minced into a paste

1 teaspoon Dijon mustard

2 teaspoons celery seeds

Olive oil (about ½ cup)

FOR THE SALAD

½ cup red seedless grapes, sliced

2 cups button mushrooms, wiped clean with a damp paper towel and sliced

6 to 8 regular celery stalks, cut into ½-inch pieces on the bias

- Chinese celery is preferable here; it practically looks like parsley, there are so many leaves to pull from one bunch. With regular celery from the supermarket, you'll barely get enough leaves to fill ¼ cup.

To make the pesto, blanch the celery leaves in a pot of boiling water for just 10 seconds. Shock them in ice water and then, with paper towels, squeeze them dry. Add the almonds and garlic to a blender and blend until you get a paste. Add the celery leaves and a pinch of salt and, with the motor running on low, slowly drizzle olive oil in through the opening in the lid until it forms a pesto. Taste and adjust the seasoning.

- It may need a hit of lemon juice; steal some from the dressing.

To make the salad dressing, either blend or whisk all the ingredients except the oil, and then slowly drizzle in the oil until the dressing reaches a consistency that you like. Taste and adjust the seasoning.

- Don't add oil here because you don't want the grapes or the mushrooms to fry; you want them to get a *grilled* taste.

To make the salad, get a grill pan or cast-iron skillet very hot and, first, add the grapes by themselves. Grill just until they get a little color—2 or 3 minutes—and then set aside. Add the mushrooms to the pan and, again, grill until they turn a nice burnished color, 4 to 5 minutes. In a medium bowl, toss both the grapes and the mushrooms with the pesto.

- Because celery is so resilient, you can actually toss it with the dressing early and it will hold up.

In a separate bowl, toss the celery with the dressing and plate; top with the grapes and mushrooms.

Red Tomato Spaetzle in Yellow Tomato Coconut Sauce

Serves 4

Cooking with color isn't something most of us set out to do, but it's a totally worthwhile (and vitamin-rich) way to think about the food that you make at home. This dish embodies that philosophy: make a bright red tomato spaetzle using tomato paste, water, and flour and heat it up in a sauce of yellow tomatoes, coconut milk, and Berber seasoning (an exotic, dynamic blend of spices; see Resources, page 371). The Berber turns the yellow sauce a funky shade of orange, and by the time you add the red tomato spaetzle, this won't look like anything you've ever made or eaten before. The topping—a slaw made with Brussels sprouts and preserved lemons—adds crunch and even more color.

● You can use red tomatoes here—even canned tomatoes—and it will taste great, but it won't look as sharp (all that red on red). It's worth your time to seek out yellow tomatoes.

FOR THE SPAETZLE

¾ cup tomato paste

1¼ cups water

1¾ cups all-purpose flour

2 teaspoons kosher salt

1 tablespoon olive oil

FOR THE YELLOW TOMATO COCONUT SAUCE

2 tablespoons olive oil

1 small white onion, diced

2 cloves garlic, chopped

1-inch piece of ginger, peeled and chopped

Kosher salt

¾ cup toasted, shredded coconut (not sweetened)

2 tablespoons Berber seasoning (see Resources, page 371)

1 stalk of lemongrass, bruised and cut into 1-inch pieces

8 large yellow tomatoes, chopped and lightly processed in a blender

2 cups coconut milk, well stirred

Zest of 2 lemons

¼ teaspoon crushed red pepper flakes

FOR THE BRUSSELS SPROUTS SLAW

5 or 6 Brussels sprouts, sliced extra thin on a mandoline slicer

1 cup peeled and small-diced jicama (optional)

2 tablespoons diced preserved lemon (see Resources)

A splash of olive oil

Kosher salt

To make the spaetzle, whisk together the tomato paste and the water in a medium bowl until there aren't any clumps. Sift the flour and salt into the bowl and continue to whisk just until a batter comes together (you don't want to overmix). Let sit for 10 minutes.

Bring a large pot of water to a gentle boil and set a bowl of ice water on the side.

Hold a metal colander over the gently boiling water and press the spaetzle batter through the holes, sliding a bench scraper or another tool back and forth to help it along. When the spaetzle rise to the top and the water has returned to a gentle boil (3 to 4 minutes), drain and place the spaetzle immediately into the ice water. Strain the spaetzle again, toss them with the olive oil, and refrigerate until you're ready to use them.

● If the spaetzle are very sticky and clumping together, rinse and drain them a few times.

290

To make the sauce, heat the olive oil in a pot or Dutch oven over medium heat. Add the onions, garlic, and ginger with a pinch of salt and sauté until the onions are translucent, 4 to 5 minutes. Add the shredded coconut, mix well, and cook for another 5 minutes.

Add the Berber seasoning and the lemongrass and let cook for another 5 minutes.

Add the rest of the sauce ingredients and another pinch of salt and bring to a gentle simmer. Cook for 30 minutes, stirring occasionally and tasting for balance.

Meanwhile, make the Brussels sprouts slaw in a bowl by combining all of the slaw ingredients and adjusting for salt, acid, and oil. Set aside.

Put the cooked yellow tomato sauce through a strainer or a chinois into a large bowl. Adjust the seasoning one more time.

To finish, spoon some of the sauce into a small sauté pan. Heat the sauce on medium heat, then add the spaetzle, cooking together just until the spaetzle are heated through. Spoon into bowls and top with a big mound of the slaw. Serve immediately.

Linton Hopkins

Chef-owner, Restaurant Eugene
Atlanta, Georgia

Valuation **is a word** that means a great deal to chef Linton Hopkins. He brings it up when I first meet him at a table at his Restaurant Eugene. "Compromise is dangerous," he tells me. "You can't turn a blind eye to things; it's all about *valuation*." When we part ways a few hours later, he calls after me: "Don't forget. *Valuation*." (My interpretation: it's all about knowing what things are worth.)

Hopkins, a round, bespectacled Southerner, is like a cross between a friendly Southern farmer and a formidable French chef. As if to confirm that latter half of his persona, he tells me that early in his career, he would have sous-chefs measure his cuts. "A julienne means one eighth of an inch by one eighth of an inch by two inches."

The friendly-Southern-farmer part of his persona comes through in the way he holds forth on a variety of topics, including restaurant cooking versus home cooking ("At home, you have to clean everything yourself"), pickling ("I'm a big believer in preservation; I want to open a restaurant with zero refrigeration"), and taking pride in his profession ("This is a real guild; there's a code of honor and respect").

But it's the subject of *valuation* that gets him the most worked up. "You can put lime juice and hot sauce on something crunchy and say 'that's good,'" he explains, "but that's not enough."

Learning how to value food properly requires a certain amount of discrimination. You have to notice the difference between a red radish from the supermarket and a Spanish black radish straight from the farm; you have to feel the difference between a conventional yellow onion dusty in its supermarket bin and a fresh Vidalia onion so sweet, says Hopkins, "My daughter eats them like apples, straight from the ground."

With those two farm-fresh ingredients—the radishes and the onions—Hopkins illustrates the way that he values good food, pickling them to preserve them. "In the South," he says, "it's all about pickles."

Hopkins approaches pickling with a casual enthusiasm that's infectious. "You just sort of wing it," he says.

On his shelves, he has kumquats pickled with garlic and chilies, and pickled fennel stalks ("They make great straws for bloody Marys"). Later, he'll use his pickled garlic and pickled banana peppers to prepare a vibrant dish of greens. He'll also make a seared trout with a watercress puree that doesn't have pickles in it, but that gets a hit of acid from an orange and a lemon.

It's *valuation,* though, that underscores everything that happens in Hopkins's kitchen. At one point he opens the lid of his garbage can and asks, "What have I thrown away?" He peers inside. "The stems from those leeks." He pauses and reflects, "I could've put them in a stock. I could've made a leek broth."

The fact that Hopkins can muster such pathos over wasted leek greens reveals the purity of his mission, the sincerity behind his ethos—an ethos built around a simple word, but a word that matters: *valuation.*

"Recipes no more make a good cook than sermons make a saint."

Pickled Black Radishes and Vidalia Onions

Makes one 8-ounce jar of pickles

This is just one example of the many things you can do if you start pickling the produce you find at the farmer's market. Because black radishes and Vidalias were in season when I met with Hopkins, this is what we cooked together, but you don't need to follow this recipe precisely. The important part is the ratio of vinegar to sugar to water; memorize this and you can pickle all kinds of things, from kumquats to fennel stems. This recipe is wonderful with fish or pork or, even better, mixed with mayo and spread on a sandwich. Once you start pickling, the possibilities are endless.

3 or 4 large black radishes	1 cup sugar
2 small spring Vidalia onions or an equal amount of cleaned leeks	1 cup water
2 cups distilled white vinegar	A pinch of kosher salt

Prepare a jar by either washing it really well with soap and water and then boiling it, along with the lid, for several minutes or—an easier option—running the jar and lid through the dishwasher. The jar should be warm when you fill it.

To prepare the vegetables, use the julienne blade on a mandoline slicer and create a kind of radish-onion relish or simply slice the radishes and onions very thin into rounds and rings. Whichever method you choose, fill the jar alternating between the radishes and the onions, so you see separate layers of black and green. Pack the layers tightly.

In a pot, combine the vinegar, sugar, water, and salt and taste it for balance. (Does it need more vinegar? More sugar?) Bring to a boil over high heat and then pour over the vegetables in the jar, leaving room at the very top for a vacuum to form. Seal with the lid.

Put the jar right into the refrigerator; as it sits, it will get more and more intense. It won't be shelf-stable, though, and will only last a few weeks.

If you think you'll eat these pickles, or any pickles you make, over the course of 1 or 2 weeks, you can skip the jar and just use a clean bowl. Simply cover with plastic wrap and store in the refrigerator.

If you want to put up these pickles so they last for months, create a "shelf" at the bottom of a pot (you can make one with aluminum foil) for the jar to rest on (the bottom of the jar should not touch the bottom of the pot). Fill the pot with water and bring it to a boil. Place the filled, sealed jar on the shelf and keep the water boiling for 20 minutes. With tongs, remove the jar to the counter and wait: you should hear a pop or see the top of the jar pop up. The pickles will keep this way at room temperature for 6 to 8 months (though you should refrigerate after opening).

Sautéed Georgia Trout with Watercress Puree and Mandarin Salad

Serves 4

With the bright green cream sauce, the crisp seared trout, and the elegant orange salad on top, this is a restaurant-worthy dish through and through. But don't be intimidated: it's doable at home, too. Once you understand the components, you'll realize how easy it is. The colors will pop, the flavors will meld, and you'll wonder how something so impressive could be so simple to make.

FOR THE WATERCRESS PUREE

4 tablespoons (½ stick) unsalted butter

1 bay leaf

1 large leek, cleaned and cut into rings

½ cup heavy cream, plus more if necessary

Kosher salt

1 head of watercress, cleaned, roots chopped off

Juice of 1 lemon

FOR THE MANDARIN SALAD

2 small mandarin oranges, cut into supremes (see page 66)

¼ cup whole parsley leaves

¼ cup chopped dill

¼ fennel bulb, cored and thinly sliced

1 radish, thinly sliced

A pinch of salt

FOR THE TROUT

4 trout fillets, skin on, bones removed

Kosher salt

Canola, vegetable, or other neutral oil

● Hopkins says you could substitute parsley to make an equally delicious parsley puree.

● This is important: you don't want the bay leaf in your puree.

To make the watercress puree, melt the butter in a pan along with the bay leaf and when the butter's thoroughly melted, add the leeks. Cook them gently on medium-low heat for 5 minutes or so.

When the leeks are nice and soft, add the cream and season with salt. Bring the cream to a boil and remove the bay leaf. Add the watercress and stir to coat. If it's not coated, add more cream while the pan is still on the boil.

When the watercress has wilted slightly after just a minute or two, add the watercress and most of the liquid to a blender. Carefully blend (cover the hole in the lid with a towel) and adjust the consistency: it should be almost soupy. If it's not, add more of the remaining liquid. Add the lemon juice, blend one more time, then taste for seasoning. Set aside.

continued

Sautéed Georgia Trout with Watercress Puree and Mandarin Salad (continued)

- If you don't have two cast-iron skillets, you can do this with two nonstick pans; just add the oil before you start heating.

- Don't go crazy with the puree. A little goes a long way.

For the mandarin salad, simply toss all the ingredients together in a large bowl, adjust for salt, and set aside.

Finally, run your finger along the length of the trout to check for bones. If you find bones, use pliers or your fingers to remove them carefully.

Season the fish on both sides with salt. Heat 2 cast-iron skillets on high heat until very hot. Add a splash of oil and then 2 trout fillets per pan, skin side down, and press the fish into the pan with your hands or a spatula.

Cook until the trout is almost completely opaque and the skin is crisp, 3 to 4 minutes. To finish, carefully flip the fish over and cook for a few seconds on the flesh side.

Spoon the watercress puree onto 4 plates. Top with the trout and then pile the salad over it. Serve immediately.

Braised Winter Greens with Tasso and Pickled Banana Peppers

Serves 4

There's so much going on in this recipe—four kinds of greens; a porky, bacon-y base; pickled garlic; chilies; and pickled chilies on top—it takes greens from black-and-white to Technicolor. Even though the elements here are specific (the tasso, the pickled banana peppers), they're all easy to substitute. Or you can just pick and choose the elements you like. Whatever you do, there's one thing for certain: these greens won't be boring.

1 bunch of collard greens	1 onion, chopped
1 bunch of mustard greens	2 dried red chilies
1 bunch of kale	2 pickled cloves garlic, chopped
1 bunch of greens from spring Vidalias (or, alternatively, scallions)	Approximately 1 cup chicken stock (enough to cover the greens)
1 tablespoon peanut oil	Kosher salt
½ cup cubed tasso (see Resources, page 371) or pancetta	Apple cider vinegar
	3 pickled banana peppers, cut into rings

- The pickled garlic is made using the same formula, and the same ratio of vinegar to water to sugar to salt, as the pickle recipe on page 294. When pickling garlic, you want to be extra careful of cleanliness (to avoid botulism); Hopkins suggests washing the garlic cloves first with water. Alternatively, you can use regular garlic for the greens.

- Tasso is a Southern cured pork product, similar to pancetta but coated in a Creole seasoning.

- The same rule applies to these peppers as to the garlic: you can make them by using the pickle formula. Or substitute Brandon Pettit's pickled peppers (page 31).

Triple-wash the greens by filling a large bowl or sink with cold water and dunking the greens in, a bunch at a time. Shake under water and then shake out of the water. All the dirt will go to the bottom of the bowl; pour the water down the sink, refill, and repeat the process 2 more times until the greens are super clean. (Nothing ruins dinner more than dirt in your greens.)

Once the greens are clean, remove the stems and give the leaves a rough chop.

In a pan large enough to hold everything, add the peanut oil and the tasso. Raise the heat to medium high and let the fat render. When the tasso is caramelized and deep golden brown, add the onions. Raise the heat a bit: you want to cook the onions aggressively for 3 to 4 minutes.

When the onions are softened, add all of the greens. You should hear a loud sizzle. Add the dried chilies and the pickled garlic. Add enough chicken stock to cover the greens and season with salt and a splash of vinegar.

Bring the mixture to a boil, lower to a simmer, and cook for 15 minutes. There should still be some liquid at the end.

Taste the greens one last time to adjust for salt and acid. Spoon into serving bowls and top with the pickled banana peppers. Serve immediately.

- This is called potlikker (or pot liquor) and it's a Southern delicacy. Hopkins suggests sopping it up with corn bread.

299

Charles Phan

**Chef-owner, the Slanted Door,
Out the Door, and Heaven's Dog
San Francisco, California**

Upstairs from one of his San Francisco restaurants, chef Charles Phan lives with his wife and children. "That's the way it is in most of the world," he tells me. "You buy a building, you live upstairs, and you work downstairs."

When we're cooking and we need some shrimp heads for a Vietnamese caramelized shrimp dish, he sends his assistant down to the restaurant to get some. For Phan, there's no real dividing line between work and home, between cooking for his customers and cooking for his family.

In fact, Phan employs twenty-two relatives. "My mom will call and say, 'Your cousin so-and-so just moved here; give him a job!'" And Phan does, though he doesn't play favorites if they don't do good work. "I'll still fire them," he says. "You have to have rules."

When it comes to cooking, Phan isn't a rule follower as much as he is a casual technician. With a large cleaver, he hacks apart a chicken for our first dish, steamed chicken with fermented black beans, a dish Phan ate as a child in Vietnam. Part of what informs his cooking is his quest to re-create these childhood dishes. "If you know the flavor profiles," he explains, "it's much easier to work on things. You eventually get it right."

The chicken gets tossed with olive oil, salt, rice wine, cornstarch, soy sauce, white pepper, preserved black beans, ginger, garlic, and scallions. Then it's placed in one of Phan's favorite cooking vessels, a dish that not only can withstand the heat of a steamer or the stove, but that's beautiful enough for presentation: a deep clay bowl.

"I love cooking in clay bowls," he says, showing me a collection of various shallow clay bowls, some from Chinatown, some from Spain. "The transfer of heat is really slow, and by the time you take it to the table, it's so hot that whatever you're serving continues to bubble. It keeps the heat."

Phan adds the chicken mixture to one of these clay bowls and places it in a bamboo steamer sitting in a wok filled with simmering water. "You want to make sure you can see the water," he advises, "because if it all evaporates, your steamer will burn."

While the chicken cooks, he places another clay bowl directly on the stove and adds canola oil and sugar. This is the start of his caramel shrimp dish, and it's surprising how resilient that clay bowl is, sitting right on the flame.

The sugar turns dark brown and Phan adds a shallot, ginger, and the shrimp heads. Soon the chicken dish is done and Phan finishes up the shrimp dish with lemongrass, chili, and fish sauce. Finally, in a large wok, I stir-fry bok choy with shiitakes and garlic. And just as the food's all done, the door bursts open and Phan's wife comes home with their children.

One starts playing the piano, another tells Phan about the diorama he helped her build for school. Downstairs, customers are dining, and upstairs, the family is contemplating dinner. At the Phan residence, it's difficult to tell where work begins and where family life ends. Everything is blurred and Phan is at the center, feeding everyone—wife, children, friends, customers; it's all one and the same to him.

> ## "It doesn't take a lot of money to eat good food. If you know what you're doing."

Steamed Chicken with Preserved Black Beans and Ginger

Serves 2

What's remarkable about this dish is that instead of developing flavor step-by-step, you stir together a bunch of ingredients—chicken, ginger, soy sauce, preserved black beans heated with garlic in olive oil—and pour them into a clay bowl that you place into a steamer. Thirty to forty minutes after steaming, you have fall-apart chicken that's been infused with all of those other components and, because it all happens in one vessel, it makes its own sauce. Serve the steaming hot clay bowl at the table and marvel at how the food stays hot as you devour it.

1 whole chicken, 3 to 4 pounds
Olive oil
Kosher salt
2 tablespoons rice wine or sherry
1½ tablespoons cornstarch
1 tablespoon soy sauce
A pinch of white pepper
1-inch knob of ginger, peeled and grated

3 scallions, sliced, white and light green parts
½ teaspoon sugar
1 shallot, sliced
2 tablespoons chopped garlic
¼ cup preserved black beans, crushed slightly with the back of a knife
Cilantro leaves, for garnish
Steamed rice, for serving

Cut the chicken with a large sharp knife or a cleaver, separating the wings, legs, thighs, and back from the body. Cut all of these into 2-inch pieces, slicing through the bone, including the back. Save the breast for another use.

In a large bowl, toss the chicken with a splash of olive oil, a big pinch of salt, the rice wine, cornstarch, soy sauce, white pepper, ginger, scallions, sugar, and shallots.

In a small pot or skillet, heat ¼ cup olive oil and add the garlic. As it becomes fragrant, add the preserved black beans and cook for a minute, stirring, until the flavors combine. Pour over the chicken, stir everything together, and allow the dish to sit, covered, for 2 to 3 hours at room temperature.

Transfer the chicken to a clay bowl that's wide and deep enough to hold everything along with the juices that will come out when it cooks. Fill a wok halfway with water and bring to a simmer over medium-low heat. Place a bamboo steamer in the water and put another bamboo steamer on top; the second steamer will not touch the water. In that steamer, place the clay bowl and cover with the bamboo top. Allow to cook like this, monitoring the water (you don't want it all to evaporate), for about 30 minutes or until the chicken is cooked through.

When it's ready, very carefully remove the clay bowl from the steamer. (It's hot!) Garnish the chicken with some cilantro leaves and serve with steamed rice.

It's important that the pieces be relatively the same size so everything cooks at the same time.

If you don't want to buy a bamboo steamer, you can cook this dish in a traditional steamer set over a pot (as long as it fits the clay pot). If you can't get the pot's lid on, you can tent everything tightly with foil.

Cut into a few pieces of chicken just to make sure; all of the chicken should look opaque. If it's pink or translucent, keep cooking.

Caramel Shrimp with Lemongrass, Thai Chili, and Ginger

Serves 2

Most of us associate caramel with dessert. In this dish, when you stop the cooking process with fish sauce, you get a marvelous caramely sauce that's sweet and savory, briny and smoky, and a staple of Vietnamese cooking. Phan prepares this in a clay bowl, but if you don't have one, use a Dutch oven. Just be extra careful with the caramel; not only does it go from dark to burned in a matter of seconds, the melted sugar is *piping* hot and sticky. Serve with lots of rice for soaking up the sauce.

1 teaspoon canola oil

2 tablespoons sugar

1 sliced shallot

1 tablespoon peeled and slivered ginger

Shrimp heads from 1 pound of shrimp (optional)

1 tablespoon fish sauce

⅓ cup very finely chopped lemongrass (about ½ stalk)

1 fresh red chili, chopped

1 pound shrimp, peeled and deveined

Black pepper

Steamed rice, for serving

● Clay bowls don't like to be shocked.

Place a clay bowl or pot directly on medium-low heat and <u>allow it to heat up slowly</u>.

As the bowl is heating, add the oil and sugar and watch it carefully; eventually, the sugar will melt and start to color. When it's a deep dark-brown caramel, add the shallots, ginger, and shrimp heads, if you're using them. Stir together for a minute and then add the fish sauce, lemongrass, chili, shrimp, and a sprinkling of black pepper.

Stir and cook until the shrimp are cooked through, 2 to 3 minutes; they'll grow firmer and pinker as they cook. Add a little water if it needs more liquid. Serve at the table in the clay dish with steamed rice on the side.

Stir-Fried Bok Choy and Shiitakes with Garlic and Rice Wine

Serves 2

Phan's take on bok choy includes shiitakes, garlic, and rice wine. It's as simple to make as it seems, but the flavor is deep and complex.

1 tablespoon canola oil	½ cup sliced shiitake mushrooms
2 cloves garlic, chopped	Rice wine
1 bunch of bok choy, washed, carefully dried, and sliced	Fish sauce

● You'll know it's hot enough when a flick of water evaporates immediately.

Heat a wok on very high heat.

Swirl oil down the sides with the wok still on high heat. Add the garlic and watch it carefully; you barely want it to color. As soon as it looks like it's ready to darken, add all the bok choy and shiitakes and use tongs to toss them, shaking the pan while you do.

Add a little water, a splash of rice wine, and a splash of fish sauce, continuing to toss the vegetables. When the bok choy is wilted (less than a minute) and flavored properly (taste to find out), serve right away.

Anita Lo

Chef-owner, Annisa
New York, New York

Lo's Kitchen Know-How

IT'S EASY to blend various world cuisines when you know the similarities between them. Both French food and Korean food, for example, have things that are fermented: France has cheese, Korea has chili paste. In both cultures, a julienne is still a julienne, it's just called something different.

USE A BONING KNIFE to segment fruit; the flexibility of the blade really allows you to get in between the membranes.

HAWAIIAN PINK SALT is good for finishing dishes in which you want to add some crunch. Use it, for example, on the tuna carpaccio on page 308.

In 2009, Chef Anita Lo had a terrible year.

In February, her restaurant Bar Q went out of business. A few months later, her mother passed away. And then, in July, her flagship restaurant, Annisa, a West Village staple and critical darling, burned down to the ground after an electrical fire. "It was a really bad year," she tells me when she recounts the story.

But Lo didn't give in to the misfortune. Instead, she used the time between the fire and the restaurant's reopening (almost a year later) to develop new dishes, to reflect on her career, and to travel. "You don't have a choice," she tells me in Annisa's basement, where there's a second kitchen and a walk-in refrigerator. "That's life."

Lo wears a perpetual game face; she seems ready for anything and everything, as if she knows disaster's likely to strike again any second and this time she'll be prepared. When we start cooking together, she also seems to invite danger: she cooks a Japanese eggplant on an open flame.

"Isn't that hazardous?" I ask.

"There are hazards to cooking," she responds matter-of-factly.

The Japanese eggplant is part of a dish that reflects Lo's style: eggplant two different ways, smoked over an open flame and steamed.

The steamed eggplant, which remains a magnificent purple color, gets cut into mini-towers and then stuffed with a mixture of red onion, garlic, lemon juice, olive oil, and a sweet Turkish seasoning called maras-biber; the smoked eggplant gets stuffed with fried shallots, lemon juice, garlic, olive oil, and a smoky Turkish pepper called urfa-biber. Lo staggers the smoked eggplant with the steamed eggplant on the plate and tops everything with yogurt mixed with lemon zest and garlic; she uses yogurt water (which comes out when she strains the yogurt) as a broth. The finished plate is quirky and vivid, the flavors big and bold and memorable.

Lo embraces multiculturalism in her food. "I once had a Turkish girlfriend," she explains when I ask her how she got the idea for this dish. "And I wanted to use some Turkish flavors."

Her curiosity about the world is what feeds her culinary ambition, though sometimes she goes for the familiar. "This is something my mom used to make," she explains later as she makes an almond jelly, stirring milk, almond extract, and sugar together on the stove. The resulting dish, served with candied fennel and segmented grapefruit, is probably a far cry from anything Lo saw in her childhood kitchen.

And though Lo's voice is somber and sad when she talks about the recent tragedies she's been through, she's clearly been invigorated by them too. Her food is energetic and exciting and, most important, future-focused (the reopened Annisa earned a solid two stars in *The New York Times*).

Some restaurant food merely shows off a chef's knowledge; Lo's food shows off her wisdom. Heaven knows it was hard-earned.

"It's all about esoteric ingredients. I'm always excited by new things I've never had before."

Tuna Carpaccio
with Kohlrabi Slaw

Serves 4

Why is it that we gladly eat raw fish at restaurants but rarely do it at home? I suspect it has something to do with trust; while we trust a restaurant to carefully purchase its seafood, we don't trust ourselves to do the same. That's a shame, though, because if you track down sushi-grade tuna from a local seafood shop that you trust, you can serve this cooling, surprising carpaccio at home with very little effort.

1 kohlrabi (or, if you can't find it, fennel or radishes), julienned (it helps to use a mandoline)

3 mint leaves, cut into a chiffonade

1 clove garlic, very finely minced

Juice of 1 lemon, plus more to taste

¼ cup dried currants

Kosher salt and freshly ground black pepper

¼ cup olive oil, plus more for drizzling

1 pound sushi-grade tuna or Spanish mackerel

Hawaiian pink salt (see Resources, page 371) or other coarse sea salt

- To make a chiffonade, stack the leaves, roll like a cigar, and slice crosswise into thin strips.

- Lo uses Spanish mackarel, but it's probably easier to find sushi-grade tuna at the store.

In a bowl, mix together the kohlrabi, mint, garlic, lemon juice, dried currants, kosher salt and pepper to taste, and the olive oil. Taste and adjust the seasoning.

Slice the fish against the grain into ¼-inch slices. Arrange on chilled plates and drizzle the fish with olive oil, squeeze on a little more lemon juice, then top with the slaw and some coarse salt. Serve immediately.

Eggplant
Two Ways

I found these spices at Kalustyan's in New York (see Resources, page 371).

Serves 4

Warning: this recipe asks you to do a lot. First, the shopping. You must track down two obscure Turkish spices, maras-biber (a hot and sweet bright red spice) and urfa-biber (the blackened, smoky version of maras-biber). Lo builds the dish around these two spices, pairing the maras-biber with steamed eggplant and the urfa-biber with charred eggplant. It makes for a dish so unusual and so worth the effort, you'll never look at eggplant the same way again. Be sure to strain the yogurt the night before you make this.

1 cup plain yogurt	¼ cup red onion, minced
¼ cup vegetable oil	3 cloves garlic, minced
2 shallots, peeled and sliced thin	Zest and juice of 1 lemon
Kosher salt	Olive oil
4 large Japanese eggplants of relatively equal size and thickness, stems removed	2 tablespoons urfa-biber
2 tablespoons maras-biber	Chives, sliced into small strips

The day before you make this, line a sieve with cheesecloth and place the sieve over a bowl. Pour in the yogurt and place in the refrigerator overnight, allowing the yogurt to strain.

Heat the vegetable oil in a small frying pan on high heat until you see bubbles around the handle of a wooden spoon when you place it in the oil. Carefully add the shallots and fry until crispy, stirring them as they cook. Remove them to paper towels, season with salt, and set aside.

Set up a steamer by filling a pot with 1 inch of water, bringing it to a simmer on medium-low heat, and placing a steamer basket with a lid on top.

Cut off the ends of two of the eggplants and slice them into rounds about 2 inches wide. Season with salt and place in the steamer, covering with the lid. Cook until a knife goes through them easily, about 10 minutes. Remove to a plate.

One at a time, using tongs, cook the other 2 eggplants over an open gas flame on your stovetop. (Be careful! Sparks may fly.) If this makes you nervous, or if you have an electric stove, you can also use the broiler or a grill, but the point is to get the whole exterior of the eggplant black and the interior cooked. It takes 10 minutes or so and you should rotate the eggplant around as you do it. When the eggplant is limp and blackened, set aside. Allow to cool and then, using your hands and a paring knife, remove the skin and slice the eggplant into rounds the same size as the ones that are in the steamer. Season with salt.

You can skip this step if you buy thick Greek yogurt, but you won't have the yogurt water Chef Lo uses when she serves it.

continued

Eggplant
Two Ways (continued)

To make the filling for the steamed eggplant, in a small bowl, mix together the maras-biber, red onion, 1 clove of the minced garlic, 1 tablespoon of the lemon juice, and enough olive oil to make a runny paste. Taste and adjust the seasoning.

To make the smoked eggplant filling, mix the fried shallots, 1 clove of the minced garlic, the urfa-biber, 1 tablespoon of the lemon juice, and enough olive oil to make a runny paste. Taste and adjust the seasoning.

Using chopsticks, poke holes through the centers of all the eggplant pieces. Spoon about a teaspoon of the appropriate filling into those holes (maras for the steamed, urfa for the smoked), pushing down with a chopstick, so that there is filling in every bite.

Mix together the strained yogurt (reserve the water), 1 tablespoon lemon zest, and the final clove of minced garlic. Adjust for salt and acid.

Serve in bowls. First pour in some of the reserved yogurt water. Stagger pieces of the smoked eggplant and the steamed eggplant on each bowl and top with a dollop of the yogurt mixture and the chives. (Lo serves hers with a fried eggplant chip, but that's not necessary at home.) You can serve this warm, at room temperature, or chilled.

Almond Jelly
with Candied Fennel
and Grapefruit

Serves 6

The most challenging thing about this recipe is the name. When I told friends that I was serving "Almond Jelly" for dessert one night, they looked at me worriedly as if this required some explanation. It's noteworthy, then, that Lo also calls this recipe "Blancmange," which sounds much more appetizing. Trust me, no matter what you call it, this combination of gelatin, milk, and almond extract is a terrific canvas for the unexpected combination of the candied fennel, the grapefruit, and my favorite of all liqueurs, St-Germain.

● St-Germain is made from elderflowers picked in the French Alps. It is available at liquor and specialty stores.

FOR THE JELLY

2½ cups whole milk

2 teaspoons almond extract

1½ cups water

½ cup sugar

A pinch of kosher salt

2 tablespoons powdered gelatin, bloomed in a small bowl with ¾ tablespoon warm water

FOR THE CANDIED FENNEL

1 cup sugar

1 cup water

1 tablespoon fresh lemon juice

A pinch of kosher salt

1 cup fennel, cut into a small dice, with the fronds reserved

TO FINISH

⅓ cup St-Germain liqueur

1 pink grapefruit, supremed

● Lo taught me how to supreme with a boning knife; the idea is to carve off the exterior of the grapefruit and then to cut between the membranes to release clean, perfect, smooth segments of grapefruit.

To make the jelly, whisk together the milk, almond extract, water, and sugar in a large saucepan over medium-high heat. Bring to a boil, whisking every so often and watching carefully so it doesn't bubble up. Once you see active bubbles, whisk in the bloomed gelatin and strain into a separate bowl. Pour into six 4-ounce ramekins that have been prepared with cooking spray. Refrigerate for 4 or 5 hours, until they're set.

To make the candied fennel, place the sugar and water in a pot and bring to a boil over medium heat to make a simple syrup, stirring occasionally. Add the lemon juice, salt, and fennel and simmer until the fennel is cooked through and soft, about 5 minutes. (Test by removing a piece of fennel to a plate, letting it cool, and then tasting to see if it's tender.) Allow to cool and then strain, saving the syrup. Set the candied fennel aside.

Mix the syrup with the St-Germain and pour over the grapefruit segments in a bowl.

To serve, run a knife around the edge of each ramekin and invert onto a small soup plate or bowl. Surround each with the pink grapefruit and a small amount of the syrup and sprinkle with the candied fennel and the fennel fronds.

● The leftover syrup can be used to make drinks with Prosecco, so don't throw it out.

Daniel Patterson

Chef-owner, Coi
San Francisco, California

The chefs in chef Daniel Patterson's kitchen at Coi (pronounced "kwa") are highly alert and deeply engrossed in their various kitchen tasks: one chef holds a cherry log over a fire, and once it catches, he runs to a metal tin that contains olive oil, drops in the log, and covers it with plastic. ("That's for smoked olive oil for our bread crumbs," explains Patterson.) Another chef vigorously presses solids through a chinois, extracting every last morsel of flavor from the stock she's been making.

And as Patterson weaves his way through the kitchen, the chefs are constantly aware of him. His power comes not from a maniacal nature (he has a subdued but intense manner); it comes from the force of his vision, a vision that he articulates rather clearly when I ask him the name of one of the dishes he's teaching me.

"That's not the most important thing about what's been going on here," he says. "It's about ingredients and paying attention and adapting to the situation."

Ingredients are, indeed, at the heart of Patterson's cuisine. The first dish that he makes is a simple assembly of radishes, turnips, fennel, and wild greens. But the attention that he pays to each of these elements is nothing short of fanatic.

"How many people pay attention to the vegetable on the cutting board?" he asks me at one point. "What's the texture? What's the flavor?"

Demonstrating this, he tastes each vegetable before adding it to the salad. First the fennel: "It's pretty good." Then a black radish: "Normally I'd cook this, but it's nice and sweet." A breakfast radish: "I don't like this. It's old; it's not nice."

The greens that Patterson adds to the salad—field sorrel, miner's lettuce, borage, chickweed—were foraged for the restaurant. When I express concern about my ability to do the same at home, he answers, "This grows all over the country. This grows in Central Park."

Most home cooks dump cans of tomatoes and cartons of cream into a pot, turn up the heat, and, thirty minutes later, call it soup. Patterson's approach is more like that of the painter Georges Seurat, who painted his masterpiece, *A Sunday Afternoon on the Island of La Grande Jatte,* dot by dot. Patterson cooks the same way.

And each dot matters. Take the cheese that Patterson shaves on top of that same salad. As we cook, the woman who makes the cheese—Soyoung Scanlan from Andante Dairy—comes to visit the Coi kitchen. She talks about a newer cheese she's trying out, and Patterson samples it. Their rapport makes it clear that Patterson values this relationship with the person whose cheese he'll soon be shaving over his salad.

That cheese has a story. So does the radish. So does the wood sorrel. It's a peculiar kind of cooking, but the kind of cooking we should all be aware of as we cook in our own kitchens. If a finished dish is the sum of its parts, Patterson asks us to really care about those parts. Then, as with a Seurat painting, we can stand back and admire the entire creation.

"Al dente
vegetables
are a big hoax,
an excuse for
sloppy cooking."

Raw Vegetable Salad with Aged Goat's-Milk Cheese

Serves 2

This salad is all about procuring. What goes into your salad depends on what you find at the farmer's market, in your own garden, or even in the fields near your home. The ingredients listed are just a place to start. Use what you have and make sure you taste everything, as Patterson does, before adding it to the bowl. From there, it's a simple matter of dressing it and seasoning it to draw out the natural flavors.

- Patterson uses McEvoy Ranch olive oil, "the best in the country."

- Etude from Andante Dairy is used at Coi.

A combination of 4 to 5 radishes (breakfast, black, watermelon)

2 to 3 small white turnips

½ small fennel bulb, core removed

A combination of interesting greens (field sorrel, miner's lettuce, borage, chickweed)

Zest and juice of 1 Meyer lemon or regular lemon

Freshly ground black pepper

Rice wine vinegar

Good, freshly pressed olive oil

Kosher salt

Aged goat's-milk cheese

Radish flowers (optional)

Wash all the vegetables and greens in a bowl of cold water, scrubbing off any dirt. Dry them on a tray lined with paper towels (this also allows you to set them out so you can study them before you bring them together in the salad).

For the radishes, study their qualities to decide the best ways to serve them. For example, you might cut a black radish into matchsticks so you don't get too much of it at once (and to have some black and white on each piece). Cut a red radish into quarters; a watermelon radish (peel it first) into half-moons.

For the turnips, trim the tops slightly, keeping some green, and slice them on a mandoline from top to bottom, so you get some of that top part in each slice.

Slice the fennel bulb on the mandoline crosswise so you don't get tough fibrous pieces.

Place all the sliced vegetables in a large bowl and add the zest and juice of the Meyer lemon. Grind in some pepper, add a splash of rice wine vinegar, drizzle in some olive oil, and sprinkle with salt. Toss with your hands (your best tool for this job) and taste! Adjust for salt and vinegar.

Lift the turnips, radishes, and fennel into 2 serving bowls and use the dressing left in the larger bowl to dress the greens. Add those to the bowls with the vegetables, toss gently, and peel the aged goat cheese on top using a vegetable peeler. Top with radish flowers, if using.

Orange, Yellow, and Purple Carrots Braised in Brown Butter

Serves 2

This carrot dish is a spectacular way to showcase multicolored carrots without sacrificing their color—which normally happens when you peel them. Served with the raw vegetable salad on page 317 and the grilled brassica on page 320, this makes a vegetarian dinner that's unlike any you've probably served at home before.

3 slices of white bread, crusts removed

8 tablespoons (1 stick) unsalted butter, plus 1 tablespoon melted butter

Kosher salt

A small head of green garlic, intact and unpeeled (the equivalent of 1 or 2 regular cloves garlic in size)

3 purple carrots, cleaned but not peeled

3 orange carrots, cleaned but not peeled

3 yellow carrots, cleaned but not peeled

Champagne vinegar

Neutral olive oil

Radish sprouts (optional)

Wood sorrel (optional)

- If the carrots are really dirty on the outside, and washing isn't enough to get them clean, use a knife to scrape off the dirty parts. You don't want to lose the color, so only scrape the parts that are dirty.

- If you can't find green garlic, you can use Chuy Valencia's technique of cooking a garlic clove still in its skin in a cast-iron skillet (see page 252). When it's soft inside, use it in place of the green garlic here.

- Although it may sound exotic, Patterson says wood sorrel is "the most common herb in the country."

- You don't necessarily need three pots. You can do the purple carrots first, set them aside, clean the pot, etc., but that'll take a lot longer.

- Patterson calls this "the cardboard stage," referring to the cardboard-like smell that the butter emits when it turns this color.

Preheat the oven to 325°F. Lay the bread on a cookie sheet, brush with the melted butter, and toast in the oven until the bread is a nice golden brown, 5 to 10 minutes. Remove from the oven, allow to cool, and then blitz with some salt in a food processor. Set aside.

Heat a grill or a cast-iron skillet over medium heat and when it's hot, add the green garlic. Cook until slightly caramelized on the outside and soft on the inside, 3 to 4 minutes. Set aside.

Now get three pots ready: you'll need one for the purple carrots (which will turn the butter a dark purple color), one for the orange and yellow carrots, and one to make a brown butter sauce. Add about 2 tablespoons of the butter to the first pot and cook it until it's a nice chestnut brown, then add ½ cup water along with a big pinch of salt. Add the purple carrots, cover the pan, and lower the heat. Simmer gently until a cake tester (or a thin knife) goes through easily, 10 to 12 minutes. Repeat with 2 tablespoons of the butter, ½ cup water, a pinch of salt, and the orange and yellow carrots in a second pot.

While the carrots are cooking, make the dressing. Peel away the outer skin of the green garlic and chop the pulp into a paste (the pulp should be very soft so this is an easy task). Add the garlic paste to a small bowl with a splash of champagne vinegar and a pinch of salt and stir. Add ½ cup olive oil and whisk. Taste, adjust the seasoning, and set aside.

Once the carrots have finished cooking, remove them from the pans but save the yellow-orange carrot liquid. In a clean pot, heat 2 tablespoons of the butter on medium heat and let it cook to a dark brown color. Add ½ cup of the yellow-orange carrot liquid and a pinch of salt. Whisk it over medium heat and add a splash of champagne vinegar, along with the final 2 tablespoons of butter. Continue to whisk and taste: if it's too acidic, add more butter. If it's too buttery, add some water.

To plate, carefully toss the carrots with some of the green garlic dressing. Lift the carrots onto plates, distributing the purple and orange and yellow equally. Spoon the brown butter sauce on top and sprinkle with the reserved bread crumbs. If you're using the radish sprouts and wood sorrel, place them on top and spoon on more of the green garlic dressing; serve immediately.

Grilled Brassica with Dandelion-Green Vinaigrette

Serves 2

Words can be deceiving when it comes to food. Patterson referred to this dish as "grilled brassica," which sounds intimidating and exotic, like some kind of fish you can only find in Europe. In fact, *Brassica* is the name of the genus of vegetables that includes broccoli, cauliflower, and their various relatives. The idea is that you go to the market, find members of this family, and grill them up, serving them with a pungent dandelion-green vinaigrette that also gets tossed with some cooked bulgur wheat. It's an easy dish that's also a creative, outside-of-the-box meal for vegetarians. When your vegan friends ask what it is, say: "*Brassica* . . . it's okay, it was raised humanely."

½ cup dandelion greens, blanched quickly in salted water, shocked in ice water, squeezed dry in a towel, and very finely chopped

1 shallot, minced

1 teaspoon champagne vinegar, plus more to taste

2 lemons

1 caperberry, chopped

¼ cup olive oil, plus more as necessary

Kosher salt

Crushed red pepper flakes

About 2 cups of florets from different members of the *Brassica* family, such as broccoli, cauliflower, romanesco broccoli, broccoli di rape, and broccoli di cicco

½ cup cooked bulgur wheat

¼ cup almonds, toasted and chopped

In a small bowl, stir together the dandelion greens, shallot, champagne vinegar, the juice of 1 lemon, the caperberry, the olive oil, a pinch of salt, and a pinch of red pepper flakes. Adjust for seasoning and consistency (it should look like a chunky pesto).

Heat a grill or a cast-iron pan on medium-high heat, add a splash of olive oil, and then add all of the *Brassica* with a pinch of salt. Spread out the vegetables and don't move them until they start to color, at least 1 minute. Allow them to brown on all sides, a few minutes more, until thoroughly cooked (a knife should go through them easily), 7 to 8 minutes total. Set aside.

In a small bowl, stir the bulgur together with some of the dandelion dressing.

Spoon the bulgur onto plates and top with more dressing. Squeeze the second lemon all over the hot *Brassica* and then spoon the vegetables on top of the bulgur. Drizzle with more dressing, sprinkle with the almonds, and serve immediately.

Patterson serves this in such a lovely way, it's worth noting: he spoons the bulgar in a C-shape just around the perimeter of the round plate. Then he tops it with the vegetables and the almonds, so it only takes up a fraction of the plate's surface but makes the presentation that much more dramatic. That said, it's totally fine to serve this family-style on a large platter (as pictured).

Curtis Duffy

Chef-owner, Grace
Chicago, Illinois

Duffy's Kitchen Know-How

THEY LOOK LIKE kumquats, but finger limes are far more precious and difficult to find. If you can find them, though, they elevate a dish with their citrusy, caviar-like interiors.

AVAILABLE IN most health food stores, xanthan gum is a natural thickener that allows you to control viscosity. You can use it to thicken ingredients that wouldn't thicken naturally by themselves. For example, you can use it to make a great fat-free salad dressing by mixing balsamic vinegar, herbs, and ⅛ teaspoon xanthan gum— just enough so it thickens. Instead of a 3:1 ratio of oil to vinegar, you get a thickened dressing with zero fat.

AT HOME, when cooking for his family, Duffy often does away with his complex techniques and esoteric ingredients. He grills chicken and serves it with quinoa that's tossed with chopped toasted hazelnuts and assorted dried fruit (it's a good meal for you to try, too).

When chef Curtis Duffy focuses, he's quiet and intense. After greeting me in the entryway of Avenues (his former restaurant), he asks me to wait a few minutes and then goes to a table to concentrate on his own work.

Because of his focus, Duffy creates food that puts him at the very forefront of his profession. His dishes are wildly imaginative: White Chocolate–Covered Sudachi Spheres, and Cassia Bud with Tropical Notes and African Blue Basil, to name a couple. He's worked with some of the country's greatest chefs, including Charlie Trotter and Grant Achatz, with whom Duffy helped open Alinea in 2005, a restaurant *Gourmet* once called the best in the United States.

When Duffy finally finishes his work, I can tell his mind has now shifted to the task at hand: teaching me how to cook the way that he cooks. The first dish we make together, a corn soup that's anything but simple, has more elements in it than I have ingredients in my kitchen at home. The finished dish contains corn shoots, coriander blossoms, a plum puree, diced peaches, freeze-dried corn, finger limes (a peculiar ingredient that produces what looks like lime caviar), a corn-flavored sponge cake made in the microwave, and a coconut ginger dome made with liquid nitrogen and infused with a burnt-corn-husk oil. Oh, and popcorn too.

How does a dish like this come into being? Again, *focus*.

"You start with the ingredient," explains Duffy, "and you ask, 'What goes with that ingredient? What's common? What's extreme?'" He shows me his notebook, in which he writes the main ingredient at the top of the page and supporting elements below. Somehow, by focusing intensely on how something tastes, he arrives at a dish that's surprising (the chill of the coconut dome, the sweetness of the peach, the tartness of the finger lime), and yet still a successful meditation on the star ingredient, corn.

"Okay," I say, pointing at a box of heirloom tomatoes. "So I just bought heirloom tomatoes at the farmer's market and made a salad in which I cut them into wedges, tossed them with olive oil and vinegar, and added some onion and basil. How would I Curtis Duffy that dish?"

"Well, what goes with tomatoes? Tarragon, vinegar, basil, bread. You start there. Then you ask: How can I present the tomato in different ways? You could juice them and turn them into tomato water. You can add gelatin to some of that water and whip it or maybe freeze it. You could add olive oil infused with mandarin oranges. You could make a tarragon puree and freeze it with liquid nitrogen."

By meditating on the main ingredients and then free-associating outward, it *is* possible to create food like this. But in a million years, I'd never come up with the other dishes Duffy teaches me: crab with *togarashi,* cucumber juice, and orange blossom floral cream, and braised short ribs with fried broccoli florets and a lime puree.

Focus, it turns out, is only part of the equation; when making food on this level, it also helps to be a genius.

"It's never been about the technique, just the ingredient."

Crab and Cucumber

Serves 4

This is a wonderfully light dish that works a subtle and refreshing magic. It's especially good to eat when it's warm outside. The cucumber juice is clean and pure tasting and it's pepped up by the pickled cucumber coins. If you have trouble finding *togarashi,* you can skip it, though it certainly adds an unusual note to the whole affair. This, of course, is a stripped-down version of Duffy's work of art (see photograph, left)—a dish that included a layer of crystallized sugar, and a floral cream shot through a whipped cream canister—but I think you'll find this take on it very satisfying and doable.

3 cucumbers, peeled

½ cup white wine vinegar

½ cup sugar

Kosher salt

1 red jalapeño, sliced very thin

½ pound fresh lump crabmeat

Togarashi (Japanese spice mix; see Resources, page 371)

Trout roe (optional)

● *Togarashi* is a Japanese condiment with a spicy, citrusy kick, made with orange peel, sesame seeds, cayenne, ginger, Szechuan pepper, and nori.

Lay a cucumber horizontally on the cutting board. Plunge an apple corer into it vertically, removing several rods of cucumber. Cut those rods into coins about ¼ inch thick, discarding any that have too many seeds. Continue with the other cucumbers until you have ½ cup of cucumber coins. In a bowl, whisk together the white wine vinegar, sugar, and ½ cup water. Add the cucumber and let it soak as you continue the recipe.

Take the hollowed-out cucumbers and chop them roughly. Toss them into a blender with ½ cup water and a big pinch of salt and blend just to break them down (you want a chunky mixture).

Strain the mixture through a sieve—pressing hard to release all the cucumber juice—and taste for seasoning.

To serve, pour cucumber juice into each serving dish and place a few jalapeño rings in the liquid along with a few pickled cucumber rods. Place a scoop of crab on top of each dish, sprinkle with *togarashi,* and, if you have it, garnish with a spoonful of trout roe.

Chilled
Corn Soup

Serves 4

This is the best corn soup I've ever had, hands down. The focus here is on the corn, so use the freshest and sweetest corn you can find in the peak of summer. This soup, all by itself, is a wonder: thick and creamy, and the only ingredients used are corn, olive oil, sugar, salt, lime juice, black pepper, and cilantro. The key is extracting all of the starch so that when you cook it, the soup thickens.

10 ears of sweet corn
Olive oil
Kosher salt
Sugar

Juice of 1 lime
Freshly ground black pepper
Cilantro leaves (optional)

Using a serrated knife, cut off the kernels from the corn. Reserve 1 cup of kernels and place the rest of the kernels in the blender. Using the back side of a paring knife, scrape down all the cobs and release the various clingy bits—they'll look like white flakes—onto the cutting board. Add these to the blender too.

Blend the kernels, the white flakes, and just enough water so the liquid comes out of the corn. You may need to add more water; the mixture should look like a wet smoothie.

Strain all the liquid from the corn through a chinois or strainer into a pot; using a rubber spatula, press hard to release all of the liquid. Meanwhile, rinse out the blender.

Bring the corn liquid to a boil, whisking constantly over medium-high heat. This heating process will cook off the starch; allow it to come to a full boil and cook for about a minute until it starts to resemble a soft custard. Transfer it to the blender.

Blend for 1 minute, being careful not to cover the blender entirely or the top will blow off (hold a towel over the open hole). Add a splash of olive oil and a big pinch of salt, blend, and taste. Not sweet enough? Add some sugar. Keep blending and adjusting it until you love the way it tastes.

To quickly chill the soup, put it in a bowl and rest it in a larger bowl of ice water or (the easier option) put it in the refrigerator. Allow the soup to chill until it's cool.

Boil the reserved cup of kernels in a pot of boiling salted water for 2 to 3 minutes, until the starch is cooked out but they're still firm. Strain and place in a bowl, tossing the kernels with olive oil, lime juice, salt, and pepper to taste. Allow to cool to room temperature.

To finish, spoon some of the corn kernels into 4 soup bowls. Pour the soup over and garnish with a few cilantro leaves, if you'd like.

Duffy says, "It's a tedious process, but the end result is a really solid soup." Those clingy bits not only have a lot of flavor but also contain much of the starch that'll make the soup thick.

Keep in mind that because this will be served chilled, the flavors will mellow later on, so be bold.

Try a few creative garnishes based on what Duffy serves. Add cubed corn bread, freeze-dried corn, and/or popcorn to the finished bowls.

Short Ribs Braised in Coconut Milk

Serves 4

One might think that Duffy's short rib, shellacked with a lime glaze and surrounded by a lime meringue, cilantro blossoms, confited purple Peruvian potatoes, and a pine nut puree, would be the furthest you could possibly get from a comforting home-cooked meal. Yet, if you focus on just the short rib and its cooking method—braised, as it is, in coconut milk with lots of spices and ginger and garlic—suddenly you have a sophisticated one-pot meal that's easy to make at home. Be careful, though, to keep the coconut milk at a low simmer; if you get it too hot, the sauce will break.

FOR THE CURE

5 cloves garlic, roughly chopped

1 large shallot, roughly chopped

1-inch knob of ginger, peeled and roughly chopped

1 tablespoon whole allspice berries

1 tablespoon fennel seeds

1 whole star anise

5 cardamom pods

½ cup kosher salt

½ cup sugar

4 beef short ribs, on the bone

FOR THE BRAISE

Vegetable oil

1 onion, chopped

1 carrot, peeled and chopped

Kosher salt

3 cloves garlic, chopped

1-inch knob of ginger, peeled and chopped

1 tablespoon whole allspice berries

1 tablespoon fennel seeds

1 whole star anise

5 cardamom pods

Zest of 1 lime (use a vegetable peeler and be careful to only extract the thin green skin and none of the pith)

2 cups chicken stock

1 (15-ounce) can coconut milk, well stirred

¼ cup fresh lime juice, plus more if needed

2 cups cooked rice

Mixture of whole cilantro and mint leaves and scallions, slightly chopped, for garnish

Four to six hours before you plan to cook the short ribs, make the cure by first combining the garlic, shallot, and ginger in a blender or food processor. Add the allspice, fennel, star anise, and cardamom pods and continue to blend. With a rubber spatula, scrape the paste into a bowl and stir together with the salt and sugar.

● If it doesn't blend up easily, add some vegetable oil to help it form a paste.

In a plastic container with a lid or in a resealable plastic bag, rub the cure all over the short ribs; cover and refrigerate for 4 to 6 hours.

Rinse the cure off the short ribs and dry them very well with paper towels.

In a Dutch oven, heat a few tablespoons of vegetable oil over medium-high heat until hot. Sear the short ribs, 2 to 3 minutes a side, until they are deep golden brown all over.

Lift the short ribs onto a plate and pour off any extra oil or fat, leaving about 1 tablespoon in the pan. On medium heat, add the onion, carrot, and a pinch of salt and sauté until the vegetables have softened and darkened slightly, 3 to 4 minutes. Add the garlic and ginger and continue to sauté for another minute, then add all the spices and the lime zest. Stir and then add the chicken stock and coconut milk and another pinch of salt. Bring to a simmer, put the short ribs back in, and cover the pan. Braise over low heat for 2½ to 3 hours, stirring every so often to make sure the coconut milk doesn't separate.

After 2½ hours, check the short ribs with two forks: you should be able to take the meat off easily. If the short ribs are indeed fork-tender, remove them to a plate and strain the sauce into a separate pot. Bring the sauce to a simmer and allow it to reduce slightly, 5 minutes or so, then season with more salt and lime juice, starting with ¼ cup, until the flavor is intense and bright.

To serve, spoon cooked rice onto each plate, top with a short rib and a ladleful of the sauce, and scatter with the fresh herbs. Serve immediately.

Because of the sugar in the cure, the sear will happen more quickly than normal, so make sure to pay attention. Use a pair of tongs to lift up the short ribs to see how dark they're getting.

José Andrés

Chef-owner, American Eats Tavern, Minibar, Bazaar, Jaleo, and E
Washington, D.C., Los Angeles, California, and Las Vegas, Nevada

You can't learn passion. You can learn craft, you can learn the history of your chosen field, you can even learn *style,* but passion? You've got to have it in your bones.

Chef José Andrés, the legendary Spanish chef, is nothing if not passionate. When he answers the door for me at his home in Bethesda, Maryland, he grunts. As he leads me into his kitchen, I ask about his philosophy when it comes to food and cooking.

"Cooking is not a philosophy," he says. "It's a lifestyle."

In his kitchen, beautifully arrayed with bowls of fruit and an Ibérico ham on a stand, Andrés says, "Let's go," and begins adding water to a big bowl of coarse salt.

"Take the leaves off the stem," he tells me, handing me sprigs of rosemary. Soon, I'm mixing all the salt, water, and herbs together by hand and packing them around a pork loin that rests in a baking dish.

As Andrés places it in the oven, he explains that the size of the meat doesn't matter as much as the radius: how far the distance is from the outside to the center. "That is what determines how it cooks," he says. "Not how big it is. That's why you can't always follow recipes."

Then he repeats his mantra: "Let's go."

While the pork cooks, we go to the juicer and Chef Andrés has me juice a pile of oranges and grapefruits while he grabs a pitcher and ice. When he comes back, he asks, "Do you always cook with your hand in your pocket?"

I look down and see my hand in my pocket.

"Um," I stammer.

"Don't," he says.

He pours Hendrick's gin into the pitcher with the juice that I've juiced, then adds torn basil, brown sugar, and cava. He stirs it all together, tastes it, and pours it into two martini glasses. "Taste," he commands and I do, even though it's 9:30 a.m. It's sunny, fizzy, and not at all too sweet.

Finally, we proceed to the dish that Andrés is best known for: his deconstructed gazpacho. Only don't use the word *deconstructed* or he'll get testy. "What is 'deconstructed'?" he asks, and I'm not sure how to answer. We're at the table at this point, eating the food we've cooked. I decide to change the subject.

We talk more about his charity work—Andrés has worked for fifteen years with the D.C. Central Kitchen, an organization that helps ex-prisoners learn cooking skills. I comment that it's nice that someone so successful uses his success to help others.

He's quiet for a second, brooding. "I don't see myself as successful," he says, almost to himself. "I don't know how to define success."

It's a truly genuine moment, one that speaks to the depths within this man who cooks food for a living. When I taste the gazpacho—a clear liquid (he uses a juicer) artfully plated with tomato seeds, cucumber sliced from the core, and edible flowers—there's a clarity and intensity of flavor that could only come from someone so passionate about everything he does.

If the question is "How do you cook with passion?," the answer seems to be staring me in the face: to cook with passion, you have to care as much as José Andrés does.

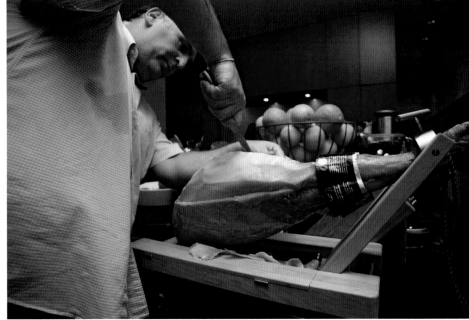

"When is the last
time you spoke
to a tomato?
Never, right?
You need to
speak to your
produce."

Citrus
Gin Cocktail

Serves 4

There's nothing cloying about this cocktail of orange juice, grapefruit juice, gin, and Champagne. In fact, it's rather bracing. Add sugar for sweetness, but use restraint. At the start of the meal, this drink is a terrific palate cleanser: the sharpness of the citrus and the fizz of the Champagne get you ready for whatever you're planning to eat next.

½ cup freshly squeezed orange juice

½ cup freshly squeezed grapefruit juice

¼ cup Hendrick's gin, straight from the freezer

1 cup Champagne or Prosecco

Approximately ¼ cup brown sugar

3 or 4 torn basil leaves

Mix all ingredients in a large pitcher and adjust to taste. Serve in chilled martini glasses.

Juiced
Gazpacho

Serves 4

Gazpacho is normally an easy dish to make: you blend the ingredients together, taste, and adjust the seasoning. This gazpacho asks you to do more. Everything is juiced; Andrés uses an industrial-strength juicer, but you can use a blender and a strainer. This produces a remarkably clear liquid instead of the muddier gazpacho most of us know. The cucumber is cut into cylindrical rounds and the tomato—well, according to Andrés, you have to talk to it. When you talk to it, you'll discover that you can "open the door" and remove the seed packet inside (further instruction below). What results is a gazpacho that you can make at home, filtered through the perspective of a great culinary artist.

2 cucumbers, peeled	½ cup olive oil
1 green bell pepper, cored, seeded, and cut into chunks	¼ cup sherry vinegar
1 clove garlic	Kosher salt
4 large red tomatoes	Edible flowers (optional)

● These are always best from the farmer's market (or grown yourself) in summer.

Lay a cucumber horizontally on the cutting board. Plunge an apple corer into it vertically, removing several rods of cucumber. Cut those rods into coins about ¼ inch thick, discarding any that have too many seeds. Lay a few cucumber coins into each of the four bowls.

Cut the leftover cucumber into chunks and place in a blender with the green pepper and the garlic. Add ½ cup water and blend for 30 seconds. Press through a chinois or strainer into a pitcher.

Prepare the tomatoes: slice the top and bottom off each tomato so you create two flat surfaces. When you do this, make sure to expose the seed packets on the inside (so cut at least an inch off the top and bottom). Then, cut a vertical slice next to one of the membranes all the way down so you can open the tomato like a book to reveal the seed packet inside (this is the gelatin-like substance holding all the seeds together). Remove the seed packet with the blade of the knife, keeping it together and lowering it carefully into the presentation bowl. Repeat so that each bowl has 3 seed packets.

● Andrés called this "the most amazing gelatin in the history of mankind."

Cut the remaining tomato parts into chunks and place in the blender. Blend on a very low speed for 30 seconds. Strain into the same pitcher with the cucumber, green pepper, and garlic juice.

Whisk the olive oil into the pitcher along with the sherry vinegar. Add salt and taste to adjust.

● If the mixture is really foamy (from all the aeration that happens in the blender), use a spoon to remove the foamy top layer.

Pour the finished mixture into the serving bowls over the cylindrical cucumber rounds and tomato seed packets. Garnish with edible flowers, if using, and serve immediately.

Salt-Crusted Pork Loin with Ibérico Ham and Asparagus

Serves 4 to 6

Cooking isn't just about making dinner, it's also about the sights, the smells, and the feel of the ingredients between your fingers. This dish offers you the chance to get your hands dirty in a very fun way: wet kosher salt until it's the consistency of damp snow and then pack it around a pork loin before roasting it in the oven. The result is a very moist, very flavorful piece of pork that makes for a dramatic presentation when you crack it open at the table. Don't skip the accoutrement: Andrés serves this with Ibérico ham he carves off the pig leg itself. Since not many of us can afford to have a seven-hundred-dollar Ibérico ham waiting for us in our kitchen, Serrano ham (if you can find it) is a totally adequate substitution, as is prosciutto. You're looking for a contrast between the smoky cured meat and the pure flavor of the salt-roasted meat.

Kosher salt

2 tablespoons fresh rosemary leaves, plus a few extra

2 tablespoons fresh thyme leaves, plus a few extra

2- to 3-pound boneless pork loin with some fat on it, at room temperature

Freshly ground black pepper

Extra virgin olive oil

The thin tops (1-inch pieces) from 1 bunch of skinny asparagus

12 or so thin slices Jamón Ibérico, Serrano ham or, if you can't find Spanish ham, prosciutto

Preheat the oven to 450°F.

In a large bowl, add 5 cups salt and enough cold water to create the consistency of wet snow. Once the salt is wet and moldable, add the rosemary and thyme.

In a large baking dish, place the pork loin. Sprinkle with black pepper and a few of the reserved rosemary leaves and thyme leaves and then pack the salt all around it. Make sure there's an even layer of salt everywhere: that's what will help it cook evenly. Roast for 30 to 45 minutes, until the salt is a solid block just starting to brown.

While the meat is cooking, heat a grill pan or a cast-iron skillet on medium-high heat. When it's very hot, add a splash of olive oil and the asparagus. Leave the asparagus alone and let it brown on one side, 3 to 4 minutes; when it does, push all the asparagus to one side, season with salt and pepper, and turn off the heat.

To plate, layer slices of the ham on each plate. Crack open the salt crust (you may want to do this tableside—it's dramatic!) and remove the pork, leaving behind any extra salt. Slice the pork thin and layer on top of the ham. Top with the browned asparagus.

- Stir with your hands while you add the water; add less at first, because it's easier to add more water later than to add more salt.

- If you want, you can insert a probe thermometer into the meat and cook it until the interior is 135 to 140°F.

- Make sure the pan is wide enough so the asparagus doesn't crowd. If necessary, cook the asparagus in batches.

- To clean the baking dish, just run scalding hot water over everything. The salt will melt.

Naomi Pomeroy

Chef-owner, Beast
Portland, Oregon

To say that chef Naomi Pomeroy has strong opinions about food would be a profound understatement.

On a bright day in December, we're in the kitchen of her hugely popular Portland restaurant, Beast, and Pomeroy is prepping onions for the French onion soup she'll be serving later that night to her forty-eight dinner guests. In the time we spend together, she spends most of it prepping these onions: there's a giant plastic crate full of them. She needs that many onions because they'll cook down into a golden, concentrated mass to which she'll add her wildly intense meat stock. She'll season it with Tabasco and thirty-year-aged balsamic vinegar, and it will be the best French onion soup I've ever had, but right now she's peeling off onion skin and talking to me about the weather.

"Weather is a big influence on what I cook," she tells me. "On a rainy day, I like comfort foods, something meaty. On a hot day, I like lighter foods. I don't want to cook inside, so I'll grill."

The discussion about food and weather leads to a conversation about balancing a menu. "When you plan a menu, you have to think start to finish. You don't serve a creamy pork entrée and then serve chocolate for dessert."

I pause for a second. Didn't I do that once? "What do you serve?"

"Something fruity and bright."

She informs me that chefs frequently judge customers who order the wrong dessert to follow their entrée or, in other cases, the wrong glass of wine.

"There's nothing more painful," she says, "than making a beautiful velouté of asparagus, sending it out, and watching someone wash it down with a big glass of Cabernet."

She tenses up. "I want to scream: 'That wine is ruining your soup and your soup is ruining that wine!'" She pauses and concludes, "Sometimes people need to be told what to do."

Which is why Beast is the perfect vehicle for Pomeroy to channel her need for control. Eating dinner at Beast is like going to someone's house for dinner. The menu is prewritten (so no one can order the wrong dessert) and there are no substitutions.

"I throw a dinner party every night," says Pomeroy. "That's all we do here."

Except, most dinner parties we all normally go to involve a thrown-together lasagna; Pomeroy's dinner party starts with that dazzling French onion soup, moves on to foie gras bonbons, steak tartare and quail egg toast, and pig's-head terrine. It continues with dry-aged, grass-fed beef wrapped in bacon and served with lentils and turnips, relaxes into butter lettuce salad with fried Meyer lemons, and finishes with a cheese plate and, for dessert, an elegant chocolate soufflé that's also a bit scruffy. ("There's digital cooking and analog," says Pomeroy. "We're very analog. We like the scratches and pops.")

Control is a tricky issue for many eaters. After all, eating is an intimate act: most diners want to have some say in what they feed their bodies. But when you put yourself

"My number one pet peeve is when an element is on the plate just for the color."

into the hands of someone who knows what they're doing, or, inversely, when you let others put themselves into *your* hands, the results can be sublime. "You can just feel it," Pomeroy tells me before I leave that night. "You can just tell when food is made with a measure of love in the heart."

Like a mother who meddles in her children's lives because she wants the very best for them, Pomeroy meddles with her dinner plates until they're exactly what she thinks should be eaten. Some may call her a control freak, but it's her insistence on control that makes her food taste so good.

French
Onion Soup

Serves 4

Accuse me of hyperbolizing, I don't care. This is the French onion soup of your dreams, the one you fantasize about slurping in your Parisian fantasy where, on a cold winter's day, you stumble into a bistro and warm up over a bowl of *soupe à l'oignon*. What makes it so good? It all comes down to the rich and flavorful meat stock. Make sure, at the end, to pump up the flavor with the balsamic and Tabasco before ladling it into the bowls. It pays to make a lot: this soup goes fast.

6 tablespoons (¾ stick) unsalted butter

6 to 8 onions, peeled and sliced into thin half-moons

Kosher salt

6 cups Beast Stock (page 342)

Tabasco sauce

30-year-aged balsamic vinegar or the best balsamic you have

4 slices toasted ciabatta bread or French bread (toast on a grill or under a broiler)

1 cup shredded Gruyère cheese

In a large stockpot or Dutch oven, melt the butter on high heat and then add all the onions. Add a light sprinkling of salt and stir, coating the onions, and allow them to cook until they start to brown, stirring frequently. As soon as you see a little color, 5 to 10 minutes, lower the heat to medium low and continue to cook, stirring and scraping the bottom of the pan, until the onions are a very dark shade of brown, 30 to 45 minutes.

Add all the stock and another sprinkling of salt. Bring to a simmer on medium heat, then turn the heat down to low and allow the soup to cook for another 30 minutes.

Taste the soup and adjust it with salt, Tabasco, and the balsamic. This is your chance to make the soup taste as great as possible.

Preheat the oven to 500°F and place 4 ovenproof soup bowls on a cookie sheet. Add a piece of toasted bread to each bowl and then ladle the soup over the bread, filling each bowl three quarters of the way. Top each bowl with some of the grated cheese and pop into the oven.

Bake until the cheese is melted and starting to brown. Serve the soup piping hot.

Besides using a rich, flavorful, homemade meat stock, this is the other key step in making a world-class French onion soup. You have to let the onions get dark, but it has to happen gradually.

Porcini-Rubbed Roast Beef with Demi-Glace and Caramelized Turnips

Serves 4

This is a special-occasion dish, the kind of meal you make when dinner really matters. Truth be told, once you make a demi-glace (see page 342) all you need to do is season the meat, sear it and roast it, and then caramelize the turnips. Just make sure to follow Pomeroy's directive about letting the meat rest: "If you're eating meat that's hot, it hasn't been properly rested. Get the plate hot and the sauce hot and let the meat rest for twenty minutes."

FOR THE BEEF

½ cup dried porcini mushrooms, ground in a spice grinder (to yield ¼ cup porcini powder)

Kosher salt

¼ cup coarsely ground black pepper

1 tablespoon truffle salt (see Resources, page 371), plus more for later (optional)

4- to 5-pound prime rib of beef

Olive oil

FOR THE TURNIPS

3 tablespoons unsalted butter

8 medium turnips, cleaned and quartered (no need to peel)

Maple sugar (see Resources) or muscovado sugar

Freshly ground black pepper

TO SERVE

Demi-glace (see page 342)

Fleur de sel or other finishing salt

Chopped parsley

• Pomeroy cooks this with a grass-fed New York strip that she butterflies and then rolls up, so that the porcini–truffle salt mixture is spread more evenly throughout the meat. While it's excellent, the prime rib is a better option to make at home.

In a bowl, combine the porcini powder, ½ cup kosher salt, the coarsely ground pepper, and the truffle salt, if you're using it. Rub the mixture all over the outside of the prime rib. Allow the meat to sit and come to room temperature, at least 1 hour.

Preheat the oven to 350°F.

In a roasting pan large enough to hold the beef, heat 1 to 2 tablespoons olive oil over high heat until almost smoking. Sear the meat on all sides until crusty and brown all over. When it's seared, place the pan in the oven and roast until it reaches an internal temperature of 120°F, about 1 hour. Tent the meat with foil and allow to rest for at least 20 minutes.

In a large sauté pan, heat the butter until foamy and hot and then add the turnips. Sprinkle with the maple sugar and cook, stirring often to keep the sugar from burning, until bronzed on the outside and just cooked through, 10 to 15 minutes. Season with lots of kosher salt and pepper.

• You can mix the sugar with a little water to make a "slurry" to even things out before pouring it over the turnips; but Pomeroy emphasizes you should use just a little water or it'll disrupt the caramelization.

Heat the demi-glace in a small pan.

Drizzle demi-glace over the serving plates, slice the meat into thick slices, and place the meat atop the sauce. Spoon the turnips on the side and drizzle more demi-glace onto the meat; sprinkle with fleur de sel and parsley. Serve immediately.

Lentilpalooza

Serves 4 to 6

This dish is so named because every time I turned my back, Pomeroy added another ingredient. "What is that?" "Oh, just some anchovies." "And that?" "Lamb belly." And so it went as I cooked with her. The end result is a lentil dish that's sweet from the sun-dried tomatoes, briny from the anchovies, and porky from the pancetta. You can make this a few hours ahead and let the flavors meld before eating—just reheat with a splash of water.

2 cups dried green lentils

1 carrot, plus 2 carrots finely chopped

1 celery stalk, plus 2 stalks finely chopped

½ medium yellow onion, plus 1 medium yellow onion cut into ¼-inch dice

¼ cup olive oil

½ cup diced pancetta

A pinch of crushed red pepper flakes

A pinch or two of maple sugar (see Resources, page 371) or muscovado sugar

6 sun-dried tomatoes packed in olive oil

3 anchovies, chopped

3 cloves garlic, sliced

½ cup kale, blanched, squeezed dry, and chopped

A squeeze of fresh lemon juice

A splash of first-press olive oil (or the freshest olive oil you have)

- Pomeroy left these whole, but I like to slice them.

- This is Pomeroy's replacement for the cubed lamb belly she regularly uses. "Most people aren't going to have lamb belly," she concedes.

- Add a few pinches of salt now, and then again when they're almost done.

- Don't add the garlic too early, Pomeroy says. "People do that and it makes everything taste weird. The garlic gets burned."

Start by par-cooking the lentils. In a large pot, add the lentils, the carrot, the celery, and the onion half and cover with cold water by at least an inch. Bring up the heat slowly to a simmer and cook the lentils until just al dente, 15 to 20 minutes. Drain, discard the vegetables, and set the lentils aside.

In a large pan, heat the olive oil with the pancetta over medium-high heat until very hot and the pancetta starts to render. Allow it to cook until the pancetta is crisp and has released most of its fat, 4 to 5 minutes.

Remove the pancetta to a plate and add the chopped carrot and celery and the diced onion. Sprinkle with the red pepper flakes and the maple sugar; cook, stirring, for 1 to 2 minutes.

Add the tomatoes, fry for a minute, then add the anchovies and the garlic. Cook until the anchovies dissolve and the garlic just starts to brown, another 2 minutes or so.

Pat the lentils dry and add them to the pan, frying them in the hot oil until they start to crisp up a bit, 3 to 4 minutes.

Add the pancetta and the kale and cook, stirring, for another 2 minutes. If the lentils are getting too brown, you can add some water at this point.

Taste for seasoning, squeeze the lemon juice over everything, and drizzle with the great olive oil. Serve hot.

Beast Stock and Demi-Glace

Makes about 4 quarts of stock and about 1 cup of demi-glace

Pssst . . . lean in close, I don't want to be too loud about this. What you're about to receive here, in this recipe, are the *keys to the kingdom*. These keys open the door to the intimidating world of classic French cooking techniques—techniques that stretch all the way back to Escoffier and live on today in the kitchens of the world's greatest restaurants. Make this Beast Stock from Pomeroy's Beast restaurant and you will have an elixir that will not only make for the best French onion soup of your life (see page 338), but will also provide the basis for a demi-glace—a concentrated, syrupy, meaty sauce—that will elevate any and every meat dish you make forevermore. Welcome to the big leagues.

FOR THE STOCK

10 pounds veal bones

2 onions, chopped

2 carrots, chopped

1 celery stalk, chopped

6 tablespoons tomato paste

½ bottle good red wine

10 whole black peppercorns

1 whole head of garlic, unpeeled, kept intact

3 sprigs of thyme

FOR THE DEMI-GLACE

30-year-aged balsamic vinegar

Truffle salt (see Resources, page 371)

Preheat the oven to 500°F.

Arrange the bones in a single layer in a roasting pan. Roast for 1 to 1½ hours, until the bones are a nice brown color, but be careful not to let them burn; you may need to flip them over every so often.

Add the onions, carrots, celery, and tomato paste to the pan, stir, and continue to roast for another 30 to 45 minutes, until all the vegetables have browned.

Remove the roasting pan and, with a pair of tongs or a large spoon, transfer the contents of the pan to a large stockpot. Carefully set the roasting pan on 2 burners, turn on medium heat, and add the wine, peppercorns, garlic, and thyme. Cook, scraping the bottom of the pan with a wooden spoon until the wine has reduced slightly. Pour the wine, peppercorns, garlic, and thyme into the stockpot with the bones.

Add 6 to 8 quarts cold water to the stockpot (it should just cover the bones when you add it). Turn on the heat to medium low and bring the liquid to the gentlest of gentle simmers, half-covering the pot with a lid. When you get to the gentle simmer, lower the heat to as low as it goes. Cook like this for as many hours as you can afford: at least 8 and up to 12. Skim the top every so often.

- If you can, substitute 3 pounds duck bones for 3 pounds of the veal bones (though duck bones may be hard to come by). You'll get a more complex flavor.

- Of course, if you don't want to spend the money on thirty-year-aged balsamic vinegar or truffle salt, this is still worth making. Use any balsamic and use regular salt. The end result will still amaze you; it just won't be quite the same as Pomeroy's.

- Pomeroy uses a hotel pan (a wide, deep pan that looks like a cross between a roasting pan and a cookie sheet), and then, instead of transferring everything to a stockpot, she returns the pan—after it gets deglazed with the red wine and refilled with the bones and water—covered with parchment and aluminum foil to a 300°F oven and leaves it overnight to cook. If you have a hotel pan, this method will result in a more even stock (with fewer impurities because of the consistent temperature).

- Burnt bones will give your stock a bitter flavor, which won't be good.

- If you let it get too hot, the stock will turn cloudy and murky. You don't want that.

Strain the stock into 2 pots or large bowls. Discard the solids. Reserve one quarter of the stock for making the demi-glace (see the next step) and the rest for the French onion soup, if making. Any stock that you don't use now, you can freeze; it will keep for up to 6 months.

Pour the stock reserved for the demi-glace into a pot. Turn up the heat to medium and bring the stock to an active simmer. Let it reduce (this will take a few hours) until it coats a spoon fully but not to the point that it's sticky. If it gets too thick, you can fix it with a little water. Season with the aged balsamic and truffle salt until it tastes mind-blowingly wonderful. Use immediately or reserve for later. It will keep for up to a week, covered, in the refrigerator and for up to 3 months in the freezer.

Hugh Acheson

Chef-partner, Five & Ten and Empire State South
Athens, Georgia, and Atlanta, Georgia

When one thinks Southern cooking, kimchi doesn't necessarily come to mind. Chef Hugh Acheson, creator of the legendary Five & Ten restaurant in Athens, Georgia, and the proprietor of the new Empire State South in Atlanta, wants to change that.

"This is the *burgeoning* South," says Acheson, from a table in the dining room. "This is the South of Buford Highway [a main artery of Atlanta known for its multiethnic community]; this is the South as a mosaic. There are so many different cultures here, and I want to use that to reinterpret the things that are the staples all around us."

Reinterpret Acheson does, with flair. In his kitchen, which is large and full of excited energy, Acheson uses a hodgepodge of techniques and ingredients that blend seamlessly together in his elegantly composed dishes.

For example, that kimchi gets folded into rice grits, an ingredient that Acheson's executive chef Ryan Smith explains to me as he begins prepping his *mise en place*. "Back during slavery times," says Smith, "the slaves would have to sift the rice. The owners got the good rice, and whatever fell through went to the slaves. And it's from that broken rice that we get rice grits."

Acheson, who's clearly taken with Southern food culture and lore (he's devoted his career to it), is not, by blood, a Southerner. "I grew up in Ottawa, Canada," he tells me, explaining that he moved to Georgia after marrying his wife, who was from Athens. "But being an outsider lets me approach this food from a whole new angle."

If Acheson had only set out to dutifully re-create Southern staples, he might have quickly become discouraged or, worse, disinterested. "I'm learning every day," he says. "But we do it our way. If not, we get bored."

That notion—avoiding boredom—is one that few of us consider in the kitchen. But cooking should divert you, it should engage you, and, at its best, it should enrich you.

For example, Acheson uses classic French techniques to take his food to a higher level. When he and I sear scallops in a hot pan with oil, Acheson begins preparations for a classic beurre blanc sauce. In a small pot, he reduces white wine vinegar and white wine with a shallot, garlic, bay leaf, and thyme. He strains that into another pot set over a low flame and then he hands me a small whisk.

I get to work as he adds small cubes of very cold butter. As the sauce begins to emulsify, Acheson watches, careful not to add too much butter at once or the sauce might break. Even though you would find this technique in stuffy old French cooking textbooks, this activity is anything but boring. It is, in fact, fun.

At the end we have two composed restaurant dishes—scallops with parsnip puree and beurre blanc, and pork belly with kimchi rice grits—and one home-cooking dish, chicken braised with vinegar. These aren't reverent re-creations of Southern staples; these dishes are something new, something exciting.

As an outsider who takes liberties with Southern food, Acheson proves that if you're not bored with what you're doing you will make food that's anything but boring.

"Never get locked into a recipe. The halibut sucks, but there's a stunning grouper. So make grouper instead."

Chicken Thighs Braised in Cider Vinegar with Fennel and Radish

Serves 2

This is an intensely flavorful chicken dinner, easy enough for a weeknight, and the result of several factors that all work together. Factor #1: You use chicken thighs, which, when braised, become wonderfully tender. Factor #2: You brown them slowly, so the fat renders out completely. Factor #3: You braise them in a combination of chicken stock and cider vinegar, which packs a huge punch. Don't skip the fennel or the radish: they absorb all that liquid and extend the deliciousness by many extra bites. Also, make sure to brown the chicken well at the beginning; it will pay off in the end.

4 large chicken thighs, skin on, bone in

Kosher salt

2 tablespoons canola oil

1 tablespoon unsalted butter, cut into cubes, plus 1 tablespoon for later

¼ cup minced shallots (from two large shallots)

1 cup cider vinegar (such as Bragg's; which you can buy directly on their Web site, www.bragg.com)

1 bay leaf

1 to 2 cups homemade chicken stock

½ medium fennel, quartered, cored, and sliced thin horizontally

1 radish, sliced very thinly

Good olive oil

¼ cup chopped parsley

Preheat the oven to 325°F. Season the chicken well with salt.

Heat an ovenproof pan or a Dutch oven on high heat, then add the canola oil. Add the chicken skin side down—it should sizzle right away—then lower the heat to between medium and medium low. You want the fat to render slowly; otherwise you'll leave pockets of fat behind. Monitor the heat so there's a steady sizzle, but not an aggressive one.

Add the butter and, without moving the chicken around, use a spoon to baste the chicken as it browns. When the skin is a deep golden brown, 3 to 4 minutes, flip the chicken over. If the skin is properly cooked, it should detach easily. Brown on the other side, 2 minutes, and then remove the chicken to a plate.

Add the shallots and cook until softened. Then add the cider vinegar and the bay leaf, raising the heat and reducing the mixture slightly. The vinegar will get sweeter as it reduces: taste it to see how much chicken stock you want to add so the liquid doesn't lose its edge. Add at least 1 cup of the chicken stock and then return the chicken to the pan, skin side up. The chicken should be halfway covered (you may need to add more stock).

Cover the pan and bake for 40 minutes. Add the fennel and the final tablespoon of butter. Stir, cover, and return to the oven for another 10 minutes.

When the chicken and fennel are fork-tender, use a slotted spoon to remove the chicken to a plate.

Place the pan with the liquid and the fennel on a burner and turn up the heat to high. Reduce the liquid to intensify it and when it's flavorful, after 3 to 4 minutes (make sure to taste it for salt), remove the bay leaf and add the radish. Return the chicken to the pan, lower the heat, and let everything warm through for another 2 to 3 minutes.

When it's time to serve, place the chicken on warm plates with the radish and fennel and drizzle with good olive oil, then sprinkle with parsley. This dish goes well with crusty bread, lightly browned under a broiler and drizzled with olive oil.

Seared Scallops with Mustard Greens, Parsnip Puree, and Beurre Blanc

Serves 4

This is a fancy restaurant dish, something that an upscale place might charge you thirty dollars to eat. But let me tell you a secret: when you break it down into components, this is pretty easy to cook at home. If you make the parsnip puree ahead and make the beurre blanc ahead, too, all you have to do is quickly sauté some mustard greens and sear the scallops. Look for scallops labeled as "dry" scallops (the other kind, which are treated with sodium tripolyphosphate and are usually sitting in liquid, won't brown up as well).

● Slice the parsnips in half vertically and then cut out the tough core at the thick end.

FOR THE PARSNIP PUREE

4 medium parsnips, peeled, cored, and roughly chopped

⅔ cup milk

½ cup heavy cream

Salt

FOR THE BEURRE BLANC

¼ cup white wine vinegar

¼ cup dry white wine

1 shallot, peeled

2 cloves garlic, peeled

1 bay leaf

A few sprigs of thyme

4 tablespoons (½ stick) very cold unsalted butter, cubed

1 tablespoon chopped parsley

FOR THE MUSTARD GREENS

2 tablespoons unsalted butter

1 shallot, chopped

1 cup mustard greens, cleaned and chopped

A pinch of salt

FOR THE SCALLOPS

12 scallops

Salt

2 tablespoons olive oil

2 tablespoons canola oil

2 tablespoons unsalted butter

To make the parsnip puree, place the parsnips in a pot and cover completely with the milk and cream. Add a pinch of salt and bring the mixture to a boil over medium-high heat, reduce to a simmer, and cook until the parsnips are just tender, about 15 minutes. You'll know they're cooked when you can smash one with a wooden spoon.

Strain the parsnips, reserving some liquid, and puree them in a blender. If it's too chunky and won't blend up, add a little of the liquid. If, on the other hand, it looks too thin, don't worry: the mixture will thicken when you heat it up later. Taste and adjust for salt.

To make the beurre blanc, in a small pot, bring the white wine vinegar, wine, shallot, garlic, bay leaf, and thyme to a boil over high heat. Let it reduce from ½ cup of liquid to ¼ cup, 5 to 10 minutes.

Strain the liquid into another small pot and then, on low heat, begin whisking in the butter 1 cube at a time. It's important you do this gradually so you achieve emulsification. Watch the sauce as you do this: it should look creamy and homogeneous, though still rather liquid. Add the parsley and taste to adjust. Set aside.

To make the greens, in a small skillet, melt the butter over medium heat. Add the shallots, cook until soft, and then add the mustard greens with the salt. Cook just until the greens have wilted, 2 to 3 minutes.

To cook the scallops, pat them dry with paper towels and season with salt. In a clean skillet, combine the olive oil and canola oil. Heat until smoking hot. Lower the scallops in, individually, away from you, making sure not to crowd the pan.

Add some of the butter and baste the scallops as they cook. You want to cook them 85 percent of the way on the first side (they'll turn a deep, dark, beautiful brown), about 2 minutes. When they're mostly opaque, carefully turn the scallops over, tilting the pan away from you and flipping the scallops with a spoon. Continue to baste the scallops with fat, and when they're cooked all the way (they'll be firm and totally opaque), remove to a plate lined with paper towels to remove some of the grease.

To plate, reheat the parsnip puree on very low heat and then spoon a little of it on each plate. Pile on the cooked mustard greens, top with two or three scallops, and spoon on the beurre blanc. Serve right away.

Cured Pork Belly with Kimchi Rice Grits

Serves 4

My friend Mark wrote me an e-mail the day after I served him this dish for dinner: "That pork belly haunted my dreams." For good reason! This is the ultimate way to serve up the ultimate part of the pig; every step of the process is intuitive and simple. You cure the belly with salt and sugar, confit it in olive oil, press it in the refrigerator to distribute the fat more evenly, and then, when you're ready to eat, you slice it up and sear it. As for the kimchi rice grits, you can certainly try making this with just rice, but there's something special about ordering a product from a company as well respected as Anson Mills.

Start this dish at least a day before you plan to serve it.

FOR THE RUB

1 teaspoon whole white peppercorns

1 teaspoon crushed red pepper flakes

1 cup kosher salt

½ cup sugar

1 teaspoon freshly grated nutmeg

FOR THE BELLY

2-pound piece of pork belly

4 cups olive oil or duck fat, plus more as needed

FOR THE RICE GRITS

2 cups chicken stock or water

1 cup Anson Mills rice grits (see Resources, page 371)

A pinch of kosher salt

½ cup chopped kimchi

¼ cup heavy cream

Juice of 1 lime

TO FINISH

¼ cup canola oil

¼ cup olive oil

Pickled black radish (see page 294; optional)

● Ask for one with good marbling, otherwise you may get a piece of pure fat.

● You're making a confit—a preservation technique in which you cook something in fat. Store the cooked pork belly covered in the fat, in the refrigerator, for several weeks.

You'll need to start this dish at least 24 hours before you plan to serve it. To make the rub, in a spice grinder, grind the white peppercorns and red pepper flakes into a powder. Stir them together with the salt, sugar, and nutmeg. Use this rub to season the pork belly aggressively and allow the pork belly to sit, coated with the rub and covered with plastic wrap, at room temperature for 2 hours.

Preheat the oven to 300°F. Brush the rub off the pork belly and then, in a Dutch oven or a similar pan, submerge the belly in room-temperature olive oil or duck fat. (Pork fat will work really well here too.) If 4 cups doesn't cover it, you'll need to add more fat: the belly needs to be completely submerged.

continued

Cured Pork Belly with Kimchi Rice Grits (continued)

This step ensures that the fat is evenly distributed throughout the pork belly. Otherwise, one bite might yield a piece with just fat, and another piece that's all meat and no fat.

You can add more kimchi and cream here, if you'd like. Use your best judgment.

The popping and spraying here is the *mean* kind of popping and spraying. Instead of a general fizz of spray, every so often it'll go "POP" and shoot scalding hot oil at you. You may want to use a splatter guard.

Roast uncovered for 2½ to 3 hours. You'll know it's done when a knife or skewer goes through the meat easily.

While the belly is warm, place it on a tray lined with plastic wrap. Cover it with more plastic wrap and top it with another tray that you line with some heavy cans to put weight on top of the belly. Refrigerate overnight.

The next day, cook the grits by bringing the 2 cups of chicken stock to a boil over high heat. Slowly stir in the grits and the salt. Lower the heat and cook until the grits are thick and creamy; taste so you know. If the liquid is gone before the grits are cooked, add more stock or water. Continue cooking until the grits taste cooked through, about 20 minutes. Add the chopped kimchi and cream.

Remove the pork belly from the tray and cut into individual portions. In a large skillet, heat the canola oil and olive oil until very hot but not smoking.

Add the pork belly to the oil and cook very fast—it will pop and spray, 30 seconds to a minute per side. You want to just brown it all over without rendering too much fat.

To finish, add lime juice to the grits to taste and adjust the salt. Spoon grits onto plates. Top with the browned pork belly and, if you're using it, the pickled radish.

Nils Noren
& Dave Arnold

Instructors, the International Culinary Center
New York, New York

In psychology there's the ego, the superego, and the id. The superego advocates for what you should do, the id advocates for what you shouldn't do, and the ego arbitrates between them.

When chefs Nils Noren and Dave Arnold get together, similar antics ensue. Noren is a classically trained, Swedish-born chef who, for several years, was chef de cuisine at New York's Aquavit and who minces chives into such tiny specks they look like subatomic particles. Arnold is an obsessive, gadget-loving sort who entered the food world not by staging at The French Laundry, but by dreaming up a food museum.

At the International Culinary Center (where Noren was the vice president of culinary and pastry arts and Arnold is currently the director of culinary technology), ideas bounce back and forth between them at such rapid speed, it's difficult to keep up.

Consider the dish that they call Eggs on Eggs. Essentially, they work six different egg preparations into one dish: steamed egg-yolk cakes are dipped in an eggy custard and fried like French toast, then topped with poached eggs, hollandaise, egg whites cooked in a pressure cooker, and trout roe.

"How did you come up with this?" I ask them as I dig into the version that they make for me, a dish as satisfying as the best eggs Benedict.

"We got lucky," says Arnold.

Lucky, yes, but also this dish is the result of their unique process. Noren and Arnold aren't afraid to follow their indulgent impulses (id), but in doing so they apply sound culinary knowledge and technique (superego). That's a good strategy for anyone who likes to take chances in the kitchen at home: be as outlandish as you want to be, but do it within a logical framework.

For Arnold, that framework is built with science. When he explains the immersion circulator (a water bath with a controlled temperature for cooking food that's been vacuum-sealed), he speaks like a scientist: "Advantages of technique: when guests come, dinner's always a minute away from being finished."

For Noren, that framework is built with traditional cooking methods. His knife skills are flawless, and he makes hollandaise with as much ease as most of us feel when we open a jar of mayonnaise. "You have to know the rules before you can break the rules," he tells me.

And break the rules, Noren and Arnold do. At an event at the famous architect Philip Johnson's house, Noren served French onion soup for dessert. "When you cook onion in a pressure cooker with milk," he tells me, "it gets sweet. So I made French onion soup ice cream."

The wicked grin on both their faces as Noren tells me about his dessert suggests the real delight they both take in pushing the culinary envelope. Too many chefs and home cooks break the rules before they know them; but when you know them as well as Noren and Arnold do, you can break them that much bigger.

"People who have their kitchen appliances put away never use them."
—Dave Arnold

Eggs on Eggs

Serves 6

- Noren and Arnold put six egg elements into their dish (including egg whites cooked in a pressure cooker). The five egg elements in this version are brioche, French toast batter, poached eggs, the hollandaise, and trout roe.

How many eggs can you get into one dish? This is the culinary challenge Noren and Arnold set out for themselves as they created this dish, which would work well for breakfast or as an appetizer for a dinner party. Their technique for making hollandaise—which they learned from food-science legend Harold McGee—is worth memorizing. It's faster, and the results are just as good as, if not better than, hollandaise made using the more traditional method.

FOR THE HOLLANDAISE

7 tablespoons cold unsalted butter, cut into cubes

2 egg yolks, cold

Kosher salt

Juice of ½ lemon, plus more to taste

Cayenne pepper

FOR THE REST OF DISH

8 eggs

½ cup milk

3 tablespoons sugar

A pinch of kosher salt

2 tablespoons unsalted butter

6 thick slices of brioche or challah bread, 2-inch rounds cut out of each slice

A splash of white wine vinegar

1 tablespoon minced chives

Trout roe (optional)

To make the hollandaise, place the butter cubes, egg yolks, and a pinch of salt in a large pot. Turn the heat to low and begin whisking; as the butter melts, the whole thing will emulsify. Don't stop whisking! When it's all melty and starting to come together, keep cooking it until it thickens, another 2 to 3 minutes. When it's creamy and smooth, remove it from the heat and add the lemon juice, a pinch of cayenne, and salt to taste. Set aside but keep an eye on it, whisking every so often if it starts to separate.

Make a batter by combining 2 of the eggs, the milk, sugar, and salt in a shallow pan.

Melt the butter in a skillet or frying pan over medium heat. Dip each bread round into the batter and then fry in the skillet until it's brown on both sides, about 2 minutes per side. Place the rounds on a serving plate.

Finally, poach the remaining 6 eggs. In a wide pan, bring 2 inches of water to a simmer over medium-low heat. Add a splash of vinegar to the water and then crack the eggs in, using a spoon to help wrap the whites around the yolks. Cook just until the whites are set and the yolks still look runny, approximately 4 minutes.

Place a poached egg on top of each bread round. Spoon the hollandaise over the top and garnish with the chives and, if you're using it, the trout roe. Serve hot.

Rib-eye Steak
Cooked Sous-Vide

Serves 2

Count me among the many who are wary of sous-vide cooking at home. Sure, it's fine at fancy restaurants, but at home? It always seems too ambitious and too impractical. Well, Noren and Arnold changed all that by showing me how to cook sous-vide with a resealable plastic bag, a pot of water, and a thermometer. The result is flawless meat that's bright pink on the inside and, because of a quick flash fry, crusty and caramelized on the outside. Be sure to make this along with their French fries (recipe follows); you can use the oil from the fries to finish the steak.

- If you want to save money, Noren and Arnold say you can use this same technique with hanger steak or skirt steak.

2 (20-ounce) rib-eye steaks

Coarsely ground black pepper

Kosher salt

3 tablespoons vegetable oil, plus more for frying

4 tablespoons melted unsalted butter

3 tablespoons natural, unsweetened peanut butter, pecan butter, or almond butter

3 tablespoons unsalted butter, at room temperature

Juice of 1 lemon

¼ cup chopped parsley

Fleur de sel (optional)

Aggressively season the steaks first with pepper and then with kosher salt.

Heat a cast-iron skillet or a frying pan on high heat until extremely hot, add the oil, and sear the steaks, one at a time, for about 1 minute per side so they have a caramelized exterior. This is both to create flavor and to kill any bacteria before cooking sous-vide.

Let the steak cool slightly and then place each steak into its own resealable plastic freezer bag with 2 tablespoons of the melted butter in each bag.

- Arnold says you want to use a freezer bag "that doesn't have a thingamjig." By that, he means a zipper contraption that sticks out of the bag. Use the freezer bags with the red and blue lines that come together cleanly when you press them.

Fill the biggest pot you have with water (that'll help keep the temperature consistent). Now you're going to create a vacuum seal with a cool technique. Zip the first bag almost all the way up, except leave a space for your finger at the end. Lower the bag carefully into the water, leaving the part with your finger in it outside the water. The pressure from the water should help you push all the air out (use your other hand). When that happens, pull your finger out, zip up the bag, and look at your work. The bag should be clinging to the meat and there should be very little to zero air (and zero water) in the bag. Repeat with the second bag.

Set the bags aside on the counter and raise the temperature of the water to 134°F on medium heat, adjusting the heat as necessary. You want to be exact here; the temperature is the most important part.

Lower the steak bags into the water, turn off the heat, cover the pot, and cook the steaks for a minimum of 45 minutes (although if it stays in a little longer, it won't hurt the result).

Meanwhile, make a compound butter. In a small bowl, using a rubber spatula, combine the peanut butter, the 3 tablespoons of regular butter, the lemon juice, the parsley, and kosher salt and pepper to taste. Set aside.

When the steaks are cooked, remove from the bags and set aside.

Bring a large pot of vegetable or canola oil to 340°F.

Using a spider or another heat-proof device, lower the steaks one at a time into the oil. Cook them just until they develop a crusty brown exterior, 1 to 2 minutes.

Slice the steak against the grain, sprinkle with fleur de sel, if using, and serve with the compound butter on top.

French Fries

Serves 4

Normally, French fries are fried twice, once at a lower temperature (to poach the fries and cook them through) and then at a higher temperature to crisp the outsides. This method adds a cooking step: the fries are boiled in salty water first. Though that may sounds strange, what happens is the fries becomes infused with the salty water (you don't have to salt them afterward) and the results speak for themselves. Just be sure not to cool the boiled fries too much before frying them; you'll get what Arnold calls "the dreaded hollow fry," which is a fry that lacks a mashed potato–like interior.

Salt

6 Russet or Idaho potatoes, peeled and cut into French fries (keep potatoes submerged in cold water when not using them or they will brown)

Pectinex Ultra SP-L (optional; see Resources, page 371)

Fry oil or vegetable oil or, if you have it, duck fat

Fill a large pot with water and bring to a very rapid boil over high heat. Add a lot of salt; you want the water to taste salty like seawater.

Drop in the potatoes and boil—again, a rapid boil—on high heat for 8 to 10 minutes, just until the potatoes are cooked through but not falling apart.

Drain and allow the potatoes to air-dry in single layers on cookie sheets for 20 minutes. Don't dry too much, though, or you'll get the dreaded "hollow fry."

Fill a large pot halfway with frying oil. Set up a thermometer so you can monitor the temperature. Bring it to 320 to 340°F and drop in the fries (if your pot is large enough, you can do them all at once; otherwise, work in batches). You don't want the fries to turn brown, just to blond up a little, so only fry for 3 to 4 minutes. Shake the oil off as you remove them to a cookie sheet (they absorb oil as they are drying). At this point, you can freeze them for later use or continue cooking.

Raise the temperature of the same oil to somewhere between 365 to 380°F. Drop the fries in for a second fry and cook for 45 seconds or so until they're crispy and brown.

Remove the fries to a plate and, remember, there should be no need to salt them; they're good to go! Serve with sumac mayo or ketchup.

That's ⅜ inch wide and however long the potato is.

Noren and Arnold add Pectinex Ultra SP-L to the water that they use to store their cut fries to break down the pectin so it forms a better crust. If you decide to use this, use 4 grams per liter of water and let them sit for 30 minutes.

The potatoes may fall apart, but don't worry: even broken potato pieces taste good when fried.

To make a sumac mayo (sumac is a dried spice with a sour taste; see Resources, page 371), simply mix 1 tablespoon sumac with ½ cup mayonnaise.

Elizabeth Falkner

Chef, Krescendo
Brooklyn, New York

Chef, Krescendo
Brooklyn, New York

Falkner's Kitchen Know-How

AN EASY WAY to get a hard- or soft-boiled egg out of its shell is to crack it on the counter and submerge it in water. The water will get between the shell and the egg and help you peel it when you're ready.

THINK ABOUT temperature when creating a dish: for example, with the puntarelle salad (see page 364), Falkner wanted cold puntarelle (she added ice to get it even colder) and hot candied bacon for contrast. She uses a similar approach with her plated desserts.

TO ADD an extra dose of flavor, inject the inside of your cupcakes using a piping bag. For example, you could inject lemon curd into a lemon cupcake or raspberry jam into red velvet cupcakes.

The element of surprise is a powerful tool when it comes to cooking. Many chefs delight in their ability to throw diners off: from chef Ferran Adrià in Spain, who serves olives that look like the real thing but are really made of olive oil, to chef Elizabeth Falkner, who blindfolds me in the kitchen of Orson (her former restaurant).

"Here," says Falkner. "Rub this on your wrists."

I do as I'm told, and suddenly the scent of cocoa wafts over me (I later learn it's a cocoa-flavored essential oil). "Now eat this," she says, placing a chocolate bonbon that's been rolled in Calvados syrup and vanilla sugar in my mouth.

"Whoa," I say, getting caught up in the experience. This is a dessert called Bon Bondage, which Falkner served at a Valentine's Day dinner to give couples an interactive experience. "I'm very turned on right now," I add as Falkner bursts out laughing.

Falkner's sense of humor and sense of fun make her a perfect candidate for making the kind of food that can have a sense of humor and a sense of fun: dessert.

"With dessert, I can do anything," she tells me later as we begin cooking together. "I just have to know what I want to achieve."

For example, once a chef annoyed her and she decided to slap him, metaphorically, with her food. So she came up with "Citrus Rose Slap"—a brown sugar–braised pineapple pureed with an oil infused with Szechuan peppercorns, ginger, chili, cloves, and ginger. She served it, naturally, with her "Chocolate Ninja Bitch."

The surprising nature of Falkner's food is there by design. That's abundantly clear when it comes to her red velvet cupcakes. "I'm not a red velvet person," she declares. "And I don't like the color pink."

Her solution is to work raspberry vinegar into the batter and pomegranate molasses into the icing and then to top the whole thing with dehydrated blackberry powder. It's a red velvet cake in which the red color actually has a flavor, and most people don't see it coming.

But to really get a sense of how Falkner weaves elements of surprise into her work, you have to watch her create a dish from scratch, as she does with some yogurt, dried cherries, and chocolate. "Let's rehydrate the cherries in something," she says, zooming around her kitchen. "Maybe a little water? With a drop of balsamic?"

She places blood orange peel into a pot with the dried cherries and water and changes her mind about the balsamic, using honey instead. By the time she's finished she has a cooling bowl of yogurt with fruity bits—segmented blood orange in addition to the cherries—toasted hazelnuts, and chocolate that she's treated so it's soft.

The textures and flavors are, of course, surprising. But comforting, too. "You could do it with frozen yogurt," she says. "Or mix in goat cheese!"

Falkner's free-spiritedness allows for the unexpected to take hold. And that's what makes her food, in particular her desserts, so delightful to eat.

"Dessert is allowed to be more obnoxious than most foods because it's only there for fun. You don't have to have it to survive."

Puntarelle with Candied Bacon, Soft-Cooked Eggs, and Ricotta Salata

Serves 2 to 4

A study in extremes, this salad has it all: cold bitter puntarelle (chickory), sweet bacon, and warm, creamy soft-cooked eggs. You can substitute another lettuce for the puntarelle, but you really want to play off the sweetness of the bacon, so shoot for something bitter.

● Good substitutions are dandelion greens or kale.

3 eggs

½ pound thick smoked bacon

½ loaf of sourdough bread

Olive oil

Kosher salt

½ cup good-quality maple syrup

White wine vinegar

Dijon mustard

Zest and juice of 1 lemon

Freshly ground black pepper

1 head of puntarelle, leaves washed, dried, and cut into bite-size pieces

¼ pound ricotta salata

Place the eggs in a pot of cold water. Bring the pot to a slow boil on medium-high heat, then reduce the heat to low and allow the eggs to simmer for 3 minutes. Turn off the heat and allow the eggs to sit, uncovered, for 15 minutes. Drain out the hot water, fill the pot with very cold water, crack the eggs slightly, and allow them to sit in the water (see Kitchen Know-How, page 362). Set aside.

Cut the bacon crosswise into lardoons (bite-size strips). Add to a cold cast-iron pan or skillet (do not use nonstick) and slowly raise the heat, allowing the bacon fat to slowly render and the bacon to crisp, 5 to 8 minutes, stirring occasionally.

Cut the crusts off the bread and then cut the bread into ½-inch cubes. In a skillet, add a layer of olive oil and add all the bread, tossing it all around, with some salt. Turn up the heat and cook, stirring every so often, until the croutons are toasted on all sides, 3 to 4 minutes. Set aside.

When the bacon has rendered and it's crispy and mostly cooked through, pour off most of the bacon fat into a bowl and set aside. Add the maple syrup and a sprinkling of salt to the pan with the bacon. Turn up the heat and stir until the bacon is coated. Watch carefully or the sugar might burn! When the bacon is coated, 1 to 2 minutes, remove from the heat.

To the reserved bacon fat, add the white wine vinegar, a little Dijon mustard, some lemon juice, and a little pepper. Stir and carefully taste for balance and then set the bowl aside.

Add the puntarelle to a salad bowl. Pour some of the bacon-fat dressing over the puntarelle. Toss and taste and add more dressing as necessary.

Lift the salad onto plates and top with the reserved croutons and the candied bacon. Peel the eggs and cut them in half, placing them on top of the salads. Grate the ricotta salata over everything and sprinkle with lemon zest. Sprinkle with more salt and pepper and serve.

Yogurt with Blood Oranges, Raspberries, Cherries, and Chocolate

Serves 2 to 4

What *is* this dish of yogurt served with rosewater-infused cherries, segmented blood oranges, crunchy hazelnuts, and soft bits of chocolate? Is it breakfast? Yes. Is it dessert? Yes, it's a dessert too. Is it an afternoon snack? Sure, it can be, and you can mix-and-match other ingredients as you like. Take the reins and make this dish all your own.

4 ounces bittersweet chocolate, roughly chopped or broken

1 teaspoon canola oil

¼ cup hazelnuts

½ cup dried cherries

¼ cup water

1 tablespoon sugar

2 tablespoons honey

A pinch of freshly ground black pepper

3 blood oranges, plus a strip of blood orange peel (use a vegetable peeler)

½ teaspoon rosewater

¼ teaspoon vanilla extract

1 cup plain Greek yogurt

¼ cup raspberries, sliced in half

It's just a pot of simmering water with a metal bowl resting on top. The bowl should not come in contact with the water.

Over a double boiler, melt the chocolate with the canola oil 80 percent of the way. Remove from the heat, stir until the rest of the chocolate melts, and then spread the chocolate out on a parchment-lined cookie sheet. Place in the refrigerator until it firms up, 30 minutes to 1 hour.

Preheat the oven to 325°F and, on a cookie sheet, roast the hazelnuts until fragrant, 8 to 10 minutes. Use paper towels to rub them until the skins come off. Then coarsely chop the nuts and set aside.

In a saucepan, combine the dried cherries, water, sugar, honey, and black pepper. Segment the blood oranges by cutting their skins away with a sharp knife and then cutting between the membranes so the fruit falls out into a bowl. Squeeze any juicy bits of skin into the pot with the cherries. Add a strip of blood orange peel (no white).

Bring the heat on the pan to medium and simmer for 10 minutes, or until the mixture is reduced by half. Add the rosewater.

Stir the vanilla into the yogurt and divide the yogurt among the serving bowls. Add some of the blood oranges, cherries, cherry liquid, and raspberries.

Cut the chocolate into small square-like chunks. Sprinkle the chocolate over the yogurt along with the hazelnuts. Serve cold or store in the fridge for several hours, covered with plastic wrap.

Red Velvet Cupcakes with Cream Cheese Frosting

Makes approximately 18 cupcakes

Why do people love red velvet cake so much? It's a question that baffles Falkner as much as it baffles me. Well, it did baffle me until I learned how to make this version, in which the cupcake is about so much more than the bold color: it's packed with flavor to match. The raspberry vinegar and the pomegranate molasses give everything a slight tang, and the dehydrated berries add a fruity kick. These cupcakes are destined to raise a small fortune at your next bake sale.

- This doesn't make a ton of frosting; if you think you might want more, simply double the recipe. It's never a bad idea to have extra frosting, right?

- Take the butter, cream cheese, and eggs out of the fridge an hour before you start; leave them on the kitchen counter, and by the time you're ready to bake, they'll be at the right temperature.

- To make your own pomegranate molasses, simply pour 2 cups pomegranate juice into a small pot with ¼ cup sugar and the juice from ½ lemon. Bring to a simmer and cook, gently, until it becomes syrupy, about 1 hour. Allow it to cool completely before using it in the frosting.

- Use red wine vinegar if you need a substitution.

- You can also use a handheld mixer at medium speed.

FOR THE CUPCAKES

1¾ cups sugar

8 tablespoons (1 stick) unsalted butter, at room temperature

½ cup canola oil

2 eggs, at room temperature

2 tablespoons cocoa powder

1 tablespoon red food coloring (about ½ small bottle)

2½ cups sifted cake flour (measured after sifting)

1 teaspoon salt

1 cup well-shaken buttermilk

1 teaspoon vanilla extract

½ teaspoon baking soda

1 tablespoon raspberry vinegar

FOR THE FROSTING

6 tablespoons (¾ stick) unsalted butter, at room temperature

3 ounces cream cheese, at room temperature

1½ cups powdered sugar, sifted

2 tablespoons pomegranate molasses (optional)

½ teaspoon vanilla extract

A pinch of salt

1 drop red food coloring (to turn the frosting pink; optional)

1 tablespoon dehydrated or freeze-dried blackberries or raspberries, ground to a powder in a food processor or clean coffee grinder (optional)

Preheat the oven to 325°F. Spray 2 muffin tins with cooking spray, then line them with cupcake liners; lightly spray the inside of the cupcake liners too.

In the bowl of a stand mixer using the paddle attachment, cream the sugar, butter, and canola oil until light and fluffy, 3 to 4 minutes. Add the eggs, one at a time, and mix well. Add the cocoa powder and red food coloring and continue to mix to incorporate.

continued

367

Red Velvet Cupcakes with Cream Cheese Frosting (continued)

In a medium bowl, combine the flour and salt with a whisk. Mix the buttermilk and vanilla in another bowl. With the mixer on low speed, starting with the flour, alternate between adding the flour and the buttermilk, ending with the flour. Combine the baking soda and vinegar in a small bowl (it will fizz) and add it right away to the mixer bowl, blending just until incorporated.

Using an ice cream scoop, scoop the batter into the muffin tins, filling them up two thirds of the way. Bake for 20 to 25 minutes, or until a cake tester comes out completely clean. Allow the cupcakes to cool completely on a wire rack.

While the cupcakes are cooling, make the frosting. In a clean bowl, add the butter and cream cheese and beat with the paddle attachment until light and fluffy. Add the powdered sugar in two additions, beating until just incorporated. Add the pomegranate molasses, vanilla, salt, and, if you're using it, the food coloring.

When the cupcakes are cool, spread the icing on each with an offset spatula or, to make them more professional, use a piping bag.

Finish by sprinkling the cupcakes with the blackberry or raspberry powder, if using.

● If you don't have a piping bag, use a plastic freezer bag with a corner cut out and a piping tip inserted. Pipe some icing into the center of the cupcake, make circles outward, and finish by circling back in.

Afterword

The changes were, at first, subtle. In April, I went to the farmer's market and bought broccoli rabe because it was in season. I brought it home and displayed it on my kitchen counter. When dinnertime came, I sautéed it with garlic and crushed red pepper flakes, loosely inspired by Lidia Bastianich's ziti recipe (see page 46). Only I served it on Anson Mills corn grits that I'd purchased along with the rice grits that I bought for Hugh Acheson's pork belly dish (see page 351) and topped it with pickled red jalapeños I've been making ever since I made them for Brandon Pettit's pizza (see page 31). The end result looked a bit like Linton Hopkins's greens (see page 299), but this was something entirely different, something I had improvised based on everything I had learned writing this cookbook.

Pretty soon I was using all the various techniques I learned cooking with all these incredible chefs—toasting tortillas over an open flame, slicing vegetables with a mandoline, juicing fruits and vegetables by blending them with a little water and pressing them through a sieve—to make up dishes of my own: breakfast tacos (with eggs, jalapeños, sour cream, and cilantro), spring radish crostini (broiling the bread as I learned to because I don't have a grill), and a raw rhubarb daiquiri ("juiced" rhubarb heated with just a little sugar until it dissolves, then cooled and shaken with white rum). I went into this cooking journey a pretty strict recipe follower and emerged a confident recipe creator of my own. Not only that; before, I was slightly fearful at the stove, and now I'm entirely in command.

I hope this happens for you. All of the chefs in this book started somewhere. True, many of them went to culinary school, but many of them didn't. And though many come from families of great cooks or spent years working in restaurants, the key element is experience: cook, cook, and cook some more. The more you cook, the more you'll know, and the more you know, the more you can start stepping out on your own.

And even if you don't, ultimately, feel confident enough to cook like a chef, writing this book taught me that cooking is, as José Andrés said, a lifestyle. A very rich and rewarding lifestyle. It means you'll constantly be surrounded by friends, family, neighbors, and other assorted loved ones who will relish the opportunity to eat your food and share your table. For that reason and that reason alone, I hope this book and its lessons make you more of a cook than you were before.

It all boils down to an absurdly simple notion, but a valid one, nonetheless: Cooks cook. That's all there is to it.

Resources

The following are suggestions for where to find the more difficult-to-track-down ingredients in this book. I use many of these sources myself; in the other cases, they have been specifically recommended by the chefs. Take some time to click around the various Web sites to see what else piques your interest; it's always more fun to receive a package of assorted ingredients in the mail than just the one you need.

Anson Mills

Based out of Columbia, South Carolina, Anson Mills is celebrated for its grits and rice, supplying chefs such as Thomas Keller, Charlie Trotter, and Tom Colicchio. The great news is that you can have the same access as these chefs do to Anson Mills' wonderful products.

1922-C Gervais Street
Columbia, SC 29201
(803) 467-4122
www.ansonmills.com

BDBazar.com

A South Asian shopping site, this is your best bet for finding *Reshampatti* chili powder online. (There's also an excellent selection of Bollywood movies, if you're so inclined.)

90-34 Vanderveer Street #B
Queens Village, NY 11428
(646) 233-4198
www.bdbazar.com

Buon Italia

This is where Nancy Silverton buys her *alici di menaica* for her mozzarella salad (see page 71), but it's also a great resource for dried pastas, olive oil, and cured meats.

75 Ninth Avenue
New York, NY 10011
(212) 633-9090
www.buonitalia.com

Chefshop.com

The first "education-focused, content-driven e-commerce site focused on real food," chefshop.com was recommended to me by Brandon Pettit (page 22) for tracking down the Colline di Santa Cruz olive oil he uses to finish his pizza. It's also a great resource for many other high-end ingredients listed in this book: *truffle salt, gray salt, aged balsamic vinegar, bigoli, canned escargot, pumpkin seed oil,* and *good olive oil.*

1425 Elliott Avenue West
Seattle, WA 98119
(800) 596-0885
www.chefshop.com

D'Artagnan

For various meat products in this book—*pancetta, chorizo, tasso,* even *demi-glace* (if you don't want to make your own)—D'Artagnan is an excellent resource. Their products are available in many high-end stores and big markets, but if you can't find what you're looking for, they ship.

280 Wilson Avenue
Newark, NJ 07105
(800) 327-8246
www.dartagnan.com

Dean & Deluca

This legendary gourmet store, which originated in New York's SoHo neighborhood (you can still visit it there), is particularly great for more common spices, such as *whole nutmeg, cinnamon sticks,* and *Mexican oregano.*

For mail orders:
Dean & Deluca
Attn: Customer Care
4115 E. Harry
Wichita, KS 67218
(316) 821-3200
Toll Free: (800) 221-7714
www.deandeluca.com

FGPizza.com

Go here to find double-zero flour and *Caputo Tipo 00 flour,* which, if you can't find freshly ground flour, is ideal for making the pizza dough on page 24 or pasta dough (see page 138).

(925) 402-4800

www.fgpizza.com

Food Service Direct

Though this Web site sells items in bulk for restaurants, you'll find good deals on some of the very specific ingredients listed in this book's recipes; for example, you can get twelve jars of *La Valle Passata di Pomodoro* (listed as Tomato Puree). They also have *Calrose rice.*

905 G. Street

Hampton, VA 23661

(757) 245-7675

www.foodservicedirect.com

Gusmer Enterprises

This is where Dave Arnold (page 354) goes to order *Pectinex Ultra SP-L,* which will make French fries (see page 361) extra crispy.

81 M Street

Fresno, CA 93721

(559) 485-2692

www.gusmerenterprises.com

iGourmet.com

If you can't find *Plugra European-style butter* at your local grocery store, you can get it here.

508 Delaware Avenue

West Pittston, PA 18643

(877) 446-8763

www.igourmet.com

Kalustyan's

If you visit Manhattan, you must make a pilgrimage to Kalustyan's on Lexington Avenue. You'll find shelves full of finishing salts, hot sauces, esoteric spices, and other ingredients, specifically *urfa-biber* and *maras-biber, Berber seasoning, garam masala, preserved lemons, curry leaves, Yucateco hot sauce, maple sugar, sumac, Hawaiian pink salt,* and *shredded coconut.* Even if you're not in New York, though, much of Kalustayn's inventory is available for order online.

Marhaba International, Inc.

123 Lexington Avenue

New York, NY 10016

(212) 685-3451

Toll Free: (800) 352-3451

www.kalustyans.com

Koa Mart

A good resource for Korean specialty ingredients, like the Korean crushed red pepper and chili paste in Roy Choi's Sweet Chili Sauce (page 177).

905 E. Eighth Street, #12

Los Angeles, CA 90021

www.koamart.com

La Tienda

Despite being based out of Williamsburg, Virginia, La Tienda focuses on food from Spain (though they're an excellent resource for many of the non-Spanish dishes in this book). Look here for *pickled white anchovies* (listed online as *boquerones*) and *Ibérico ham.*

1325 Jamestown Road

Williamsburg, VA 23185

(800) 710-4304

www.tienda.com

Nueske's

You know the *smoked bacon* at Nueske's has to be good if two chefs in this book specifically order from there for their restaurants. Nueske's isn't limited to bacon, though; they also have smoked hams, turkey, poultry, and other gourmet specialties.

To contact by mail:

Attn: Customer Service

203 N. Genesee Street

Wittenberg, WI 54499

(800) 392-2266

www.nueskes.com

Red Mule Grits

This is where Peter Dale (page 56) gets his polenta for The National in Athens, Georgia; the product gets its name from Luke, the small red mule that powers the corn mill. The mill's polenta, cornmeal, and grits must be refrigerated upon arrival because they're made from fresh corn. Red Mule also sells English porridge.

Mills Farm

150 Harve Mathis Road

Athens, GA 30601

(706) 543-8113

www.redmulegrits.us

The Shepherd's Grain

This is where Brandon Pettit gets the flour for his pizza.

info@shepherdsgrain.com

www.shepherdsgrain.com

South Mountain Creamery

Excellent *milk* is yours to be had (this is where Tim Artz, page 100, gets his), but you have to live in Maryland, D.C., Virginia, West Virginia, or Pennsylvania to have it delivered.

8305 Bolivar Road

Middletown, MD 21769

(301) 371-8565

www.southmountaincreamery.com

The Spice House

What you can't find at Kalustyan's, you will most likely find here, including *maple sugar, vanilla paste, habanero powder,* and *toasted sesame seeds (geh).*

Retail locations in Chicago, Evanston, and Geneva, Illinois; and in Milwaukee, Wisconsin.

(847) 328-3711

www.thespicehouse.com

Uwajimaya

For those who don't have a Chinatown convenient to where they live, here's where you'll find various Asian ingredients that show up in many recipes in this book: *sriracha hot sauce, Lee Kum Kee oyster sauce, Kikkoman organic soy sauce, togarashi, dried shiitakes,* and *coconut milk.*

Retail locations in Seattle, Renton, and Bellevue, Washington, and Beaverton, Oregon.

www.uwajimaya.com

WokShop.com

Grace Young (page 50) recommends this San Francisco–based store for buying a *wok* (if you can't make it to K. K. Discount in New York's Chinatown).

718 Grant Avenue

San Francisco, CA 94108-2114

(415) 989-3797

www.wokshop.com

Acknowledgments

If some books take a village, this book took a small city.

Thank you to everyone at Stonesong and my wonderful agent, Alison Fargis, who nurtured a book proposal out of me with tough love and well-seasoned patience. She was a huge emotional crutch for me as I wrote this book, convinced as I was that I'd never be able to cook with 50 chefs and test 150 recipes before my deadline. I'll be forever grateful for her kindness, humor, and constant availability.

Judy Pray, my editor, is any cookbook author's dream editor: a delight to be around, but absolutely ferocious on the page. She pushed me to do great work not only in the writing of this book but over the whole cookbook-writing process, engaging with me about chefs and recipes every step of the way. Thank you to Kevin Brainard, who designed this book, and to Susan Baldaserini, Michelle Ishay, Laurin Lucaire, and Nancy Murray, who brought it to its beautiful completion. Thanks to my copy editor, Janet McDonald, and Sibylle Kazeroid, my production editor, for going over this book with a fine-tooth comb. Also thanks to Ann Bramson and everyone else at Artisan for making this experience so pleasant. And thank you to Peter Workman for his early vision that set this book in motion.

My constant companion over the course of my cookbook journey was Elizabeth Leitzell, this book's snapshot photographer. Together Lizzie and I flew on planes, rented cars, and stuffed our faces side by side in the kitchens of the nation's best chefs. Lizzie became not only a great friend but also a terrific collaborator and adviser, helping us navigate from one chef's home to the next without ever losing her sunny disposition (and keeping me awake when we drove from the Seattle airport to Portland late at night with games of G-H-O-S-T and "Would you rather?"). I'm so happy to provide her a showcase for her brilliant work. To the talented team who worked on the styled food pictures for this book—Johnny Miller (photographs), Justin Conly (who assisted), Lesley Stockton (food stylist), Johanna Rockwell (her assistant), and Michelle Wong (prop stylist)—I had so much fun working with you all. And your hard work speaks for itself.

The beautiful props came from Le Creuset, ABC Carpet & Home, and dbO Home.

Tyla Fowler volunteered to be my "cookbook intern" before I was sure what my cookbook intern would do. Turns out, she did a lot: from researching potential chefs and travel options to joining me in my kitchen to test recipes. Tyla is a talented writer in her own right; one day I'll be interning on her cookbook.

We couldn't have visited as many cities as we did without the generosity of the following friends and kindhearted souls who let us stay with them as we crossed the country: Robin Lasher and Vaughn Sterling; Benson Wright and Andy Cole; Molly Wizenberg and Brandon Pettit; David and Celia Russo; Nicole Miller; Chris, Liz, and Katie Herron; and Kristen, Felix, and Anders Lo.

The recipes in this book wouldn't work as well as they do if it weren't for the many recipe testers who tried them out in their own kitchens. Many thanks to Anthony Jackson, Sarah Landrum, Katya Schapiro, Catherine Hull, Yelena Malcolm, Paula Lee, Chris Killoran, Lisa Lacy, Graye Pelletier, Gabrielle Amette, Susan Stromberg, Becky Goldstein-Glaze, Jason Greenberg, Melissa Holsinger, and Alejandra Guanipa. Also thanks to Diana Fithian, Patty Jang, Lauren Gutterman, Morgan Tingley, and Leland Scruby, all of whom lent a hand in the kitchen during my recipe-testing process.

This paragraph is devoted to the endless list of people who offered suggestions, tips, advice, and connections that helped form this book's roster of chefs and home cooks. There are too many people to name here (from food writers to bloggers to folks on Twitter, Facebook, and my blog) but, obviously, I couldn't have written this book without their help. I will enthusiastically thank them all in person.

Thank you to Jonathan Rubinstein and the good people at Joe (New York's best coffee shop, located on Waverly Place just off of Sixth Avenue) for letting me commandeer a table as often as I did over the course of writing this book. Joe was my office and my refuge when writing became too tedious at home.

A big thank-you to my family for their constant support and enthusiasm. My mother and grandmother may not cook, but they treat meals with as much passion and dedication as any of the chefs in this book. In doing so, they make everyone feel loved and well cared for. And my father, while pretty unadventurous at the table, has expanded his horizons for my sake—and for that I'm very grateful.

Endless thanks to Craig for being there every step of the way, from the early days of "Will I ever finish this book?" to the final days of "What will I do when I'm done?" Craig was the ultimate arbiter of whether these recipes work for the home cook. If he was happy, I knew you'd be happy too.

Finally, and most important, a bottomless thank-you, once again, to all of the chefs and home cooks who shared their kitchens, their stories, and their recipes for this book. My time spent with all of them was positively life-changing, and I hope one day to do for others what they did for me. I'm honored to include them all in these pages.

Index

Acheson, Hugh, 344–53, *345, 350*

Admony, Einat, 62–67, *63*

Allegretti, Alain, 128–33, *129*

almond flour (note), 132

almonds:

Almond Jelly with Candied Fennel and Grapefruit, 312, *313*

Crispy White Asparagus with Orange and Marcona Almonds, 236, *237*

Lemon Semifreddo with Blackberries and Honey, 92, *93*

anchovies:

Bagna Cauda with Vegetables, 91

Crostini with Sugar Snap Peas, Radishes, and Anchovies, 96

Lentilpalooza, 340, *341*

Mozzarella with Meyer Lemon, Celery Salad, and Alici di Menaica, 71

Raw Dandelion Salad with Hard-Boiled Eggs and Pickled White Anchovies, 173

Andrés, José, 331–35, *332*

appetizers and snacks:

Baba Ghanouj Bruschetta with Citrus Herb Salad, 66, *67*

Bagna Cauda with Vegetables, 91

Braised Winter Greens with Tasso and Pickled Banana Peppers, *298,* 299

Buckwheat Blinis with Smoked Salmon and Caviar, *114,* 115

Ceviche, 251

Chicken Liver Mousse, 160, 161

Crostini with Sugar Snap Peas, Radishes, and Anchovies, 96

Fried Olives with Labneh and Harissa Oil, 64

Gibanica with Feta, Goat Cheese, and Kajmak Cheese, 154, *155*

Kaya Toast, 188–89, *189*

Pickled Black Radishes and Vidalia Onions, 294

P'tit Basque with Chorizo and Grilled Garlic Bread, 84

Sautéed Medjool Dates, 210, *211*

Stuffed Focaccia, 204–5, *205*

Tortilla Española with Chorizo, 274, *275*

apple(s):

Beet Salad with Pecans, Herbs, and Apple, 146, *147*

French Apple Tart, 164–65, *165*

Arnold, Dave, 354–61, *355*

Artz, Tim, 100–105, 101

Arugula Salad with Heirloom Tomatoes, 12

asparagus:

Asparagus Soup with Spinach and Tarragon, 116, *117*

Crispy White Asparagus with Orange and Marcona Almonds, 236, *237*

Salt-Crusted Pork Loin with Ibérico Ham and Asparagus, 334, *335*

avocado:

Charred and Cheesy Garden Salad Tacos, 35

Funky Lettuce Salad with Beets, Feta, and Creamy Meyer Lemon Dressing, 85

Baba au Rhum with Grapes and Crème Fraîche, 267–68, *269*

Baba Ghanouj Bruschetta with Citrus Herb Salad, 66, *67*

bacon:

Garganelli with Speck and Cream, 280, *281*

Puntarelle with Candied Bacon, Soft-Cooked Eggs, and Ricotta Salata, 364

Spinach Salad with Pear, Curried Cashews, and Bacon, 256–57, *257*

Bagna Cauda with Vegetables, 91

banana: Choi's Favorite Banana Milk Shake, 176

basil:

Margherita Pizza, 28, *29*

Trofie with Basil and Cilantro Pesto, 97

Bastianich, Lidia, 44–49, *45*

beans:

Cavatappi with Mussels, *282,* 283

Oxtail Cassoulet, 216–17

Pasta Fagioli, 266

Spring Vegetable Confit, 124, *125*

Steamed Chicken with Preserved Black Beans and Ginger, 302, *303*

Thoren with Carrots and Green Beans, 242, *243*

Beast Stock and Demi-Glace, 342–43

beef:

Beef Ularthiyathu, 241

Beef with Tomato Stir-Fry, 52, *53*

Braciola, 170, *171,* 172

Flank Steak with Guajillo Chili Sauce, 252–53

Oxtail Cassoulet, 216–17

Porcini-Rubbed Roast Beef with Demi-Glace and Caramelized Turnips, 339

Rib-Eye Steak Cooked Sous-Vide, 358–59, *360*

Short Ribs Braised in Coconut Milk, 328–29

Tortellini with Pork in Creamy Meat Ragù, 278–79
beets:
Beet Salad with Pecans, Herbs, and Apple, 146, *147*
Funky Lettuce Salad with Beets, Feta, and Creamy Meyer Lemon Dressing, 85
Beurre Blanc, 348–49
blackberries: Lemon Semifreddo with Blackberries and Honey, 92, *93*
blinis: Buckwheat Blinis with Smoked Salmon and Caviar, *114*, 115
Blueberry Crostada, 118–19, *119*
bok choy:
Stir-Fried Bok Choy and Shiitakes with Garlic and Rice Wine, 305
Stir-Fried Bok Choy with Ginger, 55
Bone Marrow and Escargot, 272
bones, for stock, 38
bowls, 4, 112
Braciola (Rolled Beef with Garlic and Parsley Braised in Tomato Sauce), 170, *171*, 172
branzino: Pan-Seared Branzino with Fennel Salad, 131
breads:
Bread Salad with Tuna, Capers, and Olives, 228, *229*
Carrot Dumplings, 286–87
Country Bread (Pain de Campagne), 226–27
Kaya Toast, 188–89, *189*
pita chips (note), 85
P'tit Basque with Chorizo and Grilled Garlic Bread, 84

Stuffed Focaccia, 204–5, *205*
tortillas, frying, 231
yeast (note), 224
broccoli: Grilled Brassica with Dandelion-Green Vinaigrette, 320, *321*
broccoli rabe: Ziti with Broccoli Rabe and Sausage, 46
Brooklyn Pizza, 30
Brussels Sprouts Slaw, 290–91
Buckwheat Blinis with Smoked Salmon and Caviar, *114*, 115
butter, 4
Buttermilk-Marinated Roast Chicken, 136–37, *137*
Butternut Squash Tortellini, *140*, 141–42, *143*

cabbage: Chowchow, 17
calamari: Pantesca Salad, 206, *207*
Canora, Marco, 166–73, *167*
Caramel Shrimp with Lemongrass, Thai Chili, and Ginger, 304
carrots:
Braised Rabbit with Carrots and Mushrooms, 152–53, *153*
Carrot Dumplings, 286–87
Carrot-Hoisin Dipping Sauce, 286–87
Orange, Yellow, and Purple Carrots Braised in Brown Butter, 318–19, *319*
Thoren with Carrots and Green Beans, 242, *243*
West Indies–Style Hot Sauce, 102
cashews: Spinach Salad with Pear, Curried Cashews, and Bacon, 256–57, *257*
Cassoulet, Oxtail, 216–17
Cavatappi with Mussels, *282*, 283

Cavatelli with Pesto, Peas, and Ricotta Salata, 130
caviar: Buckwheat Blinis with Smoked Salmon and Caviar, *114*, 115
celery:
Celery Salad with Mushrooms and Grapes in a Celery Leaf Pesto, 288, *289*
Mozzarella with Meyer Lemon, Celery Salad, and Alici di Menaica, 71
celery root (celeriac):
Lamb Shanks Roasted with Root Vegetables, 148
Porcini-Crusted Rack of Lamb with Celeriac-Potato Gratin, 261
Ceviche, 251
Chai Tea, 240
Chanterelle and Cremini Mushroom Gratin, 197
Charles, Rebecca, 106–11, *107*
cheese:
The Brooklyn Pizza, 30
Butternut Squash Tortellini, *140*, 141–42, *143*
Cavatelli with Pesto, Peas, and Ricotta Salata, 130
Charred and Cheesy Garden Salad Tacos, 35
French Onion Soup, 338
Frico with Potato, 47
Funky Lettuce Salad with Beets, Feta, and Creamy Meyer Lemon Dressing, 85
Garganelli with Speck and Cream, 280, *281*
Gibanica with Feta, Goat Cheese, and Kajmak Cheese, 154, *155*

cheese *(continued)*

homemade (note), 100

Lamb Meatballs (Kafta) with Baked Feta and Pomegranate Molasses, 192, *193*

Mozzarella in Panna with Pesto and Slow-Roasted Tomatoes, 72, *73*

Mozzarella with Meyer Lemon, Celery Salad, and Alici di Menaica, 71

P'tit Basque with Chorizo and Grilled Garlic Bread, 84

Puntarelle with Candied Bacon, Soft-Cooked Eggs, and Ricotta Salata, 364

Raw Vegetable Salad with Aged Goat's-Milk Cheese, 317

Smoked Herring Caesar Salad, 273

Spinach Calzone with Two Cheeses, 103

Spring Vegetable Confit, 124, *125*

Stuffed Focaccia, 204–5, *205*

Swiss Chard and Ricotta Dumplings, 198, *199*

Tagliatelle with Cherry Tomatoes, 203

Ziti with Broccoli Rabe and Sausage, 46

cherries:

Chocolate Cherry Clafoutis, 132, *133*

Yogurt with Blood Oranges, Raspberries, Cherries, and Chocolate, 365

chicken:

Buttermilk-Marinated Roast Chicken, 136–37, *137*

Chicken Croquettes, 104, *105*

Chicken Thighs Braised in Cider Vinegar with Fennel and Radish, 346–47, *347*

Chicken with Rosemary, Fennel Pollen, and Balsamic-Braised Radicchio, 78–79

cutting up (note), 18

deboning a breast (note), 158

Fried Chicken, 18, *19*

Jamaican Squash Soup with Chicken and "Spinners," 219–20, *221*

marinade (note), 178

Mushroom-Crusted Chicken Breasts with Mushroom Jus, 184, *185*

Steamed Chicken with Preserved Black Beans and Ginger, 302, *303*

Stir-Fried Chicken Henhouse Bowl, 178, *179*

Stuffed Chicken Breasts, 163

Tomatillo Chicken Tamales, 248, *249*, 250

chicken livers:

Chicken Liver Mousse, 160, *161*

Tortellini with Pork in Creamy Meat Ragù, 278–79

chickpea(s):

Chickpea and Salt Cod Stew, 126–27, *127*

Chickpeas and Okra with Harissa and Yogurt, 60

Chilaquiles, *230*, 231

chilies:

Caramel Shrimp with Lemongrass, Thai Chili, and Ginger, 304

Chilaquiles, *230*, 231

Flank Steak with Guajillo Chili Sauce, 252–53

notes, 150, 242, 246

Sweet Chili Sauce, 177

chocolate:

Chocolate Cherry Clafoutis, 132, *133*

Yogurt with Blood Oranges, Raspberries, Cherries, and Chocolate, 365

Choi, Roy, 174–81, *175*

Choi's Favorite Banana Milk Shake, 176

chorizo:

P'tit Basque with Chorizo and Grilled Garlic Bread, 84

Shrimp and Polenta with Chorizo, 58, *59*

Tortilla Española with Chorizo, 274, *275*

Chowchow, 17

Chowder, Scallop, 108

citrus fruits:

Baba Ghanouj Bruschetta with Citrus Herb Salad, 66, *67*

Citrus Gin Cocktail, 332

how to supreme (notes), 66, 312

clams:

Black Pepper Clams, *190*, 191

Mussels and Clams Triestina, 48, *49*

Clark, Melissa, 94–99, *95*

coconut: Red Tomato Spaetzle in Yellow Tomato Coconut Sauce, 290–91

coconut milk: Short Ribs Braised in Coconut Milk, 328–29

cod:

Chickpea and Salt Cod Stew, 126–27, *127*

Cracker-Crusted Cod with Corn, Sugar Snap Peas, and Tomatoes, 110, *111*

Fish Stew with Cod, Swordfish, and Mussels, 13

Cohen, Amanda, 284–91, *285*

Collard Greens, Vegetarian, 16

corn:

Chilled Corn Soup, 326, *327*

Corn Stock (note), 246

Cracker-Crusted Cod with Corn, Sugar Snap Peas, and Tomatoes, 110, *111*

Creamed Corn, 81

Country Bread (Pain de Campagne), 226–27

Crab and Cucumber, *324*, 325

Crab Cakes with Lemon and Dill, 258, *259*, 260

Creamed Corn, 81

crème fraîche, 194

    Baba au Rhum with Grapes and Crème Fraîche, 267–68, *269*

Croquettes, Chicken, 104, *105*

Crostini with Sugar Snap Peas, Radishes, and Anchovies, 96

cucumbers:

    Crab and Cucumber, *324*, 325

    Juiced Gazpacho, 333

    Smoked Fish Salad, 109

    Tsatsiki (note), 40

Dale, Peter, 56–61, *57*

dandelion:

    Grilled Brassica with Dandelion-Green Vinaigrette, 320, *321*

    Raw Dandelion Salad with Hard-Boiled Eggs and Pickled White Anchovies, 173

Danko, Gary, 112–19, *113*

dates: Sautéed Medjool Dates, 210, *211*

Davis, Kevin, 232–37, *233*

Demi-Glace, 342–43

DePalma, Gina, 88–93, *89*

desserts:

    Almond Jelly with Candied Fennel and Grapefruit, 312, *313*

    Baba au Rhum with Grapes and Crème Fraîche, 267–68, *269*

    Blueberry Crostada, 118–19, *119*

    Chocolate Cherry Clafoutis, 132, *133*

Choi's Favorite Banana Milk Shake, 176

French Apple Tart, 164–65, *165*

Fresh Pecan Pie, 21

Jamaican Rum Cake, 222–23, *223*

Lemon Semifreddo with Blackberries and Honey, 92, *93*

Orange-Poached Peaches with a Graham Cracker Crust, 149

Pineapple with Lime Sugar, Cane Syrup, and Pomegranate Seeds, 61

Plum Dumplings with a Brown Sugar Crust, 156–57, *157*

Red Velvet Cupcakes with Cream Cheese Frosting, *366*, 367–68, *369*

Yogurt with Blood Oranges, Raspberries, Cherries, and Chocolate, 365

Dieterle, Harold, 74–81, *75*, *80*

Dorrier, Bill, 276

Dotolo, Vinny, 82–87, *83*

Douglas, Tom, 254–61, *255*

duck:

    Herb-Cured Duck Breast with Baby Turnips and Meyer Lemon, 264–65

    Seared Duck Breast with Garam Masala and Grapes, 98, *99*

Duffy, Curtis, 322–29, *323*

Dufour, Hugue, 270–75, *271*

dumplings:

    Braised Rabbit with Carrots and Mushrooms, 152–53, *153*

    Carrot Dumplings, 286–87

    dough (note), 284

    Plum Dumplings with a Brown Sugar Crust, 156–57, *157*

    Swiss Chard and Ricotta Dumplings, 198, *199*

eggplant:

    Baba Ghanouj Bruschetta with Citrus Herb Salad, 66, *67*

    Eggplant Two Ways, 309–10, *311*

    Fried Eggplant with Honey, 123

    Gnocchi with Eggplant and Tomatoes, 10, *11*

eggs, 5

    beating egg whites (note), 112

    Chocolate Cherry Clafoutis, 132, *133*

    Eggs on Eggs, 356, *357*

    how to hard-boil (note), 71

    Lemon Semifreddo with Blackberries and Honey, 92, *93*

    Olive Oil–Fried Eggs with a Crown of Herbs, 36, *37*

    Puntarelle with Candied Bacon, Soft-Cooked Eggs, and Ricotta Salata, 364

    Raw Dandelion Salad with Hard-Boiled Eggs and Pickled White Anchovies, 173

    Shakshouka, 65

    Stir-Fried Chicken Henhouse Bowl, 178, *179*

    Tortilla Española with Chorizo, 274, *275*

equipment, 2, 4

Erickson, Renee, 208–13, *209*

escargot: Bone Marrow and Escargot, 272

Falkner, Elizabeth, 362–69, *363*

Farmer's Market Salad with Garlic Vinaigrette, 34

Feniger, Susan, 186–93, *187*

fennel:

    Almond Jelly with Candied Fennel and Grapefruit, 312, *313*

fennel *(continued)*

Chicken Thighs Braised in Cider Vinegar with Fennel and Radish, 346–47, *347*

Herb-Cured Duck Breast with Baby Turnips and Meyer Lemon, 264–65

Pan-Seared Branzino with Fennel Salad, 131

Raw Vegetable Salad with Aged Goat's-Milk Cheese, 317

fish and shellfish:

Black Pepper Clams, *190*, 191

Bone Marrow and Escargot, 272

Buckwheat Blinis with Smoked Salmon and Caviar, *114*, 115

Caramel Shrimp with Lemongrass, Thai Chili, and Ginger, 304

Cavatappi with Mussels, *282*, 283

Ceviche, 251

Chickpea and Salt Cod Stew, 126–27, *127*

Crab and Cucumber, *324*, 325

Crab Cakes with Lemon and Dill, 258, *259*, 260

Cracker-Crusted Cod with Corn, Sugar Snap Peas, and Tomatoes, 110, *111*

Fish Stew with Cod, Swordfish, and Mussels, 13

Fried Rice with Dried Scallops and Shiitake Mushrooms, 54

Mussels and Clams Triestina, 48, *49*

Mussels with Cider, Cream, and Mustard, 213

Pan-Seared Branzino with Fennel Salad, 131

Pantesca Salad, 206, *207*

Poached Halibut with Pistachio–Meyer Lemon Pesto, 212

Salt-and-Pepper Shrimp, 235

Sautéed Georgia Trout with Watercress Puree and Mandarin Salad, 295–96, *297*

Scallop Chowder, 108

Seared Scallops with Mustard Greens, Parsnip Puree, and Beurre Blanc, 348–49

Shrimp and Polenta with Chorizo, 58, *59*

Smoked Fish Salad, 109

Smoked Herring Caesar Salad, 273

Trout David, 234

Tuna Carpaccio with Kohlrabi Slaw, 308

Flank Steak with Guajillo Chili Sauce, 252–53

Focaccia, Stuffed, 204–5, *205*

French Apple Tart, 164–65, *165*

French Fries, 361

French Onion Soup, 338

Frico with Potato, 47

Garganelli with Speck and Cream, 280, *281*

garlic, 5; notes, 13, 22

Braciola, 170, *171*, 172

confit, 66

Farmer's Market Salad with Garlic Vinaigrette, 34

Lentil Soup with Sausage, Chard, and Garlic, 90

P'tit Basque with Chorizo and Grilled Garlic Bread, 84

Stir-Fried Bok Choy and Shiitakes with Garlic and Rice Wine, 305

Trofie with Basil and Cilantro Pesto, 97

Gazpacho, Juiced, 333

Gibanica with Feta, Goat Cheese, and Kajmak Cheese, 154, *155*

gin: Citrus Gin Cocktail, 332

ginger:

Caramel Shrimp with Lemongrass, Thai Chili, and Ginger, 304

Steamed Chicken with Preserved Black Beans and Ginger, 302, *303*

Stir-Fried Bok Choy with Ginger, 55

gnocchi:

Gnocchi with Eggplant and Tomatoes, 10, *11*

Light-as-Air Potato Gnocchi, 168–69, *169*

Gomez, Asha, 238–45, *239*

grapefruit: Almond Jelly with Candied Fennel and Grapefruit, 312, *313*

grapes:

Baba au Rhum with Grapes and Crème Fraîche, 267–68, *269*

Celery Salad with Mushrooms and Grapes in a Celery Leaf Pesto, 288, *289*

Seared Duck Breast with Garam Masala and Grapes, 98, *99*

greens:

Braised Winter Greens with Tasso and Pickled Banana Peppers, *298*, 299

Chickpea and Salt Cod Stew, 126–27, *127*

Grilled Brassica with Dandelion-Green Vinaigrette, 320, *321*

Lentil Soup with Sausage, Chard, and Garlic, 90

Seared Scallops with Mustard Greens, Parsnip Puree, and Beurre Blanc, 348–49

Shakshouka, 65

Swiss Chard and Ricotta Dumplings, 198, *199*

Vegetarian Collard Greens, 16

see also salads; spinach

halibut: Poached Halibut with Pistachio–Meyer Lemon Pesto, 212

ham: Salt-Crusted Pork Loin with Ibérico Ham and Asparagus, 334, *335*

harissa, 60

Chickpeas and Okra with Harissa and Yogurt, 60

Fried Olives with Labneh and Harissa Oil, 64

Hearts of Palm Salad with Mango and Macadamia Nuts, 76, 77

Hellen, Bobby, 38–44, *39*

Herb-Cured Duck Breast with Baby Turnips and Meyer Lemon, 264–65

herring: Smoked Herring Caesar Salad, 273

Hollandaise Sauce, 356, *357*

honey:

Fried Eggplant with Honey, 123

Lemon Semifreddo with Blackberries and Honey, 92, *93*

Hopkins, Linton, 292–99, *293*

ingredients, 4–5, 6; sources, 7, 371–73

Israel, Christopher, 194–99, *195*

Jamaican Rum Cake, 222–23, *223*

Jamaican Squash Soup with Chicken and "Spinners," 219–20, *221*

Jovancicevic, Ana, 150–57, *151*

Juiced Gazpacho, 333

kafta: Lamb Meatballs (Kafta) with Baked Feta and Pomegranate Molasses, 192, *193*

Kaya Toast, 188–89, *189*

kimchi: Cured Pork Belly with Kimchi Rice Grits, 351–52, *353*

knives, 2; notes, 158, 186

kohlrabi: Tuna Carpaccio with Kohlrabi Slaw, 308

labneh: Fried Olives with Labneh and Harissa Oil, 64

lamb:

Lamb Meatballs (Kafta) with Baked Feta and Pomegranate Molasses, 192, *193*

Lamb Shanks Roasted with Root Vegetables, 148

Lamb Stock, 41

Leftover Lamb BLT, 42, *43*

Porcini-Crusted Rack of Lamb with Celeriac-Potato Gratin, 261

Yogurt-Marinated Leg of Lamb, 40

lemon(s):

Crab Cakes with Lemon and Dill, 258, *259*, 260

Funky Lettuce Salad with Beets, Feta, and Creamy Meyer Lemon Dressing, 85

Herb-Cured Duck Breast with Baby Turnips and Meyer Lemon, 264–65

Lemon Semifreddo with Blackberries and Honey, 92, *93*

Mozzarella with Meyer Lemon, Celery Salad, and Alici di Menaica, 71

Poached Halibut with Pistachio–Meyer Lemon Pesto, 212

lemonade (note), 14

lemongrass: Caramel Shrimp with Lemongrass, Thai Chili, and Ginger, 304

lentils:

Lentilpalooza, 340, *341*

Lentil Soup with Sausage, Chard, and Garlic, 90

limes: Pineapple with Lime Sugar, Cane Syrup, and Pomegranate Seeds, 61

Lo, Anita, 306–13, *307*

mango: Hearts of Palm Salad with Mango and Macadamia Nuts, 76, 77

Mantuano, Tony, 200–207, *201*, *202*

Margherita Pizza, 28, *29*

Martin, Anthony, 144–49, *145*

milk shake: Choi's Favorite Banana Milk Shake, 176

Montero, Eder, 120–27, *121*

mortar and pestle (note), 82

Moulton, Sara, 158–65, *159*

mozzarella:

The Brooklyn Pizza, 30

Margherita Pizza, 28, *29*

Mozzarella in Panna with Pesto and Slow-Roasted Tomatoes, 72, *73*

Mozzarella with Meyer Lemon, Celery Salad, and Alici di Menaica, 71

Sausage and Pickled Pepper Pizza, 31

mushrooms:

Braised Rabbit with Carrots and Mushrooms, 152–53, *153*

Celery Salad with Mushrooms and Grapes in a Celery Leaf Pesto, 288, *289*

Chanterelle and Cremini Mushroom Gratin, 197

mushrooms *(continued)*
Chicken Croquettes, 104, *105*
Fried Rice with Dried Scallops and
Shiitake Mushrooms, 54
Mushroom-Crusted Chicken Breasts
with Mushroom Jus, 184, *185*
Mushroom Stock, 182
Porcini-Crusted Rack of Lamb with
Celeriac-Potato Gratin, 261
Porcini-Rubbed Roast Beef with
Demi-Glace and Caramelized Turnips,
339
Stir-Fried Bok Choy and Shiitakes with
Garlic and Rice Wine, 305
mussels:
Cavatappi with Mussels, *282*, 283
eating (note), 208
Fish Stew with Cod, Swordfish, and
Mussels, 13
Mussels and Clams Triestina, 48, *49*
Mussels with Cider, Cream, and
Mustard, 213

nigella seeds (note), 62
nochino (walnut liqueur), note, 100
Noren, Nils, 354–61, *355*
Nosrat, Samin, 134–43, *135*

oils, 4, 5; thyme oil, 219
okra, 56
Chickpeas and Okra with Harissa and
Yogurt, 60
Olive Oil–Fried Eggs with a Crown of
Herbs, 36, *37*
olive powder (note), 266
olives:

Bread Salad with Tuna, Capers, and
Olives, 228, *229*
Fried Olives with Labneh and Harissa
Oil, 64
Stuffed Focaccia, 204–5, *205*
onions:
caramelizing (note), 186
French Onion Soup, 338
Pickled Black Radishes and Vidalia
Onions, 294
orange(s):
Crispy White Asparagus with Orange
and Marcona Almonds, 236, *237*
Orange-Poached Peaches with a Graham
Cracker Crust, 149
Sautéed Georgia Trout with Watercress
Puree and Mandarin Salad, 295–96, *297*
Yogurt with Blood Oranges, Raspberries,
Cherries, and Chocolate, 365
Oxtail Cassoulet, 216–17

Pantesca Salad, 206, *207*
parsley: Persillade, 272
parsnips: Seared Scallops with Mustard
Greens, Parsnip Puree, and Beurre
Blanc, 348–49
pasta:
Butternut Squash Tortellini, *140*,
141–42, *143*
Cavatappi with Mussels, *282*, 283
Cavatelli with Pesto, Peas, and Ricotta
Salata, 130
Garganelli with Speck and Cream, 280,
281
Gnocchi with Eggplant and Tomatoes,
10, *11*

Light-as-Air Potato Gnocchi, 168–69,
169
Pasta Fagioli, 266
Tagliatelle with Cherry Tomatoes, 203
Tortellini with Pork in Creamy Meat
Ragù, 278–79
Trofie with Basil and Cilantro Pesto, 97
Ziti with Broccoli Rabe and Sausage, 46
Pasta Dough, 138–39
Patterson, Daniel, 314–21, *315*, *316*
peaches: Orange-Poached Peaches with a
Graham Cracker Crust, 149
pear(s):
Prosciutto San Daniele with Warren
Pear and Pomegranate Seeds, 70
Spinach Salad with Pear, Curried
Cashews, and Bacon, 256–57, *257*
peas:
Cavatelli with Pesto, Peas, and Ricotta
Salata, 130
Cracker-Crusted Cod with Corn, Sugar
Snap Peas, and Tomatoes, 110, *111*
Crostini with Sugar Snap Peas, Radishes,
and Anchovies, 96
pecans:
Beet Salad with Pecans, Herbs, and
Apple, 146, *147*
Fresh Pecan Pie, 21
peppers:
Braised Winter Greens with Tasso and
Pickled Banana Peppers, *298*, 299
Chickpeas and Okra with Harissa and
Yogurt, 60
Chowchow, 17
Juiced Gazpacho, 333
pickled (note), 31

Sausage and Pickled Pepper Pizza, 31

Shakshouka, 65

Shrimp and Polenta with Chorizo, 58, *59*

West Indies–Style Hot Sauce, 102

Ziti with Broccoli Rabe and Sausage, 46

Persillade, 272

pesto:

Cavatelli with Pesto, Peas, and Ricotta Salata, 130

Celery Salad with Mushrooms and Grapes in a Celery Leaf Pesto, 288, *289*

Mozzarella in Panna with Pesto and Slow-Roasted Tomatoes, 72, *73*

Poached Halibut with Pistachio–Meyer Lemon Pesto, 212

Trofie with Basil and Cilantro Pesto, 97

Pettit, Brandon, 22–31, *23, 26*

Phan, Charles, 300–305, *301*

Pickled Black Radishes and Vidalia Onions, 294

Pineapple with Lime Sugar, Cane Syrup, and Pomegranate Seeds, 61

pizza, 22–31

The Brooklyn Pizza, 30

Homemade Pizza Dough, 24–25

Margherita Pizza, 28, *29*

Pizza Sauce, 27

Sausage and Pickled Pepper Pizza, 31

Plum Dumplings with a Brown Sugar Crust, 156–57, *157*

polenta: Shrimp and Polenta with Chorizo, 58, *59*

pomegranates, 56

pomegranate seeds:

Pineapple with Lime Sugar, Cane Syrup, and Pomegranate Seeds, 61

Prosciutto San Daniele with Warren Pear and Pomegranate Seeds, 70

Pomeroy, Naomi, 336–43, *337*

pork:

Braised Winter Greens with Tasso and Pickled Banana Peppers, *298, 299*

Cured Pork Belly with Kimchi Rice Grits, 351–52, *353*

Salt-Crusted Pork Loin with Ibérico Ham and Asparagus, 334, *335*

Sweet-and-Sour Balsamic-Glazed Spareribs, 86, *87*

Tortellini with Pork in Creamy Meat Ragù, 278–79

potato(es):

French Fries, 361

Frico with Potato, 47

Lamb Shanks Roasted with Root Vegetables, 148

Light-as-Air Potato Gnocchi, 168–69, *169*

Pantesca Salad, 206, *207*

Plum Dumplings with a Brown Sugar Crust, 156–57, *157*

Porcini-Crusted Rack of Lamb with Celeriac-Potato Gratin, 261

Potato Risotto, 183

Scallop Chowder, 108

Tortilla Española with Chorizo, 274, *275*

pots and pans, 2, 4, 50, 56, 270

Powell, Omar, 214–23, *215, 218*

pressure cooker (note), 120

Prosciutto San Daniele with Warren Pear and Pomegranate Seeds, 70

P'tit Basque with Chorizo and Grilled Garlic Bread, 84

pumpkin seeds: Radish Salad with Toasted Pumpkin Seeds and Pumpkin Seed Oil, 196

Puntarelle with Candied Bacon, Soft-Cooked Eggs, and Ricotta Salata, 364

Quatrano, Anne, 262–69, *263*

quenelles (note), 144

rabbit: Braised Rabbit with Carrots and Mushrooms, 152–53, *153*

radicchio: Chicken with Rosemary, Fennel Pollen, and Balsamic-Braised Radicchio, 78–79

radishes:

Chicken Thighs Braised in Cider Vinegar with Fennel and Radish, 346–47, *347*

Crostini with Sugar Snap Peas, Radishes, and Anchovies, 96

Pickled Black Radishes and Vidalia Onions, 294

Radish Salad with Toasted Pumpkin Seeds and Pumpkin Seed Oil, 196

Raw Vegetable Salad with Aged Goat's-Milk Cheese, 317

Raij, Alex, 120–27, *121*

raspberries: Yogurt with Blood Oranges, Raspberries, Cherries, and Chocolate, 365

Red Velvet Cupcakes with Cream Cheese Frosting, 366, 367–68, *369*

Rib-Eye Steak Cooked Sous-Vide, 358–59, *360*

rice:

Fried Rice with Dried Scallops and Shiitake Mushrooms, 54

rice *(continued)*

Stir-Fried Chicken Henhouse Bowl, 178, *179*

washing (note), 174

Yogurt Rice, *244*, 245

rice grits: Cured Pork Belly with Kimchi Rice Grits, 351–52, *353*

Richard, Michel, 180–85, *181*

Rodriguez, Jessamyn Waldman, 224–31, *225*

rum:

Baba au Rhum with Grapes and Crème Fraîche, 267–68, *269*

Jamaican Rum Cake, 222–23, *223*

Rum Syrup, 267

salads:

Arugula Salad with Heirloom Tomatoes, 12

Baba Ghanouj Bruschetta with Citrus Herb Salad, 66, *67*

Beet Salad with Pecans, Herbs, and Apple, 146, *147*

Bread Salad with Tuna, Capers, and Olives, 228, *229*

Brussels Sprouts Slaw, 290–91

Celery Salad with Mushrooms and Grapes in a Celery Leaf Pesto, 288, *289*

Charred and Cheesy Garden Salad Tacos, 35

Farmer's Market Salad with Garlic Vinaigrette, 34

Funky Lettuce Salad with Beets, Feta, and Creamy Meyer Lemon Dressing, 85

Hearts of Palm Salad with Mango and Macadamia Nuts, 76, *77*

Mozzarella with Meyer Lemon, Celery Salad, and Alici di Menaica, 71

Pan-Seared Branzino with Fennel Salad, 131

Pantesca Salad, 206, *207*

Prosciutto San Daniele with Warren Pear and Pomegranate Seeds, 70

Puntarelle with Candied Bacon, Soft-Cooked Eggs, and Ricotta Salata, 364

Radish Salad with Toasted Pumpkin Seeds and Pumpkin Seed Oil, 196

Raw Dandelion Salad with Hard-Boiled Eggs and Pickled White Anchovies, 173

Raw Vegetable Salad with Aged Goat's-Milk Cheese, 317

Sautéed Georgia Trout with Watercress Puree and Mandarin Salad, 295–96, *297*

Smoked Fish Salad, 109

Smoked Herring Caesar Salad, 273

Spinach Salad with Pear, Curried Cashews, and Bacon, 256–57, *257*

Tuna Carpaccio with Kohlrabi Slaw, 308

salmon: Buckwheat Blinis with Smoked Salmon and Caviar, *114*, 115

Salsa, Tomatillo, 231

salt, 4; pink salt, 306; sea salt, 208

Salt-and-Pepper Shrimp, 235

Salt-Crusted Pork Loin with Ibérico Ham and Asparagus, 334, *335*

sauces:

Beurre Blanc, 348–49

Braciola, 170, *171*, 172

Carrot-Hoisin Dipping Sauce, 286–87

Flank Steak with Guajillo Chili Sauce, 252–53

Hollandaise Sauce, 356, *357*

Pizza Sauce, 27

Red Tomato Spaetzle in Yellow Tomato Coconut Sauce, 290–91

Rum Syrup, 267

Sweet-and-Sour Balsamic-Glazed Spareribs, 86, *87*

Sweet Chili Sauce, 177

Tomatillo Sauce, 248, 250

Tortellini with Pork in Creamy Meat Ragù, 278–79

West Indies–Style Hot Sauce, 102

sausage:

Fried Rice with Dried Scallops and Shiitake Mushrooms, 54

Lentil Soup with Sausage, Chard, and Garlic, 90

Oxtail Cassoulet, 216–17

P'tit Basque with Chorizo and Grilled Garlic Bread, 84

Sausage and Pickled Pepper Pizza, 31

Shakshouka, 65

Shrimp and Polenta with Chorizo, 58, *59*

Tortilla Española with Chorizo, 274, *275*

Ziti with Broccoli Rabe and Sausage, 46

scales (notes), 112, 226

scallops:

Fried Rice with Dried Scallops and Shiitake Mushrooms, 54

Scallop Chowder, 108

Seared Scallops with Mustard Greens, Parsnip Puree, and Beurre Blanc, 348–49 seasoning, "two-finger pinch," 174

seeds, toasting (note), 196

Shakshouka, 65

Shallot Puree, 272

shallots (note), 174

Shook, Jon, 82–87, *83*

Short Ribs Braised in Coconut Milk, 328–29

shrimp:

    Caramel Shrimp with Lemongrass, Thai Chili, and Ginger, 304

    Salt-and-Pepper Shrimp, 235

    Shrimp and Polenta with Chorizo, 58, *59*

Silverton, Nancy, 68–73, *69*

Smoked Fish Salad, 109

soups and stews:

    Asparagus Soup with Spinach and Tarragon, 116, *117*

    bones for stock, 38

    Braised Rabbit with Carrots and Mushrooms, 152–53, *153*

    Chickpea and Salt Cod Stew, 126–27, *127*

    Chilled Corn Soup, 326, *327*

    Corn Stock (note), 246

    Fish Stew with Cod, Swordfish, and Mussels, 13

    French Onion Soup, 338

    Jamaican Squash Soup with Chicken and "Spinners," 219–20, *221*

    Juiced Gazpacho, 333

    Lamb Stock, 41

    Lentil Soup with Sausage, Chard, and Garlic, 90

    Mushroom Stock, 182

    Oxtail Cassoulet, 216–17

    Pasta Fagioli, 266

    Scallop Chowder, 108

sous-vide cooking: Rib-Eye Steak Cooked Sous-Vide, 358–59, *360*

spaetzle: Red Tomato Spaetzle in Yellow Tomato Coconut Sauce, 290–91

spareribs: Sweet-and-Sour Balsamic-Glazed Spareribs, 86, *87*

speck: Garganelli with Speck and Cream, 280, *281*

spices, 5

spinach:

    Asparagus Soup with Spinach and Tarragon, 116, *117*

    Spinach Calzone with Two Cheeses, 103

    Spinach Salad with Pear, Curried Cashews, and Bacon, 256–57, *257*

    Stuffed Chicken Breasts, 163

Spring Vegetable Confit, 124, *125*

squash:

    Butternut Squash Tortellini, *140*, 141–42, *143*

    Jamaican Squash Soup with Chicken and "Spinners," 219–20, *221*

stir-fry:

    Beef with Tomato Stir-Fry, 52, *53*

    Fried Rice with Dried Scallops and Shiitake Mushrooms, 54

    Stir-Fried Bok Choy and Shiitakes with Garlic and Rice Wine, 305

    Stir-Fried Bok Choy with Ginger, 55

    Stir-Fried Chicken Henhouse Bowl, 178, *179*

stocks:

    Beast Stock and Demi-Glace, 342–43

    bones for, 38

    Corn Stock (note), 246

    Lamb Stock, 41

Mushroom Stock, 182

sugar, 5

    Pineapple with Lime Sugar, Cane Syrup, and Pomegranate Seeds, 61

    Plum Dumplings with a Brown Sugar Crust, 156–57, *157*

    Sweet-and-Sour Balsamic-Glazed Spareribs, 86, *87*

Swiss chard:

    Lentil Soup with Sausage, Chard, and Garlic, 90

    Swiss Chard and Ricotta Dumplings, 198, *199*

swordfish: Fish Stew with Cod, Swordfish, and Mussels, 13

Tagliatelle with Cherry Tomatoes, 203

tamales: Tomatillo Chicken Tamales, 248, *249*, 250

tasso: Braised Winter Greens with Tasso and Pickled Banana Peppers, *298*, 299

Tea, Chai, 240

thermometer, 40

Thoren with Carrots and Green Beans, 242, *243*

tomatillos:

    Tomatillo Chicken Tamales, 248, *249*, 250

    Tomatillo Salsa, 231

    Tomatillo Sauce, 248, 250

tomato(es), 56

    Arugula Salad with Heirloom Tomatoes, 12

    Beef with Tomato Stir-Fry, 52, *53*

    Bread Salad with Tuna, Capers, and Olives, 228, *229*

tomato(es) *(continued)*
    Cracker-Crusted Cod with Corn, Sugar Snap Peas, and Tomatoes, 110, *111*
    Gnocchi with Eggplant and Tomatoes, 10, *11*
    how to peel (note), 128
    Juiced Gazpacho, 333
    Leftover Lamb BLT, 42, *43*
    Lentil Soup with Sausage, Chard, and Garlic, 90
    Mozzarella in Panna with Pesto and Slow-Roasted Tomatoes, 72, *73*
    Pantesca Salad, 206, *207*
    Pizza Sauce, 27
    Red Tomato Spaetzle in Yellow Tomato Coconut Sauce, 290–91
    Shakshouka, 65
    Shrimp and Polenta with Chorizo, 58, *59*
    Tagliatelle with Cherry Tomatoes, 203
    Tortellini with Pork in Creamy Meat Ragù, 278–79
tortellini:
    Butternut Squash Tortellini, *140*, 141–42, *143*
    Tortellini with Pork in Creamy Meat Ragù, 278–79
Tortilla Española with Chorizo, 274, *275*
tortillas, frying, 231
Trofie with Basil and Cilantro Pesto, 97

trout:
    Sautéed Georgia Trout with Watercress Puree and Mandarin Salad, 295–96, *297*
    Trout David, 234
Tsatsiki (note), 40
tuna:
    Bread Salad with Tuna, Capers, and Olives, 228, *229*
    Tuna Carpaccio with Kohlrabi Slaw, 308
turnips:
    Herb-Cured Duck Breast with Baby Turnips and Meyer Lemon, 264–65
    Porcini-Rubbed Roast Beef with Demi-Glace and Caramelized Turnips, 339
    Raw Vegetable Salad with Aged Goat's-Milk Cheese, 317

vacuum sealer (note), 106
Valencia, Chuy, 246–53, *247*
vanilla paste (note), 144
veal:
    Beast Stock and Demi-Glace, 342–43
    Tortellini with Pork in Creamy Meat Ragù, 278–79
vegetables:
    Bagna Cauda with Vegetables, 91
    foraging for, 314
    Lamb Shanks Roasted with Root Vegetables, 148
    Spring Vegetable Confit, 124, *125*

Vegetarian Collard Greens, 16
vinegar, 5, 344

watercress, Sautéed Georgia Trout with Watercress Puree and Mandarin Salad, 295–96, *297*
Waters, Alice, 32–37, *33*
Waxman, Jonathan, 8–13, *9*
West Indies–Style Hot Sauce, 102
White, Michael, 276–83, *277*
Wilson, Angelish, 14–21, *15*, *20*
woks, 50, 300; to season, 52

xanthan gum (note), 322

yeast (note), 224
yogurt:
    Chickpeas and Okra with Harissa and Yogurt, 60
    Eggplant Two Ways, 309–10, *311*
    Fried Olives with Labneh and Harissa Oil, 64
    Yogurt with Blood Oranges, Raspberries, Cherries, and Chocolate, 365
    Yogurt-Marinated Leg of Lamb, 40
    Yogurt Rice, *244*, 245
Young, Grace, 50–55, *51*

zaatar (note), 62
Ziti with Broccoli Rabe and Sausage, 46